Natural Experiments in the S

This unique book is the first comprehensive guide to the discovery, analysis, and evaluation of natural experiments—an increasingly popular methodology in the social sciences. Thad Dunning provides an introduction to key issues in causal inference, including model specification, and emphasizes the importance of strong research design over complex statistical analysis. Surveying many examples of standard natural experiments, regression-discontinuity designs, and instrumental-variables designs, Dunning highlights both the strengths and potential weaknesses of these methods, aiding researchers in better harnessing the promise of natural experiments while avoiding the pitfalls. Dunning also demonstrates the contribution of qualitative methods to natural experiments and proposes new ways to integrate qualitative and quantitative techniques. Chapters complete with exercises, and appendices covering specialized topics such as cluster-randomized natural experiments, make this an ideal teaching tool as well as a valuable book for professional researchers.

Thad Dunning is Associate Professor of Political Science at Yale University and a research fellow at Yale's Institution for Social and Policy Studies and the Whitney and Betty MacMillan Center for International and Area Studies. He has written on a range of methodological topics, including impact evaluation, econometric corrections for selection effects, and multi-method research in the social sciences, and his first book, *Crude Democracy: Natural Resource Wealth and Political Regimes* (Cambridge University Press, 2008), won the Best Book Award from the Comparative Democratization Section of the American Political Science Association.

Strategies for Social Inquiry

Natural Experiments in the Social Sciences: A Design-Based Approach

Editors
Colin Elman, *Maxwell School of Syracuse University*
John Gerring, *Boston University*
James Mahoney, *Northwestern University*

Editorial Board
Bear Braumoeller, David Collier, Francesco Guala, Peter Hedström, Theodore Hopf, Uskali Maki, Rose McDermott, Charles Ragin, Theda Skocpol, Peter Spiegler, David Waldner, Lisa Wedeen, Christopher Winship

This new book series presents texts on a wide range of issues bearing upon the practice of social inquiry. Strategies are construed broadly to embrace the full spectrum of approaches to analysis, as well as relevant issues in philosophy of social science.

Published Titles
John Gerring, *Social Science Methodology: A Unified Framework*, 2nd edition
Michael Coppedge, *Democratization and Research Methods*
Carsten Q. Schneider and Claudius Wagemann, *Set-Theoretic Methods for the Social Sciences: A Guide to Qualitative Comparative Analysis*

Forthcoming Titles
Diana Kapiszewski, Lauren M. MacLean and Benjamin L. Read, *Field Research in Political Science*
Jason Seawright, *Multi-Method Social Science: Combining Qualitative and Quantitative Tools*

Natural Experiments in the Social Sciences

A Design-Based Approach

Thad Dunning

CAMBRIDGE UNIVERSITY PRESS

CAMBRIDGE
UNIVERSITY PRESS

University Printing House, Cambridge CB2 8BS, United Kingdom

Cambridge University Press is part of the University of Cambridge.

It furthers the University's mission by disseminating knowledge in the pursuit of education, learning and research at the highest international levels of excellence.

www.cambridge.org
Information on this title: www.cambridge.org/9781107698000

© Thad Dunning 2012

This publication is in copyright. Subject to statutory exception
and to the provisions of relevant collective licensing agreements,
no reproduction of any part may take place without the written
permission of Cambridge University Press.

First published 2012
5th printing 2015

Printed in the United Kingdom by Clays, St Ives plc.

A catalog record for this publication is available from the British Library

Library of Congress Cataloging in Publication data
Dunning, Thad, 1973–
Natural experiments in the social sciences: a design-based approach / Thad Dunning.
  p. cm. – (Strategies for social inquiry)
Includes bibliographical references and index.
ISBN 978-1-107-69800-0
1. Social sciences – Experiments. 2. Social sciences – Research. 3. Experimental design. I. Title.
H62.D797   2012
300.72′4–dc23

2012009061

ISBN 978-1-107-01766-5 Hardback
ISBN 978-1-107-69800-0 Paperback

Additional resources for this publication at www.cambridge.org/dunning

Cambridge University Press has no responsibility for the persistence or
accuracy of URLs for external or third-party internet websites referred to
in this publication, and does not guarantee that any content on such
websites is, or will remain, accurate or appropriate.

Dedicated to the memory of David A. Freedman

Contents

Detailed table of contents		*page* ix
List of figures		xiv
List of tables		xv
List of boxes		xvi
Preface and acknowledgements		xvii
1	Introduction: why natural experiments?	1

Part I Discovering natural experiments 39

2	Standard natural experiments	41
3	Regression-discontinuity designs	63
4	Instrumental-variables designs	87

Part II Analyzing natural experiments 103

5	Simplicity and transparency: keys to quantitative analysis	105
6	Sampling processes and standard errors	165
7	The central role of qualitative evidence	208

Part III Evaluating natural experiments 233

8	How plausible is as-if random?	235
9	How credible is the model?	256
10	How relevant is the intervention?	289

Part IV Conclusion   311

11 Building strong designs through multi-method research   313

References   338
Index   353

Detailed table of contents

	Preface and acknowledgements	page xvii
1	**Introduction: why natural experiments?**	**1**
1.1	The problem of confounders	5
	1.1.1 The role of randomization	6
1.2	Natural experiments on military conscription and land titles	8
1.3	Varieties of natural experiments	15
	1.3.1 Contrast with quasi-experiments and matching	18
1.4	Natural experiments as design-based research	21
1.5	An evaluative framework for natural experiments	27
	1.5.1 The plausibility of as-if random	27
	1.5.2 The credibility of models	28
	1.5.3 The relevance of the intervention	29
1.6	Critiques and limitations of natural experiments	32
1.7	Avoiding conceptual stretching	34
1.8	Plan for the book, and how to use it	35
	1.8.1 Some notes on coverage	37

Part I Discovering natural experiments — 39

2	**Standard natural experiments**	**41**
2.1	Standard natural experiments in the social sciences	43
2.2	Standard natural experiments with true randomization	48
	2.2.1 Lottery studies	49
2.3	Standard natural experiments with as-if randomization	53
	2.3.1 Jurisdictional borders	57
	2.3.2 Redistricting and jurisdiction shopping	59
2.4	Conclusion	60
	Exercises	61

3 Regression-discontinuity designs — 63
- 3.1 The basis of regression-discontinuity analysis — 63
- 3.2 Regression-discontinuity designs in the social sciences — 68
  - 3.2.1 Population- and size-based thresholds — 72
  - 3.2.2 Near-winners and near-losers of close elections — 77
  - 3.2.3 Age as a regression discontinuity — 79
  - 3.2.4 Indices — 80
- 3.3 Variations on regression-discontinuity designs — 81
  - 3.3.1 Sharp versus fuzzy regression discontinuities — 81
  - 3.3.2 Randomized regression-discontinuity designs — 82
  - 3.3.3 Multiple thresholds — 83
- 3.4 Conclusion — 84
- Exercises — 85

4 Instrumental-variables designs — 87
- 4.1 Instrumental-variables designs: true experiments — 91
- 4.2 Instrumental-variables designs: natural experiments — 92
  - 4.2.1 Lotteries — 94
  - 4.2.2 Weather shocks — 95
  - 4.2.3 Historical or institutional variation induced by deaths — 97
- 4.3 Conclusion — 101
- Exercises — 102

Part II Analyzing natural experiments — 103

5 Simplicity and transparency: keys to quantitative analysis — 105
- 5.1 The Neyman model — 107
  - 5.1.1 The average causal effect — 109
  - 5.1.2 Estimating the average causal effect — 112
  - 5.1.3 An example: land titling in Argentina — 115
  - 5.1.4 Key assumptions of the Neyman model — 118
  - 5.1.5 Analyzing standard natural experiments — 121
- 5.2 Analyzing regression-discontinuity designs — 121
  - 5.2.1 Two examples: Certificates of Merit and digital democratization — 123
  - 5.2.2 Defining the study group: the question of bandwidth — 127
  - 5.2.3 Is the difference-of-means estimator biased in regression-discontinuity designs? — 128

		5.2.4 Modeling functional form	133
		5.2.5 Fuzzy regression discontinuities	134
	5.3	Analyzing instrumental-variables designs	135
		5.3.1 Natural experiments with noncompliance	136
		5.3.2 An example: the effect of military service	143
		5.3.3 The no-Defiers assumption	148
		5.3.4 Fuzzy regression-discontinuities as instrumental-variables designs	149
		5.3.5 From the Complier average effect to linear regression	150
	5.4	Conclusion	153
	Appendix 5.1	Instrumental-variables estimation of the Complier average causal effect	154
	Appendix 5.2	Is the difference-of-means estimator biased in regression-discontinuity designs (further details)?	158
		Exercises	160
6		**Sampling processes and standard errors**	165
	6.1	Standard errors under the Neyman urn model	166
		6.1.1 Standard errors in regression-discontinuity and instrumental-variables designs	173
	6.2	Handling clustered randomization	175
		6.2.1 Analysis by cluster mean: a design-based approach	179
	6.3	Randomization inference: Fisher's exact test	186
	6.4	Conclusion	191
	Appendix 6.1	Conservative standard errors under the Neyman model	192
	Appendix 6.2	Analysis by cluster mean	195
		Exercises	201
7		**The central role of qualitative evidence**	208
	7.1	Causal-process observations in natural experiments	210
		7.1.1 Validating as-if random: treatment-assignment CPOs	212
		7.1.2 Verifying treatments: independent-variable CPOs	219
		7.1.3 Explaining effects: mechanism CPOs	222
		7.1.4 Interpreting effects: auxiliary-outcome CPOs	224
		7.1.5 Bolstering credibility: model-validation CPOs	225
	7.2	Conclusion	228
		Exercises	230

Part III Evaluating natural experiments — 233

8 How plausible is as-if random? — 235
- 8.1 Assessing as-if random — 236
  - 8.1.1 The role of balance tests — 239
  - 8.1.2 Qualitative diagnostics — 243
- 8.2 Evaluating as-if random in regression-discontinuity and instrumental-variables designs — 244
  - 8.2.1 Sorting at the regression-discontinuity threshold: conditional density tests — 245
  - 8.2.2 Placebo tests in regression-discontinuity designs — 246
  - 8.2.3 Treatment-assignment CPOs in regression-discontinuity designs — 248
  - 8.2.4 Diagnostics in instrumental-variables designs — 248
- 8.3 A continuum of plausibility — 249
- 8.4 Conclusion — 252
- Exercises — 254

9 How credible is the model? — 256
- 9.1 The credibility of causal and statistical models — 258
  - 9.1.1 Strengths and limitations of the Neyman model — 259
  - 9.1.2 Linear regression models — 263
- 9.2 Model specification in instrumental-variables regression — 269
  - 9.2.1 Control variables in instrumental-variables regression — 277
- 9.3 A continuum of credibility — 278
- 9.4 Conclusion: how important is the model? — 283
- Appendix 9.1 Homogeneous partial effects with multiple treatments and instruments — 285
- Exercises — 287

10 How relevant is the intervention? — 289
- 10.1 Threats to substantive relevance — 293
  - 10.1.1 Lack of external validity — 293
  - 10.1.2 Idiosyncrasy of interventions — 297
  - 10.1.3 Bundling of treatments — 300
- 10.2 A continuum of relevance — 303
- 10.3 Conclusion — 306
- Exercises — 309

Part IV Conclusion — 311

11 Building strong designs through multi-method research — 313
    11.1 The virtues and limitations of natural experiments — 315
    11.2 A framework for strong research designs — 318
        11.2.1 Conventional observational studies and true experiments — 319
        11.2.2 Locating natural experiments — 321
        11.2.3 Relationship between dimensions — 324
    11.3 Achieving strong design: the importance of mixed methods — 326
    11.4 A checklist for natural-experimental research — 328

    References — 338
    Index — 353

Figures

1.1	Natural experiments in political science and economics	*page* 2
1.2	Typology of natural experiments	31
3.1	Examples of regression discontinuities	66
5.1	The Neyman model	113
5.2	A regression-discontinuity design	124
5.3	Potential and observed outcomes in a regression-discontinuity design	129
5.4	Noncompliance under the Neyman model	140
6.1	Clustered randomization under the Neyman model	177
8.1	Plausibility of as-if random assignment	250
9.1	Credibility of statistical models	280
10.1	Substantive relevance of intervention	303
11.1	Strong research designs	318
11.2	A decision flowchart for natural experiments	329

Tables

1.1	Death rates from cholera by water-supply source	*page* 13
2.1	Typical "standard" natural experiments	44
2.2	Standard natural experiments with true randomization	45
2.3	Standard natural experiments with as-if randomization	46
3.1	Selected sources of regression-discontinuity designs	69
3.2	Examples of regression-discontinuity designs	70
4.1	Selected sources of instrumental-variables designs	90
4.2	Selected instrumental-variables designs (true experiments)	92
4.3	Selected instrumental-variables designs (natural experiments)	93
4.4	Direct and indirect colonial rule in India	98
5.1	The effects of land titles on children's health	117
5.2	Social Security earnings in 1981	145
6.1	Potential outcomes under the strict null hypothesis	187
6.2	Outcomes under all randomizations, under the strict null hypothesis	188

Boxes

4.1	The intention-to-treat principle	*page* 88
5.1	The Neyman model and the average causal effect	111
5.2	Estimating the average causal effect	115
6.1	Standard errors under the Neyman model	170
6.2	Code for analysis by cluster means	181

Preface and acknowledgements

Natural experiments have become ubiquitous in the social sciences. From standard natural experiments to regression-discontinuity and instrumental-variables designs, our leading research articles and books more and more frequently reference this label. For professional researchers and students alike, natural experiments are often recommended as a tool for strengthening causal claims.

Surprisingly, we lack a comprehensive guide to this type of research design. Finding a useful and viable natural experiment is as much an art as a science. Thus, an extensive survey of examples—grouped and discussed to highlight how and why they provide the leverage they do—may help scholars to use natural experiments effectively in their substantive research. Just as importantly, awareness of the obstacles to successful natural experiments may help scholars maximize their promise while avoiding their pitfalls. There are significant challenges involved in the analysis and interpretation of natural-experimental data. Moreover, the growing popularity of natural experiments can lead to conceptual stretching, as the label is applied to studies that do not very credibly bear the hallmarks of this research design. Discussion of both the strengths and limitations of natural experiments may help readers to evaluate and bolster the success of specific applications. I therefore hope that this book will provide a resource for scholars and students who want to conduct or critically consume work of this type.

While the book is focused on natural experiments, it is also a primer on design-based research in the social sciences more generally. Research that depends on *ex post* statistical adjustment (such as cross-country regressions) has recently come under fire; there has been a commensurate shift of focus toward design-based research—in which control over confounding variables comes primarily from research design, rather than model-based statistical adjustment. The current enthusiasm for natural experiments reflects this renewed emphasis on design-based research. Yet, how should such research be conducted and evaluated? What are the key assumptions behind design-based inference, and what causal and statistical models are appropriate for this style of research? And can such design-based approaches help us make progress on big, important substantive topics, such as the causes and consequences of democracy or socioeconomic development? Answering such questions is critical for sustaining the credibility and relevance of design-based research.

Finally, this book also highlights the potential payoffs from integrating qualitative and quantitative methods. "Bridging the divide" between approaches is a recurring theme in many social sciences. Yet, strategies for combining multiple methods are not always carefully explicated; and the value of such combinations is sometimes presumed rather than demonstrated. This is unfortunate: at least with natural experiments, different methods do not just supplement but often *require* one another. I hope that this book can clarify the payoffs of mixing methods and especially of the "shoe-leather" research that, together with strong designs, makes compelling causal inference possible.

This book grows out of discussions with many colleagues, students, and especially mentors. I am deeply fortunate to have met David Freedman, to whom the book is dedicated, while finishing my Ph.D. studies at the University of California at Berkeley. His impact on this book will be obvious to readers who know his work; I only wish that he were alive to read it. While he is greatly missed, he left behind an important body of research, with which every social scientist who seeks to make causal inferences should grapple.

I would also like to thank several other mentors, colleagues, and friends. David Collier's exemplary commitment to the merger of qualitative and quantitative work has helped me greatly along the way; this book grew out of a chapter I wrote for the second edition of his book, *Rethinking Social Inquiry*, co-edited with Henry Brady. Jim Robinson, himself a prominent advocate of natural-experimental research designs, continues to influence my own substantive and methodological research. I would especially like to thank Don Green and Dan Posner, both great friends and colleagues, who read and offered detailed and incisive comments on large portions of the manuscript. Colin Elman organized a research workshop at the Institute for Qualitative and Multi-Method Research at Syracuse University, where John Gerring and David Waldner served as very discerning discussants, while Macartan Humphreys and Alan Jacobs convoked a book event at the University of British Columbia, at which Anjali Bohlken, Chris Kam, and Ben Nyblade each perceptively dissected individual chapters. I am grateful to all of the participants in these two events. For helpful conversations and suggestions, I also thank Jennifer Bussell, Colin Elman, Danny Hidalgo,

Macartan Humphreys, Jim Mahoney, Ken Scheve, Jay Seawright, Jas Sekhon, Rocío Titiunik, and David Waldner. I have been privileged to teach courses and workshops on related material to graduate students at the Institute for Qualitative and Multi-Method Research and at Yale, where Natalia Bueno, Germán Feierherd, Nikhar Gaikwad, Malte Lierl, Pia Raffler, Steve Rosenzweig, Luis Schiumerini, Dawn Teele, and Guadalupe Tuñón, among others, offered insightful reactions. I have also enjoyed leading an annual short course on multi-method research at the American Political Science Association with David Collier and Jay Seawright. These venues have provided a valuable opportunity to improve my thinking on the topics discussed in this book, and I thank all the participants in those workshops and courses for their feedback.

I would also like to thank my editor on this book, John Haslam of Cambridge University Press, as well as Carrie Parkinson, Ed Robinson, and Jim Thomas, for their gracious shepherding of this book to completion. I am particularly grateful to Colin Elman, John Gerring, and Jim Mahoney, who approached me about writing this book for their Strategies of Social Inquiry series. For their steadfast love and support, my deepest gratitude goes to my family.

1 Introduction: why natural experiments?

> If I had any desire to lead a life of indolent ease, I would wish to be an identical twin, separated at birth from my brother and raised in a different social class. We could hire ourselves out to a host of social scientists and practically name our fee. For we would be exceedingly rare representatives of the only really adequate natural experiment for separating genetic from environmental effects in humans—genetically identical individuals raised in disparate environments.
>
> —Stephen Jay Gould (1996: 264)

Natural experiments are suddenly everywhere. Over the last decade, the number of published social-scientific studies that claim to use this methodology has more than tripled (Dunning 2008a). More than 100 articles published in major political-science and economics journals from 2000 to 2009 contained the phrase "natural experiment" in the title or abstract—compared to only 8 in the three decades from 1960 to 1989 and 37 between 1990 and 1999 (Figure 1.1).[1] Searches for "natural experiment" using Internet search engines now routinely turn up several million hits.[2] As the examples surveyed in this book will suggest, an impressive volume of unpublished, forthcoming, and recently published studies—many not yet picked up by standard electronic sources—also underscores the growing prevalence of natural experiments.

This style of research has also spread across various social science disciplines. Anthropologists, geographers, and historians have used natural experiments to study topics ranging from the effects of the African slave trade to the long-run consequences of colonialism. Political scientists have explored the causes and consequences of suffrage expansion, the political effects of military conscription, and the returns to campaign donations. Economists, the most prolific users of natural experiments to date, have scrutinized the workings of

---

[1] Such searches do not pick up the most recent articles, due to the moving wall used by the online archive, JSTOR.
[2] See, for instance, Google Scholar: http://scholar.google.com.

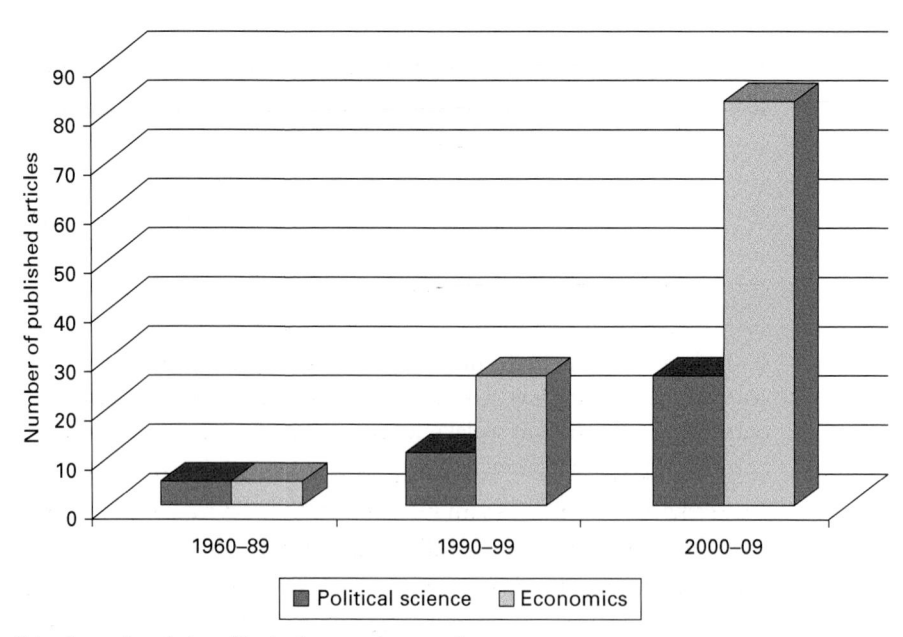

Figure 1.1 Natural experiments in political science and economics
Articles published in major political science and economics journals with "natural experiment" in the title or abstract (as tracked in the online archive JSTOR).

labor markets, the consequences of schooling reforms, and the impact of institutions on economic development.[3]

The ubiquity of this method reflects its potential to improve the quality of causal inferences in the social sciences. Researchers often ask questions about cause and effect. Yet, those questions are challenging to answer in the observational world—the one that scholars find occurring around them. Confounding variables associated both with possible causes and with possible effects pose major obstacles. Randomized controlled experiments offer one possible solution, because randomization limits confounding. However, many causes of interest to social scientists are difficult to manipulate experimentally.

Thus stems the potential importance of natural experiments—in which social and political processes, or clever research-design innovations, create

---

[3] According to Rozenzweig and Wolpin (2000: 828), "72 studies using the phrase 'natural experiment' in the title or abstract issued or published since 1968 are listed in the *Journal of Economic Literature* cumulative index." A more recent edited volume by Diamond and Robinson (2010) includes contributions from anthropology, economics, geography, history, and political science, though several of the comparative case studies in the volume do not meet the definition of natural experiments advanced in this book. See also Angrist and Krueger (2001), Dunning (2008a, 2010a), Robinson, McNulty, and Krasno (2009), Sekhon (2009), and Sekhon and Titiunik (2012) for surveys and discussion of recent work.

situations that approximate true experiments. Here, we find observational settings in which causes are randomly, or as good as randomly, assigned among some set of units, such as individuals, towns, districts, or even countries. Simple comparisons across units exposed to the presence or absence of a cause can then provide credible evidence for causal effects, because random or as-if random assignment obviates confounding. Natural experiments can help overcome the substantial obstacles to drawing causal inferences from observational data, which is one reason why researchers from such varied disciplines increasingly use them to explore causal relationships.

Yet, the growth of natural experiments in the social sciences has not been without controversy. Natural experiments can have important limitations, and their use entails specific analytic challenges. Because they are not so much planned as discovered, using natural experiments to advance a particular research agenda involves an element of luck, as well as an awareness of how they have been used successfully in disparate settings. For natural experiments that lack true randomization, validating the definitional claim of as-if random assignment is very far from straightforward. Indeed, the status of particular studies as "natural experiments" is sometimes in doubt: the very popularity of this form of research may provoke conceptual stretching, in which an attractive label is applied to research designs that only implausibly meet the definitional features of the method (Dunning 2008a). Social scientists have also debated the analytic techniques appropriate to this method: for instance, what role should multivariate regression analysis play in analyzing the data from natural experiments? Finally, the causes that Nature deigns to assign at random may not always be the most important causal variables for social scientists. For some observers, the proliferation of natural experiments therefore implies the narrowing of research agendas to focus on substantively uninteresting or theoretically irrelevant topics (Deaton 2009; Heckman and Urzúa 2010). Despite the enthusiasm evidenced by their increasing use, the ability of natural experiments to contribute to the accumulation of substantively important knowledge therefore remains in some doubt.

These observations raise a series of questions. How can natural experiments best be discovered and leveraged to improve causal inferences in the service of diverse substantive research agendas? What are appropriate methods for analyzing natural experiments, and how can quantitative and qualitative tools be combined to construct such research designs and bolster their inferential power? How should we evaluate the success of distinct natural experiments, and what sorts of criteria should we use to assess their strengths and limitations? Finally, how can researchers best use natural experiments to build strong research designs, while avoiding or mitigating the potential limitations of the method? These are the central questions with which this book is concerned.

In seeking to answer such questions, I place central emphasis on natural experiments as a "design-based" method of research—one in which control over confounding variables comes primarily from research-design choices, rather than *ex post* adjustment using parametric statistical models. Much social science relies on multivariate regression and its analogues. Yet, this approach has well-known drawbacks. For instance, it is not straightforward to create an analogy to true experiments through the inclusion of statistical controls in analyses of observational data. Moreover, the validity of multivariate regression models or various kinds of matching techniques depends on the veracity of causal and statistical assumptions that are often difficult to explicate and defend—let alone validate.[4] By contrast, random or as-if random assignment usually obviates the need to control statistically for potential confounders. With natural experiments, it is the research design, rather than the statistical modeling, that compels conviction.

This implies that the quantitative analysis of natural experiments can be simple and transparent. For instance, a comparison of average outcomes across units exposed to the presence or absence of a cause often suffices to estimate a causal effect. (This is true at least in principle, if not always in practice; one major theme of the book is how the simplicity and transparency of statistical analyses of natural experiments can be bolstered.) Such comparisons in turn often rest on credible assumptions: to motivate difference-of-means tests, analysts need only invoke simple causal and statistical models that are often persuasive as descriptions of underlying data-generating processes.

Qualitative methods also play a critical role in natural experiments. For instance, various qualitative techniques are crucial for discovering opportunities for this kind of research design, for substantiating the claim that assignment to treatment variables is really as good as random, for interpreting, explaining, and contextualizing effects, and for validating the models used in quantitative analysis. Detailed qualitative information on the circumstances that created a natural experiment, and especially on the process by which "nature" exposed or failed to expose units to a putative cause, is often essential. Thus, substantive and contextual knowledge plays an important role at every

---

[4] Matching designs, including exact and propensity-score matching, are discussed below. Like multiple regression, such techniques assume "selection on observables"—in particular, that unobserved confounders have been measured and controlled.

stage of natural-experimental research—from discovery to analysis to evaluation. Natural experiments thus typically require a mix of quantitative and qualitative research methods to be fully compelling.

In the rest of this introductory chapter, I explore these themes and propose initial answers to the questions posed above, which the rest of the book explores in greater detail. The first crucial task, however, is to define this method and distinguish it from other types of research designs. I do this below, after first discussing the problem of confounding in more detail and introducing several examples of natural experiments.

1.1 The problem of confounders

Consider the obstacles to investigating the following hypothesis, proposed by the Peruvian development economist Hernando de Soto (2000): granting *de jure* property titles to poor land squatters augments their access to credit markets, by allowing them to use their property to collateralize debt, thereby fostering broad socioeconomic development. To test this hypothesis, researchers might compare poor squatters who possess titles to those who do not. However, differences in access to credit markets across these groups could in part be due to confounding factors—such as family background—that also make certain poor squatters more likely to acquire titles to their property.

Investigators may seek to control for such confounders by making comparisons between squatters who share similar values of confounding variables but differ in their access to land titles. For instance, a researcher might compare titled and untitled squatters with parallel family backgrounds. Yet, important difficulties remain. First, the equivalence of family backgrounds is difficult to assess: for example, what metric of similarity should be used? Next, even supposing that we define an appropriate measure and compare squatters with equivalent family backgrounds, there may be other difficult-to-measure confounders—such as determination—that are associated with obtaining titles and that also influence economic and political behaviors. Differences between squatters with and without land titles might then be due to the effect of the titles, the effect of differences in determination, or both.

Finally, even if confounders *could* all be identified and successfully measured, the best way to "control" for them is not obvious. One possibility is stratification, as mentioned above: a researcher might compare squatters who have equivalent family backgrounds and measured levels of determination—but who vary with respect to whether or not they have land titles. However, such stratification is often infeasible, among other reasons because the number of potential confounders is usually large relative to the number of data points (that is, relative to the number of units).[5] A cross-tabulation of titling status against every possible combination of family background and levels of determination would be likely to have many empty cells. For instance, there may be no two squatters with precisely the same combination of family attributes, such as parental education and income, and the same initial determination, but different exposures to land titles.

Analysts thus often turn to conventional quantitative methods, such as multivariate regression or its analogues, to control for observable confounders. The models essentially extrapolate across the missing cells of the cross-tabulations, which is one reason for their use. Yet, typical regression models rely on essentially unverifiable assumptions that are often difficult to defend. As I discuss in this book, this is an important difficulty that goes well beyond the challenge of identifying and measuring possible confounders.

1.1.1 The role of randomization

How, then, can social scientists best make inferences about causal effects? One option is true experimentation. In a randomized controlled experiment to estimate the effects of land titles, for instance, some poor squatters might be randomly assigned to receive *de jure* land titles, while others would retain only de facto claims to their plots. Because of randomization, possible confounders such as family background or determination would be balanced across these two groups, up to random error (Fisher [1935] 1951). After all, the flip of a coin determines which squatters get land titles. Thus, more determined squatters are just as likely to end up without titles as with them. This is true of all other potential confounders as well, including family background. In sum, randomization creates *statistical independence* between these confounders and treatment assignment—an important concept discussed later in the book.[6] Statistical independence implies that squatters who are likely to do poorly even if they are granted titles are initially as likely to receive them as not to receive them. Thus, particularly when the number of squatters in each group is large and so the role of random error is small, squatters with titles and without titles should be nearly indistinguishable as groups—save for the

---

[5] This stratification strategy is sometimes known as "exact matching." One reason exact matching may be infeasible is that covariates—that is, potential confounders—are continuous rather than discrete.

[6] In Chapter 5, when I introduce the idea of *potential outcomes*, I discuss how randomization creates statistical independence of potential outcomes and treatment assignment.

presence or absence of titles. *Ex post* differences in outcomes between squatters with and without land titles are then most likely due to the effect of titling.

In more detail, random assignment ensures that any differences in outcomes between the groups are due either to chance error or to the causal effect of property titles. In any one experiment, of course, one or the other group might end up with more determined squatters, due to the influence of random variation; distinguishing true effects from chance variation is the point of statistical hypothesis testing (Chapter 6). Yet, if the experiment were to be repeated over and over, the groups would not differ, on average, in the values of potential confounders. Thus, the average of the average difference of group outcomes, across these many experiments, would equal the true difference in outcomes—that is, the difference between what would happen if every squatter were given titles, and what would happen if every squatter were left untitled. A formal definition of this causal effect, and of estimators for the effect, will await Chapter 5. For now, the key point is that randomization is powerful because it obviates confounding, by creating *ex ante* symmetry between the groups created by the randomization. This symmetry implies that large post-titling differences between titled and untitled squatters provide reliable evidence for the causal effect of titles.

True experiments may offer other advantages as well, such as potential simplicity and transparency in the data analysis. A straightforward comparison, such as the difference in average outcomes in the two groups, often suffices to estimate a causal effect. Experiments can thus provide an attractive way to address confounding, while also limiting reliance on the assumptions of conventional quantitative methods such as multivariate regression—which suggests why social scientists increasingly utilize randomized controlled experiments to investigate a variety of research questions (Druckman et al. 2011; Gerber and Green 2012; Morton and Williams 2010).

Yet, in some contexts direct experimental manipulation is expensive, unethical, or impractical. After all, many of the causes in which social scientists are most interested—such as political or economic institutions—are often not amenable to manipulation by researchers. Nor is true randomization the means by which political or economic institutions typically allocate scarce resources. While it is not inconceivable that policy-makers might roll out property titles in a randomized fashion—for example, by using a lottery to determine the timing of titling—the extension of titles and other valued goods typically remains under the control of political actors and policy-makers (and properly so). And while examples of randomized interventions are becoming more frequent (Gerber and Green 2012), many other causes continue to be allocated by social and political process, not by experimental researchers. For scholars concerned with the effects of causes that are difficult to manipulate, natural experiments may therefore provide a valuable alternative tool.

1.2 Natural experiments on military conscription and land titles

In some natural experiments, policy-makers or other actors do use lotteries or other forms of true randomization to allocate resources or policies. Thus, while the key intervention is not planned and implemented by an experimental researcher—and therefore these are observational studies, not experiments—such randomized natural experiments share with true experiments the attribute of randomized assignment of units to "treatment" and "control" groups.[7]

For instance, Angrist (1990a) uses a randomized natural experiment to study the effects of military conscription and service on later labor-market earnings. This topic has important social-scientific as well as policy implications; it was a major source of debate in the United States in the wake of the Vietnam War. However, the question is difficult to answer with data from standard observational studies. Conscripted soldiers may be unlike civilians; and those who volunteer for the military may in general be quite different from those who do not. For example, perhaps soldiers volunteer for the army because their labor-market prospects are poor to begin with. A finding that ex-soldiers earn less than nonsoldiers is then hardly credible evidence for the effect of military service on later earnings. Confounding factors—those associated with both military service and economic outcomes—may be responsible for any such observed differences.

From 1970 to 1972, however, the United States used a randomized lottery to draft soldiers for the Vietnam War. Cohorts of 19- and 20-year-old men were randomly assigned lottery numbers that ranged from 1 to 366, according to their dates of birth. All men with lottery numbers below the highest number called for induction each year were "draft eligible," while those with higher numbers were not eligible for the draft. Using earnings records from the Social Security Administration, Angrist (1990a) estimates modest negative effects of draft eligibility on later income. For example, among white men who were

---

[7] I use the terms "independent variable," "treatment," and "intervention" roughly synonymously in this book, despite important differences in shades of meaning. For instance, "intervention" invokes the idea of manipulability—which plays a key role in many discussions of causal inference (e.g., Holland 1986)—much more directly than "independent variable."

eligible for the draft in 1971, average earnings in 1984 were $15,813.93 in current US dollars, while in the ineligible group they were $16,172.25. Thus, assignment to draft eligibility in 1971 caused an estimated decrease in average yearly earnings of $358.32, or about a 2.2 percent drop from average earnings of the assigned-to-control group.[8]

The randomized natural experiment plays a key role in making any causal inferences about the effects of military conscription persuasive. Otherwise, initial differences in people who were or were not drafted could explain any *ex post* differences in economic outcomes or political attitudes.[9] The usefulness of the natural experiment is that confounding should not be an issue: the randomization of draft lottery ensures that on average, men who were draft eligible are just like those who were not. Thus, large *ex post* differences are very likely due to the effects of the draft.

Of course, in this case not all soldiers who were drafted actually served in the military: some were disqualified by physical and mental exams, some went to college (which typically deferred induction during the Vietnam War), and others went to Canada. By the same token, some men who were not drafted volunteered. It might therefore seem natural to compare the men who actually served in the military to those who did not. Yet, this comparison is again subject to confounding: soldiers self-select into military service, and those who volunteer are likely different in ways that matter for earnings from those who do not. The correct, natural-experimental comparison is between men randomly assigned to draft eligibility—whether or not they actually served—and the whole assigned-to-control group. This is called "intention-to-treat" analysis—an important concept I discuss later in this book.[10] Intention-to-treat analysis estimates the effect of draft eligibility, not the effect of actual military service. Under certain conditions, the natural experiment can also be used to estimate the effects of draft eligibility on men who would serve if drafted, but otherwise would not.[11] This is the goal of instrumental-variables analysis, which is discussed later in this book—along with the key assumptions that must be met for its persuasive use.

Not all natural experiments feature a true randomized lottery, as in Angrist's study. Under some conditions, social and political processes may

---

[8] The estimate is statistically significant at standard levels; see Chapters 4 and 6.
[9] An interesting recent article by Erikson and Stoker (2011) uses this same approach to estimate the effects of draft eligibility on political attitudes and partisan identification.
[10] See Chapters 4 and 5.
[11] These individuals are called "Compliers" because they comply with the treatment condition to which they are assigned (Chapter 5).

assign units to treatment and control groups in a way that is persuasively *as-if* random. In such settings, ensuring that confounding variables do not distort results is a major challenge, since no true randomizing device assigns units to the treatment and control groups. This is one of the main challenges—and sometimes one of the central limitations—of much natural-experimental research, relative for instance to true experiments. Yet, social or political processes, or clever research-design innovations, sometimes do create such opportunities for obviating confounding. How to validate the claim that assignment to comparison groups is plausibly as good as random in such studies is an important focus of this book.

Galiani and Schargrodsky (2004, 2010) provide an interesting example on the effects of extending property titles to poor squatters in Argentina. In 1981, squatters organized by the Catholic Church occupied an urban wasteland in the province of Buenos Aires, dividing the land into similar-sized parcels that were then allocated to individual families. A 1984 law, adopted after the return to democracy in 1983, expropriated this land, with the intention of transferring title to the squatters. However, some of the original owners then challenged the expropriation in court, leading to long delays in the transfer of titles to the plots owned by those owners, while other titles were ceded and transferred to squatters immediately.

The legal action therefore created a "treatment" group—squatters to whom titles were ceded immediately—and a "control" group—squatters to whom titles were not ceded.[12] Galiani and Schargrodsky (2004, 2010) find significant differences across these groups in subsequent housing investment, household structure, and educational attainment of children—though not in access to credit markets, which contradicts De Soto's theory that the poor will use titled property to collateralize debt. They also find a positive effect of property rights on self-perceptions of individual efficacy. For instance, squatters who were granted land titles—for reasons over which they apparently had no control!—disproportionately agreed with statements that people get ahead in life due to hard work (Di Tella, Galiani, and Schargrodsky 2007).

Yet, what makes this a natural experiment, rather than a conventional observational study in which squatters with and without land titles are compared? The key definitional criterion of a natural experiment, as we shall see below, is that the assignment of squatters to treatment and control

---

[12] I use the terms "treatment" and "control" groups here for convenience, and by way of analogy to true experiments. There is no need to define the control group as the absence of treatment, though in this context the usage makes sense (as we are discussing the presence and absence of land titles). One could instead talk about "treatment group 1" and "treatment group 2," for example.

groups—here, squatters with and without titles—was as good as random. In some natural experiments, like the Angrist (1990a) study discussed above, there is indeed true randomization, which makes this claim highly credible. In others—including many so-called "regression-discontinuity designs" I will discuss below—the a priori case for as-if random is quite strong. Notice that in Galiani and Schargrodsky's (2004) study, however—as in many other natural experiments—this claim may not be particularly persuasive on a priori grounds. After all, no true coin flip assigned squatters to receive *de jure* titles or merely retain their de facto claims to plots. Instead, the social and political processes that assigned titles to certain poor squatters and not to others are simply alleged to be like a coin flip. How, then, can we validate the claim of as-if random?

The Argentina land-titling study gives a flavor of the type of evidence that can be compelling. First, Galiani and Schargrodsky (2004) show that squatters' "pre-treatment characteristics," such as age and sex, are statistically unrelated to whether squatters received titles or not—just as they would be, in expectation, if titles were truly assigned at random. (Pre-treatment characteristics are those thought to be determined before the notional treatment of interest took place, in this case the assigning of land titles; they are not thought to be themselves potentially affected by the treatment.) So, too, are characteristics of the occupied parcels themselves, such as distance from polluted creeks. Indeed, the Argentine government offered very similar compensation in per-meter terms to the original owners in both the treatment and the control groups, which also suggests that titled and untitled parcels did not differ systematically. In principle, more determined or industrious squatters could have occupied more promising plots; if titles tended systematically to be granted (or withheld) to the occupiers of such plots, comparisons between titled and untitled squatters might overstate (or understate) the impact of titles. Yet, the quantitative evidence is not consistent with the existence of such confounders: it suggests balance on potentially confounding characteristics, such as the quality of plots.

Just as important as this quantitative assessment of pre-treatment equivalence, however, is qualitative information about the process by which plots and titles were obtained in this substantive context. In 1981, Galiani and Schargrodsky (2004) assert, neither squatters nor Catholic Church organizers could have successfully predicted which *particular* parcels would eventually have their titles transferred in 1984 and which would not. Thus, industrious or determined squatters who were particularly eager to receive titles would not have had reason to occupy one plot over another. Nor did the quality of the plots or attributes of the squatters explain the decisions of some owners and not others to challenge expropriation: on the basis of extensive interviews and other qualitative fieldwork, the authors argue convincingly that idiosyncratic factors explain these decisions. I take up this substantive example in more detail elsewhere. For present purposes, a key initial point is simply that fine-grained knowledge about context and process is crucial for bolstering the case for as-if random assignment.

In sum, in a valid natural experiment, we should find that potential confounders are balanced across the treatment and control group, just as they would be in expectation in a true experiment. Note that this balance occurs *not* because a researcher has matched squatters on background covariates—as in many conventional observational studies—but rather because the *process* of treatment assignment itself mimics a random process. However, various forms of quantitative and qualitative evidence, including detailed knowledge of the process that led to treatment assignment, must be used to evaluate the claim that squatters were assigned to treatment and control groups as-if by a coin flip. Much of this book focuses on the type of evidence that validates this claim—and what sort of evidence undermines it.

If the claim of as-if random assignment is to be believed, then the natural experiment plays a key role in making causal inferences persuasive. Without it, confounders could readily explain *ex post* differences between squatters with and without titles. For example, the intriguing findings about the self-reinforcing (not to mention self-deluding) beliefs of the squatters in meritocracy could have been explained as a result of unobserved characteristics of those squatters who did or did not successfully gain titles.

Snow on Cholera

The structure of Galiani and Schargrodsky's (2004) study bears a striking resemblance to a third, classic example of a natural experiment from a distinct substantive domain, which is also worth reviewing in some detail. John Snow, an anesthesiologist who lived through the devastating cholera epidemics in nineteenth-century London (Richardson [1887] 1936: xxxiv), believed that cholera was a waste- or waterborne infectious disease—contradicting the then-prevalent theory of "bad air" (miasma) that was used to explain cholera's transmission. Snow noted that epidemics seemed to follow the "great tracks of human intercourse" (Snow [1855] 1965: 2); moreover, sailors who arrived in a cholera-infested port did not become infected until they disembarked, which provided evidence against the miasma theory. During London's cholera outbreak of 1853–54, Snow drew a map showing addresses of deceased victims;

Table 1.1 Death rates from cholera by water-supply source

Company	Number of houses	Cholera deaths	Death rate per 10,000
Southwark and Vauxhall	40,046	1,263	315
Lambeth	26,107	98	37
Rest of London	256,423	1,422	56

Note: The table shows household death rates during London's cholera outbreak of 1853–54. Households are classified according to the company providing water service.
Source: Snow ([1855] 1965: table IX, p. 86) (also presented in Freedman 2009).

these clustered around the Broad Street water pump in London's Soho district, leading Snow to argue that contaminated water supply from this pump contributed to the cholera outbreak. (A rendition of Snow's spot map provides the cover image for this book.)

Snow's strongest piece of evidence, however, came from a natural experiment that he studied during the epidemic of 1853–54 (Freedman 1991, 1999). Large areas of London were served by two water companies, the Lambeth company and the Southwark & Vauxhall company. In 1852, the Lambeth company had moved its intake pipe further upstream on the Thames, thereby "obtaining a supply of water quite free from the sewage of London," while Southwark & Vauxhall left its intake pipe in place (Snow [1855] 1965: 68). Snow obtained records on cholera deaths in households throughout London, as well as information on the company that provided water to each household and the total number of houses served by each company. He then compiled a simple cross-tabulation showing the cholera death rate by source of water supply. As shown in Table 1.1, for houses served by Southwark and Vauxhall, the death rate from cholera was 315 per 10,000; for houses served by Lambeth, it was a mere 37 per 10,000.

Why did this constitute a credible natural experiment? Like Galiani and Schargrodsky's study of land titling in Argentina, Snow presented various sorts of evidence to establish the pre-treatment equivalence of the houses that were exposed to pure and contaminated sources of water supply. His own description is most eloquent:

> The mixing of the (water) supply is of the most intimate kind. The pipes of each Company go down all the streets, and into nearly all the courts and alleys. A few houses are supplied by one Company and a few by the other, according to the decision of the owner or occupier at that time when the Water Companies were in active

competition. In many cases a single house has a supply different from that on either side. Each company supplies both rich and poor, both large houses and small; there is no difference either in the condition or occupation of the persons receiving the water of the different Companies ... It is obvious that no experiment could have been devised which would more thoroughly test the effect of water supply on the progress of cholera than this. (Snow [1855] 1965: 74–75)

While Snow did not gather data allowing him to systematically assess the empirical balance on potential confounders (such as the condition or occupation of persons receiving water from different companies) or present formal statistical tests investigating this balance, his concern with establishing the pre-treatment equivalence of the two groups of households is very modern—and contributes to validating his study as a natural experiment.

At the same time, qualitative information on context and on the process that determined water-supply source was also crucial in Snow's study. For instance, Snow emphasized that decisions regarding which of the competing water companies would be chosen for a particular address were often taken by absentee landlords. Thus, residents did not largely "self-select" into their source of water supply—so confounding characteristics of residents appeared unlikely to explain the large differences in death rates by company shown in Table 1.1. Moreover, the decision of the Lambeth company to move its intake pipe upstream on the Thames was taken before the cholera outbreak of 1853–54, and existing scientific knowledge did not clearly link water source to cholera risk. As Snow puts it, the move of the Lambeth company's water pipe meant that more than 300,000 people of all ages and social strata were

divided into two groups *without their choice, and, in most cases, without their knowledge*; one group being supplied with water containing the sewage of London, and, amongst it, whatever might have come from the cholera patients, the other group having water quite free from such impurity. (Snow [1855] 1965: 75; italics added)

Just as in the land-titling study in Argentina, here neighbors were sorted into differing treatment groups in a way that appears as-if random. The process of treatment assignment itself appears to obviate confounding variables.

Like Galiani and Schargrodsky's study, Snow's study of cholera transmission suggests some possible lessons in the virtues of successful natural experiments. If assignment to receive a source of water supply is really as good as random, then confounding is not an issue—just as in true experiments. Straightforward contrasts between the treatment and control groups may then suffice to demonstrate or reject a causal effect of land titling. For instance,

Table 1.1 suggests that the difference in average death rates may be used to estimate the effect of water-supply source—and thus provide credible evidence that cholera is a water-borne disease. With strong natural experiments, the statistical analysis may be straightforward and transparent, and it can rest on credible assumptions about the data-generating process—a theme I explore in detail elsewhere in this book. Snow used quantitative techniques such as two-by-two tables and cross-tabulations that today may seem old-fashioned, but as Freedman (1999: 5) puts it, "it is the design of the study and the magnitude of the effect that compel conviction, not the elaboration of technique."

1.3 Varieties of natural experiments

What, then, are natural experiments? As the discussion above has implied, this method can be best defined in relation to two other types of research design: true experiments and conventional observational studies. A randomized controlled experiment (Freedman, Pisani, and Purves 2007: 4–8) has three hallmarks:

(1) The response of experimental subjects assigned to receive a treatment is compared to the response of subjects assigned to a control group.[13]
(2) The assignment of subjects to treatment and control groups is done at random, through a randomizing device such as a coin flip.
(3) The manipulation of the treatment—also known as the intervention—is under the control of an experimental researcher.

Each of these traits plays a critical role in the experimental model of inference. For example, in a medical trial of a new drug, the fact that subjects in the treatment group take the drug, while those in the control group do not, allows for a comparison of health outcomes across the two groups. Random assignment establishes *ex ante* symmetry between the groups and therefore obviates confounding. Finally, experimental manipulation of the treatment condition establishes further evidence for a *causal* relationship between the treatment and the health outcomes.[14]

Some conventional observational studies share the first attribute of true experiments, in that outcomes for units bearing different values of independent

---

[13] The control condition is often defined as the absence of a treatment, but again, it need not be defined this way. There may also be multiple groups, and multiple treatment conditions.
[14] For a discussion of the role of manipulation in accounts of causation, see Goldthorpe (2001) and Brady (2008).

variables (or "treatment conditions") are compared. Indeed, such comparisons are the basis of much social science. Yet, with typical observational studies, treatment assignment is very far from random; self-selection into treatment and control groups is the norm, which raises concerns about confounding. Moreover, there is no experimental manipulation—after all, this is what makes such studies observational. Thus, conventional observational studies do not share attributes (2) and (3) of experiments.

Natural experiments, on the other hand, share attribute (1) of true experiments—that is, comparison of outcomes across treatment and control conditions—and they at least partially share (2), since assignment is random or as good as random. This distinguishes natural experiments from conventional observational studies, in which treatment assignment is clearly *not* as-if random. Again, how a researcher can credibly claim that treatment is as good as randomized—even when there is no true randomizing device—is an important and tricky matter. As a definitional and conceptual matter, however, this is what distinguishes a natural experiment from a conventional observational study, and it makes natural experiments much more like true experiments than other observational studies. However, unlike true experiments, the data used in natural experiments come from "naturally" occurring phenomena—actually, in the social sciences, from phenomena that are often the product of social and political forces. Because the manipulation of treatment variables is not generally under the control of the analyst, natural experiments are, in fact, observational studies. Hallmark (3) therefore distinguishes natural experiments from true experiments, while hallmark (2) distinguishes natural experiments from conventional observational studies.

Two initial points are worth making about this definition, one terminological and the other more conceptual. First, it is worth noting that the label "natural experiment" is perhaps unfortunate. As we shall see, the social and political forces that give rise to as-if random assignment of interventions are not generally "natural" in any ordinary sense of that term.[15] Second, natural experiments are observational studies, not true experiments, again, because they lack an experimental manipulation. In sum, natural experiments are neither natural nor experiments. Still, the term "natural" may suggest the serendipity that characterizes the discovery of many of these research designs; and the analogy to

---

[15] Rosenzweig and Wolpin (2000) distinguish "natural" natural experiments—for instance, those that come from weather shocks—from other kinds of natural experiments.

experiments is certainly worth making.[16] This standard term is also widely used to describe the research designs that I discuss in this book. Rather than introduce further methodological jargon, I have therefore retained use of the term.

A second point relates to the distinction between true experiments and randomized natural experiments. When the treatment is truly randomized, a natural experiment fully shares attributes (1) and (2) of true experiments. Yet, the manipulation is not under the control of an experimental researcher. This does appear to be an important distinguishing characteristic of natural experiments, relative to many true experiments. After all, using natural experiments is appealing precisely when analysts wish to study the effects of independent variables that are difficult or impossible to manipulate experimentally, such as political regimes, aspects of colonial rule, and even land titles and military service.[17]

To some readers, the requirement that the randomized manipulation be under the control of the researcher in true experiments may seem unnecessarily restrictive. After all, there are true experiments in which researchers' control over the manipulation is far from absolute; there are also natural experiments in which policy-makers or other actors implement exactly the manipulation for which researchers might wish.

Yet, the planned nature of the intervention is an important conceptual attribute of true experiments, and it distinguishes such research designs from natural experiments. With true experiments, planning the manipulation may allow for comparison of complex experimental treatment conditions (as in factorial or variation-in-treatment experimental designs) that are not available with some natural experiments. The serendipity of many natural-experimental interventions, in contrast, gives rise to special challenges. As we will see later in the book, the fact that the manipulation is not under the control of natural-experimental researchers can raise important issues of interpretation—precisely because "Nature" often does *not* design to design a manipulation exactly as researchers would wish. It therefore seems useful to maintain the distinction between randomized controlled experiments and natural experiments with true randomization.

Within the broad definition given above, there are many types of natural experiments. Although there are a number of possible classifications, in this book I divide natural experiments into three categories:

---

[16] Below I contrast "natural experiments" with another term that draws this analogy—"quasi-experiments"—and emphasize the important differences between these two types of research design.

[17] The latter such variables might in principle be experimentally manipulated, but typically they are not.

- *"Standard" natural experiments* (Chapter 2). These include the Argentina land-titling study, Snow's study of cholera transmission, and a range of other natural experiments. These natural experiments may be truly randomized or merely as-if randomized. This is by design a heterogeneous category that includes natural experiments that do not fall into the next two types.
- *Regression-discontinuity designs* (Chapter 3). In these designs, the study group is distinguished by virtue of position just above or below some threshold value of a covariate that determines treatment assignment. For instance, students scoring just above a threshold score on an entrance exam may be offered admission to a specialized program. The element of luck involved in exam outcomes suggests that assignment to the program may be as good as random—for those exam-takers just above and just below the threshold. Thus, comparisons between these two groups can be used to estimate the program's impact.
- *Instrumental-variables designs* (Chapter 4). In these designs, units are randomly or as-if randomly assigned not to the key treatment of interest but rather to a variable that is correlated with that treatment. In the military draft example, men were assigned at random to draft eligibility, not to actual military service. Yet, draft eligibility can be used as an instrumental variable for service; under some nontrivial assumptions, this allows for analysis of the effects of military service, for a particular set of subjects. Instrumental variables may be viewed as an analytic technique that is often useful in the analysis of standard natural experiments as well as some regression-discontinuity designs. Yet, in many natural experiments, the focus is placed on the as-if random assignment of values of variables that are merely correlated with treatment, rather than on the as-if random assignment of values of the key treatment variable itself. It is therefore useful to separate the discussion of instrumental-variables designs from standard natural experiments and regression-discontinuity designs.

This categorization of varieties of natural experiments provides a useful framework for surveying existing studies, as I do in Part I of the book.

1.3.1 Contrast with quasi-experiments and matching

Before turning to the questions posed at the beginning of the chapter, it is also useful to contrast natural experiments with some observational research designs with which they are sometimes mistakenly conflated. My definition of natural experiments distinguishes them from what Donald Campbell and his colleagues called "quasi-experiments" (Campbell and Stanley 1966). With the latter research design, there is no presumption that policy interventions have been assigned at random or as-if random. Indeed, Achen's (1986: 4) book on the statistical analysis of quasi-experiments defines these as studies "characterized by *nonrandom* assignment" (italics in the original). While some analysts continue to refer to natural experiments like Angrist's (1990a) as *quasi*-experiments, it nonetheless seems useful to distinguish these terms. In this book, I therefore use the term "natural experiment" rather than "quasi-experiment" advisedly.

Indeed, it is instructive to compare the natural experiments introduced above to standard quasi-experimental designs. Consider the famous quasi-experiment in which Campbell and Ross (1970) investigated the effects of a speeding law passed in Connecticut in the 1960s. There, the question was the extent to which reductions in traffic fatalities in the wake of the law could be attributed to the law's effects; a key problem was that the timing and location of the speeding law was not random. For example, the law was passed in a year in which Connecticut experienced an especially high level of traffic fatalities—perhaps because legislators' constituents tend to be more demanding of reforms when deaths are more visible. Some of the subsequent reduction in fatalities could thus be due to the "regression to the mean" that would tend to follow an unusually high number of traffic deaths. The nonrandom application of the intervention—the fact that legislators passed the law after a period of especially high fatalities—therefore raises the inferential difficulties that Campbell and Ross discuss in connection with this quasi-experiment. Precisely because of this nonrandomness of the intervention, Campbell developed his famous list of "threats to internal validity"—that is, sources of errors that could arise in attributing the reduction in traffic fatalities to the causal effects of the law.

Campbell usefully suggested several research-design modifications that could be made in this context, for example, extending the time series to make pre-intervention and post-intervention comparisons, acquiring data on traffic fatalities in neighboring states, and so on. However, such refinements and controlled comparisons do not make the study a natural experiment, even if they are successful in eliminating confounding (which, of course, cannot be verified, because the confounding may be from unobservable variables). This is not to gainsay the value of such strategies. Yet, this example does suggest a key difference between studies in which apparently similar comparison groups are found or statistical controls introduced, and those in which the process of treatment assignment produces statistical independence of treatment assignment and potential confounders—as in the Vietnam draft-lottery study or, arguably, the Argentina land-titling study. The key point is that with quasi-experiments, there is no presumption of random or as-if random assignment; threats to internal validity arise precisely because treatment assignment is not randomized.

Natural experiments must also be distinguished from the "matching" techniques increasingly used to analyze the data from conventional observational studies, for similar reasons. Matching, like standard regression analysis, is a strategy of controlling for known confounders through covariate adjustment. For example, Gilligan and Sergenti (2008) study the effects of UN peacekeeping missions in sustaining peace after civil war. Recognizing that UN interventions are nonrandomly assigned to countries experiencing civil wars, and that differences between countries that receive missions and those that do not—rather than the presence or absence of UN missions per se—may explain postwar differences across these countries, the authors use matching to adjust for nonrandom assignment. Cases where UN interventions took place are matched—i.e., paired—with those where they did not occur, applying the criterion of having similar scores on measured variables such as the presence of non-UN missions, the degree of ethnic fractionalization, or the duration of previous wars. The assumption is then that whether a country receives a UN mission—within the strata defined by these measured variables—is like a coin flip.[18]

In matching designs, then, assignment to treatment is neither random nor as-if random. Comparisons are made across units exposed to treatment and control conditions, while addressing observable confounders—that is, those researchers can observe and measure. In contrast to natural experiments—in which as-if random assignment allows the investigator to control for both observed and unobserved confounders—matching relies on the assumption that analysts can measure and control the relevant (known) confounders. Some analysts suggest that matching yields the equivalent of a study focused on twins, in which one sibling gets the treatment at random and the other serves as the control (Dehejia and Wahba 1999; Dehejia 2005). Yet, while matching seeks to approximate as-if random by conditioning on observed variables, unobserved variables may distort the results. If statistical models are used to do the matching, the assumptions behind the models may play a key role (Smith and Todd 2005; Arceneaux, Green, and Gerber 2006; Berk and Freedman

---

[18] The study yields the substantive finding that UN interventions are effective, at least in some areas.

2008).[19] In successful natural experiments, in contrast, there may be no need to control for observable confounders—a theme I take up presently.[20]

The contrast between matching designs and natural experiments again underscores the importance of understanding the *process* that determines treatment assignment. With natural experiments, the onus is on analysts to explain how social and political forces end up allocating treatments in a random or as-if random way. Often, as we will see, detailed institutional knowledge is crucial for recognizing and validating the existence of a natural experiment. Unlike with matching, the focus is not on what the analyst does to adjust the data—after the fact—to confront confounding or other threats to valid causal inference. Rather, it is on how the *ex ante* assignment process itself generates statistical independence between treatment assignment and potential confounders, thereby making inferences about the causal effects of treatment assignment persuasive.

Thus, at the heart of natural-experimental research is the effort to use random or as-if random processes to study the effects of causes—instead of attempting to control for confounders statistically. At least in principle, this distinguishes natural experiments from conventional observational studies, including quasi-experiments and matching designs.

1.4 Natural experiments as design-based research

What, then, explains the recent growth of natural experiments in the social sciences? Their prominence may reflect three interrelated trends in social-science methodology. In the last decade or so, many methodologists and researchers have emphasized:

(1) the often-severe problems with conventional regression analysis (Achen 2002; Brady and Collier 2010; Freedman 2006, 2008, 2009; Heckman 2000; Seawright 2010; Sekhon 2009);

---

[19] An example is propensity-score matching, in which the "propensity" to receive treatment is modeled as a function of known confounders. See also the special issue on the econometrics of matching in the *Review of Economics and Statistics* (February 2004), vol. 86, no. 1.

[20] Researchers sometimes suggest that Nature generates an as-if random assignment process conditional on covariates. For instance, elections secretaries may take account of race or partisanship while redistricting constituencies; conditional on covariates such as race or partisanship, assignment to a particular constituency may be as-if random. However, a difficulty here often involves constructing the right model of the true assignment process: what functional form or type of "matching" does an elections secretary use to take account of race or partisanship, when doing redistricting? Such issues are not straightforward (see Chapters 2 and 9).

(2) the importance of strong research designs, including both field and natural experiments, as tools for achieving valid causal inferences (Freedman 1999; Gerber and Green 2008; Morton and Williams 2008; Dunning 2008a);
(3) the virtues of multi-method research, in which qualitative and quantitative methods are seen as having distinct but complementary strengths (Collier, Brady, and Seawright 2010; Dunning 2010a; Paluck 2008).

The first topic bears special emphasis, because it runs against the grain of much social-scientific practice. Over the last several decades, among quantitatively oriented researchers, multivariate regression analysis and its extensions have provided the major vehicle for drawing causal inferences from observational data. This convention has followed the lead of much technical research on empirical quantitative methods, which has focused, for example, on the estimation of complicated linear and non-linear regression models. Reviewing this trend, Achen (2002: 423) notes that the "steady gains in theoretical sophistication have combined with explosive increases in computing power to produce a profusion of new estimators for applied political researchers."

Behind the growth of such methods lies the belief that they allow for more valid causal inferences, perhaps compensating for less-than-ideal research designs. Indeed, one rationale for multivariate regression is that it allows for comparisons that approximate a true experiment. As a standard introductory econometrics text puts it, "the power of multiple regression analysis is that it allows us to do in non-experimental environments what natural scientists are able to do in a controlled laboratory setting: keep other factors fixed" (Wooldridge 2009: 77).

Yet, leading methodologists have questioned the ability of these methods to reproduce experimental conditions (Angrist and Pischke 2008; Freedman 1991, 1999, 2006, 2009), and they have also underscored other pitfalls of these techniques, including the more technically advanced models and estimators—all of which fall under the rubric of what Brady, Collier, and Seawright (2010) call mainstream quantitative methods. There are at least two major problems with such "model-based" inference, in which complicated statistical models are used to measure and control confounding factors.[21]

---

[21] A "statistical model" is a probability model that stipulates how data are generated. In regression analysis, the statistical model involves choices about which variables are to be included, along with assumptions about functional form, the distribution of (unobserved) error terms, and the relationship between error terms and observed variables.

First, with such techniques, statistical adjustment for potential confounders is assumed to produce the conditional independence of treatment assignment and unobserved causes of the outcomes being explained. Roughly, conditional independence implies that within the strata defined by the measured confounders, assignment to treatment groups is independent of other factors that affect outcomes. Yet, conditional independence is difficult to achieve: the relevant confounding variables must be identified and measured (Brady 2010). To recall the examples above, what are the possible confounders that might be associated with military service and later earnings? Or with land titles and access to credit markets? And how does one reliably measure such potential confounders? In the multiple regression context, as is well known, failure to include confounders in the relevant equation leads to "omitted-variables bias" or "endogeneity bias." On the other hand, including irrelevant or poorly measured variables in regression equations may also lead to other problems and can make inferences about causal effects even less reliable (Clarke 2005; Seawright 2010).

This leads to the major problem of identifying what particular confounders researchers should measure. In any research situation, researchers (and their critics) can usually identify one or several potential sources of confounding. Yet, reasonable observers may disagree about the importance of these various threats to valid inference. Moreover, because confounding is from unobserved or unmeasured variables, ultimately the direction and extent of confounding is unverifiable without making strong assumptions. The use of so-called "garbage-can regression," in which researchers attempt to include virtually all potentially measureable confounders, has properly fallen into disrepute (Achen 2002). However, this leaves researchers somewhat at a loss about what particular variables to measure, and it may not allow their readers to evaluate reliably the results of the research.

A second, perhaps even deeper problem with typical model-based approaches is that the models themselves may lack credibility as persuasive depictions of the data-generating process. Inferring causation from regression requires a theory of how the data are generated (i.e., a *response schedule*—Freedman 2009: 85–95; Heckman 2000). This theory is a hypothetical account of how one variable would respond if the scholar intervened and manipulated other variables. In observational studies, of course, the researcher never actually intervenes to change any variables, so this theory remains, to reiterate, hypothetical. Yet, data produced by social and political processes can be used to estimate the expected magnitude of a change in one variable that would arise if one were to manipulate other variables—assuming, of course, that the researcher has a correct theory of the data-generating process.

The requirement that the model of the data-generating process be correct goes well beyond the need to identify confounders, though this is certainly a necessary part of constructing a valid model. Assumptions about the functional form linking alternative values of the independent variable to the dependent variable are also part of the specification of the model. Perhaps even more crucial is the idea that the parameters (coefficients) of regression equations tell us how units would respond if a researcher intervened to change values of the independent variable—which is sometimes called the invariance of structural parameters to intervention. Whether and how various models can provide credible depictions of data-generating processes is an important theme of later chapters of this book (e.g., Chapters 5, 6, and 9).

In light of such difficulties, the focus on complex statistical models and advanced techniques for estimating those models appears to be giving way to greater concern with simplicity and transparency in data analysis, and in favor of more foundational issues of research design—the trend (2) identified above. This approach is a far cry from more conventional practice in quantitative research, in which the trend has been towards more complex statistical models in which the assumptions are difficult to explicate, rationalize, and validate.

Of course, the importance of research design for causal inference has long been emphasized by leading texts, such as King, Keohane, and Verba's (1994; see also Brady and Collier 2010). What distinguishes the current emphasis of some analysts is the conviction that if research designs are flawed, statistical adjustment can do little to bolster causal inference. As Sekhon (2009: 487) puts it, "without an experiment, natural experiment, a discontinuity, or some other strong design, no amount of econometric or statistical modeling can make the move from correlation to causation persuasive."

Here we find one rationale for "design-based" research—that is, research in which control over confounders comes primarily from appropriate research-design choices, rather than *ex post* statistical adjustment (Angrist and Krueger 2001; Dunning 2008b, 2010a). Without random or as-if random assignment, unobserved or unmeasured confounders may threaten valid causal inference. Yet, if units are instead assigned at random to treatment conditions, confounders are balanced in expectation across the treatment groups. This implies that the researcher is no longer faced with the difficult choice of what potential variables to include or exclude from a regression equation: randomization balances all potential confounders, up to random error, whether those confounders are easy or difficult to measure. In the quote from Sekhon above, we thus find a contrast between two strategies—one in which statistical modeling is used to attempt to move from correlation to causation, and another in which researchers rely on the strength of the research design to control observed *and* unobserved confounders. The capacity of the first, modeling strategy to control for confounding variables has encountered increasing scepticism in several social-science disciplines. Thus, while methodologists continue to debate the strengths and limitations of experiments and various kinds of natural experiments, there is considerable sympathy for the view that strong research designs provide the most reliable means to mitigate the problem of confounding. This is one reason for the recent excitement for experimental and natural-experimental research.

Yet, there is a second important rationale for the growth of design-based research in the social sciences, one that relates closely to the second difficulty mentioned above in relation to model-based inference (Dunning 2008a). If treatment assignment is truly random or as good as random, a simple comparison of average outcomes in treatment and control groups can often suffice for valid causal inference.[22] Moreover, this simplicity rests on a model of data-generating processes that is often credible for experiments and natural experiments. In later chapters, I describe a simple model that often is the right starting point for natural experiments—the so-called Neyman potential outcomes model, also known as the Neyman–Holland–Rubin model—and examine the conditions under which it applies to the analysis of natural-experimental data. When this model applies, analysts may sidestep the often-severe problems raised by model-based inference, in which complicated causal and statistical models are instead used to control confounding factors (Chapter 5).

In sum, research designs such as strong natural experiments are often amenable to simple and transparent data analysis, grounded in credible hypotheses about the data-generating process. This constitutes an important potential virtue of this style of research, and in principle, it distinguishes natural experiments and design-based research more generally from model-based inference. In practice, nonetheless, complex regression models are sometimes still fit to the data produced by these strong research designs. How the simplicity, transparency, and credibility of the analysis of natural-experimental data can be bolstered is thus an important theme of the book.

This also takes us to the third and final topic listed above, the importance and utility of multi-method research. Persuasive natural experiments typically involve the use of multiple methods, including the combination of

---

[22] Put differently, a difference-of-means test validly estimates the average causal effect of treatment assignment.

quantitative and qualitative methods for which many scholars have recently advocated. For instance, while the analysis of natural experiments is sometimes facilitated by the use of statistical and quantitative techniques, the detailed case-based knowledge often associated with qualitative research is crucial both to recognizing the existence of a natural experiment and to gathering the kinds of evidence that make the assertion of as-if random compelling. Moreover, qualitative evidence of various kinds may help to validate the causal and statistical models used in quantitative analysis. Exhaustive "shoe-leather" research involving both qualitative and quantitative techniques may be needed to gather various kinds of data in support of causal inferences (Freedman 1991). Like other research designs, natural experiments are unlikely to be compelling if they do not rest on a foundation of substantive expertise.

Yet, the way quantitative and qualitative methods are jointly used in natural experiments differs from other kinds of research, such as studies that combine cross-national or within-country regressions or formal models with case studies and other qualitative work (Fearon and Laitin 2008; Lieberman 2005; Seawright and Gerring 2008). The simple and transparent quantitative analysis involved in successful natural experiments rests on the Neyman potential outcomes models described above. Yet, qualitative methods are often crucial for motivating and validating the assumptions of these models. In addition, specific kinds of information about the context and the process that generated the natural experiment are critical for validating the as-if random assumption in many natural experiments. Following Brady, Collier, and Seawright (2010), such nuggets of information about context and process may be called "causal-process observations" (see also Mahoney 2010).[23]

In this book, I develop a typology to describe the important role of several types of causal-process observations, including what I label "treatment-assignment CPOs" and "model-validation CPOs" (Chapter 7). Along with quantitative tools like difference-of-means tests or balance tests, these are helpful for analyzing and evaluating the success of particular natural experiments. My goal here is to put the contributions of qualitative methods to natural experiments on a more systematic foundation than most previous methodological research has done and to emphasize the ways in which the use of multiple methods can make design-based research more compelling.

---

[23] Collier, Brady, and Seawright (2010) contrast such causal-process observations, which are nuggets of information that provide insight into context, process, or mechanism, with "data-set observations," that is the collection of values on dependent and independent variables for each unit (case).

1.5 An evaluative framework for natural experiments

The discussion above suggests a final issue for consideration in this introductory chapter: how should the success of natural experiments be evaluated? To answer this question, it is useful to think about three dimensions along which research designs, and the studies that employ them, may be classified—involving what will be called plausibility, credibility, and relevance (see Dunning 2010a). Thus, the dimensions include (1) the plausibility of as-if random assignment to treatment; (2) the credibility of causal and statistical models; and (3) the substantive relevance of the treatment. A typology based on these three dimensions serves as the basis for Part III of the book; it is useful to discuss these dimensions briefly here to set the stage for what follows.

Each of these three dimensions corresponds to distinctive challenges involved in drawing causal inferences in the social sciences: (i) the challenge of confounding; (ii) the challenge of specifying the causal and/or stochastic process by which observable data are generated; (iii) the challenge of generalizing the effects of particular treatments or interventions to the effects of similar treatments, or to populations other than the one being studied, as well as challenges having to do with interpretation of the treatment. While this overarching framework can be used to analyze the strengths and limitations of any research design—including true experiments and observational studies—it is particularly helpful for natural experiments, which turn out to exhibit substantial variation along these dimensions.

1.5.1 The plausibility of as-if random

In some natural experiments, such as those that feature true randomization, validating as-if random assignment is fairly straightforward. With lottery studies, barring some failure of the randomization procedure, assignment to treatment truly is randomized. Still, since randomization is often not under the control of the researcher but rather some government bureaucrat or other agent—after all, these are natural experiments, not true experiments—procedures for evaluating the plausibility of as-if random are nonetheless important.[24]

---

[24] For instance, in the 1970 Vietnam-era draft lottery, it was alleged that lottery numbers were put in a jar for sampling month by month, January through December, and that subsequent mixing of the jar was not sufficient to overcome this sequencing, resulting in too few draws from later months (see Starr 1997). Of course, birth date may still be statistically independent of potential outcomes (i.e., earnings that would occur under draft eligibility and without it; see Chapter 5). Yet, if there is any failure of the

Later in the book, I describe both quantitative and qualitative procedures that can be used to check this assertion.

Without true randomization, however, asserting that assignment is as good as random may be much less plausible—in the absence of compelling quantitative and qualitative evidence to the contrary. Since as-if random assignment is the definitional feature of natural experiments, the onus is therefore on the researcher to make a very compelling case for this assertion (or to drop the claim to a natural experiment), using the tools mentioned earlier in this chapter and discussed in detail later in the book. Ultimately, the assertion of as-if random is only partially verifiable, and this is the bane of some natural experiments relative, for instance, to true experiments.

Different studies vary with respect to this criterion of as-if random, and they can be ranked along a continuum defined by the extent to which the assertion is plausible (Chapter 8). When as-if random is very compelling, natural experiments are strong on this definitional criterion. When assignment is something less than as-if random, analysts may be studying something less than a natural experiment, and causal inferences drawn from the study may be more tenuous.

1.5.2 The credibility of models

The source of much skepticism about widely used regression techniques is that the statistical models employed require many assumptions—often both implausible and numerous—that undermine their credibility. In strong natural experiments, as-if randomness should ensure that assignment is statistically independent of other factors that influence outcomes. This would seem to imply that elaborate multivariate statistical models may often not be required. With natural experiments, the Neyman potential outcomes model (introduced in Chapter 5) often provides an appropriate starting point—though this model also involves important restrictions, and the match between the model and the reality should be carefully considered in each application. If the Neyman model holds, the data analysis can be simple and transparent—as with the comparison of percentages or of means in the treatment and the control groups.

Unfortunately, while this is true in principle, it is not always true in practice. Empirical studies can also be ranked along a continuum defined by the credibility of the underlying causal and statistical models (Chapter 9). Like

---

randomization, this assumption is less secure. The lesson is that analysts should assess the plausibility of as-if random, even in randomized natural experiments.

the dimension of plausibility of as-if random, ranking studies along this second dimension inevitably involves a degree of subjectivity. Yet, the use of such a continuum gives texture to the idea that the presence of a valid natural experiment does not necessarily imply data analysis that is simple, transparent, and founded on credible models of the data-generating process.

Note that because the causal and statistical models invoked in typical natural experiments often involve an assumption of as-good-as-random assignment, the first evaluative dimension—the plausibility of as-if random—could be seen as derivative of this second dimension, the credibility of models. After all, if a statistical model posits random assignment and the assumption fails, then the model is not credible as a depiction of the data-generating process. However, there are two reasons to discuss the plausibility of as-if random separately from the credibility of models. First, as the discussion in this book makes clear, plausible as-if random assignment is far from sufficient to ensure the credibility of underlying statistical and causal models. There are many examples of plausible as-if random assignment in which underlying models lack credibility, and sometimes studies in which assignment is not plausibly random may employ more persuasive models than studies with true random assignment. Thus, the first dimension of the typology is not isomorphic with the second. Second, because of the definitional importance of the as-if random assumption for natural experiments, it is useful to discuss this dimension in isolation from other modeling assumptions.

1.5.3 The relevance of the intervention

A third dimension along which natural experiments may be classified is the substantive relevance of the intervention. Here one may ask: To what extent does as-if random assignment shed light on the wider theoretical, substantive, and/or policy issues that motivate the study?

Answers to this question might be a cause for concern for a number of reasons. For instance, the type of subjects or units exposed to a natural-experimental intervention might be more or less like the populations in which we are most interested. In lottery studies of electoral behavior, for example, levels of lottery winnings may be randomly assigned among lottery players, but we might doubt whether lottery players are like other populations (say, all voters). Next, the particular treatment might have idiosyncratic effects that are distinct from the effects of greatest interest. To continue the same example, levels of lottery winnings may or may not have similar effects on, say, political attitudes as income earned through work (Dunning 2008a, 2008b).

Finally, natural-experimental interventions (like the interventions in some true experiments) may "bundle" many distinct treatments or components of treatments. This may limit the extent to which this approach isolates the effect of the explanatory variable about which we care most, given particular substantive or social-scientific purposes. Such ideas are often discussed under the rubric of "external validity" (Campbell and Stanley 1966), but the issue of substantive relevance involves a broader question: i.e., whether the intervention—based on as-if random assignment deriving from social and political processes—in fact yields causal inferences about the real causal hypothesis of concern, and for the units we would really like to study.

Thus, for some observers, the use of natural experiments and related research designs can sharply limit the substantive and theoretical relevance of research findings (Deaton 2009). Indeed, clever studies in which as-if assignment is compelling, but that have only limited substantive relevance, do not meet a high standard of research design. Yet, natural-experimental studies also vary in the relevance of the key intervention. This suggests that existing research can also be ranked—albeit with some lack of precision—along a continuum defined by the relevance of the treatment (Chapter 10).

These three dimensions together define an evaluative framework for strong research designs (Figure 1.2). In the lower-left-hand corner are the weakest research designs, in which as-if random assignment is not compelling, causal models are not credible, and substantive relevance is low; the strongest research designs, which are compelling on all three of these criteria, appear in the upper-right corner. All three of these dimensions define important desiderata in social-scientific research. There may be trade-offs between them, and good research can be understood as the process of balancing astutely between these dimensions. Yet, the strongest natural-experimental research achieves placement near the upper-right corner of the cube. How best to leverage both quantitative and qualitative tools to move from the "weak-design" corner of the cube in Figure 1.2 towards the "strong-design" corner constitutes one broad focus of this book.

To see how these three dimensions might be used to evaluate a natural experiment, consider again the Argentina land-titling study. First, details of the process by which squatting took place and titles were assigned—as well as statistical evidence on the pre-treatment equivalence of titled and untitled squatters—suggest the plausibility of the claim that assignment to titles was as-if random. Of course, without actual randomization, this claim may not be as credible as in a true experiment; the prospect that unobserved confounders may distort results cannot be entirely discounted. Second, however, as-if

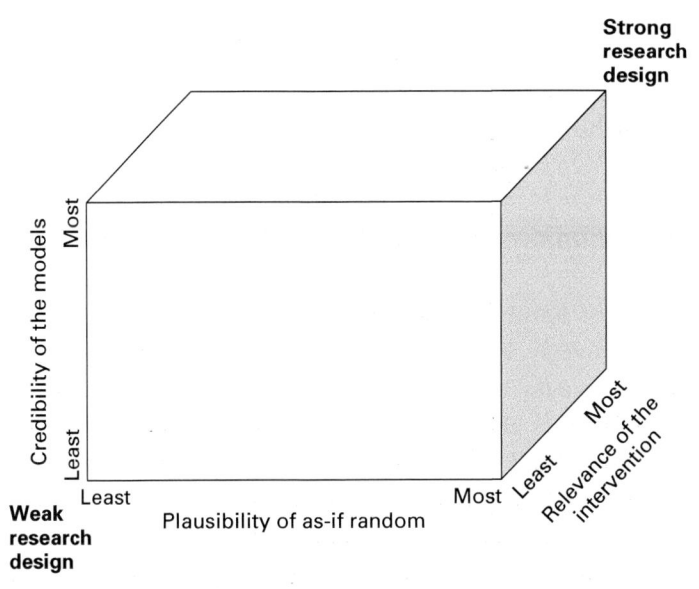

Figure 1.2 Typology of natural experiments

random is not enough: the model that defines causal parameters—such as the average causal effect, that is, the difference between the outcome we would observe if all the squatters were assigned titles and the outcome we would observe if no squatters were assigned titles—must also be correct. For example, this model assumes that squatters assigned to the control group are not influenced by the behaviors of squatters in the treatment group: each squatter's response is impacted only by whether he or she is assigned a title. Yet, if the reproductive behaviors or beliefs in self-efficacy of untitled squatters are affected by their interactions with their (titled) neighbors, this assumption is not valid. The causal and statistical model of the process that generated observable data posits other assumptions as well. The credibility of such assumptions must therefore be investigated and validated, to the extent possible. Finally, whether the effect of land-titling for squatters in Argentina can generalize to other settings—such as those in which local financial institutions may be more developed, and thus the use of titled property to collateralize access to capital may be more feasible—or whether there are special aspects of the intervention in this context are open questions. These should also be assessed using a priori arguments and evidence, to the extent possible.

In evaluating the success of a given natural experiment, then, all three of the desiderata represented by the dimensions of this typology should be considered. Achieving success on one dimension at the expense of the others does not produce the very strongest research designs.

1.6 Critiques and limitations of natural experiments

The growth of natural experiments in the social sciences has not been without controversy. For instance, many scholars have questioned the ability of both experimental and natural-experimental research to yield broad and cumulative insights about important theoretical and substantive concerns. Analysts have argued that the search for real-world situations of as-if random assignment can narrow analytic focus to possibly idiosyncratic contexts; this criticism parallels critiques of the embrace of randomized controlled experiments in development economics and other fields. As the Princeton economist Angus Deaton (2009: 426) puts it,

> under ideal circumstances, randomized evaluations of projects are useful for obtaining a convincing estimate of the average effect of a program or project. The price for this success is a focus that is too narrow and too local to tell us "what works" in development, to design policy, or to advance scientific knowledge about development processes.

From a somewhat different perspective, the econometricians James Heckman and Sergio Urzúa (2010: 27–28) suggest

> Proponents of IV [instrumental variables] are less ambitious in the range of questions they seek to answer. The method often gains precision by asking narrower questions ... the questions it answers are ... [not] well-formulated economic problems. Unspecified "effects" replace clearly defined economic parameters.

The political scientist Francis Fukuyama (2011) has also weighed in on this point, noting that

> Today, the single most popular form of development dissertation in both economics and political science is a randomized micro-experiment in which the graduate student goes out into the field and studies, at a local level, the impact of some intervention like the introduction of co-payments for malaria mosquito netting or changes in electoral rules on ethnic voting. These studies can be technically well designed, and they certainly have their place in evaluating projects at a micro level. But they do not

aggregate upwards into anything that can tell us when a regime crosses the line into illegitimacy, or how economic growth is changing the class structure of a society. We are not, in other words, producing new Samuel Huntingtons, with the latter's simultaneous breadth and depth of knowledge.

Many defenders of true as well as natural experiments take a position that contrasts sharply with these critiques. For these supporters, studying randomly or as-if randomly assigned interventions may not tell us everything we need to know about processes of social and political change—but it offers the most reliable way to learn about causal effects in a world in which it is very difficult to make valid inferences about the effects of economic or political causes. Moreover, for these advocates, the alternative may be little short of speculation. Causal effects estimated for a particular natural-experimental study group may indeed be local average treatment effects (LATEs), in the sense that they only characterize causal parameters for particular units, such as those located at the key threshold in regression-discontinuity designs (see Chapter 5). Yet, at least true experiments and natural experiments offer us opportunities actually to learn about the direction and size of these causal effects, which alternative approaches may not. The title of an essay by Imbens (2009)—"Better LATE than Nothing"—is telling in this regard.

Unsurprisingly, this defense has not satisfied the critics. As Deaton (2009: 430) notes,

I find it hard to make any sense of the LATE. We are unlikely to learn much about the processes at work if we refuse to say anything about what determines [causal effects]; heterogeneity is not a technical problem calling for an econometric solution but a reflection of the fact that we have not started on our proper business, which is trying to understand what is going on. (430)

Thus, here we find two broadly contrasting positions in contemporary writings on true and natural experiments. Detractors suggest that while these methods may offer reliable evidence of policy impacts at the micro level, the findings from natural experiments and from design-based research more generally are unlikely to aggregate into broader knowledge. Moreover, even at the level of single studies, the interventions being studied may lack substantive or theoretical relevance, in that they do not allow us to study "interesting" economic or political parameters. Advocates for true experiments and natural experiments, in contrast, suggest that these methods offer the most reliable route to secure causal inference. Even if some of the causes that analysts study appear trivial, the alternative to using true and natural experiments to make causal inferences is even less promising.

This book advances a middle-ground argument positioned between these two extremes. Valid causal inference—secured by settings in which confounding is obviated, models of the data-generating process are credible, and data analysis is preferably simple and transparent—is important. So is the ability to say something about the effect of interventions that are relevant, in both theoretical and substantive terms. Achieving these important desiderata at the same time is not easy. That is why many studies may not fully reach the "strong-research-design" corner of the cube in Figure 11.2 (Chapter 11).

Yet, reaching that corner of the cube should nonetheless remain an aspiration. Neither as-if random assignment nor substantive relevance alone can position a study at the strong-research-design corner of the cube. Gains on any single dimension should be weighed against losses on the others. Sometimes, analytic or substantive choices can help scholars strengthen their research on all three dimensions. How best to achieve research designs that are strong on each dimension—and how to manage trade-offs between them that inevitably come up in doing real research—is therefore an important theme of the book.

1.7 Avoiding conceptual stretching

A final point is important to make in this introductory chapter. The potential strengths of natural experiments—and the excitement and interest that their use attracts among contemporary social scientists—can sometimes lead to misapplication of the label. As we will see in this book, natural experiments have been successfully used to study many important causal relations; and many more valid natural experiments may await researchers alert to their potential use. Yet, analysts have also sometimes claimed to use natural experiments in settings where the definitional criterion of the method—random or as-if random assignment—is not plausibly met. To the extent that assignment to treatment is something less than as-if random, analysts are likely studying something less than a natural experiment.

Calling such studies "natural experiments" is not productive. An analogy to an earlier surge of interest in quasi-experiments is useful here. The eminent scholar Donald Campbell came to regret having popularized the latter term; as he put it,

It may be that Campbell and Stanley (1966) should feel guilty for having contributed to giving quasi-experimental designs a good name. There are program evaluations in which the authors say proudly, "We used a *quasi*-experimental design." If responsible, Campbell and Stanley should do penance, because in most social settings, there are many equally or more plausible rival hypotheses ... (Campbell and Boruch 1975: 202)

As with the previous use of the label quasi-experiment, the growing use of the term "natural experiment" may well possibly reflect a keener sense among researchers of how to make strong causal inferences. Yet, it may also reflect analysts' desire to cover observational studies with the glow of experimental legitimacy. Thus, there is a risk of conceptual stretching, as researchers rush to call their conventional observational studies "natural experiments." Delimiting the scope of natural-experimental research—and helping to protect the integrity of the concept—is therefore an important additional goal.

1.8 Plan for the book, and how to use it

The initial discussion in this chapter raises several questions about the strengths and limitations of natural experiments. In exploring these questions, the book has three principle aims.

First, it seeks to illustrate where natural experiments come from and how they are uncovered. Part I of the book—on "Discovering Natural Experiments"—therefore provides a non-exhaustive survey of standard natural experiments as well as regression-discontinuity and instrumental-variables designs, drawn from a number of social-scientific disciplines. Since the art of discovery is often enhanced by example, these chapters may serve as a valuable reference guide for students and practitioners alike. However, readers who are already familiar with natural experiments or who are interested primarily in tools for analysis and evaluation may wish to skim or skip Chapters 2–4.

Second, the book seeks to provide a useful guide to the analysis of natural-experimental data. Part II turns to this topic; Chapters 5 and 6 focus on quantitative tools. The emphasis here is on the credibility of models and the potential simplicity and transparency of data analysis. Thus, Chapter 5 introduces the Neyman potential outcomes model and focuses on the definition of the average causal effects in standard natural experiments. It also discusses a standard extension to this model that defines the average causal effect for Compliers and broaches several issues in the analysis of regression-discontinuity designs.

Chapter 6 then covers chance processes and the estimation of standard errors, with a focus on issues of special relevance to natural experiments, such as the analysis of cluster-randomized natural experiments. It also discusses useful hypothesis tests in settings with relatively small numbers of units, such as those based on randomization inference (e.g. Fisher's exact test). The discussion of statistical estimation is entirely developed in the context of the Neyman urn model, which is often a credible model of stochastic data-generating processes in natural experiments. However, limitations of this approach are also emphasized. As the discussion emphasizes, the veracity of causal and statistical assumptions must be investigated on a case-by-case basis.

The material in Chapters 5 and 6 is mostly nonmathematical, with technical details left to appendices. However, the details are important, for they distinguish design-based approaches based on the Neyman model from, for instance, standard regression models, both in well-known and less obvious ways. Readers looking for guidance on models for quantitative analysis of natural-experimental data may find Chapters 5 and 6 particularly useful. Exercises appear at the conclusion of most chapters in this book, and several may be useful for assimilating methods of quantitative analysis.

Chapter 7, by contrast, focuses on qualitative methods. In particular, it develops a typology of causal-process observations (Collier, Brady, and Seawright 2010) that play an important role in successful natural experiments. This chapter seeks to place the contribution of these methods on a more systematic foundation, by conceptualizing the different contributions of qualitative methods to successful natural experiments. This chapter and subsequent discussion demonstrate that successful natural experiments often require the use of multiple methods, including quantitative and qualitative techniques.

Finally, the third part of the book seeks to provide a foundation for critical evaluation of natural experiments. Readers particularly interested in a deeper discussion of strong research design may therefore be most interested in Part III, which develops in more detail the three-dimensional typology introduced in this chapter. Thus, Chapter 8 focuses on the plausibility that assignment is as good as random; Chapter 9 interrogates the credibility of statistical and causal models; and Chapter 10 asks how substantively or theoretically relevant is the key natural-experimental treatment. These chapters also rank several of the studies discussed in Part I of the book along the continua defined by these three dimensions. Readers interested in the quantitative analysis of natural experiments may find Chapters 8 and 9 especially relevant.

This ordering of the book raises the question: how can the natural-experimental designs discussed in Part I and the various analytic tools discussed in Part II best be used and combined to afford strength along each of the dimensions discussed in Part III? The concluding Chapter 11 returns to this question, describing the important role of multiple methods in achieving strong research designs for social-scientific research.

1.8.1 Some notes on coverage

The evaluative framework developed in this book is intentionally broad, and it may apply to other kinds of research designs—including true experiments as well as conventional observational studies. Some of the material on the combination of quantitative and qualitative methods also applies to many research settings. The book is intended as a primer on design-based research more generally; for instance, much of the discussion of data-analytic tools applies to true experiments as well. However, it is also appropriate to delineate the book's domain of focus. Much of the advice applies primarily to studies with some claim to random or as-if random assignment but which lack an experimental manipulation. In other words, this is a book about natural experiments.

The book builds on a burgeoning literature on design-based research, yet it is distinguished from those efforts in a number of ways. Unlike recent books that are focused primarily on econometric issues (Angrist and Pischke 2008), this book focuses instead primarily on foundational issues in the design of natural experiments; unlike "how-to" manuals for impact evaluations (e.g., Khandker, Koolwal, and Samad 2010), the applications discussed in the book delve into a range of social-science questions. A number of articles and book chapters by economists and political scientists have also sought to evaluate natural experiments and related research designs.[25] Yet, these also focus mainly on data-analytic issues or else are not comprehensive enough to serve as a reference for those seeking to employ this methodology themselves. In its focus on making causal inferences with strong research designs and relatively weak assumptions, the book also forms a natural complement to recent and forthcoming volumes on field experimentation, such as Gerber and Green's (2012) excellent book.

---

[25] See, e.g., Angrist and Krueger 2001; Deaton 2009; Diamond and Robinson 2010; Dunning 2008a, 2010a; Gerber and Green 2008; Heckman 2000; Robinson, McNulty, and Krasno 2009; Rosenzweig and Wolpin 2000.

Every book requires choices about coverage, and some topics are not discussed adequately here. For example, I largely omit discussion of sensitivity analysis (Manski 1995); I also give regrettably short shrift to mediation analysis (for excellent discussions of the latter, see Bullock and Ha 2011 or Green, Ha, and Bullock 2010). One could also say much more about the various econometric and data-analytic issues raised in Chapters 5, 6, 8, and 9. Several methodological topics that arise in the design of true experiments—such as "blocking," a technique whereby units are sorted into strata and then randomized to treatment or control within those strata—do not apply in many natural experiments, where the researcher does not design the randomization.[26] On the other hand, issues such as clustered randomization are crucial for natural experiments (and this topic is discussed extensively in Chapter 6). In my defense, these omissions reflect the focus of the book on perhaps more foundational issues of research design.

The book is not highly technical (though a few of the exercises require intermediate knowledge of regression analysis). Readers without a statistical background would nonetheless benefit from reference books such as Freedman, Pisani, and Purves (2007) or Freedman (2009). The sequencing of the book also implies that the formal definition of causal effects and discussion of their estimators awaits Part II. This makes the discussion in Part I somewhat imprecise—but this may also have the advantage of greater accessibility. The end-of-chapter exercises also sometimes preview material that will be taken up in more detail later in the book; thus, they need not be considered in the order they appear. The book seeks to preserve a compromise between important foundational issues in causal inference, which have received attention from many methodologists, and the practical choices that arise in conducting real research. Beginning with real applications in Part I, returning to foundational issues in Part II, and then building an evaluative framework in Part III seemed to be the appropriate way to strike this balance.

---

[26] However, some natural experiments—for instance, those in which lotteries take place in different regions or jurisdictions and the data are analyzed across jurisdictions—are effectively block-randomized natural experiments. See Gerber and Green (2012) for discussion.

Part I

Discovering natural experiments

2 Standard natural experiments

The title of this part of the book—"Discovering Natural Experiments"—suggests a first foundational issue for discussion. The random or as-if random assignment that characterizes natural experiments occurs as a feature of social and political processes—not in connection with a manipulation planned and carried out by an experimental researcher. This is what makes natural experiments observational studies, not true experiments.

For this reason, however, researchers face a major challenge in identifying situations in which natural experiments occur. Scholars often speak not of "creating" a natural experiment, but of "exploiting" or "leveraging" an opportunity for this kind of approach in the analysis of observational data. In an important sense, natural experiments are not so much designed as discovered.

How, then, does one uncover a natural experiment? As the survey in Part I of the book will suggest, new ideas for sources of natural experiments—such as close elections or weather shocks—seem to arise in unpredictable ways. Moreover, their successful use in one context does not guarantee their applicability to other substantive problems. The discovery of natural experiments is thus as much art as science: there appears to be no algorithm for the generation of convincing natural experiments, and analysts are challenged to think carefully about whether sources of natural experiments discovered in one context are applicable to other settings.

Yet, the best way to recognize the potential for using a natural experiment productively is often through exposure to examples. This can generate ideas for new research, as existing approaches are modified to suit novel contexts and questions, and it can also lead researchers to recognize new sources of natural experiments. Part I of the book therefore surveys and discusses in detail existing research, as a way to broach the central topic of how to discover natural experiments.

It is important to note that the emphasis on discovering natural experiments is not without potential problems. For some observers, the idea of scouring the landscape for instances of as-if random assignment threatens to substantially narrow the scope of substantive inquiry. Rather than pose "questions in search of variations," some observers suggest that researchers using natural experiments tend to focus on "variations in search of questions." According to these critics, as discussed in the introduction, the recent focus among some social scientists on identifying natural experiments divorces empirical work from theory, and thus leads to the estimation of causal parameters that are not theoretically relevant (see Chapters 1 and 10; Deaton 2009).

Not all scholars share this skeptical view. If the number of interesting questions is large, while the number of plausible instances of as-if random assignment is small—and if random or as-if random assignment is a *sine qua non* of successful causal inference—then perhaps analysts really should begin by identifying the natural experiments, and then find interesting questions that can be answered with those natural experiments. For some researchers, finding instances in which social and political processes have assigned interesting causes at random is the best—perhaps the only—way to make progress in answering otherwise intractable causal questions (for discussion, see Angrist and Pischke 2008; Imbens 2009; also Gelman and Hill 2007).

As with the broader critiques discussed in the introduction, this book adopts a middle position between these extremes. Not all research projects should or will include the use of natural experiments (or true experiments), since not all questions can be answered using these methods. This is as it should be: methods should be chosen to suit the research question, and various empirical strategies, from the conventionally observational to the truly experimental, can be useful in different contexts and for different purposes. Yet, natural experiments may serve as one vital component of a multi-method research strategy, and many more natural experiments may await researchers who are alert to their potential uses. As suggested by the ever-growing list of new applications—many of them discussed in this section of the book—the number of potentially useful natural experiments may also be quite large. Thus, scholars pursuing various research questions would do well to familiarize themselves with the logic of the natural-experimental approach. I return to these topics in more detail in the final part of the book.

The survey in Part I of the book is not intended to be exhaustive—the range of applications is now far too extensive for that—nor does it make a pretense of being representative (for example, it is not a random sample from the universe of existing studies). However, I have made every effort to include many of the studies of which I am aware and, particularly, to include natural experiments with varied substantive foci and varied sources of random or as-if random assignment. Besides possibly generating ideas for new natural experiments, this survey serves another purpose: the examples provide useful points of reference in the second two parts of the book, when I turn to issues of analysis and interpretation. In particular, since different studies may vary with respect to the three evaluative dimensions discussed in the Introduction—the plausibility of as-good-as-random assignment, the credibility of statistical models, and the substantive or theoretical relevance of the key intervention—having a range of examples will help to give some sense to the possible trade-offs and tensions involved in using natural experiments to achieve strong research designs. In this chapter, I focus on "standard" natural experiments, in which units are assigned at random or as-if at random to categories of a key independent (treatment) variable. In subsequent chapters, I discuss two specific variants of natural experiments, the so-called regression-discontinuity and instrumental-variables designs.

2.1 Standard natural experiments in the social sciences

Natural experiments in the social sciences involve a range of interventions. Random or as-if random treatment assignment may stem from various sources, including a procedure specifically designed to randomize, such as a lottery; the nonsystematic implementation of certain interventions; and the arbitrary division of units by jurisdictional borders. The plausibility that assignment is indeed as-if random—considered here to be one of the definitional criteria for this type of study—varies greatly. Table 2.1 describes a number of characteristic sources of "standard" natural experiments; Table 2.2 and Table 2.3 list specific applications according to the substantive focus, the source of the natural experiment, and the geographical location of the study. (The latter two tables also code whether a simple, unadjusted difference-of-means test is used to estimate causal effects; I return to this topic in later chapters.)

By "standard" natural experiments, I have in mind various natural experiments in which units are assigned at random or as-if at random to categories of the independent variable—that is, to treatment and control groups. In fact, this is an umbrella, "catch-all" category that encompasses many different types of designs. Yet, these studies are usefully distinguished from two more specific types of natural experiments discussed in subsequent chapters: the regression-discontinuity and instrumental-variables designs. Thus, standard

Table 2.1 Typical "standard" natural experiments

Source of natural experiment	Random or as-if random	Units in study group	Outcome variables
Lotteries	Random		
Military drafts		Soldiers	Earnings
Electoral quotas		Politicians	Public spending
Term lengths		Politicians	Legislative productivity
School vouchers		Students	Educational achievement
Prize lotteries		Lottery players	Political attitudes
Program roll-outs	Random	Municipalities, villages, others	E.g., voting behavior
Policy interventions	As-if random		
Voting locations		Voters	Turnout
Election monitors		Candidates	Electoral fraud
Property titles		Squatters	Access to credit markets
Number of police		Criminals	Criminal behavior
Jurisdictional borders	As-if random	Voters, citizens, others	Ethnic identification, employment
Electoral redistricting	As-if random	Voters, candidates	Voting behavior
Ballot order	Random or as-if random	Candidates	Voting behavior
Institutional rules	As-if random	Countries, voters, politicians	Economic development
Historical legacies	As-if random	Citizens, countries, regions	Public goods provision

Note: The table provides a non-exhaustive list of sources of standard natural experiments. Specific studies are listed in Tables 2.2 and 2.3.

natural experiments constitute a residual category including all studies that meet the definition of a natural experiment, yet do not include the distinctive features of regression-discontinuity and instrumental-variables designs.

With this definition in place, it is also useful to distinguish standard natural experiments that feature true randomization from those in which treatment assignment is merely alleged to be "as good as random." These two distinct kinds of natural experiments can raise quite different issues of analysis and interpretation. For instance, validating the assertion of as-good-as-random assignment is substantially more challenging in natural experiments that lack randomization—while natural experiments with true randomization might sometimes raise issues related to substantive relevance, one of the dimensions of the evaluative typology discussed in the Introduction.

Standard natural experiments

Table 2.2 Standard natural experiments with true randomization

Authors	Substantive focus	Source of natural experiment	Country	Simple difference of means?
Angrist (1990a, 1990b)	Effects of military induction on later labor-market earnings	Randomized Vietnam-era draft lottery	US	Yes
Angrist et al. (2002); *Angrist, Bettinger, and Kremer* (2006)	Effects of private school vouchers on school completion rates and test performance	Allocation of vouchers by lottery	Colombia	Yes[a]
Chattopadhyay and Duflo (2004)	Effects of electoral quotas for women	Random assignment of quotas for village council presidencies	India	Yes
Dal Bó and Rossi (2010)	Effect of tenure in office on legislative performance	Randomized term lengths in some sessions of legislature	Argentina	Yes
De la O (forthcoming)	Effect of length of time in conditional cash transfer program on voter turnout and support for incumbent	Comparison of early- and late-participating villages based on randomized roll-out of program	Mexico	No[b]
Doherty, Green, and Gerber (2006)	Effect of lottery winnings on political attitudes	Random assignment of lottery winnings, among lottery players	US	No[c]
Erikson and Stoker (2011)	Effects of military conscription on political attitudes and partisan identification	Randomized Vietnam-era draft lottery	US	Yes
Galiani, Rossi, and Schargrodsky (2011)	Effects of military conscription on criminal behavior	Randomized draft lottery for military service in Argentina	Argentina	No
Ho and Imai (2008)	Effect of ballot position on electoral outcomes	Randomized ballot order under alphabet lottery in California	US	Yes
Titiunik (2011)	Effects of term lengths on legislative behavior	Random assignment of state senate seats to two- or four-year terms	US	Yes

Note: The table lists selected natural experiments with true randomization. The final column codes whether a simple difference-of-means test is presented, without control variables.

[a] The 2002 study includes a regression with cohort dummies.
[b] Nonoverlapping units of assignment and outcome lead to estimation of interaction models.
[c] The treatment variables are continuous.

Table 2.3 Standard natural experiments with as-if randomization

Authors	Substantive focus	Source of natural experiment	Country	Simple difference of means?
Ansolabehere, Snyder, and Stewart (2000)	The personal vote and incumbency advantage	Electoral redistricting	US	Yes
Banerjee and Iyer (2005)	Effect of landlord power on development	Land tenure patterns instituted by British in colonial India	India	No[a]
Berger (2009)	Long-term effects of colonial taxation institutions	The division of northern and southern Nigeria at 7°10' N	Nigeria	No
Blattman (2008)	Consequences of child soldiering for political participation	Abduction of children by the Lord's Resistance Army	Uganda	No
Brady and McNulty (2011)	Voter turnout	Precinct consolidation in California gubernatorial recall election	US	Yes
Cox, Rosenbluth, and Thies (2000)	Incentives of Japanese politicians to join factions	Cross-sectional and temporal variation in institutional rules in Japanese parliamentary houses	Japan	Yes
Di Tella and Schargrodsky (2004)	Effect of police presence on crime	Allocation of police to blocks with Jewish centers after terrorist attack in Buenos Aires	Argentina	No
Ferraz and Finan (2008)	Effect of corruption audits on electoral accountability	Public release of corruption audits in Brazil	Brazil	Yes[a]
Galiani and Schargrodsky (2004, 2010); also Di Tella, Galiani, and Schargrodsky (2007)	Effects of land titling for the poor on economic activity and attitudes	Judicial challenges to transfer of property titles to squatters	Argentina	Yes (*Galiani and Schargrodsky 2004*); No (*Di Tella, Galiani, and Schargrodsky 2007*; *Galiani and Schargrodsky 2010*)
Glazer and Robbins (1985)	Congressional responsiveness to constituencies	Electoral redistricting	US	No

Grofman, Brunell, and Koetzle (1998)	Midterm losses in the House and Senate	Party control of White House in previous elections	US	No
Grofman, Griffin, and Berry (1995)	Congressional responsiveness to constituencies	House members who move to the Senate	US	Yes
Hyde (2007)	The effects of international election monitoring on electoral fraud	Assignment of election monitors to polling stations in Armenia	Armenia	Yes
Krasno and Green (2008)	Effect of televised presidential campaign ads on voter turnout	Geographic spillover of campaign ads in states with competitive elections to some but not all areas of neighboring states	US	No[b]
Lyall (2009)	Deterrent effect of bombings and shellings	Allocation of bombs by drunk Russian soldiers	Chechnya	No
Miguel (2004)	Nation-building and public goods provision	Political border between Kenya and Tanzania	Kenya/ Tanzania	No
Posner (2004)	Political salience of cultural cleavages	Political border between Zambia and Malawi	Zambia/ Malawi	Yes
Snow ([1855] 1965)	Incidence of cholera in London	Allocation of water to different houses	UK	Yes
Stasavage (2003)	Bureaucratic delegation, transparency, and accountability	Variation in central banking institutions	Cross-national	No

Note: The table lists selected natural experiments with alleged as-if randomization. The final column codes whether a simple differences-of-means test is presented, without control variables.

[a] Includes state fixed effects.
[b] The treatment conditions are continuous in this study, complicating the calculation of differences-of-means.

Finally, it is also useful to distinguish natural experiments that feature true randomization from field experiments and other true experiments. The control of researchers over the design and implementation of a randomized intervention is the basis for the distinction.[1] In some cases, this may seem like splitting hairs. Nonetheless, as discussed in the introductory chapter, the distinction is both conceptually and practically important. Policy-planners often do not implement precisely the policy intervention that social scientists might desire for their own purposes. As I discuss in later chapters (especially Chapter 10), this can lead to important issues of interpretation. The lack of researcher control over the nature of the treatment poses one potential limitation of natural experiments, relative to other kinds of studies such as field experiments (while natural experiments may present other kinds of advantages, relative to field experiments). Thus, defining randomized studies in which researchers do not control the design and implementation of the intervention as natural experiments—and, thus, as observational studies—seems well advised.

2.2 Standard natural experiments with true randomization

In one important class of natural experiments, researchers study situations in which an actual randomizing device with a known probability distribution assigns subjects to the treatment and control conditions. Such natural experiments with true randomization often—though not always—arise from public-policy interventions in which randomization of program eligibility is an explicit aspect of the program. These lotteries are sometimes rationalized by virtue of equity considerations (in the case of allocating benefits) and/or burden-sharing (in the case of allocating costs). In any case, various policies are sometimes allocated by lottery across different substantive settings. The goal of this subsection is simply to give an initial flavor for the types of policies and programs that have been allocated in this way, across a range of

---

[1] Hyde (2010), for example, randomized election observers to voting locations in Indonesia, in a study of the effect of election monitoring on the presence and displacement of electoral fraud. By my definition, this qualifies as a field experiment, rather than a natural experiment with true randomization—because the randomized assignment of election observers to voting centers and polling places was under the control of the investigator (even though, as it turned out, many monitors did not comply with their treatment assignment). On the other hand, Hyde's (2007) study of Armenia is a natural experiment with as-if randomization, because the researcher did not control the assignment of observers to voting locations.

substantive contexts; subsequent sections and chapters will return to discuss these examples in greater depth.

2.2.1 Lottery studies

In the Introduction, I discussed Angrist's (1990a) study of the effects of military conscription during the Vietnam War on later labor-market earnings. Erikson and Stoker (2011) provide an interesting example of this same approach, this time in a study of the effects of the Vietnam-era draft lottery on political attitudes and partisan identification.[2] These authors studied political attitudes among young men who were potentially subject to the 1969 Vietnam draft lottery; data are from the Political Socialization Panel Study, which surveyed high-school seniors from the class of 1965 before and after the national draft lottery was instituted. According to Erikson and Stoker (2011: 221), "Males holding low lottery numbers became more antiwar, more liberal, and more Democratic in their voting compared to those whose high numbers protected them from the draft. They were also more likely than those [with high lottery numbers] to abandon the party identification that they had held as teenagers." Some evidence for persistent effects was also found in interviews with draft-eligible and draft-ineligible men in the 1990s. As in the Angrist (1990a) study, such effects cannot be explained by confounding—because eligibility for the draft is assigned at random in this natural experiment.

Draft lotteries have been used to study the effects of military conscription in other substantive contexts as well. Galiani, Rossi, and Schargrodsky (2011), for example, study the effects of randomized eligibility for mandatory military service in Argentina. They find that draft eligibility and actual conscription both increase the likelihood of having a criminal record later in adulthood. This may occur because of delayed labor-market opportunities for young men who are drafted. Here, then, is an example of a source of a randomization natural experiment—draft lotteries—being used in a new substantive context and to answer a different research question than in the original application.

---

[2] According to Angrist (1990a), the first researchers to study the impact of the draft lottery were Hearst, Newman, and Hulley (1986), who estimated the effects of military service on delayed (noncombat) mortality (see also Conley and Heerwig 2009). A host of researchers have now studied the effects of the Vietnam-era draft lottery on outcomes such as schooling (Angrist and Chen 2011), alcohol consumption (Goldberg et al. 1991), cigarette consumption (Eisenberg and Rowe 2009), and health (Angrist, Chen, and Frandsen 2010; Dobkin and Shabini 2009).

Natural experiments with true randomization have been used to study many other substantive questions as well; several of these studies are listed in Table 2.2, which codes the author(s), substantive focus, source of the natural experiment, and the country in which the study was located. These tables also code whether a simple unadjusted difference-of-means test was reported (though I delay discussion of this latter topic for Chapters 5 and 9). For instance, how does mandated political representation for women or minorities shape public policy? Since the passage of a constitutional amendment in India in 1993, the seats and presidencies of some local village councils must be set aside for women candidates; in certain states, moreover, presidencies are "reserved" for women through random lotteries.[3] This creates a randomized natural experiment, in which the causal effect of quotas may be estimated by comparing councils with and without quotas for women in any electoral term. Chattopadhyay and Duflo (2004) use this strategy to study the impact of quotas for women presidents in the states of West Bengal and Rajasthan. They find some evidence that having a female village-council head shapes the provision of public goods—for example, by boosting the provision of types of goods that are most preferred by female citizens (as measured by household surveys).

The study by Chattopadhyay and Duflo (2004) raises another salient point: how bureaucrats actually implement ostensible lotteries is not always transparent, and this is a potential drawback of natural experiments, relative to studies in which assignment is under the control of investigators. In Chattopadhyay and Duflo's (2004) study, for example, bureaucrats apparently ranked village councils in order of their serial numbers, and every third council was selected for a quota (see also Gerber and Green 2012). This is not, strictly speaking, a random lottery (though if the initial council were picked by lot, and every third council on the list were then selected, true randomization of treatment assignment would be maintained). Another example comes from the Angrist (1990a) study, where, as mentioned in Chapter 1, lottery numbers for the 1970 Vietnam draft were put in a jar month by month, January through December; according to some observers, insufficient mixing of the jar resulted in too few draws of birthdays from later months (see Starr 1997). In these cases, such possible failures of the randomization procedure seem quite unlikely to induce a correlation between treatment assignment and confounders (or potential outcomes; see Chapter 5), because day of birth and council serial number are unlikely to be connected

---

[3] This is not true in all Indian states; see Dunning and Nilekani (2010) or Nilekani (2010).

to potential labor-market earnings or patterns of public goods provision, respectively. Thus, as-if random assignment remains highly plausible (Chapter 8). Yet, these examples suggest the difficulties that may arise because treatment assignment is not controlled by researchers, and they underscore the value of investigating empirically the veracity of as-if random assignment, even in natural experiments featuring alleged true randomization—a topic to which I will return in later chapters

Another example comes from Doherty, Green, and Gerber (2006), who are interested in the relationship between income and political attitudes. They surveyed 342 people who had won a lottery in an Eastern state between 1983 and 2000 and asked a variety of questions about estate taxes, government redistribution, and social and economic policies more generally. Comparing the political attitudes of lottery winners to those of the general public (especially, those who do not play the lottery) is clearly a nonexperimental comparison, since people self-select as lottery players, and those who choose to play lotteries may be quite different than those who do not, in ways that may matter for political attitudes. However, among lottery players, levels of lottery *winnings* are randomly assigned.[4] This is only true within blocks defined by lottery winners who bought the same number and kind of tickets; in effect, there are many small experiments conducted for each type of lottery player. Thus, abstracting from sample nonresponse and other issues that might threaten the internal validity of their inferences, Doherty, Green, and Gerber (2006) can obtain an estimate of the relationship between levels of lottery winnings and political attitudes that is plausibly not confounded by unobserved variables.[5] They find that lottery winnings have some effects on specific political attitudes—people who win more in the lottery like the estate tax less—but not on broad attitudes towards the government in general.

Such studies may demonstrate the power of randomized lotteries to rule out alternative interpretations of the findings. In the case of Doherty, Green, and Gerber (2006), unmeasured factors that might affect political attitudes should be statistically independent of the level of lottery winnings: just as in a true experiment, randomization takes care of the confounders.[6] Yet, how often do interesting substantive problems yield themselves to the presence

---

[4] Lottery winners are paid a large range of dollar amounts. In Doherty, Green, and Gerber's (2006) sample, the minimum total prize was $47,581, while the maximum was $15.1 million, both awarded in annual installments.
[5] See Doherty, Green, and Gerber (2006) for further details.
[6] Again, lottery winnings are randomly assigned conditional on the kind of lottery tickets bought, so randomization takes place among subgroups; see Doherty, Green, and Gerber (2006) for details.

of randomized prize lotteries? In fact, a number of studies in economics and political science have been able to make interesting use of such lotteries. For example, researchers have used lotteries to study the effects of income on health (Lindahl 2002), happiness (Brickman, Janoff-Bulman, and Coates 1978; Gardner and Oswald 2001), and consumer behavior (Imbens, Rubin, and Sacerdote 2001).

Various public policies are also sometimes assigned at random. For instance, De la O (forthcoming) studies the effect of the PROGRESA (National Program for Education, Health and Nutrition) antipoverty program in Mexico on voter turnout and support for the political incumbent. Political participation among early- and late-entering municipalities in the program was compared; since the identity of the early entrants was chosen at random by policy-makers, *ex post* differences in aggregate voting and turnout behavior can be attributed to the effect of length of time in the antipoverty program. Schooling programs are also sometimes allocated by lottery. In Bogotá, Colombia, for instance, vouchers that partially covered the cost of private secondary school were allocated by lottery to students who met certain academic requirements. Angrist et al. (2002: 1535) found that three years after the lotteries, "winners were about 10 percentage points more likely to have finished 8th grade, primarily because they were less likely to repeat grades, and scored 0.2 standard deviations higher on achievement tests. There is some evidence that winners worked less [outside of school] than losers and were less likely to marry or cohabit as teenagers." A follow-up study (Angrist, Bettinger, and Kremer 2006) found some evidence of persistent effects on academic achievement. Like the draft-lottery study above, one feature of such voucher studies is that not all eligible students choose to use vouchers. Under some conditions, assignment to a voucher can be used as an instrumental variable for attending private schools.[7]

A final set of illustrations comes from legislatures, which sometimes use randomization to allocate term lengths. This may open the possibility of studying the impact of tenure in office on legislative productivity or responsiveness to constituents. In the Argentine Chamber of Deputies, for instance, term lengths were assigned randomly after the return to democracy in 1983: in order to develop a staggered system, in which every two years half of the Chamber would be up for reelection for four-year terms, some legislators were randomly assigned two-year initial terms. A similar natural experiment was initiated in the Senate as a result of a constitutional reform; in 2001, senators were randomly assigned initial two-year terms, four-year terms, or six-year

---

[7] See Chapters 4 and 5.

terms. Dal Bó and Rossi (2010) develop various measures of legislative output and argue that longer terms enhance legislative performance; they interpret this as evidence for a "political investment" logic on the part of legislators.[8] Titiunik (2011), in a study of the effects of term lengths on legislative behavior, uses the random assignment of some US state senate seats to two- or four-year terms after reapportionment. She also finds that shorter terms do not improve legislative performance; for instance, senators with shorter terms abstain more often and introduce fewer bills. In this case, part of the explanation lies in the fact that legislators with shorter terms spend more time campaigning.

As the examples surveyed in this section suggest, many interesting natural experiments feature true randomization of assignment to treatment. In this class of natural experiment—unlike the Argentina land-titling study or Snow's study of cholera transmission (Introduction)—researchers do not need to depend on a priori reasoning or empirical evidence to defend the assumption of as-if random assignment of subjects to treatment and control conditions. They can often simply appeal to the true randomization of treatment assignment. (Of course, it is not a bad idea to use evidence to check for possible failures of the randomization procedure; see Chapters 7 and 8.)

This does not imply that other important issues of interpretation and analysis do not arise in randomized natural experiments, however. As I discuss extensively in later chapters, the substantive and theoretical relevance of the randomized intervention may vary across different studies, depending in part on the research question being asked; and different studies may vary in terms of the credibility of the models that undergird analysis of the data. Such randomized natural experiments are typically quite strong on one of the three dimensions of strong research designs discussed in the Introduction, however: the plausibility of random assignment.

2.3 Standard natural experiments with as-if randomization

Nonetheless, many interventions that constitute the basis of credible natural experiments in the social sciences involve treatments that are assigned only as-if at random, rather than through an actual randomizing device. We have already seen two examples—the Argentina land-titling study and John Snow's

---

[8] Dal Bó and Rossi (2010) use six measures of legislative performance: attendance in floor sessions, participation in floor debates, attendance in committee sessions, participation in the production of committee bills, the number of bills each member introduced, and how many of these bills became law.

study of cholera transmission. The goal of the brief survey in this section is to give an initial idea of other sources of alleged national experiments, some of which are more compelling than others.

In principle, natural experiments with as-if randomization *may* stem from various sources—such as policy interventions, jurisdictional borders, or redistricting. Of course, most instances of these phenomena probably do not produce natural experiments. For instance, many of the interventions that could in principle provide the basis for plausible natural experiments in political science are the product of the interaction of actors in the social and political world. It can strain credulity to think that these interventions are independent of the characteristics of the actors involved, or are undertaken in ways that do not encourage actors to self-select into treatment and control groups in ways that are correlated with the outcome in question. However, sometimes such problems are overcome, to greater or lesser degrees.

Brady and McNulty (2011), for example, are interested in examining how the cost of voting affects turnout. Positive turnout in elections seems to contradict some rational-choice theories of voting (see Green and Shapiro 1994); however, turnout is less than the size of the electorate in virtually every election virtually everywhere, so the costs of voting may well matter. How do changes in voting costs affect participation?

In California's special gubernatorial recall election of 2003, in which Arnold Schwarzenegger became governor, the elections supervisor in Los Angeles County consolidated the number of district voting precincts from 5,231 (in the 2002 regular gubernatorial election) to 1,885. For some voters, the physical distance from residence to polling place was increased, relative to the 2002 election; for others, it remained the same.[9] Those voters whose distance to the voting booth increased—and who therefore presumably had higher costs of voting, relative to the 2002 election—constituted the "treatment" group, while the control group voted at the same polling place in both elections.

The consolidation of polling places in the 2003 election arguably provides a natural experiment for studying how the costs of voting affect turnout. A well-defined intervention—the closing of some polling places and not others—allows for a comparison of average turnout across treatment and control groups. The key question, of course, is whether assignment of voters to polling

---

[9] For a relatively small group of voters, the polling place was changed but the overall distance did not increase (or indeed decreased). This provides an opportunity to estimate the effect of pure "disruption costs" on voting turnout, which I do not discuss in detail here.

places in the 2003 election was as-if random with respect to other characteristics that affect their disposition to vote. In particular, did the county elections supervisor close some polling places and not others in ways that were correlated with potential turnout?

Brady and McNulty (2011) raise the possibility that the answer to this question is yes. Indeed, they find some evidence for a small lack of pre-treatment equivalence on observed covariates such as age across groups of voters who had their polling place changed (i.e., the treatment group) and those that did not. Thus, the assumption of as-if random assignment may not completely stand up either to Brady and McNulty's (2011) careful data analysis or to a priori reasoning (elections supervisors, after all, may try to maximize turnout). Yet, pre-treatment differences between the treatment and control groups are quite small, relative to the reduction in turnout associated with increased voting costs. After careful consideration of potential confounders, Brady and McNulty (2011) can convincingly argue that the costs of voting negatively influenced turnout, and a natural-experimental approach plays a key role in their study.

Table 2.3 catalogues many other standard natural experiments in which as-if randomization is claimed. An innovative example comes from Lyall (2009), who studies the deterrent effect of bombings and shellings by Russian soldiers in Chechnya. According to some students of civil wars, bombings do not work to deter insurgents and indeed may simply inspire greater rebel retaliation, or shift hostilities from one theater of combat to another. Lyall, however, finds that in Chechnya rebel attacks decline in the wake of Russian bombings, and they do not seem to shift to neighboring villages either.

Now, it might be that Russian soldiers anticipate rebel responses, for example, by shelling places that are weaker to begin with—so that declines in counterattacks in village that are bombed, relative to villages that are not, is simply an artifact of this selection process. Yet, Lyall argues that the allocation of bombs by Russian soldiers to the hamlets that surround their garrisons is independent of the characteristics of the garrisons. Instead, shellings seem to occur in a quite haphazard manner, and at least some of them occur at particular times—when Russian soldiers are drunk. Lyall claims that this lays the foundation for a natural experiment on the deterrent effects of bombings and shellings.

Hyde (2007) provides another example, this time on the effects of international election observers in Armenia. While election monitors did not select sites to visit by literally drawing at random from a list of polling places, according to Hyde (2007: 48–9) their method would have been highly unlikely to produce a list of assigned polling stations that were systematically different from the polling stations that observers were not assigned to visit ... Those making the lists did not possess information about polling-station attributes that would have allowed them to choose polling stations according to criteria that could have predicted voting patterns ... lists were made with two objectives in mind: (1) to distribute the observers throughout the entire country (including rural and urban areas) and (2) to give each observer team a list of polling stations that did not overlap with that of other teams ... individuals who made these lists had little knowledge of polling-station characteristics other than their general geographic location ... [and] did not have access to disaggregated data on the demographic characteristics of the Armenian voting population [or] the capability of choosing polling stations that were more or less likely to favor the incumbent or ... experience election-day fraud.

Hyde also cites the fact that Armenian politics is not predictable along partisan or demographic lines and that each team of observers was pressured to complete the entire list under its purview as factors that mitigate against selection effects and help to validate this study as a natural experiment. The results suggest that international observers reduced the vote share for the incumbent politician (President Kocharian) by an estimated 5.9 percent in the first round of the election and by more than 2 percent in the second round.[10]

Many other studies leverage such natural experiments to draw inferences about various kinds of discrete policy interventions. Blattman (2008), for example, argues that the abduction of child soldiers by the Lord's Resistance Army in Uganda followed a pattern that was as good as random and adduces various evidence in favor of this hypothesis; he finds that abducted youth are actually more frequent participants in political life after demobilization (e.g., they vote at higher rates than non-abducted youth).[11] Ferraz and Finan (2008) study the effects of the public release of corruption audits in Brazilian municipalities, comparing municipalities where audits were released before elections to those where they were released after; they find, contrary to some reports that corruption is not an electorally salient issue, that voters do punish politicians found to be corrupt by these audits. Other studies surveyed in Table 2.3 also take advantage of alleged as-if random assignment to study the causal impact of varied policy interventions; the quality of the assertion of as-if

---

[10] Both estimated effects are significantly different from zero in difference-of-means tests; see Chapters 5 and 6. There is some evidence that fraud deterrence had persistent effects: the incumbent's vote share was lower in polling places visited in the first round but not the second than in polling places that were not visited in either round.

[11] However, Blattman (2008) also suggests that age and region may be confounders.

random may vary, as I will discuss further with regard to these studies in Chapters 7 and 8.

2.3.1 Jurisdictional borders

Another increasingly common class of alleged natural experiments exploits the existence of political or jurisdictional borders that separate similar populations of individuals, communities, firms, or other units of analysis. Generally, because these units of analysis are separated by the political or jurisdictional boundary, a policy shift (or "intervention") that affects groups on one side of the border may not apply to groups on the other side. In broadest terms, those that receive the policy intervention can be thought of as having received a treatment, while those on the other side of the border are the controls. A key question is then whether treatment assignment is as-if random, that is, independent of other factors that might explain differences in average outcomes across treatment and control groups.[12]

For example, Krasno and Green (2008) exploit the geographic spillover of campaign ads in states with competitive elections to some but not all areas of neighboring states to study the effects of televised campaign ads on voter turnout. Miguel (2004) uses jurisdictional borders to study the effects of "nation-building" on public goods provision in communities in Kenya and Tanzania. A well-known example in economics is Card and Krueger (1994), who studied similar fast-food restaurants on either side of the New Jersey–Pennsylvania border; contrary to the postulates of basic theories of labor economics, Card and Krueger found that an increase in the minimum wage in New Jersey did not increase, and perhaps even decreased, unemployment.[13]

Natural experiments exploiting colonial-era borders in Africa—which were allegedly often drawn for arbitrary reasons, with little attention to the distribution of ethnic groups or other factors on the ground—are also

---

[12] Natural experiments involving jurisdictional borders are sometimes classified as regression-discontinuity designs, in which there a clear cutoff value of a covariate that determines treatment assignment (Chapter 3); see Lee and Lemieux (2010), Hahn, Todd, and Van Der Klaauw (2001), and also Black (1999). Yet, while natural experiments based on jurisdictional boundaries do share the flavor of the regression-discontinuity designs—in that position just "next to" a border determines assignment to some treatment—there is typically not a single covariate (or index based on a set of covariates) that distinguishes units assigned to treatment from those assigned to control.

[13] In 1990, the New Jersey legislature passed a minimum-wage increase from $4.25 to $5.05 an hour, to be implemented in 1992, while Pennsylvania's minimum wage remained unchanged. The estimation strategy is based on a difference-in-differences estimator, that is, the change in employment in New Jersey is compared to the change in employment in Pennsylvania.

increasingly common.[14] An innovative illustration comes from Posner (2004), who studies the question of why cultural differences between the Chewa and Tumbuka ethnic groups are politically salient in Malawi but not in Zambia. Separated by an administrative boundary originally drawn by Cecil Rhodes' British South Africa Company and later reinforced by British colonialism, the Chewas and the Tumbukas on the Zambian side of the border are apparently identical to their counterparts in Malawi, in terms of allegedly "objective" cultural differences such as language, appearance, and so on.

However, Posner finds very different intergroup attitudes in the two countries. In Malawi, where each group has been associated with its own political party and voters rarely cross party lines, Chewa and Tumbuka survey respondents report an aversion to intergroup marriage and a disinclination to vote for a member of the other group for president, and generally emphasize negative features of the other group. In Zambia, on the other hand, Chewas and Tumbukas would much more readily vote for a member of the other group for president, are more disposed to intergroup marriage, and "tend to view each other as ethnic brethren and political allies" (Posner 2004: 531).

Several characteristic issues arise with studies using jurisdictional borders. As with all natural experiments lacking true randomization, one first-order question is whether the assumption of as-if random assignment is valid. According to Posner, for example, long-standing differences between Chewas and Tumbukas located on either side of the border cannot explain the very different intergroup relations in Malawi and in Zambia; a key claim is that "like many African borders, the one that separates Zambia and Malawi was drawn purely for [colonial] administrative purposes, with no attention to the distribution of groups on the ground" (Posner 2004: 530). Such claims may be more plausible in some studies that exploit jurisdictional borders than in others: for example, in Card and Krueger's (1994) study, owners of fast-food restaurants might choose to locate on one or the other side of the border, or legislators may choose to alter minimum-wage laws, in ways that are correlated with outcomes under alternative minimum-wage laws.[15] The

---

[14] Laitin (1986) provided an important early example. See also Berger (2009), Cogneau and Moradi (2011), MacLean (2010), Miles (1994), and Miles and Rochefort (1991), among others.

[15] As Card and Krueger note, economic conditions deteriorated between 1990, when New Jersey's minimum-wage law was passed, and 1992, when it was to be implemented; New Jersey legislators then passed a bill revoking the minimum-wage increase, which was vetoed by the governor, allowing the wage increase to take effect. The legislative move to revoke the wage increase suggests that the treatment is something less than as-if random. A critique of this study can be found in Deere, Murphy, and Welch (1995).

plausibility of as-if random in such studies is evaluated at greater length elsewhere, e.g., in Chapter 8. In later chapters, I also discuss several other important issues that arise in natural experiments with jurisdictional borders, such as the clustering of treatment assignment (Chapter 6) and the bundled nature of treatment variables (the "compound treatment" problem discussed in Chapter 9). These issues have important implications for the analysis and interpretation of such studies.

2.3.2 Redistricting and jurisdiction shopping

Scholars of American politics appear to fairly frequently exploit electoral redistricting and other mechanisms as a source of alleged natural experiments. Ansolabehere, Snyder, and Stewart (2000), for example, use electoral redistricting as a natural experiment to study the influence of the personal vote on incumbency advantage.[16] The post-redistricting vote for an incumbent, among voters who were in the incumbent's district in a previous election (prior to redistricting), is compared to the vote among voters who were previously not in the district; since these groups of constituents now share the same incumbent representative in the Congress, experience the same electoral campaign, and so forth, but differ in their previous exposure to the incumbent, this comparison may be used to gauge the effect of the cultivation of the personal vote and to distinguish this effect from other sources of incumbency advantage. In terms of the natural-experimental design, a key assertion is that the voters who are brought into the incumbents' district through the electoral redistricting process are just like voters who were already in the old district, except that the latter group received the "treatment"—that is, cultivation of the personal vote (see also Elis, Malhotra, and Meredith 2009). However, as Sekhon and Titiunik (2012) point out, if new voters are sampled as-if at random from their old districts and placed into new districts, they are not comparable to old voters in those new districts; rather, they are comparable to voters in the districts they left behind. Unfortunately, this latter comparison is not useful for assessing the effect of the personal vote: new voters in new districts and old voters in old districts face different incumbents, as well as different campaigns. Thus, even if as-if random holds, it may not secure the right kind of comparison for purposes of answering questions about the personal vote as a source of incumbency advantage.

---

[16] Another study to exploit electoral redistricting is Glazer and Robbins (1985).

In other examples, the assertion of as-if random may be less compelling as well. One such example comes from Grofman, Griffin, and Berry (1995), who use roll-call data to study the voting behavior of congressional representatives who move from the House to the Senate. The question here is whether new senators, who will represent larger and generally more heterogeneous jurisdictions (i.e., states rather than House districts), will modify their voting behavior in the direction of the state's median voter. Grofman, Griffin, and Berry find that the voting records of new Senate members are close to their own previous voting records in the House, the mean voting record of House members of their party, and the voting record of the incumbent senator from the new senator's state. Among House members who enter the Senate, there is thus little evidence of movement towards the median voter in the new senator's state.

Here, however, the "treatment" is the result of a decision by representatives to switch from one chamber of Congress to another. In this context, the inevitable inferential issues relating to self-selection seem to make it much more difficult to claim that assignment of representatives to the Senate is as-if random. As the authors themselves note, "extremely liberal Democratic candidates or extremely conservative Republican candidates, well suited to homogeneous congressional districts, should not be well suited to face the less ideologically skewed statewide electorate" (Grofman, Griffin, and Berry 1995: 514). Thus characteristics of voters in states with open Senate seats, and the characteristics of House members who run for the Senate, may explain why these House members choose to run for the Senate in the first place. This sort of study therefore probably exploits something less than a natural experiment.

2.4 Conclusion

Natural experiments involving true randomization may offer persuasive evidence of causal effects—since the randomization gets rid of confounding, just as in a true experiment. Moreover, some such natural experiments involve treatment variables that would presumably be difficult to manipulate experimentally—such as military conscription or mandated political representation for minorities. Thus, some such studies can be quite compelling on the grounds of both as good as random assignment and the theoretical or substantive relevance of the intervention. Of course, other studies involving true randomization may be less compelling on other grounds, such as the relevance of the intervention.

In studies lacking true randomization, the assertion of as-if random may be more compelling in some contexts than in others. Even if a researcher demonstrates perfect empirical balance on *observed* characteristics of subjects across treatment and control groups, the possibility that *unobserved* differences across groups may account for differences in average outcomes is always omnipresent in observational settings. Since the assertion of as-if random assignment can be supported but is never confirmed by data, there clearly is no hard-and-fast rule to validate a natural experiment. This is obviously the Achilles' heel of natural experiments as well as other forms of observational research, relative to randomized controlled experiments, and it is a topic to which I will return in depth.[17]

Many standard natural experiments lacking true randomization can nonetheless lead to quite compelling causal inferences. Moreover, such natural experiments often involve interventions that are quite difficult to manipulate experimentally and that may not lend themselves to randomized natural experiments on a large scale—such as polling places, minimum-wage laws, or varieties of ethnic mobilization. What such studies may lack in persuasive as-if randomization they may sometimes gain in substantive relevance. Future chapters will consider these themes more explicitly.[18]

Exercises

2.1) One survey found that 18 out of 22 papers on the effect of police presence on crime rates found either a positive or no relationship between these variables (Cameron 1988; see Di Tella and Schargrodsky 2004). Does this evidence suggest that police do not deter—or might even encourage—crime? Why or why not? How might a natural experiment on this topic be helpful?

2.2) In a study of the effect of police presence on the incidence of crime, Di Tella and Schargrodsky (2004: 115–16) write that,

> following a terrorist attack on the main Jewish center in Buenos Aires, Argentina, in July 1994, all Jewish institutions received police protection.... Because the geographical distribution of these institutions

---

[17] See Chapter 8.   [18] See Chapters 10 and 11.

can be presumed to be exogenous in a crime regression, this hideous event constitutes a natural experiment . . .

These authors find that blocks which were allocated extra police forces due to the presence of a Jewish institution experienced lower motor vehicle theft rates. The control group consists of blocks in the same neighborhood that do not have Jewish institutions.

What do these authors mean by "presumed exogenous in a crime regression" and what is the relationship to as-if random assignment? Can the location of Jewish institutions be presumed exogenous? What are some potential threats to as-if random assignment? How might these threats be evaluated empirically?

2.3) *Snow on cholera.* The impurity of water in the Thames was a source of concern to public authorities (though it was not widely linked to cholera transmission), and the Metropolis Water Act of 1852 in fact made it unlawful for any water company to supply houses with water from the tidal reaches of the Thames after August 31, 1855. Yet, while the Lambeth's move of its intake pipe upstream was planned in the late 1840s and completed in 1852—before the cholera outbreak of 1853–54—the Southwark and Vauxhall company did not move its pipe until 1855. In other words, the Lambeth Waterworks Company chose to move its pipe upstream before it was legally required to do so, while Southwark & Vauxhall left its intake pipe in place. Could this fact pose a threat to the claim that assignment of households to pure or impure water supply—and thus risk of death from cholera—was as-if random? Why or why not? How might Snow's discussion of the process by which water was purchased and supplied counter some potential threats to the validity of the natural experiment?

2.4) Discuss the matching design on UN peacekeeping interventions described in the Introduction. In what ways is this different from a valid natural experiment? Suppose an analyst did describe this study as a potential natural experiment. What sort of evidence would cast doubt on that claim?

3 Regression-discontinuity designs

In this chapter and the next, I consider two specific kinds of natural experiments: regression-discontinuity designs in this chapter, and instrumental-variables designs in the next. When appropriately invoked, both kinds of designs meet the key definitional criterion of natural experiments—namely, random or as-if random assignment. Yet they differ in other ways, and their use tends to raise characteristic issues of discovery, analysis, and interpretation that are specific to each kind of design. This makes it valuable to discuss these two kinds of natural experiments separately in various chapters, where they can each be given more detailed attention.

The regression-discontinuity design was proposed by Thistlethwaite and Campbell (1960) and discussed extensively by Trochim (1984). Yet, for somewhat unclear reasons—and despite the extensive efforts that Donald Campbell's research team at Northwestern University put into studying it—this research design was relatively underutilized for several decades after Campbell and his team originally proposed it. However, empirical applications have exploded in the social sciences over the past decade or so. In this chapter, I survey many recent applications, as a way to shed some light on the art of discovering productive opportunities for these modes of research. Issues of analysis and interpretation are mostly postponed for Parts II and III of this book, though some mention of them is also made here.

3.1 The basis of regression-discontinuity analysis

As part of a social or political process, individuals or other units are sometimes assigned to one or the other category of the independent variable (e.g., the treatment or control groups) according to whether they are above or below a given threshold value on some covariate or pre-test. For units very near the threshold, the process that determines treatment assignment may be as good as random, ensuring that these units will be similar with respect to potential confounders. This in turn opens the possibility for a *regression-discontinuity design*, which may allow for a more compelling causal inference about the impact of the treatment on the dependent variable. The name of the design does not imply that regression analysis needs to be used to analyze data arising from such studies.

The contrast with the standard natural experiment is that as-if random assignment specifically involves the position of subjects in relation to the key threshold.[1] For example, in their study of the National Merit Scholarship program in the United States, Thistlethwaite and Campbell (1960) compared students who received public recognition of scholastic achievement with a similar group of students who did not, with the goal of inferring the impact of recognition on subsequent academic achievement. All students who scored above a given threshold on a Scholastic Aptitude Test received a Certificate of Merit—and thus had their names "published in a booklet distributed to colleges, universities, and other scholarship granting agencies and . . . received approximately two and one half times more newspaper coverage than commended students" (Thistlethwaite and Campbell 1960: 310). Students who scored below the threshold, however, merely received commendations, which confer less public recognition of scholastic achievement.

In general, students who score high on qualifying exams will be different from those who score low, in ways that matter for outcomes such as receipt of scholarships or later scholastic achievement. For instance, if high scorers have greater initial ability than low scorers, on average, then better *ex post* performance among the high scorers could be due to the effects of public recognition, differences in initial ability, or both. Comparisons between high scorers and low scorers may therefore be misleading for purposes of inferring the effect of receiving public recognition. Even comparing the change in outcomes from pre- to post-test could be misleading, for instance, if high scorers receive more coaching, invitations to apply to elite colleges, or differ in other ways besides the public recognition they receive in the form of Certificates of Merit.[2]

However, given the role of unpredictability and luck in exam performance, students just above and below the key threshold should be very similar, on average. In particular, they should not differ systematically with respect to the

---

[1] More technically, in a regression-discontinuity design, treatment assignment is determined by the value of a covariate, sometimes called a forcing variable, and there is a sharp discontinuity in the probability of receiving treatment at a particular threshold value of this covariate (Campbell and Stanley 1966: 61–64; Rubin 1977).

[2] Comparing the change on a dependent variable in the treatment and control groups, from pre-test to post-test, is *difference-in-differences* analysis.

ex post outcomes each student *would* experience if he or she were given a Certificate of Merit, or instead merely received a commendation. Thus, the outcomes that each student *would* experience in the presence and absence of public recognition should be independent of whether he or she actually received a Certificate.[3] This presumes that students cannot readily "sort" themselves on one side or another of the relevant threshold in ways that may be related to their potential outcomes; moreover, officials must not choose the threshold strategically to select particular candidates for certificates, who might differ from students in the control group in various ways. I discuss these conditions in more detail below. If such conditions hold, however, assignment to receive a Certificate of Merit can plausibly be considered as-if random in the neighborhood of the threshold. Then, comparisons near the threshold allow an estimate of the causal effects of certificates, at least for the group of students with scores near the threshold.[4]

Figure 3.1, which is similar to a figure in Thistlethwaite and Campbell (1960), shows why the "regression-discontinuity design" has this name. The figure plots average values of a hypothetical outcome variable—here, the percentage of students receiving college scholarships—against scores on the qualifying exam. The horizontal axis expresses exam scores in arbitrary units, because the specific threshold exam score varied across different US states; the vertical axis plots the average outcome for each student at each value of the exam score. Exam scores are scaled so that the key cutoff is at 11: students who scored 11 and above on the exam were awarded certificates, while those below the threshold merely received commendations. For ease of presentation, exam scores are rounded to the nearest mid-point between two integers (4.5, 5.5, and so on). The vertical dotted line above the score of 11 illustrates that this is the key value of the exam score determining assignment to certificates.

In Figure 3.1, we see three very different patterns. In Series A at the top of the figure, there is a clear jump in the value of the outcome variable between exam scores of 10 and 11. Thus, the group of students who scored 10 on the

---

[3] Chapter 5 more formally introduces the idea of *potential outcomes*. A potential outcome is the outcome a unit *would* experience, if it were assigned to treatment or control. Since each unit can only be assigned to at most one group, at least one of these potential outcomes is unobserved by the researcher.

[4] Oddly, Thistlethwaite and Campbell (1960) remove from their study group Certificate of Merit winners who also won National Merit Scholarships. Only Certificate of Merit winners were eligible for National Merit Scholarships, which are based on grades as well as exam scores. Thus, the control group includes students who *would have* won merit scholarships had they received Certificates of Merit and those who would not have, while the treatment group includes only the latter type. If type is related to potential outcomes, as seems plausible, this should lead to bias in the estimation of treatment effects (see Chapter 5).

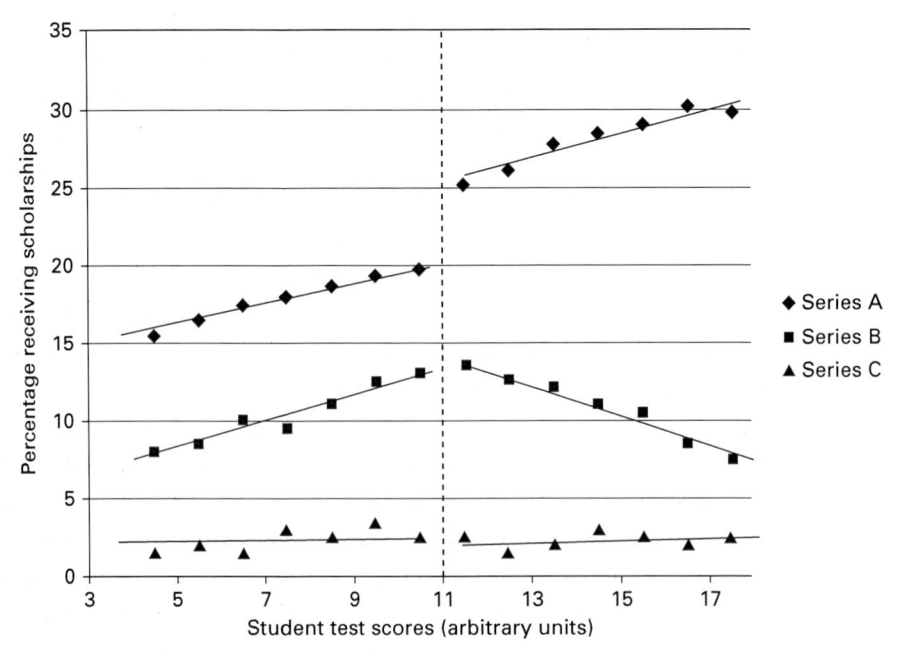

Figure 3.1 Examples of regression discontinuities

exam performed systematically worse on the outcome variable—i.e., they received proportionately fewer scholarships—than students who scored an 11 on the exam and thus received public recognition in the form of certificates. If we believe the assertion that potential outcomes are independent of exam scores for those who scored very near the threshold—and thus, assignment to certificates is as good as random—this is credible evidence for a causal effect of Certificates of Merit.

Here, the solid lines on each side of the vertical dashed line represent the regression lines relating this outcome variable to the exam score to the right and the left of the threshold.[5] Note that in Series A, the intercepts of these two regression lines—that is, the point at which they coincide with the dashed vertical line between 10 and 11—are clearly different. This discontinuity in the intercept of the regression line is in fact what gives "regression-discontinuity" designs their name. However, as we shall see in more detail in Part II, there is no need to use linear regression analysis to estimate causal effects using regression-discontinuity designs—and the use of regression can even be misleading.

---

[5] Note that the regression of the *average* outcome within each interval on the qualifying score produces the same fitted line as the regression of actual outcomes on the qualifying score, so long as the intervals are weighted by the numbers of students in each interval.

Series C at the bottom of Figure 3.1 presents an opposite case. Here, there is no detectable jump in outcomes between 10 and 11. Indeed, the regression lines on either side of the key threshold are nearly identical, as are their intercepts. While I discuss the role of sampling error in Chapters 5 and 6 and describe more systematic procedures for verifying the existence of causal effects, Series C does not seem to suggest any causal effect of certificates for students just above and just below the threshold.

Finally, Series B in the middle of Figure 3.1 seems to present a more mixed case, since the slopes of the regression lines on either side of the key threshold clearly differ: the regression line slopes up to the left of the threshold and slopes down to its right. Yet, as in Series C, the intercepts are nearly identical: there is no discernible difference in *ex post* outcomes between those who scored 10 and those who scored 11. In general, such a figure does not present compelling evidence for the effect of Certificates of Merit. For instance, recall that the outcome here is receipt of an academic scholarship. A pattern such as that in Series B might be produced if, for instance, scholarship committees tend to give scholarships to low-income students with relatively high abilities, and if income and ability are both correlated with test scores. Then, test scores might be positively associated with receipt of scholarships, up to a certain point, since low-scoring students may also tend to have low incomes. Yet beyond a certain income threshold, high-scoring students become less attractive candidates, since most of them may be too rich for scholarships. This could induce a negative relationship, on average, between test scores and receipt of scholarships among high scorers.

This last point underscores a central feature of regression-discontinuity designs: the assumption that assignment to the treatment (here, Certificates of Merit) is as-if random is typically only plausible for students just above and just below the key threshold—that is, in the neighborhood of the threshold. The problem with using the slope of regression lines to infer causal impacts in regression-discontinuity designs is that unobserved confounders, such as income, can influence the slopes of these regression lines—and even their intercepts. This suggests that the most reliable comparison group for students who scored 11 on the exam is students who scored a 10. The performance of students who scored, say, 17 or 4 may be less relevant, since many systematic differences—not just the luck of the draw on a particular exam—may distinguish these groups of students.[6]

---

[6] As Thistlethwaite and Campbell (1960: 311) put it, the effect of certificates may be "strictly demonstrated only for aptitude intervals adjacent to the cutting point, and inferences as to effects of the [Certificate of Merit] award upon persons of other ability levels would be made in hazard of unexplored interactions of award and ability level."

The example also suggests, in a cursory way, some of the potential dangers of using regression analysis to draw inferences about causal effects in regression-discontinuity designs: the slopes of the regression lines in Series B of Figure 3.1, and even their intercepts, are driven by data points that are relatively far from the key regression-discontinuity threshold—and as such, can be subject to confounding in a way that simple comparisons between students who scored 10 or 11 on the exam are not. I will return to these points in more detail in Chapters 5 and 6, when I discuss procedures for analyzing data from regression-discontinuity designs.

Finally, the example also illustrates another foundational point about regression-discontinuity designs: while limiting the analysis to students who scored 10 or 11 on the exam limits confounding—and thus bolsters the ability to draw valid inferences about the causal effect of recognition for this group of students—it may also limit the ability to say something about the effect of public recognition for students far from the cutting point. This point is typically discussed in terms of a trade-off between "internal validity" and "external validity" (Campbell and Stanley 1966). How sharp this trade-off is depends on the application: while in some settings the achievement of internal validity can come at the cost of external validity, in other settings it may not.

These central issues of analysis and interpretation are best saved for later sections of the book, however. The central goal of this chapter is to survey real social-scientific applications, as a way of answering the question: from where do regression-discontinuity designs arise?

3.2 Regression-discontinuity designs in the social sciences

Regression-discontinuity designs have become increasingly common in the social sciences over the past decade or two, particularly in economics and political science. Following Thistlethwaite and Campbell (1960), regression-discontinuity designs based on entrance exams have been used by many scholars; for instance, Matsudaira (2007) studies the effect of a remedial summer school program that is mandatory for students who score less than a cutoff level on a test (see also Jacob and Lefgren 2004).

However, scholars have greatly expanded the substantive domain of studies using this methodological approach, as Tables 3.1 and 3.2 attest. The first table lists some generic sources of regression-discontinuity designs used in recent

Table 3.1 Selected sources of regression-discontinuity designs

Source of RD design	Units in study group (at RD threshold)	Treatment variables	Outcome variables
Entrance exams	Students, others	Public recognition of scholastic achievement	Educational achievement
Population thresholds	Municipalities, citizens	Voting technologies	Effective turnout
		Federal funds	Voting behavior
		Cash transfers	Voting behavior
		Electoral rules	Voting behavior
		Politicians' salaries	Candidate entry
Size-based thresholds			
Voter numbers	Voters	Voting by mail	Voting behavior
School size	Students	Class size	Educational achievement
Firm size	Firms	Antibias laws	Productivity
Eligibility criteria			
Poverty rank	Municipalities	Antipoverty programs	Voting behavior
Criminality index	Prisoners	High-security incarceration	Recidivism
Age-based thresholds			
Voting age	Voters	Past voting	Turnout
Birth quarter	Students	Years of education	Earnings
Close elections	Candidates/parties	Incumbency	Candidates' performance
	Firms	Campaign donations	Public works contracts

Note: The table provides a non-exhaustive list of sources of regression-discontinuity designs. Specific studies are listed in Table 3.2. RD, regression discontinuity.

social-scientific research; the second provides a non-exhaustive yet large list of specific recent studies using this research design. For each study, the table lists the author(s), substantive focus, country in which the study took place, and the source of the regression discontinuity.[7] (Table 3.2 also lists whether a simple difference-of-means test is used to analyze the data, a topic for which I again postpone further discussion until later chapters.)

How are these designs discovered and leveraged in the service of diverse research agendas? As with standard natural experiments, discovering useful regression discontinuities is as much an art as a science. Yet, as the survey in this section will show, regression-discontinuity designs developed in one place or context have often served as inspiration for designs in other settings. One

---

[7] Most of these studies take place within a single country, a topic I will discuss elsewhere.

Table 3.2 Examples of regression-discontinuity designs

Authors	Substantive focus	Source of regression discontinuity	Country	Simple difference of means?
Angrist and Lavy (1999)	Effect of class size on educational achievement	Enrollment ceilings on class sizes	Israel	No
Boas and Hidalgo (2011)	Effect of incumbency on access to media	Near-winners and near-losers of close elections	Brazil	Yes
Boas, Hidalgo, and Richardson (2011)	Effect of campaign donations on access to government contracts	Near-winners and near-losers of close elections	Brazil	No
Brollo and Nannicini (2010)	Effect of partisan affiliation of incumbent mayor on federal transfers	Near-winners and near-losers of close elections	Brazil	No
Brollo et al. (2009)	Effect of federal transfers to municipalities on corruption and candidate quality	Population-based revenue-sharing formula	Brazil	No
Chamon, de Mello, and Firpo (2009)	Effects of second-round mayoral runoffs on political competition and fiscal outcomes	Population-based discontinuity in voting system	Brazil	No
Dunning (2010b), Dunning and Nilekani (2010)	Effects of caste-based quotas on ethnic identification and distributive politics	Rule rotating quotas based on caste population proportions[a]	India	Yes
Eggers and Hainmueller (2009)	Effects of holding legislative office on wealth accumulation	Near-winners and near-losers of close elections	UK	No[b]
Ferraz and Finan (2010)	Impact of monetary incentives on politician quality and performance	Salary caps for politicians based on municipal size	Brazil	No
Fujiwara (2011)	Effects of second-round runoff on first-round vote shares	Population-based discontinuity in voting system	Brazil	No[b]
Fujiwara (2009)	Effects of electronic voting technology on de facto enfranchisement and fiscal policy	Thresholds based on numbers of registered voters	Brazil	No[b]
Gerber, Kessler, and Meredith (2011)	Effects of campaign mail on voter turnout and vote choice	Discontinuity in rule used to select households to receive mail[c]	US	Yes
Golden and Picci (2011)	Incumbency advantage and distribution of pork	Within-party comparisons of near-winners and near-losers	Italy	No

Hidalgo (2010)	Effects of electronic voting technology on de facto enfranchisement and fiscal policy	Thresholds based on numbers of registered voters	Brazil	Yes
Kouser and Mullin (2007), Meredith and Malhotra (2011)	Effects of voting by mail on turnout and vote choice	Population-based thresholds used to select precincts for voting by mail	US	No
Lerman (2008)	Social and political effects of incarceration in high-security prisons	Criminality index used to assign prisoners to security levels	US	Yes[d]
Litschig and Morrison (2009)	Effects of federal transfers to municipalities on incumbent reelection probabilities	Discontinuities based on population-based revenue-sharing formula	Brazil	Yes
Manacorda, Miguel, and Vigorito (2011)	The effect of a cash-transfer program on support for the incumbent government	Discontinuity in program assignment based on a pre-treatment eligibility score	Uruguay	Yes
Meredith (2009)	The effect of past voting on subsequent turnout and partisanship	Voting-age restrictions	US	No[b]
Titiunik (2009)	Incumbency advantage in mayoral elections	Near-winners and near-losers of close elections	Brazil	Yes

[a] This RD design has an element of true randomization.
[b] Local linear regression with or without covariates, or polynomial regression without covariates, is used in these studies, and graphic difference-of-means comparisons are made.
[c] The rule is a function of income and other variables.
[d] Regression-discontinuity and instrumental-variables designs are both used.

goal of this survey is therefore to familiarize readers with these ideas, so they might be used in disparate contexts.

3.2.1 Population- and size-based thresholds

One of the most common regression-discontinuity designs, broadly conceived, is one in which researchers take advantage of the fact that a policy intervention is allocated to some geographic or political units but not to others according to some function of population size—and a rigid cutoff is adopted, so that units above or below the threshold differ in their exposure to the intervention. Like students with similar pre-test scores located on either side of a threshold score for public recognition, geographic units with similar population sizes may differ sharply in their exposure to the policy intervention. Error in the measurement of population size may introduce a further element of chance into location of units just above or just below the key threshold. If assignment to one side or the other of the threshold is as good as random, comparison of units on either side of the threshold can then be used to estimate the effect of exposure to the intervention. This presumes, of course, that census officials or other policy-makers do not manipulate the measurement of population size, or that politicians do not choose the key threshold to include or exclude particular units in the intervention group.

Hidalgo (2010), for instance, uses regression-discontinuity designs to study the impact of the introduction of electronic voting machines on de facto enfranchisement, patterns of partisan support, and fiscal policy in Brazil (see also Fujiwara 2009). In the 1998 Brazilian legislative elections, municipalities with more than 40,500 registered voters used electronic ballots, while municipalities with fewer than 40,500 voters continued to use traditional paper ballots. The introduction of electronic voting machines, which feature an ATM-like interface and display of candidates' names, party affiliations, and photographs for voters' confirmation, was thought to ease the process of navigating the complex voting system for illiterate and less well-educated voters, in particular. Brazil uses an open-list proportional representation system with high district magnitudes, meaning that many candidates are often elected from the same districts. In elections to the federal Chamber of Deputies, for instance, the "districts" are states; voters in large states such as São Paulo must elect as many as 70 deputies, choosing from among more than 200 candidates. This implies a bewildering number of individual candidates from which voters may choose, a process made all the more difficult for illiterate or less well-educated voters using traditional paper ballots because of the need to write in candidates' names (or 5- or 6-digit identification numbers) for each of the offices being contested in a given election. The difficulty and inconvenience of navigating this process surely contributed to giving Brazil the highest rates of invalid or blank ballots in Latin America, reaching an average of about 33 percent of all ballots cast in the pre-reform period between 1980 and 1998 (as compared to the regional average of 8.5 percent).

The basis for the regression-discontinuity design is the use of the population threshold of 40,500 registered voters.[8] Municipalities "just above" and "just below" the threshold of 40,500 registered voters should on average be highly similar. Indeed, since the threshold was announced in May of 1998 and the number of registered voters was recorded in the municipal elections of 1996, municipalities should not have been able to manipulate their position in relation to the threshold. There is no apparent evidence that the particular threshold was chosen by municipalities to exclude or include particular municipalities in Brazil. (The threshold was applied uniformly throughout the country, with the exception of four states.) If location just above or just below the population cutoff is as good as randomly assigned, comparisons around the threshold can validly be used to estimate the impact of the voting technology.

Hidalgo (2010) and Fujiwara (2009) find that introduction of electronic voting increased the effective franchise in legislative elections by about 13–15 percentage points or about 33 percent—a massive effect that appears more pronounced in poorer municipalities with higher illiteracy rates. This is likely because electronic voting greatly simplified the process of voting, in a setting in which an open-list proportional representation electoral system with high district magnitude implied that voters would sometimes have to choose from among hundreds of candidates. In contrast to paper ballots, in which voters had to write in the name of their preferred candidate or party, voting machines use an ATM-like interface to display candidates' names, party affiliations, and photographs, which was thought to ease the voting process for illiterate voters, in particular.

Moreover, the introduction of voting machines led to substantial declines in the vote shares of incumbent "machine" parties in several Northeastern states. Thus, Hidalgo (2010) suggests that the introduction of voting machines contributed towards the strengthening of programmatic parties in Brazil.

---

[8] An earlier, more limited reform in 1996 used a population cutoff of 200,000 registered voters; see Chapter 10.

While the increasing importance of programmatic parties has been noted by several recent observers of Brazilian politics, the study by Hidalgo (2010) identifies a plausible cause of this tendency, and his use of a regression-discontinuity design suggests that it is highly unlikely that differences in de facto enfranchisement are driven by confounders, rather than by the introduction of the electronic voting technology.[9]

Regression-discontinuity research designs based on such population thresholds have also been used extensively to study the economic and political impacts of federal transfers in Latin America and other regions. T. Green (2005), for example, calculates the electoral returns of the Mexican conditional cash-transfer program, PROGRESA, using a regression-discontinuity design based on a municipal poverty ranking.[10] Litschig and Morrison (2009) study the effect of federal transfers on municipal incumbents' vote shares in Brazil, while Brollo et al. (2009) study the effect of such transfers on political corruption and on the qualities of political candidates. Both of these latter studies take advantage of the fact that the size of some federal transfers in Brazil depends on given population thresholds. Thus, these authors can construct regression-discontinuity designs in which municipalities just on either side of the relevant thresholds are compared.[11]

Scholars have also used population-based thresholds to study the political and economic impact of electoral rules. For instance, the Brazilian federal constitution states that municipalities with less than 200,000 registered voters must use a single-ballot plurality rule (a first-past-the-post system where the candidate with the most votes is elected) to elect their mayors, while municipalities with more than 200,000 voters must use the dual-ballot plurality rule (second-round "runoff"), a system where voters may vote twice. Fujiwara (2011) finds that in the neighborhood of this threshold, the change from single-ballot to second-round runoff systems increases voting for third-place finishers and decreases the difference between third-place and first- and second-place finishers—a finding consistent both with strategic voting and with the observations of Duverger (1954) and G. Cox (1997) that in elections for m seats, $m + 1$ candidates should command most of the votes. Chamon, de Mello, and Firpo (2009) extend this same idea, finding that the greater political competition induced by the discontinuous change in electoral rules in mayoral elections at the threshold of 200,000

---

[9] This study and the results are discussed more extensively elsewhere, for instance, in Chapters 5 and 10.
[10] This is the same program studied by De La O (forthcoming), as discussed in Chapter 2.
[11] See also the study in Uruguay by Manacorda, Miguel, and Vigorito (2009) discussed below.

voters induces greater investment and reduces current expenditures, particularly personnel expenditures.

Population-based thresholds have been used to study many other topics as well, among them legislative productivity and voter turnout. A constitutional amendment in Brazil sets salary caps on the wages of local legislators as a function of the population size of municipalities. Using this rule to construct a regression-discontinuity design, Ferraz and Finan (2010) find that higher wages increase legislative productivity and political entry but also increase reelection rates among incumbent politicians. Kousser and Mullin (2007) and Meredith and Malhotra (2011) take advantage of an administrative policy in California in which all voters in some precincts are assigned to vote by mail, based on an arbitrary threshold of the number of registered voters.[12] Analyzing the 2008 California presidential primary, and comparing precincts just above and below the relevant threshold, Meredith and Malhotra (2011) show that the practice of voting by mail both increases the probability of selecting withdrawn candidates and affects the relative performance of candidates remaining in the race.

This survey suggests that the use of population-based thresholds by politicians and policy-makers to allocate benefits or introduce other policy innovations has quite often provided the basis for productive regression-discontinuity designs. Obviously, opportunities will not always exist for the construction of this type of regression-discontinuity design in the context of a given substantive research agenda. Yet, the recent record suggests that the potential range of applications is very broad: many more possibilities for using this kind of design may also await researchers alert to their existence. Indeed, population-based thresholds and ceilings appear to be fairly widely used in the allocation of public benefits and other policies across a number of different countries, and scholars investigating a range of different causal hypotheses might be able to take advantage of such instances to construct regression-discontinuity designs.

Scholars have also used many other kinds of size-based thresholds, beyond those based on the populations of municipalities, to construct regression-discontinuity designs. A well-known example, which illustrates both the

---

[12] The election law states that if the number of registered voters in a precinct is no larger than 250 on a given date prior to the election, election officials may *choose* to establish voting by mail in that precinct. Because there are in fact some precincts above the 250-voter limit that also have vote-by-mail, and some below it that do not, this can be seen as an example of "fuzzy" regression-discontinuity analysis (discussed below and in Chapter 5). See Kousser and Mullin (2007) or Meredith and Malhotra (2011) for further details.

strengths and limitations of this design, is Angrist and Lavy (1999), who analyze the effects of class size on educational achievement. In general, comparing educational outcomes in schools with large classes to schools with small classes would be misleading, for purposes of inferring the impact of class size: students in schools with large classes differ in both potentially observable (income, ethnic background) and more difficult-to-measure (parental backgrounds, student motivation) ways.

However, Angrist and Lavy (1999) build on a requirement in contemporary Israel—known as Maimonides' Rule, after the twelfth-century Rabbinic scholar—that requires secondary schools to have no more than 40 students per classroom. Thus, in a school in which the total enrollment is near this threshold or its multiples—e.g., schools with just under 40, 80, or 120 students—the addition of a few students to the school through increases in overall enrollment can cause a sharp reduction in average class sizes—since more classes must be created to comply with the rule. The educational achievement of students in schools the enrollments of which are just under the threshold size of 40 (or 80 or 120) can then be compared to students in schools that are just over the threshold and who were thus reassigned to classrooms with a smaller number of students.

The key assertion is that, on average, schools just above each threshold size are just like schools below the threshold size—save for average class size. Thus, assignment to class sizes for students in these schools is as good as random, and the effect of class size can therefore be estimated in the neighborhood of the thresholds. A key feature of the design is that students probably do not self-select into smaller classrooms, since the application of Maimonides' Rule is triggered by increases in schoolwide grade enrollment. The design is interesting, and there is a plausible claim of as-if randomness in the neighborhood of the threshold—though this study also raises interesting issues of analysis and interpretation to which I turn in later chapters.

Beyond class size, scholars have used size-based thresholds to study effects for many other kinds of units. For example, Hahn, Todd, and Van Der Klaauw (1999) study the effect of an anti-discrimination law that only applies to firms with at least 15 employees. In such contexts, one must worry about confounding decisions related to the size of the firm; perhaps racist employers hold their size under 15 employees to avoid adverse consequences from the anti-discrimination law. Yet, such concerns notwithstanding, the potential range of applications of regression-discontinuity designs based on size-based thresholds also appears large.

3.2.2 Near-winners and near-losers of close elections

A different kind of regression-discontinuity design, which has also found growing use in recent years, takes advantage of the fact that in very close and fair elections, there is an element of luck and unpredictability in the outcome; thus, underlying attributes of near-winners may not differ greatly from near-losers. As Lee (2008) suggested in his study of the US Congress, near-winners and near-losers of close elections should be nearly identical, on average. Thus, comparisons of these groups can be used to estimate the effects of winning office. Indeed, due to the element of luck in very close elections, candidates and parties are plausibly assigned as-if at random to office in these elections. As with other natural experiments, whether the assumption of as-if random is valid in this kind of regression-discontinuity design should be evaluated on a case-by-case basis, using various quantitative and qualitative tools discussed in later chapters. In the context of the US House elections studied by Lee (2008), Caughey and Sekhon (2011) develop a compelling critique of the assertion of as-if randomness; in other contexts, this assertion may be more convincing.

For instance, Titiunik (2009) studies the incumbency advantage of political parties in Brazil's municipal mayor elections, comparing municipalities where a party barely lost the 2000 mayor elections to municipalities where it barely won. Contrary to findings in the US, she finds evidence of a strong *negative* effect of incumbency on both the vote share and the probability of winning in the following election; the significant estimated effect sizes range from around negative 4 percentage points of the vote share for the Liberal Front Party) to around negative 19 percentage points for the Party of the Brazilian Democratic Movement.

In a study of the relationship between political incumbency and media access, Boas and Hidalgo (2011) show that near-winners of city council elections are much more likely than near-losers to have their applications for community radio licenses approved by the federal government, a finding that reinforces previous research on the political control of the media in Brazil. Brollo and Nannicini (2010) use a related regression-discontinuity design to study the effect of partisan affiliation on federal transfers to municipalities in Brazil, comparing winners and losers of close elections and stratifying on whether the winner is a member of the president's coalition.

Beyond incumbency advantage for candidates, such designs have been used to study the effects for citizens and firms of supporting winning candidates. Boas, Hidalgo, and Richardson (2011), for example, study the effect of campaign contributions on government contracts received by donors. These authors compare the returns to donations to near-winners and near-losers of campaigns, showing that public-works companies that rely on government contracts may receive a substantial monetary return on electoral investments. The effect size is striking: firms who specialize in public works projects can expect a substantial boost in government contracts—at least 8.5 times the value of their contributions—when a recipient of campaign donations from the ruling Workers' Party wins office. Golden and Picci (2011) adapt the near-winner and near-loser framework to the study of within-party effects of incumbency advantage in Italy's open-list proportional representation system, using a regression-discontinuity design to look at the relationship between the distribution of federal spending and the reelection prospects of incumbents. Finally, Eggers and Hainmueller (2009) use a regression-discontinuity approach based on near-winners and near-losers to estimate the returns to office in the British Parliament, finding that Conservative (but not Labour) MPs profited handsomely from office through outside employment they acquired due to their political positions.

Notice that regression-discontinuity designs in which analysts compare near-winners and near-losers of close elections differ in some respects from the classic design proposed by Thistlethwaite and Campbell (1960). For example, here there is not necessarily a single value of a pre-treatment covariate (or index) that determines treatment assignment. In plurality elections with just two candidates, the difference in the votes received by the two candidates can be thought of as the assignment variable—with a value of 0 being the key cutoff, positive values indicating assignment to treatment, and negative values indicating assignment to control. With more than two candidates, the difference in votes between the first and second vote-getters can be defined as the assignment covariate (also known as the "forcing variable"). Yet the adaptation of regression-discontinuity designs to other electoral systems, such as list systems with proportional representation, may imply that the margin between near-winners and near-losers is not zero at the assignment threshold, nor is it the same in every election. (For instance, the margin between the lowest vote-getter to enter the legislature on a party's list and the highest vote-getter not to enter the legislature need not be zero).[13] Thus, graphs such as Figure 2.1 showing outcomes as a function of the assignment covariate may not be as easy to draw. Yet the estimation of the effect of treatment assignment follows a similar logic as in other regression-discontinuity designs.

---

[13] See unpublished work by Luis Schiumerini as well as Olle Folke, and Golden and Picci (2011).

Whether electoral office is really assigned as-if at random in the neighborhood of the winning margin, even in very close elections, may be debatable in some contexts (Caughey and Sekhon 2011). The claim of as-if randomness, which motivates the analysis of the data from such natural experiments, should be carefully evaluated on a case-by-case basis. I will return later in the book to the type of a priori reasoning and empirical evidence that may be useful for such regression-discontinuity designs.[14]

3.2.3 Age as a regression discontinuity

Does past voting affect subsequent turnout or partisanship among voters? Many theories of political participation suggest that the act of voting itself has important consequences for political attitudes and behavior. Evaluating such causal claims empirically might seem rather hopeless at first glance, however, since people who choose to vote—for example, when they are first eligible to do so—probably differ in many difficult-to-measure ways from those who do not. For example, they may feel greater urge to heed civic duty, which may affect both voting and other political attitudes. Thus, initial differences in affect or behavior might then be responsible for subsequent differences in turnout rates or partisan identification.

Meredith (2009), however, takes advantage of the discontinuities imposed by voting-age restrictions to identify the effect of past participation on subsequent turnout and partisan identification. Thus, this paper compares individuals who turned eighteen just before US presidential elections—and were thus eligible to vote in those elections—with those who turned eighteen just after. Those twenty-two years of age with the opportunity to cast a ballot in a given presidential election are thus divided, as-if at random, into two groups: those who were eligible to vote in the previous election and those who were ineligible to do so, on the basis of birthdays that could be separated by as little as a few days or months. Because precise date of birth should not be related to confounding factors that affect turnout decisions or partisan identification, this regression-discontinuity design appears to provide a valid natural experiment for studying the effects of past eligibility on subsequent behavior.[15] The paper finds that past presidential election eligibility increases the probability that a voter will turn out in the next election by

---

[14] See Chapters 7 and 8.
[15] It may also provide an opportunity to evaluate the effects of past *participation*—rather than simply past eligibility to participate—on subsequent partisanship and voting behavior. See the discussion of instrumental-variables analysis in Chapters 4 and 5.

between 3 and 7 percentage points, depending on the election; moreover, these effects continue to persist for several election cycles after a voter first becomes eligible. Participation in past presidential elections also appears to affect partisan identification in subsequent elections.

Other kinds of age-based cutoffs have or could be used to construct regression-discontinuity designs. For example, individuals above or below a cutoff age often pay lower prices for access to libraries, museums, and other public resources (e.g., through senior citizen discounts or discounts for children under some age limit). Similarly, eligibility for medical services through Medicare (the US public health-care program) is restricted by age, which can be used to study the effects of access to these services, by comparing those who are just eligible on the basis of age to those who are just ineligible—but are otherwise indistinguishable from the treatment group (Card, Dobkin, and Maestas 2009). Again, the range of potential applications of age-based cutoffs to the study of the political and economic effects of access to various public services appears to be very large.

3.2.4 Indices

In many examples surveyed above, the key cutoff in each regression-discontinuity design was based on the value of a single pre-treatment covariate—such as a student's score on a qualifying exam or the population of a municipality. (These are called "pre-treatment" covariates because their value is determined before the intervention of interest takes place.) While this is perhaps the most common scenario for regression-discontinuity designs, it also sometimes occurs that policy-makers or other actors combine information from several variables into an index—and the value of the index then determines program assignment, with units scoring above a threshold score on the index being assigned to treatment. For example, Manacorda, Miguel, and Vigorito (2009) use a discontinuity in program assignment based on a pre-treatment eligibility score to study the effects of cash transfers in Uruguay on support for the incumbent Frente Amplio government; the eligibility score is constructed from a range of different variables, however. They find that program beneficiaries are much more likely than nonbeneficiaries to support the incumbent, by around 11 to 14 percentage points. Similarly, Lerman (2008) exploits an index used in the California prison system to assign convicts to higher- and lower-security prisons to study the effect of high-security incarceration, finding that assignment to high-security prisons has important consequences for social attitudes and behaviors.

3.3 Variations on regression-discontinuity designs

The basic regression-discontinuity design described in Section 3.2 has a number of extensions and modifications. Perhaps the most important is the distinction between regression-discontinuity designs in which treatment receipt is a deterministic function of placement above and below the threshold—as in the original Thistlethwaite and Campbell (1960) design, where every student scoring above the key threshold received a Certificate of Merit—and those in which placement relative to the threshold influences treatment receipt but does not determine it completely. Some regression-discontinuity designs also have an element of true randomization. I mention these topics only briefly below and return to them at greater length in subsequent chapters.

3.3.1 Sharp versus fuzzy regression discontinuities

I have presented the designs above as if the key regression-discontinuity threshold must determine program participation deterministically: e.g., a policy intervention is allocated to some geographic areas but not to others according to population size—and a rigid cutoff is adopted, so that units above the threshold all participate in the intervention while those below the threshold do not. While this description aptly characterizes so-called "sharp" regression-discontinuity designs (Campbell 1969; Trochim 1984), this is not necessary for successful regression-discontinuity analysis. In some studies, the key threshold merely influences program participation in a probabilistic, rather than deterministic, fashion.[16] That is, placement just above or just below the key threshold influences treatment receipt, but does not determine it completely.

Regression-discontinuity designs in which placement relative to the threshold influences treatment receipt, but does not determine it completely, are known as "fuzzy" regression-discontinuity designs (Campbell 1969; Trochim 1984). In a study by Gerber, Kessler, and Meredith (2011), for instance, a political organization in Kansas used a rule to select households to receive mailings critical of the political incumbent. Because of this rule, individuals living in census tracts in which a certain percentage of residents had

---

[16] In this case, as I discuss in Chapter 5, program assignment acts as an instrumental variable for program participation. Thus, there is an intimate connection between fuzzy regression-discontinuity and instrumental-variables designs.

household incomes above a given threshold were substantially more likely to be assigned to receive the mailings. Yet, the threshold did not deterministically influence treatment receipt.

Such "fuzzy" regression-discontinuity designs are closely linked to instrumental-variables designs, introduced in the next chapter: as in instrumental-variables designs, random assignment to treatment does not completely determine receipt of treatment. The analysis of fuzzy regression discontinuities thus raises issues that are similar to instrumental-variables analysis. I will therefore delay further discussion of this design for subsequent chapters.

3.3.2 Randomized regression-discontinuity designs

Some regression-discontinuity designs also incorporate elements of true randomization at the key regression-discontinuity threshold. For instance, thresholds may be relatively coarse, so that a broad set of (possibly quite heterogeneous) units are eligible for assignment to a policy on the basis of a score near the key threshold. However, actual assignment may be based on a true lottery.

Dunning and Nilekani (2010) provide one example from India.[17] In village council elections in the state of Karnataka, electoral laws require some council presidencies to be reserved for lower castes and tribes, i.e., in some councils the president must come from designated castes and tribes. The quotas are assigned by ranking councils within subdistricts in descending order, on the basis of the number of council *seats* that are reserved for lower castes and tribes.[18] Thus, quotas go first to the block of councils at the top of the list. (The total number of presidencies that must be reserved in a given election is determined by the proportion of the subdistrict population from lower castes and tribes.) In subsequent elections, quotas rotate down to the next block of councils on the list.[19] Thus, in any given election, councils with particular threshold numbers of seats reserved for lower castes and tribes are "eligible" for reservation of the council presidency. As in other regression-discontinuity

---

[17] See also Dunning (2010b).
[18] The number of council seats reserved for lower castes and tribes is in turn a proxy for the population proportion of lower castes and tribes, within each council constituency. What I call subdistricts here are administrative jurisdictions called "blocks."
[19] This system of rotation began in 1994, in the first elections after the passage of a national constitutional amendment requiring such electoral quotas for marginalized castes and tribes as well as women.

designs, this threshold determines treatment assignment, since councils below the threshold do not receive quotas while those above the threshold may receive quotas (though some do not, e.g., if they had quotas in previous elections; so this is also a fuzzy regression-discontinuity design).

The element of true randomization arises because, whenever the number of councils that are eligible for quotas (on the basis of having the threshold number of seats reserved for lower-castes or lower-tribe) exceeds the number of councils to which quotas must be assigned, councils are chosen at random for quotas from among the eligible group, using a lottery. In other words, at the regression-discontinuity threshold, there is then true randomization of treatment assignment. Comparisons among councils in the eligible group—including those in which the presidency was set aside for members of lower castes and tribes and those in which the presidency was not thus reserved—can then allow valid estimation of the effects of the electoral quotas.

3.3.3 Multiple thresholds

In some regression-discontinuity designs, the particular threshold that determines treatment assignment may vary across jurisdictional areas; or different thresholds may be used for different populations, or at different points in time. In Hidalgo's (2010) study of electronic voting in Brazil, for instance, the main threshold of interest is the one located at a municipal population of 40,500; in 1998, municipalities with populations greater than this threshold switched to electronic voting. However, an earlier reform in 1996 had introduced electronic voting in municipalities with populations greater than 200,000. Thus, the causal effects of electronic voting can be estimated at this threshold for the elections held in that year. In the studies by Dunning (2011) and Dunning and Nilekani (2010) discussed above, different Scheduled Caste population thresholds are used in each subdistrict in a given election, depending on the size of the subdistrict and the overall proportion of Scheduled Caste residents. Thus, the effect of caste-based quotas is estimated at different thresholds of the assignment covariate across different subdistricts.

As discussed later in the book, one of the potential advantages of regression-discontinuity designs with multiple thresholds is that causal effects at different thresholds may be explicitly compared. In general, one limitation of many regression-discontinuity designs is that the causal effect of treatment for units located near the threshold may differ from those located far from the threshold; and regression-discontinuity designs are properly used to estimate causal effects for the former population. However, with multiple thresholds this question of external validity can, at least to some extent, be investigated empirically (see Chapter 10).

3.4 Conclusion

The recent growth of regression-discontinuity designs in the social sciences is impressive. In many contexts, the case for as-if random assignment at the threshold has strong a priori plausibility, making this a particularly useful kind of natural experiment for drawing causal inferences. Of course, as in other natural experiments, analysts are challenged to validate this assertion to the extent possible, and as-if random may be more compelling in some regression-discontinuity designs than in others.[20]

Discovering regression-discontinuity designs, as with other kinds of natural experiments, is an imprecise affair, subject to luck and inspiration. Yet, as the survey in this chapter suggests, scholars have adapted ideas developed in other contexts to study disparate substantive problems. For example, similar population-based thresholds have often provided the basis for different regression-discontinuity designs; indeed, sometimes the same threshold is used for different purposes or to study different outcomes. Comparisons of near-winners and near-losers of close elections have also been an increasingly prominent strategy for drawing inferences about the effects of a range of variables, from political incumbency to campaign donations.

Regression-discontinuity designs can have several limitations, however, and their use has inspired controversies related to both analysis and interpretation of effects. For example, there is a lively debate about strategies for analyzing data from regression-discontinuity designs: analysts have debated the virtues of simple difference-of-means tests in this context, and there are also important issues related to defining the size of the study group—essentially, how big the "window" should be around the key threshold. Such choices both depend on, and have key implications for, the claim that assignment to treatment is as good as random in a regression-discontinuity design. I return to these issues in Chapter 5.

As for interpretation, in regression-discontinuity designs the average causal effect is defined only for units near the threshold—that is, those units in the regression-discontinuity study group. Following Imbens and Angrist (1994), this parameter is sometimes called a "local average treatment effect" to

---

[20] See Chapter 8.

emphasize that it holds only for these units. Whether and under what conditions this parameter is of social-scientific interest has been subject to controversy (Deaton 2009; Imbens 2009). I take up this question later in the book as well.[21]

Exercises

3.1) Regression-discontinuity designs estimate average causal effects for particular sets of units—those whose values on a pre-treatment covariate are just above or just below the key threshold that determines treatment assignment. Pick two of the studies surveyed in this chapter and then answer the following questions:
   (a) Is the effect of treatment assignment for units located just above or just below the key threshold an interesting or relevant parameter, for either social-scientific or policy purposes? Why or why not? In answering this question, consider both the potential virtues and limitations of estimating effects for these units.
   (b) How might the relevance of this causal effect for other units—those whose covariate values do not put them just above or below the threshold for treatment assignment—be investigated empirically?

3.2) In some US states, anti-discrimination laws are enforced only for companies of a certain size—say, 15 employees and above (see Hahn, Todd, and Van Der Klaauw 1999). Consider a regression-discontinuity design in which the effects of these laws are investigated by comparing outcomes, such as employment of minority workers, by firms with 13 or 14 employees and firms with 15 and 16 employees.
   (a) Is this a valid natural experiment? What are some possible threats to as-if random?
   (b) How could these threats be investigated empirically? What sort of data or information would be relevant for the empirical tests?

3.3) An analyst makes the following statement: "In studies using jurisdictional borders to generate natural experiments, villages or other units are analyzed in the neighborhood of a threshold determining assignment to treatment groups—that is, on either side of the jurisdictional or administrative border. Therefore, such studies should be considered

---

[21] See Chapter 10.

regression-discontinuity designs." Is this claim valid? Why or why not? What, if anything, distinguishes a standard regression-discontinuity design, such as Thistlethwaite and Campbell's (1960) study, from studies using jurisdictional borders?

3.4) Campbell and Stanley (1966) describe the Connecticut crackdown discussed in this book's introductory chapter as an "interrupted time-series" design. Suppose an analyst compares traffic fatalities in a short window on either side of the passage of the traffic law. Should such a study be considered a regression-discontinuity design? Why or why not? What, if anything, distinguishes regression-discontinuity designs from standard interrupted time-series designs?

4 Instrumental-variables designs

An instrumental-variables design relies on the idea of as-if random in yet another way. Consider the challenge of inferring the impact of a given independent variable on a particular dependent variable—where this inference is made more difficult, given the strong possibility that reciprocal causation or confounding may pose a problem for causal inference. The solution offered by the instrumental-variables design is to find an additional variable—an instrument—that is correlated with the independent variable but could not be influenced by the dependent variable or correlated with its other causes. Thus, units are assigned at random or as-if at random, not to the key independent variable of interest, but rather to this instrumental variable.

Recall, for instance, Angrist's (1990 a) study of military conscription discussed in the Introduction. Eligibility for the Vietnam draft was randomly assigned to young men, via numbers from 1 to 366 that were matched to each potential draftee's birth date; men with lottery numbers above a particular cutoff value were not subject to the draft. Comparing men with lottery numbers above and below the cutoff estimates the effect of draft eligibility. This is "intention-to-treat" analysis, as described in Box 4.1: males are compared according their draft eligibility status, regardless of whether they actually served in the military. Intention to treat is a key principle of natural-experimental analysis, and intention-to-treat analysis should usually be reported in write-ups of research results.[1]

However, intention-to-treat analysis estimates the impact of draft eligibility, not actual military service. Since many soldiers who were draft eligible did not serve, while some who were not drafted volunteered, the effects of actual service may differ from the effects of eligibility for service. Intention-to-treat analysis will typically produce a conservative estimate of the effects of service.

---

[1] The jargon stems from medical trials, in which researchers intend to administer a treatment to those assigned to the treatment group (some of whom may fail to comply with the protocol). See Freedman, Petitti, and Robins (2004) for an example on breast-cancer screening.

> **Box 4.1 The intention-to-treat principle**
>
> In natural experiments, true randomization—or an as-if random process—sorts units such as individuals or municipalities into treatment and control groups. Yet, this does not imply that all units in the study group are actually exposed to the treatment regime that corresponds to these groups. For instance, the Vietnam-era draft lottery established draft eligibility, but not all draft-eligible men served in the military. Policy-makers use a lottery to assign students to receive vouchers for private schools in Colombia, yet some students who receive vouchers may fail to enroll in private schools. In regression-discontinuity designs, a population index or other pre-treatment score might establish eligibility for a program, but some individuals eligible for a program might opt out. Comparisons of people who self-select into treatment and those who do not receive the treatment are a bad idea: such comparisons are subject to confounding and may thus lead to misleading inferences about the effect of treatment.
>
> Analysis of many natural experiments thus depends on the *intention-to-treat* principle. Here, the groups created by the (as-if) randomization are compared, regardless of the choice of individual units to opt in or opt out of a program. In Angrist's (1990 a) study of the Vietnam-era draft lottery, draft-eligible men may be compared to draft-ineligible men—whether they actually served in the military or not. Intention to treat is one of the most important principles of experimental and natural-experimental analysis. Although subjects may be heterogeneous in their response to treatment assignment, the intention-to-treat analysis makes no statistical adjustments for heterogeneity. Instead, randomization or as-if randomization is relied upon to balance the treatment and control groups, up to random error. Intention-to-treat analysis is also useful for purposes of significance testing, that is, for assessing whether observed differences between the treatment and control groups could reasonably have arisen by chance. These topics are discussed further in Chapters 5 and 6.

Instrumental-variables analysis provides an alternative that is often useful. This technique estimates the average effect of actual military service for a particular set of potential soldiers—those who would serve only if they are drafted. Such people are called Compliers, because they comply with the treatment condition to which they are assigned (Imbens and Angrist 1994; Freedman 2006).

Why does this procedure work? In brief, the lottery gives us an instrumental variable—draft eligibility—that is correlated with the treatment variable (actual military service) but that could not be influenced by the dependent variable or correlated with its other causes. Notice that the impact of service on labor-market earnings or political attitudes is typically subject to confounding: those who choose to serve in the military may be different than those who do not, in ways that matter for earnings (Chapter 1). Thus, the group that receives treatment includes soldiers who would choose to serve whether or not they are drafted—that is, volunteers—while the group that receives the control regime does not include any people of this type. Self-selection therefore destroys the *ex ante* symmetry between the treatment and control groups: if propensity to volunteer for the military is correlated with potential earnings or political attitudes, then comparing people who serve in the military with people who do not leads to a biased estimate of the effects of service.

By contrast, randomization to the draft lottery restores the symmetry, since draft eligibility is randomly assigned and is therefore uncorrelated with such confounders, up to random error. The instrumental-variables procedure works because the proportion of Compliers is about the same in the assigned-to-treatment and assigned-to-control groups—due to random assignment. By examining the proportion of units in each group who actually take the treatment, we can estimate the proportion of Compliers in the study group. Using techniques discussed in detail in Chapter 5, we can then adjust the intention-to-treat analysis to estimate the effects of military service for men who would serve only if drafted.

As this discussion makes clear, instrumental variables might be viewed as an analytic strategy, rather than as a distinct type of natural-experimental design—one that may be used to estimate quantities such as the effect of treatment on Compliers in standard natural experiments in which there is imperfect compliance with treatment assignment. Nonetheless, because of the importance instrumental-variables analysis has assumed in recent years—and because some analysts mainly use natural experiments to generate instrumental variables—it is worth discussing this form of design in a separate chapter in Part I of the book. Moreover, as the discussion in subsequent chapters makes clear, instrumental-variables designs often raise specific issues of interpretation. The discussion in this chapter will therefore provide a useful reference point.

The logic of instrumental-variables analysis sometimes carries through to natural experiments with as-if randomization. In effect, the instrumental variable is treated as though it "assigns" units to values of the independent variable in a way that is as-if random, even though often no explicit randomization occurred. However, important conditions must be met for valid

Table 4.1 Selected sources of instrumental-variables designs

Source of instrumental variable	Units in study group	Treatment variable	Outcome variables
Lotteries			
Military drafts	Soldiers	Military service	Earnings, attitudes
Prize lotteries	Lottery players	Overall income	Political attitudes
Judge lotteries	Prisoners	Prison terms	Recidivism
Training invitations	Job-seekers	Job trainings	Wages
School vouchers	Students	Private-school attendance	Educational achievement
Weather shocks			
Rainfall growth	Countries	Economic growth	Civil war
Natural disasters	Countries	Oil prices	Democracy
Age			
Quarter-of-birth	Students	Education	Earnings
Twin studies			
Twin births	Mothers	Number of children	Earnings
Institutional variation			
Electoral cycles	States	Police presence	Crime
Land tenure types	States	Inequality	Public goods
Historical shocks			
Deaths of leaders	Countries	Colonial annexation	Development
Colonial settler mortality	Countries	Current institutions	Economic growth

Note: The table provides a non-exhaustive list of sources of instrumental-variables designs. See Tables 4.2 and 4.3 for references to specific studies.

instrumental-variables analysis. Without true randomization, the approach requires validating as-if randomization; as with other natural experiments, this can be tricky. Moreover, if regression models are used, the assumptions behind the models may or may not be plausible: depending on the application, instrumental-variables designs may be more "design based" or more "model based."

Other assumptions are critical as well, whether treatment assignment is truly randomized or only as-if random. For instance, the instrument must affect the outcome only by influencing treatment receipt, and this so-called "exclusion restriction" may or may not hold: for instance, draft eligibility might shape later earnings not only through actual military service but also through other channels (say, educational receipt). Finally, whether the causal effect of actual treatment for Compliers is an interesting and important parameter depends on the context and research question.

Such analytic and interpretive issues are discussed in much more detail later in the book.[2] The main goal in this chapter, as in the previous two chapters, is instead to survey applications, as a way of motivating discussion of how analysts discover instrumental-variables designs. To this end, Table 4.1 lists several generic sources of instrumental variables, while Tables 4.2 and 4.3 list specific studies that use instrumental variables in true experiments and natural experiments, respectively. The rest of this chapter briefly discusses applications of instrumental variables in true experiments, where the usage parallels that discussed for Angrist's draft lottery study; I then turn to natural experiments, organizing the discussion by the source of the instrumental variable, as in Table 4.1.

4.1 Instrumental-variables designs: true experiments

Instrumental variables are used in true randomized experiments in which some subjects do not comply with treatment assignment. In fact, one of the best ways to understand the logic of instrumental-variables analysis is by analogy to true experiments, in which a random process like a flip of a coin determines which subjects are assigned to treatment—so subjects assigned to receive the treatment are, on average, just like subjects assigned to control. Even in experiments there can be confounding, however, if subjects who accept the treatment are compared to those who refuse it. The decision to accept treatment—e.g., to take the drug if assigned to the treatment regime in a medical trial—is made by the subjects, not the experimenter, and those who choose to accept treatment may be unlike those who do not, in ways that matter for outcomes.

Analysts should therefore compare subjects randomly assigned to treatment to those randomly assigned to control—following Campbell's (1984) admonition to "analyze 'em as you randomize 'em." Again, however, intention-to-treat analysis does not take account of the fact that not all subjects receive the treatment condition to which they are assigned. In true experiments, as in some observational studies, instrumental-variables analysis may be used to estimate the effect of treatment on Compliers—those subjects who follow the treatment regime to which they are assigned. In true experiments, treatment assignment often satisfies two key requirements for an instrumental variable: it is statistically independent of unobserved causes of

---

[2] See especially Chapters 5 and 8–10.

Table 4.2 Selected instrumental-variables designs (true experiments)

Authors	Substantive focus	Source of instrument
Bloom et al. (1997)	Effect of job training participation on earnings	Random assignment of admission to training program
Burghardt et al. (2001)	Effect of participation in Job Corps program on earnings	Random assignment of admission to training program
Howell et al. (2000)	Effect of enrollment in private school on achievement test scores	Random assignment of offer of school voucher
Krueger (1999)	Effect of class size on achievement test scores	Random assignment to smaller or larger class
Powers and Swinton (1984)	Effect of hours of study on achievement test scores	Random mailing of test preparation materials
Permutt and Hebel (1984, 1989)	Effect of maternal smoking on birth weight	Random assignment of free smoker's counseling

Note: This non-exhaustive list includes published and unpublished studies in political science, economics, and cognate disciplines that analyze randomized controlled experiments, using treatment assignment as an instrument for treatment receipt.

the dependent variable, due to randomization, and it plausibly affects the outcome only through its effect on treatment receipt. Instrumental-variables analysis of true experimental data is a common strategy; Table 4.2 gives examples of a few such studies.[3]

4.2 Instrumental-variables designs: natural experiments

In observational studies, in which assignment to treatment is not under the control of the researcher, the problem of confounding is typically severe, because units self-select into the treatment and control groups. Instrumental-variables analysis can be used to recover the effect of an "endogenous" treatment, that is, a treatment variable that is correlated with confounders. Just as in true experiments, a valid instrumental variable must be independent of other causes of the dependent variable, and it must influence exposure to treatment but have no direct effect on the outcome, other than through its

---

[3] Some of the studies in Table 4.2 are known as "encouragement" designs, because subjects are randomly assigned to receive encouragement to comply with some treatment—for instance, they are sent test preparation materials to encourage them to study for tests (Powers and Swinton 1984). In such studies, the encouragement to perform some activity serves as an instrumental variable for actual performance of the activity.

Table 4.3 Selected instrumental-variables designs (natural experiments)

Authors	Random or as-if random?	Substantive focus	Source of instrument	Country
Acemoglu, Johnson, and Robinson (2001)	As-if	Effects of institutions on economic growth	Colonial settler mortality rates	Cross-national
Angrist (1990a)	Random	Effect of military service on later labor-market earnings	Randomized draft lottery numbers in the Vietnam war	US
Angrist and Evans (1998)	As-if	Effect of fertility on labor supply	Sibling-sex composition	US
Angrist and Krueger (1991)	As-if	Effect of years of schooling on earnings	Age-based school enrollment laws (quarter-of-birth is the instrument)	US
Bronars and Grogger (1994)	As-if	Effect of fertility on education and labor supply	Occurrence of twin births	US
Card (1995)	As-if	Effect of years of schooling on earnings	Proximity to college	US
Doherty, Green, and Gerber (2005)	Random	Effect of income on political attitudes	Random assignment of lottery winnings, among lottery players	US
Duflo (2001)	As-if	Effect of individual years of schooling on earnings	Region and time variation in school construction	Indonesia
Evans and Ringel (1999)	As-if	Effects of maternal smoking on birth weight	Variation in state cigarette taxes	US
Green and Winik (2010)	Random	Effects of incarceration and probation on recidivism	Random assignment of judges to cases	US
Gruber (2000)	As-if	Effect of disability insurance replacement rates on labor supply	Region and time variation in benefit rules	US
Hidalgo et al. (2010)	As-if	Effects of economic conditions on land invasions in Brazil	Shocks to economic conditions due to rainfall patterns	Brazil
Kling (2006)	Random	Effects of prison term length on employment and earnings	Random assignment of federal judges to cases	US
Levitt (1997)	As-if	Effects of policing on crime	Electoral cycles	US
McClellan, McNeil, and Newhouse (1994)	As-if	Effect of heart attack surgery on health	Proximity to cardiac care centers	US

Table 4.3 (cont.)

Authors	Random or as-if random?	Substantive focus	Source of instrument	Country
Miguel, Satyanath and Sergenti (2004)	As-if	Economic growth and civil conflict	Shocks to economic conditions due to rainfall patterns	Cross-national (Africa)
Ramsay (2011)	As-if	Effects of oil price on democracy	Shocks to oil price due to damage from natural disasters	Cross-national

Note: This non-exhaustive list includes published and unpublished studies in political science, economics, and cognate disciplines that have used ostensible natural experiments to generate instrumental variables.

effect on exposure to treatment.[4] These are often strong assumptions, which can be only partially validated from data.

Such instrumental variables can arise both in natural experiments with true randomization—such as those involving lotteries—and those with as-if randomization—for instance, in which weather shocks or other sources of instrumental variables are employed. Table 4.3 lists some examples, several of which I discuss in this section.

4.2.1 Lotteries

Randomized lotteries sometimes supply instrumental variables. In Chapter 2, for instance, I discussed the study by Doherty, Green, and Gerber (2006), who study the relationship between lottery winnings and political attitudes. In this context, we have a standard natural experiment, because the treatment—levels of lottery winnings—is randomly assigned among lottery players (given the kind and number of lottery tickets bought).

However, this lottery study could also provide the foundation for an instrumental-variables design.[5] For example, the relationship between overall income and political attitudes may be subject to confounding, since many factors—such as family background—may shape both income and attitudes. However, here we have an instrumental variable—lottery winnings—that is correlated with overall income and presumably independent of other causes of

---

[4] The latter condition is sometimes called an "exclusion restriction," in reference to the exclusion of the instrumental variable from a causal equation governing the outcome.
[5] Doherty, Green, and Gerber (2005) use instrumental variables.

political attitudes. This example underscores that whether a given study adopts a standard natural-experimental or an instrumental-variables design depends on the question being asked—for example, whether the question of interest concerns the effect of lottery winnings or of overall income. A number of different assumptions must be met for this instrumental-variables design to be valid; the strengths and limitations of instrumental variables analysis in this context are discussed further in Chapter 9 (see also Dunning 2008c).

Similarly, instrumental-variables designs may arise from lotteries in which there is imperfect compliance with treatment assignment—as in the case of the Vietnam draft lottery. Vouchers for private secondary school in Colombia were allocated by lottery, but not all winners of vouchers used them (while some students who did not receive vouchers paid for private school themselves). Here, vouchers can provide an instrumental variable for private-school attendance, for instance in a study of the effect of private secondary schooling on educational attainment (Angrist et al. 2002). Assignment to a voucher is correlated with enrollment in private secondary schools, and it is presumably independent of other influences on educational attainment—due to the randomization of the lottery. For valid use of an instrumental-variables design in this context, assignment to a voucher must not have a direct effect on educational attainment—above and beyond its influence on private secondary-school enrollment rates—and other assumptions may be required.[6]

4.2.2 Weather shocks

As-if randomization can also provide the basis for instrumental-variables designs. For example, some analysts use weather-induced shocks as instruments for a range of independent variables, from economic growth to commodities prices. Miguel, Satyanath, and Sergenti (2004) study the effect of economic growth on the probability of civil war in Africa, using annual change in rainfall as an instrumental variable. Reciprocal causation poses a major problem in this research—civil war causes economies to grow more slowly—and many difficult-to-measure omitted variables may affect both economic growth and the likelihood of civil war. As Miguel, Satyanath, and Sergenti (2004: 726) point out, "the existing literature does not adequately address the endogeneity of economic variables to civil war and thus does not convincingly establish a causal relationship. In addition to endogeneity,

---

[6] See Chapters 5 and 9.

omitted variables—for example, government institutional quality—may drive both economic outcomes and conflict, producing misleading cross-country estimates."

However, year-to-year variation in rainfall is plausibly as-if random vis-a-vis these other social and political processes, and it is correlated with economic growth. In other words, year-on-year variation in rainfall "assigns" African countries to rates of economic growth—if only probabilistically—so the predicted value of growth based on changes in rainfall can be analyzed in place of actual economic growth rates. If rainfall is independent of all determinants of civil war other than economic growth, instrumental-variables analysis may allow estimation of the effect of economic growth on conflict, at least for those countries whose growth performance is shaped by variation in rainfall.

Of course, rainfall may or may not be independent of other sources of armed conflict, and it may or may not influence conflict only through its effect on growth (Sovey and Green 2009). If floods wash away the roads, soldiers may not fight, so rainfall might have a direct influence on conflict, above and beyond its effect on growth.[7] Moreover, variation in rainfall may also influence growth only in particular sectors, such as agriculture, and the effect of agricultural growth on civil war may be quite different than the effects of growth in the urban sector (Dunning 2008c). If the model linking economic growth to conflict is incorrectly specified, using rainfall to instrument for growth may capture idiosyncratic rather than general effects.[8] Thus, caution may be advised when extrapolating results or making policy recommendations.

A similar approach is found in Hidalgo et al. (2010), who study the effects of economic growth on land invasions in Brazil. Arguing that reverse causality or omitted variables could be a concern—for instance, land invasions could influence growth, and unmeasured institutions could influence both growth and invasions—these authors use rainfall growth as an instrumental variable for economic growth. The authors find that decreases in growth, instrumented by rainfall, indeed encourage land invasions. Again, this application illuminates characteristic strengths and limitations of instrumental-variables designs. Rainfall shocks may or may not be as-if random; rainfall may or may not influence land invasions only through its effect on growth; and variation in rainfall may also influence growth only in particular sectors, such as agriculture, which may have idiosyncratic effects on the likelihood

---

[7] Miguel, Satyanath, and Sergenti (2004) consider and dismiss some such violations of the exclusion restriction.
[8] See Chapter 9 for a more detailed discussion.

of invasions (Dunning 2008c). Horiuchi and Saito (2009) use rainfall to instrument for voter turnout in Japan, in a study of the effects of turnout on federal transfers to municipalities.

Ramsay (2011) asks whether oil wealth engenders authoritarian government, as per arguments made by students of the so-called "resource curse" (Ross 2001; see also Dunning 2008d and Haber and Menaldo 2011 for dissenting views). While the political regime type may not determine countries' endowments of natural resources like oil—and while confounding variables associated with political regimes may not be closely associated with natural resource endowments—the amount of oil-based revenue available in a given country may well be a function of features of the political system. However, shocks to oil price due to worldwide damage from natural disasters may be as-if random for oil producers; as in other instrumental-variables designs, they may assign countries to levels of oil revenue in a particular year, in a way that is as-if random. If so, natural disasters may be used to instrument for oil revenue, in a study of the effects of oil revenue on the political regime type (Ramsay 2011).

4.2.3 Historical or institutional variation induced by deaths

Other apparently random, or as good as random, events—for instance, the death of political leaders from natural causes—may sometimes provide the basis for instrumental-variables analysis. Consider, for instance, the natural experiment of Iyer (2010), who compares the long-term developmental effects of two kinds of British rule in India: direct colonial control, in which British administrators collected taxes and administered local governance themselves, and indirect rule, in which native princes collected revenue on behalf of the British but otherwise retained substantial autonomy in matters of internal administration.[9]

A direct comparison of districts in India that were formerly under direct British rule and those under the so-called "native" or "princely" states suggests that the former do better, today, on a range of socioeconomic variables. Districts that were under direct rule during the colonial period are significantly more populated and denser today than districts under indirect rule (Table 4.4)—perhaps suggesting heightened processes of

---

[9] Princely states enjoyed substantial autonomy in internal administration, though not in matters of defense or external policy. They were absorbed into a single administrative structure after independence in 1947, but they retained control during the colonial period through the second half of the nineteenth century and first half of the twentieth century.

Table 4.4 Direct and indirect colonial rule in India

Variable	Direct rule: mean	Indirect rule: mean	Difference of means (SE)
Log (population)	14.42	13.83	0.59 (0.16)
Population density (persons/km^2)	279.47	169.20	110.27 (41.66)
Proportion illiterate	0.32	0.28	0.04 (0.03)
Mean annual rainfall (mm)	1,503.41	1,079.16	424.25 (151.08)

Note: The table shows the difference of means on key covariates across areas subject to direct and indirect colonial rule in India. SE, standard error.
Source: Based on Iyer (2010).

urbanization associated with socioeconomic development.[10] Moreover, they have also exhibited significantly higher agricultural investment and productivity in the postcolonial period. For example, in the several decades after independence, the average proportions of irrigated land, intensity of fertilizer usage, usage of high-yielding crop varieties, and total agricultural yields were higher in areas formerly under direct British control (Iyer 2010: 693, tables 3–4). Finally, while areas under direct rule provide slightly less in the way of public goods than areas formerly under indirect rule, the difference is not statistically significant. One might therefore conclude that direct British rule had a salutary impact on long-term development.

Yet, is this effect causal? Table 4.4 suggests that annexation of districts by the British was hardly random: for instance, districts under direct rule have about half-again as much annual rainfall as districts left to princely rulers. Annexation was a selective process, and the British may have targeted areas that were likely to be more favorable to agriculture, perhaps because these would generate greater land revenues for the colonial government (Iyer 2010: 698). Confounding factors associated with annexation and economic outcomes could therefore explain long-term developmental contrasts between areas subject to direct and indirect rule.

To confront the problem of confounding, Iyer (2010) relies on an instrumental-variables design. Between 1848 and 1856, the Governor-General of India, Lord Dalhousie, enacted a new policy regarding annexation of native states, announcing:

I hold that on all occasions where heirs natural shall fail, the territory should be made to lapse and adoption should not be permitted, excepting in those cases in which some strong political reason may render it expedient to depart from this general rule.

---

[10] However, there is no significant difference in the proportion of the population that is literate across the two types of districts (Table 4.4).

In other words, according to this so-called Doctrine of Lapse, annexation would result from the death of a ruler without a natural (nonadopted) heir. In total, 20 districts of modern-day India were ruled by colonial-era princes who died without natural heirs during Lord Dalhousie's rule; of these, 16 were permanently placed under direct rule, implying that 16/20 or 80 percent of the districts "assigned" to direct rule by the Doctrine of Lapse in fact experienced direct rule. Only 18 of the remaining 161 districts lying under native states were annexed during the colonial period, for a proportion of about 0.11. Thus, assignment to direct rule through the Doctrine of Lapse is strongly associated with actually experiencing direct rule.[11]

Districts in which the ruler died without a natural heir can be compared to districts in which no such heirless death occurred, during Lord Dalhousie's tenure as Governor. This "intention-to-treat" analysis (Box 4.1) shows a nontrivial negative effect of assignment to direct British rule: the former set of districts had significantly fewer middle schools, health centers, and roads than the latter districts in the postcolonial period. Indeed, the former districts measured five percentage points lower on a combined measure of public goods provision than the latter districts, suggesting a substantively important effect of assignment to direct rule.[12]

Iyer's instrumental-variables analysis—in which assignment to annexation by the British under the Doctrine of Lapse serves as an instrument for actual annexation—thus also suggests that direct colonial rule significantly lowered the quantity of public goods. (As we will see in Chapters 5 and 6, intention-to-treat and instrumental-variables analysis will produce estimates with the same sign and statistical significance; in effect, the instrumental-variables analysis simply upweights the intention-to-treat analysis to account for imperfect compliance with treatment assignment.) In other words, the claim that direct rule led to better development outcomes is not supported by careful scrutiny of the evidence.

As always, of course, these conclusions are only as good as the assumptions. The natural experiment presumes that the presence or absence of an heir is as-if random; in other words, the long-term development outcomes that areas *would* experience under direct and indirect rule (i.e., the potential outcomes under treatment and control) are statistically independent of

---

[11] The "net crossover rate," which estimates the proportion of compliers in the study group (Chapter 5), is therefore 0.8 − 0.11 = 0.69.

[12] However, the intention-to-treat analyses (aka reduced form regressions) are not presented without control variables, which may substantially undercut their credibility. See Iyer (2010: 705, table 10).

whether their ruler in fact died with or without an heir. Iyer suggests that while heirless death of rulers was fairly common during British rule, the Doctrine of Lapse was only enforced between 1848 and 1857, during Lord Dalhousie's rule. Together with other evidence, this may reinforce the plausibility that whether a ruler happened to die without an heir during this period is as good as random—though it is always possible that places where the ruler died without a natural heir could differ in unobservable ways that are related to long-term development. Techniques for evaluating the plausibility of as-if random are presented in Chapter 8.[13]

To use the absence of an heir as a valid instrumental variable for direct British rule, moreover, Iyer must also posit an "exclusion restriction," as discussed in subsequent chapters. That is, the presence or absence of an heir must not have a direct impact on long-term development outcomes. Iyer shows that princely states in which the ruler died without a natural heir during other historical periods—when Lord Dalhousie's doctrine of lapse was not in effect—do not do significantly worse in terms of providing public goods or lowering infant mortality. Thus, she argues, differential experience with colonial rule—and not the fact of a ruler's heirless death itself—plausibly explains why districts annexed under the Doctrine of Lapse did worse than districts retained by native states.[14]

The importance of these assumptions arises as well in other instrumental-variables designs, for instance, when historical or institutional variables are used as instrumental variables for present-day institutions or economic conditions. Acemoglu, Johnson, and Robinson (2001), in a well-known study of the effects of institutional arrangements on countries' economic performance, use colonial settler mortality rates as an instrumental variable for current institutions. These authors argue that settler mortality rates during colonial years do not affect current economic performance in former colonies, except through their effect on current institutions; they also argue that settler mortality is as good as randomly assigned, at least conditional on covariates. Since neither assumption is verifiable from the data, a combination of historical evidence and a priori reasoning must be used to try to validate, at least partially, these core assumptions. The portion of current institutions that is related to past settler mortality rates may also have idiosyncratic effects on economic growth, which could limit the generalizability of the findings

---

[13] Another study to leverage the deaths of leaders in office is Jones and Olken (2005), who ask whether such leadership transitions affect countries' growth rates.

[14] Several other familiar assumptions must also be invoked, for instance, the assumption of "no-Defiers" (Chapter 5); see Exercise 5.1.

(Dunning 2008c). Moreover, the response of one country to colonial institutions must be invariant to the assignment of institutions of other countries.[15] The importance and potential limitations of the underlying assumptions of such instrumental-variables analyses will be discussed in subsequent chapters.

4.3 Conclusion

In recent years, instrumental variables have been used to estimate causal effects in many substantive domains. As the examples surveyed in this chapter suggest, instrumental variables can provide an important tool, because they help to confront the problem of confounding—a first-order issue in the social sciences. The examples discussed in this chapter also suggest that ideas generated in one context have been exported and modified in another, sometimes to good effect.

Yet, whether an instrumental variable is valid and useful may depend on the research question and setting. Detailed institutional knowledge is often needed in each new context to evaluate the validity of the technique. The use of instrumental variables often requires strong assumptions, which can be only partially validated from data. Some empirical tests can be performed to assess the central assumption that the instrumental variable is as good as randomly assigned; for instance, the instrument may be shown to be uncorrelated with pre-treatment covariates (those that are determined before the intervention). A priori reasoning and detailed knowledge of the empirical context may also play an important role. In observational studies, because there is often no actual randomization, the validity of as-if random assignment is difficult to validate; this assertion may be classified along a spectrum from "less plausible" to "more plausible" (Chapter 8), but it is difficult to validate the placement of any given study on such a spectrum.

Additional issues arise in many applications, often in connection with the use of multiple regression models (Chapter 9). For instance, concerns about the endogeneity of a single treatment variable will typically lead researchers to use instrumental-variables regression. Yet analysts typically do not discuss the possible endogeneity of other covariates in their multiple regression models. (One reason may be that the number of instruments must equal or surpass the number of endogenous variables, and good instruments are difficult to find.) Furthermore, instruments that are truly random may not be strongly related

---

[15] This is the so-called "stable unit-treatment value assumption" (SUTVA) discussed in Chapters 5 and 9.

to an endogenous treatment; in this case, substantial small-sample bias can arise. One recommendation for practice may be to report "reduced-form" results. (Reduced-form is a synonym for intention-to-treat; here, the outcome is regressed directly on the instrumental variable.)

Another recommendation may be to report instrumental-variables regressions without covariates; with one endogenous treatment variable and one valid instrument, including covariates can be unnecessary and even be harmful. The estimand should be carefully defined, and analysts should consider difficulties that may arise when extrapolating results to other contexts and types of subjects. In multiple-regression models, the statistical model itself must be validated, to the extent possible; with regression, the identification of causal effects depends not just on the exogeneity of instrumental variables in relation to a posited regression model but also on the validity of the underlying model itself.

Finally, it is important to emphasize that neither of the core criteria for a valid instrumental variable—that it is statistically independent of unobserved causes of the dependent variable and that it only affects the dependent variable through its effect on the endogenous treatment—are directly testable from data. Analysts using instrumental variables should defend these assertions using evidence and reasoning, to the extent possible. Yet especially outside of the experimental context, instrumental-variables estimates should be interpreted with an appropriate degree of caution. I will return further to these themes in subsequent chapters.[16]

Exercises

4.1) As described in the text of this chapter, Iyer (2010) compares former native states in India in which the prince died without a natural heir during Lord Dalhousie's rule—and which were therefore eligible for annexation by the British—with areas in which native rulers did not have an heirless death.
   (a) What is "intention-to-treat" analysis in this context? In particular, what groups are compared in an intention-to-treat analysis of Iyer's (2010) natural experiment?
   (b) How is intention-to-treat analysis related to instrumental-variables analysis?

---

[16] See especially Chapters 5 and 8–10.

Part II

Analyzing natural experiments

5 Simplicity and transparency: keys to quantitative analysis

Suppose that a researcher has discovered a credible natural experiment and designed a study akin to the best examples I have surveyed in previous chapters. This researcher then faces a central question: how should the data be analyzed? This second part of the book takes up this central question.

For reasons I will discuss extensively, the analysis of natural experiments should ideally leverage both qualitative and quantitative methods. There are important choices to be made with respect to both modes of analysis. This chapter and the next discuss quantitative analysis, leaving qualitative tools to Chapter 7. In this chapter, I describe the definition and estimation of causal effects. The role of chance variability—including assumptions about sampling processes and procedures for calculating standard errors—is left for Chapter 6.

A central theme of this chapter and the next is that the quantitative analysis of natural experiments can and should be very simple. Often, a minimum of mathematical manipulation is involved. For example, straightforward contrasts between the treatment and control groups—such as the difference in average outcomes in these two groups—often suffices to provide evidence of causal effects. Such difference-of-means (or difference-of-percentages) analysis plays a central role in each kind of natural experiment, from standard natural experiments and regression discontinuities to instrumental-variables designs.

The potential simplicity of quantitative data analysis provides an important advantage of natural experiments, for a number of reasons. First, it implies that statistical results are often easy to convey and interpret. Generally, just one or a few main quantitative tests are most relevant to testing key hypotheses. Rather than presenting the estimated coefficients from multivariate models in long tables of regression results, analysts may have more space in articles to discuss the research design and substantive import of the results. Second, because the procedures involved in constructing these tests are easy to understand and report, simplicity may also breed transparency in quantitative analysis. A focus on simple estimators of key parameters may limit concerns about "data mining" that often plague multivariate regression analysis. Difference-of-means tests relevant to the key hypotheses should almost always be presented; thus, concerns that only "significant" findings have made their way into research reports may be reduced.

Finally and perhaps most importantly, however, this analytic simplicity rests on underlying causal and statistical models that are often highly credible descriptions of the data-generating process. This last point highlights a crucial foundational issue. Analyzing data from strong research designs—including true and natural experiments—requires analysts to invoke assumptions about the process that gives rise to observed data. Before a causal hypothesis can be formulated and tested, a causal model must be defined, and the link from observable variables to the parameters of that model must be posited. Statistical tests, meanwhile, depend on the stochastic process that generates the data, and this process must also be formulated as a statistical model.

The presence of a natural experiment therefore does not obviate the need to formulate a model of the data-generating process. Yet, with strong natural experiments, the models may be simpler and more flexible, and they may involve fewer untestable assumptions than with standard observational studies—such as those in which multivariate regression models are fitted to observational data. Understanding the differences between the assumptions necessary for the quantitative analysis of natural experiments and those invoked in many conventional observational studies is therefore critical.

I thus begin this chapter by describing the causal and statistical assumptions that undergird the simple and transparent analysis of natural experiments, focusing first on standard natural experiments. While the material is not excessively technical and can be followed by readers with only minimal background, the Neyman model of causal inference (Neyman et al. [1923] 1990; Rubin 1978, 1990; Holland 1986) is crucial to the analysis and is therefore discussed in some detail. In the interest of ensuring that the discussion is accessible to a wide variety of readers, formal notation and technical details are presented mostly in boxes and appendices rather than in the main text. However, these details are critical to understand: while the technical manipulations required to analyze natural-experimental data are often minimal, the causal and statistical foundations on which this simplicity relies are not trivial.

I then extend the discussion to the case of regression-discontinuity and instrumental-variables designs. Distinct issues come up for each kind of natural experiment. However, in each case the Neyman potential outcomes model provides the foundation for simple and transparent data analysis. As in standard natural experiments, straightforward comparisons such as differences-of-means should play a central role.

The simplicity and transparency of analysis and credibility of underlying models is an advantage of strong natural experiments in principle but not always in practice; as I discuss in later chapters, the credibility of the models can vary substantially across applications, as can the persuasiveness of the data analysis.[1] This raises the question of the strengths and limitations of the Neyman model for natural experiments. Here and elsewhere, I discuss this issue and contrast the simple analysis based on the Neyman model with multivariate regression. I also take up the question of when control variables should be used. (The answer is sparingly, and unadjusted differences-of-means should almost always be presented.)

In sum, this chapter and the next serve as a simple reference guide for researchers who wish to analyze data from natural experiments. They show how and why analysts should present unadjusted difference-of-means tests, along with any auxiliary analyses, and detail reasons why the calculation of standard errors should follow the design of the experiment, rather than the assumptions behind standard regression models. These practices are not always followed in social science, where analysts often develop more complex models involving assumptions that are more difficult to explicate and validate.

5.1 The Neyman model

What causal and statistical model justifies the simple, transparent, and often highly credible approaches to the analysis of quantitative data mentioned above—such as unadjusted difference-of-means tests? A sensible model for true experiments and for many natural experiments is the Neyman potential outcomes model, sometimes known as the Neyman–Holland–Rubin model (Neyman et al. [1923] 1990; Holland 1986; Rubin 1978; Freedman 2006).[2] In this section, I discuss the causal and statistical assumptions of this model and characterize the key parameters that the model defines, such as the average causal effect.

---

[1] See Chapter 9.
[2] The potential outcomes model for experiments dates at least to Neyman et al. ([1923] 1990). D. Cox (1958), Rubin (1974, 1978), and many others have proposed refinements and extensions. Holland (1986) popularized the usage of what he called the Rubin causal model, but see Rubin (1990) for discussion.

To begin this discussion, it is useful to define the *study group* in a natural experiment. The study group is simply the set of units being studied. (Sometimes, I will refer to units as "subjects," but they could be individuals, municipalities, districts, or other entities, depending on the study.) For example, in the Argentina land-titling study discussed in the Introduction, the study group consists of those poor squatters in a particular area of greater Buenos Aires who were either extended property titles or were not. In Hidalgo's (2010) regression-discontinuity study of effective enfranchisement in Brazil, the study group comprises those municipalities in most Brazilian states, the populations of which were "near" the relevant cutoff required for use of electronic voting machines. And in Angrist's (1990a) instrumental-variables study of the effects of military service during the Vietnam War, the study group is a particular set of men born in 1950, 1951, or 1952 who were randomly assigned draft lottery numbers in the drafts of 1970, 1971, or 1972.

For the moment, I will bracket discussion of where the study group comes from or how it is defined. However, it is important to point out that in almost all natural experiments—like many true experiments in the social sciences—the study group does not consist of a representative sample of some underlying population. Instead, the study group is simply some set of units being studied. Often, as in regression-discontinuity designs, there are important choices to be made by the analyst about how the study group should be defined; I will take up these issues later. The key point for now is that the process of random or as-if random assignment to treatment and control groups occurs within this set of units, however defined. It is sometimes useful to think of the study group as itself comprising a small population; as we will see, the logic of random or as-if random assignment of units to treatment and control groups is closely akin to the logic of sampling at random from the small population comprised by the study group.[3] However, I have chosen to use the term "study group" (rather than, say, "natural-experimental population") to avoid confusion with settings in which the units being studied are themselves sampled from some broader population.

The next key idea is the concept of a *potential outcome*. In the simplest version of the Neyman model, each unit in the study group has one potential outcome under treatment and another potential outcome under control. A "potential outcome under treatment" is the outcome that *would be* observed *were* a

---

[3] In experiments, for example, the study group is sometimes referred to as the "experimental population." I discuss the relationship of natural-experimental study groups to broader populations elsewhere in the book.

particular unit assigned to treatment; a potential outcome under control is the outcome that *would be* observed if a given unit *were* assigned to control. This is all in the subjunctive tense, because each subject may be assigned to treatment or control—but not typically to both. To return to the Argentina land-titling study, if a squatter named Juan Fulano receives a title to his plot, we do not observe how his savings behavior or investment decisions would have evolved had he not received title. Similarly, if he does not receive title, we cannot examine the outcome had he instead received property rights to his land.[4]

Note that potential outcomes are typically assumed to be deterministic at the unit level—that is, according to the model, one outcome would materialize for each unit if it were assigned to treatment, and one (possibly different) outcome would materialize for each unit if it were assigned to control. However, there is no requirement that the potential outcome under treatment for one unit is the same as the potential outcome under treatment for any other unit; the same comment applies to potential outcomes under control.

The *unit causal effect* is then defined as the difference between a unit's potential outcome under treatment and the unit's potential outcome under control. This parameter can never be observed, because we do not simultaneously observe any unit's potential outcome under treatment and its potential outcome under control. Holland (1986) refers to the unobservability of the unit causal effect as the "fundamental problem of causal inference."

Notwithstanding this difficulty, the idea of the unit-level causal effect embeds perhaps the most important causal idea involved in the Neyman model: a counterfactual definition of causality. Among units exposed to a cause, we do not observe what would happen in the absence of a cause. Yet, comparing what happened in the presence of a cause to what would have happened in its absence—that is, the comparison of the factual with the counterfactual—is central to causal inference under the Neyman model.

5.1.1 The average causal effect

The general impossibility of observing the unit-level causal effect does not mean that we cannot make useful causal inferences, however. Indeed, at least

---

[4] Readers might suggest that we can in principle assign a single unit to treatment at one point in time and to control at another point in time; it might therefore seem that we can observe both the potential outcome under treatment and the potential outcome under control. Yet, further reflection suggests some of the difficulties. We would have to stipulate that the potential outcomes at time t are the same as at time $t + 1$, yet conditions may change between the assignment to treatment and the assignment to control. We would also have to assume that the potential outcome under control is invariant to previous assignment to treatment (or vice versa).

three other parameters are typically of interest—and all three are estimable, as we shall see.[5] These three parameters are defined for the study group:

(1) The average response, if all subjects were assigned to treatment;
(2) The average response, if all subjects were assigned to control; and
(3) The difference between (1) and (2).

The third parameter is called the *average causal effect*. As the definition in (3) makes clear, the average causal effect is defined as the difference between the average outcome if every unit in the study group were assigned to treatment, relative to the average outcome if every unit were assigned to control. Since here we are describing the average responses to treatment assignment, (3) is also called the *intention-to-treat* parameter. (The average causal effect is also sometimes called the *average treatment effect*, though usage can be ambiguous.) Box 5.1 defines the average causal effect using formal notation.

The average causal effect is often interesting because it tells us how units, as a group, would respond to interventions. This parameter is sometimes directly relevant to policy because it can tell us the marginal returns to assigning all units to treatment. For instance, suppose policy-makers had extended land titles to all of the squatters in the Argentina land-titling study (and there had been no challenges to any of the expropriations in the Argentine courts). The average causal effect tells how much squatters on average would have gained, relative to a setting in which policy-makers extended titles to none of the squatters. Of course, if no owners had in fact challenged the expropriation in court, we would have had no basis for estimating the average causal effect. Without the natural experiment, we would have observed parameter (1) but could not have estimated parameter (3).

Knowledge of the average causal effect may matter not only for public policy but also social science. For example, the claim that extending property titles would foster broad socioeconomic development, by allowing poor squatters to use their property as collateral and thereby access capital markets (De Soto 2000), can be put to direct empirical scrutiny in a setting like the Argentina land-titling study, where estimates of the average causal effect give us some evidence for claims about the effect of titles on savings or borrowing behavior.[6]

---

[5] A parameter or a function of that parameter is "estimable" whenever there is an unbiased estimator for that parameter or function. For example, the function $f(\theta)$ is estimable is there is a function g with $E_\theta [g(X)] = f(\theta)$ for all θ. Here, X is an observable random variable, and θ is a parameter that governs the probability distribution of X. See Freedman (2009: 119) for discussion.

[6] Parameters other than the average causal effect may be of interest as well, and it is well-worth thinking through which parameters are most theoretically relevant in a given application—but the average

> **Box 5.1 The Neyman model and the average causal effect**
>
> Let T_i be the potential outcome of unit i under treatment and C_i be the potential outcome of unit i under control. Thus, T_i is the outcome unit i would experience if it were assigned to the treatment group and C_i is the outcome if it were assigned to control. In the literature on causal inference, it is common to write potential outcomes as $Y_i(1)$ in place of T_i and $Y_i(0)$ in place of C_i.
>
> Hence, the unit-level causal effect of assignment to treatment is defined as $T_i - C_i$. However, since $T_i - C_i$ is unobservable—because unit i is either assigned to the treatment group or the control group, so we can observe T_i or C_i but not both—analysts usually focus attention on a different parameter: the average causal effect. For a natural-experimental study group of size N, with units indexed by $i = 1, \ldots, N$, the average value of the potential outcomes under treatment is $\overline{T} = \frac{1}{N}\sum_{i=1}^{N} T_i$ while the average value of the potential outcomes under control is $\overline{C} = \frac{1}{N}\sum_{i=1}^{N} C_i$. The average causal effect is then defined as $\overline{T} - \overline{C}$.
>
> Notice that here the average causal effect defines the effect of treatment assignment, because $\overline{T}$ is the average outcome that would occur if all units were assigned to the treatment group—irrespective of whether they actually received the treatment—while $\overline{C}$ is the outcome that would occur if all units were assigned to the control group. For this reason, the average causal effect is also known as the *intention-to-treat* parameter (see Box 4.1).

Notice that this definition of the average causal effect highlights the impact of treatment assignment—what would happen if we assigned all the units to treatment, minus what would happen if we assigned every unit to control. In many settings, of course, treatment assignment is not the same as treatment receipt. For instance, individuals that are eligible for a poverty relief program—say, based on their position relative to a poverty index, as in many regression-discontinuity designs—may choose to opt out of the program. The average causal effect then tells us what the marginal gain might be from making more subjects eligible for the program—say, by marginally increasing the threshold score on the poverty index enough to include individuals in the control group. However, it does not directly estimate the effect on those who actually comply with their treatment assignment. (For that, as described below, we need instrumental-variables analysis.) The average causal effect is usually of interest as well. Often, average causal effects for particular subgroups of the study group are of interest; the framework is easily adapted to cover this case.

effect as defined here is therefore synonymous with the *intention-to-treat parameter*, which also measures the effect of treatment assignment. Intention to treat is a crucial idea in natural-experimental analysis, as described in Box 4.1 in Chapter 4.[7]

Analysts of true experiments and natural experiments are therefore often interested in estimating the average causal effect. Notice, however, that the average causal effect is subject to the same difficulty as the unit causal effect. After all, this effect is defined as the difference in average outcomes if every unit in the study group were assigned to treatment and if every unit in the study group were assigned to control. Yet, if every unit is assigned to treatment, none are left to assign to control—and thus, the average causal effect is unobservable, just like the unit causal effect.

5.1.2 Estimating the average causal effect

How, then, can analysts obtain information about the magnitude of the average causal effect? The answer lies in the idea of random sampling. For true experiments and strong natural experiments, the Neyman approach lends itself naturally to a sensible statistical model—that of sampling potential outcomes at random from an urn. Given this model, good estimators for the average causal effect are often available in natural experiments.

Figure 5.1 depicts the model in terms of a box of tickets.[8] Here, the tickets in the box represent the natural-experimental study group, that is, the group of units being studied. There is one ticket in the box for each unit. Each ticket shows two values: the unit's potential outcome under treatment, and the unit's potential outcome under control. Now, imagine that some tickets are sampled at random and placed into the treatment group; the remaining tickets are placed into the control group. If a ticket is placed in treatment, we observe the potential outcome under treatment; if the ticket is placed in the control group, we observe the potential outcome under control. This is indicated in the figure by placing slashes over the potential outcomes under control—denoted by C_i—for those tickets placed into the treatment group; similarly, slashes appear over the potential outcomes under treatment—the T_is—for tickets allocated to the control group.

---

[7] Below, I discuss the issues that arise from noncompliance (i.e., crossover) and contrast intention-to-treat analysis with other approaches.

[8] See Freedman, Pisani, and Purves (2007: 509) for discussion of a similar box model for randomized controlled experiments.

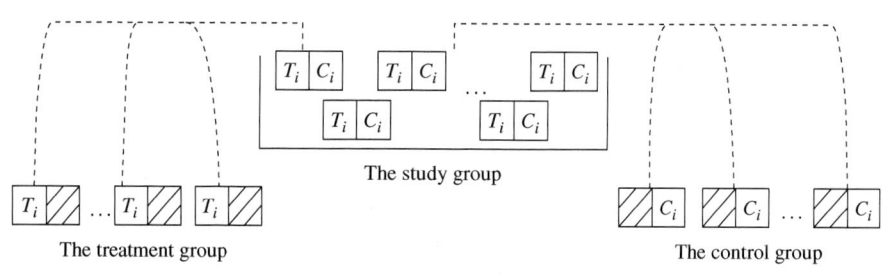

Simplicity and transparency: keys to quantitative analysis

Figure 5.1 The Neyman model.

Here, we are drawing at random from a box with N tickets. Each ticket represents one unit in the natural-experimental study group. Here, T_i and C_i are the potential outcomes under treatment and control, respectively. If unit i is sampled into treatment, we observe T_i but not C_i; if unit i is assigned to control, we observe C_i but not T_i. The average of the T_is in the treatment group estimates the average of all the T_is in the box, while the average of the C_is in the control group estimates the average of all the C_is.

Notice that according to this simple model, the treatment group and control group are both random samples of the tickets in the box. Rather than talk about sampling, analysts of true experiments and natural experiments often refer, correctly, to random *assignment* of units to treatment and control groups. Yet, under the Neyman model, the treatment and control groups can also be viewed as random samples from the box of tickets in Figure 5.1. This is an important and powerful idea to keep in mind. The logic of random sampling helps clarify the nature of causal effect estimators as well as estimates of their variability (as discussed in the next chapter).

In a true experiment, the treatment group can be viewed as a random sample from the experimental study group, as can the control group. Analogously, in a strong natural experiment, the treatment and control groups are random or as-if random samples from the natural-experimental study group—as in Figure 5.1. These are assumptions, and their credibility must be probed in each application, particularly when there is no true random device determining assignment to the treatment or control groups. Yet, with strong natural experiments, these assumptions are often tightly connected to the actual data-generating and data-collecting process. This is not necessarily so in many other observational studies, and so this represents one of the advantages of both true experiments and strong natural experiments relative to conventional observational studies.[9]

---

[9] See Chapters 7 and 8 for further discussion.

Given the model depicted in Figure 5.1, we have available ready estimators of the key parameters of the model—such as the average causal effect. We can appeal to a statistical principle:

The mean of a random sample is an unbiased estimator for the mean of the population.

This statement means that across many repeated samples, the average of the means in each sample will tend to converge to the mean of the population. In any particular random sample, of course, the sample mean may be a little too high or a little too low: this is sampling error.[10] Yet, if we were to repeat the process of drawing a random sample from the population and calculating the mean, on average across many samples the average of the sample means would tend to equal the true population mean. In fact, the expected value of each sample mean is just the population mean—a concept that statisticians use to define an unbiased estimator.

Following this principle, the average outcome in the assigned-to-treatment group—which is a random sample from the box of tickets in Figure 5.1—is an unbiased estimator for the average of the potential outcomes under treatment in the population—that is, the study group. Similarly, the average outcome in the assigned-to-control group is an unbiased estimator for the average of all the potential outcomes under control. Thus, the difference between observed outcomes in the first sample—the treatment group—and observed outcomes in the second sample—the control group—is an unbiased estimator for the average causal effect of treatment assignment in the population.[11]

To recap, the definition of the Neyman model defines three parameters for the study group: (1) the average response, if all subjects were assigned to treatment; (2) the average response, if all subjects were assigned to control; and (3) the difference between (1) and (2), which is called the *average causal effect*. Given the model, there are three unbiased estimators, one for each parameter:

(i) The average response among subjects assigned to treatment;
(ii) The average response among subjects assigned to control;
(iii) The difference between (i) and (ii).

---

[10] Further discussion of sampling error, techniques to estimate its size, and related topics such as the construction of hypothesis tests are postponed until Chapter 6.
[11] Note that in this context, we are not considering complications that may arise when units do not comply with treatment assignment: here, treatment assignment is synonymous with treatment receipt. Thus, the intention-to-treat parameter is identical to the average causal effect. In general, the intention-to-treat parameter is the average causal effect of treatment assignment.

The third quantity estimates the average causal effect. When Figure 5.1 applies, we therefore have the following conclusion:

> An unbiased estimator for the average causal effect is a difference of means.

Thus, in those strong natural experiments for which Figure 5.1 provides a credible model of the data-generating process, analysts can estimate the average causal effect by simply subtracting the average outcome among units as-if randomly assigned to control from the average outcome among units as-if randomly assigned to treatment. Box 5.2 discusses these ideas using formal notation.

Box 5.2 Estimating the average causal effect

The discussion uses the notation from Box 5.1 and refers to Figure 5.1. First, note that each ticket in Figure 5.1 represents a single unit and has two values, T_i and C_i—the potential outcomes under treatment and control, respectively. There are N tickets in the box; this is the size of the natural-experimental study group. Units are indexed by $i = 1, \ldots, N$. Now, $n < N$ tickets are sampled at random and placed in the treatment group and the remaining m tickets are placed in control, with $n + m = N$. If a ticket is placed in treatment, we observe T_i, and if a ticket is placed in control, we see C_i.

Under these assumptions, the average outcome for the n tickets in the treatment group estimates the average value for all the T_is in the study group—that is, the whole box of tickets. Similarly, the average outcome in the m units assigned to control estimates the average value of all the potential outcomes under control.

In more detail, the n elements that are assigned to treatment are a random sample of all N units in the study group; denote this random subset of $\{1, \ldots, N\}$ as A. We can then estimate the population mean $\overline{T}$ by the sample mean $Y^T = \frac{1}{n}\sum_{i \in A} T_i$, appealing to the fact that we observe T_i when units are assigned to treatment. Similarly, the m elements assigned to control are a random subset S of the N units in the study group. Thus, the sample mean $Y^C = \frac{1}{m}\sum_{i \in S} C_i$ is an unbiased estimator for the parameter $\overline{C}$. Here, Y^T and Y^C are both observable random variables, and $Y^T - Y^C$ estimates the average causal effect $\overline{T} - \overline{C}$.

5.1.3 An example: land titling in Argentina

How may these ideas be put into practice? Consider the standard natural experiment involved in the Argentina land-titling study. Galiani and

Schargrodsky (2004) are interested in the effects of land titling on children's health outcomes; they hypothesize that land titling may translate into positive effects on health through its impact on housing investments and household structure (e.g., the number of children that parents have).[12] Their main measures of children's health are standardized weight-for-height measures and height-for-age measures, based on anthropometric measurements taken by physicians at the conclusion of each household survey.[13] Drawing on the public health literature, Galiani and Schargrodsky (2004) interpret weight-for-height scores as a short-run measure of children's health status, whereas height-for-age scores are considered to reveal the accumulation of past outcomes. Their household surveys also measured pregnancy rates among teenage girls aged 14–17.

Table 5.1 shows the average outcome for children in households that were offered property rights (first column); the average outcome for children in households that were not offered property rights (second column); and the difference between these two quantities (final column). These sample quantities estimate three parameters: (1) the average health outcome, had all households in the study group been offered titles; (2) the average health outcome, had none of the households in the study group been offered titles; and (3) the difference between (1) and (2), that is, the average causal effect. Thus, as these authors correctly note, "the simple comparison of sample means consistently estimates the causal effect of land titling on [health] outcome[s]" (Galiani and Schargrodsky 2004: 363).[14] Notice also that this is intention-to-treat analysis: children are compared according to whether a property title was offered to their household (Property title offer=1) or not (Property title offer=0), not according to whether the household actually opted to receive the property title.[15]

---

[12] See Galiani and Schargrodsky (2004) and Di Tella, Galiani, and Schargrodsky (2007) for other dependent variables.

[13] These standardized Z-scores subtract average weight-for-height in a reference population from each respondent's weight-for-height, then divide by the standard deviation in the reference population. Thus, scores above zero indicate an above-average weight, given height.

[14] The meaning of "consistently estimates" here is the following: if more and more subjects were (hypothetically) included in the study group and a fixed fraction were assigned to the treatment and control groups, the mean of the probability distribution for the sample averages would converge to the true means in the study group. That is, the estimator of the average causal effect is asymptotically unbiased. However, if the assumption of as-if random sampling holds, the estimator is also exactly unbiased, even in small samples.

[15] In 108 out of 1,839 parcels in the geographical area under consideration, the original squatters who were offered titles missed the opportunity to receive titles because they had moved or died, had not fulfilled some of the required registration steps, or for other reasons (Galiani and Schargrodsky 2004: 356–7).

Table 5.1 The effects of land titles on children's health

	Property title offer=1	Property title offer=0	Difference of means
Weight-for-height Z-score	0.279	0.065	0.214
	(239)	(132)	(371)
Height-for-age Z-score	0.398	0.314	0.084
	(277)	(147)	(424)
Teenage pregnancy rate	0.079	0.208	−0.129
	(63)	(24)	(87)

Note: In the first two rows, data for children ages 0–11 are shown; in the third row, data for teenage girls aged 14–17 are shown. The number of observations is in parentheses.

This simple analysis shows some evidence of property titling on short-run health outcomes, with a difference-in-means of the weight-for-height Z-scores of 0.214 across households that were offered titles and those that were not. (I do not reproduce the standard errors in Table 5.1, since this topic is postponed until Chapter 6; the authors report a difference that is statistically significant at the 0.1 level.)[16] However, there is little or no evidence on longer-run outcomes, as measured by height-for-age Z-scores. There is some evidence of effects on teenage fertility: among households offered property titles, the female teenage pregnancy rate is 7.9 percent, while among households not offered titles, it is 20.8 percent.[17]

The point here is not so much about the presence or absence of particular causal effects, or their substantive interpretation. Rather, the point is that these simple comparisons can provide credible evidence of average causal effects. Indeed, the structure of this analysis recalls Snow's study of death from cholera, where a simple difference of means provides evidence of the causal effect of water supply source (see Table 1.1 in Chapter 1). These comparisons of means (or percentages) are motivated and justified by the Neyman model, and they provide a simple and transparent way to estimate average causal effects in strong natural experiments.

---

[16] Galiani and Schargrodsky (2004) do not appear to account for the cluster-randomized nature of their data—some households contain more than one child, and property titles were offered to households—in calculating the standard errors for the differences-of-means (see Chapter 6). They do cluster standard errors by household in their multivariate regressions, however.

[17] This difference is not statistically significant, perhaps due to the small number of girls age 14–17 in the sample. Galiani and Schargrodsky (2004) also estimate multivariate regression models with controls, in which the point estimate is statistically signfcant. The issue of discrepancies between simple difference-of-means estimates and multivariate modeling is discussed below.

Of course, readers may rightly wonder about confounding. Perhaps there are variables associated with assignment to the treatment or control groups—and that are also related to potential outcomes. Suppose, for instance, that tickets in Figure 5.1 with particularly high potential outcomes under treatment and control are systematically assigned to the treatment group, while tickets with particularly low potential outcomes under treatment and control tend to be assigned to the control group. In the Argentina example, households with healthier children might have been offered land titles, while those with less healthy children were not. In this case, Figure 5.1 does not apply—because the treatment and control groups are not like random samples from the population of units in the study group.

Yet, the whole point of a natural experiment is that such concerns about confounding should be limited by the research design. With natural experiments, analysts posit random or as-if random assignment of units to treatment. Use of the simple Neyman model is predicated on the veracity of this assumption. In Chapters 7 and 8, I discuss tools for evaluating the credibility of this assumption, through a combination of a priori reasoning, quantitative empirical analysis, and knowledge of causal process; while in Chapter 9, I return to a broader discussion of the credibility of underlying models for analysis of natural-experimental data. This chapter instead discusses modeling assumptions and analytic techniques that are appropriate for valid natural experiments.

The bottom line for present purposes is that if as-if random does not hold in any study, then the analyst is working with something less than a strong natural experiment.[18] For now, it is simply worth noting that if as-if random holds, no adjustment for confounders is needed—for that is what a strong natural experiment, with random or plausible as-if random assignment, buys us. In this case, Figure 5.1 provides a good model of the data-generating process, and there is no bias from confounding. In particular, the assertion of random sampling implies that there are no variables that cause tickets with especially high or low values of the potential outcomes to go systematically to the treatment or control groups.

5.1.4 Key assumptions of the Neyman model

Several other initial points can be made about the model depicted in Boxes 5.1 and 5.2 and in Figure 5.1. First, although I have focused on the simplest case

---

[18] There may be some studies, such as those involving redistricting, in which assignment to treatment and control is conditional on covariates, yet these may be few in number; a further difficulty is that the true assignment rule may be difficult to discern (see Chapters 1 and 9).

for the Neyman model, where there is one treatment condition and one control condition, this model can be readily extended to experiments or natural experiments with any finite number of treatments. For instance, suppose there are three treatments in a natural experiment (or two treatments and a control condition). Then, each ticket in the box in Figure 5.1 would have three values—showing one potential outcome for each treatment condition. Tickets would be sampled at random and placed into one of the three groups. For each group, we would observe the potential outcomes associated with the corresponding treatment condition. Then, for each treatment condition, the average potential outcome in the study group—that is, the average across all tickets in the box—would be estimated by the averages in each of the three samples. Since each of the three groups is a random sample from the study group, the sample means are unbiased estimators for the population averages—that is, the averages in the study group. The effect of any particular treatment relative to another can be estimated by comparing the relevant sample averages. The model is thus both flexible and general.[19]

Second, however, it is important to point out one feature of the model that can be restrictive—and unrealistic for some natural experiments: potential outcomes are assumed to be unaffected by the responses to treatment or the treatment-assignment status of other units in the study group. Following D. Cox (1958), this important assumption can be referred to as "noninterference" between natural-experimental units (though other labels have been applied to this assumption as well); other scholars, following Rubin (1978), have called it the "stable unit-treatment value assumption" (SUTVA). The assumption can be summarized as follows:

> Noninterference: potential outcomes for unit i depend only on the treatment assignment of unit i (and not $j \neq i$).

In some contexts, the assumption of noninterference is more restrictive than others. Consider again the Argentina land-titling study. Here, because treatment and control subjects live in close proximity and may interact frequently with each other, one could imagine that the noninterference assumption is not valid. For example, the economic, political, or health-related behaviors of squatters who do not receive land titles might well be affected by the behavior of those squatters who do receive land titles. If titles encourage squatters in the treatment group to save more of their incomes, access capital markets, or have fewer

---

[19] As discussed in later chapters, various analysts have also extended the Neyman model to real-valued treatment variables and parametric models, including linear causal relationships.

children, some of this behavior might "spill over" to subjects in the control group. For instance, squatters in the control group might borrow or invest more, or have fewer children, simply because their neighbors in the treatment group are doing so. This may lead us to understate the contrast between average potential outcomes under treatment and average potential outcomes under control—that is, to underestimate the causal effect of assigning all units in the study group to treatment, relative to assigning all units to control. The larger point here is that the modeling assumption of noninterference might not hold. In later chapters, I discuss the kind of evidence that might be helpful for evaluating the credibility of such modeling assumptions (e.g., in Chapter 7).

In other contexts, the assumption of noninterference may be less problematic. For example, the geographic proximity of treatment and control subjects may not be an issue, or relevant communication between subjects assigned to the different groups might be limited. Unfortunately, natural-experimental researchers often do not have the capacity to tweak their research designs to detect and estimate the size of such spillovers empirically—as experimental researchers sometimes do (Nickerson 2008). However, knowledge of context and substance, as well as other empirical techniques, can often provide researchers with some ability to assess how big an issue interference might be—and its potential importance will vary in different natural experiments. I return to this topic in later chapters, especially Chapter 9.

It is also important to point out that the inferential issues raised by interference between units are not unique to the Neyman model. An analogous noninterference assumption is true of standard multivariate regression models as well: there, unit i's outcome is typically assumed to be a function of unit i's treatment-assignment status, covariate values, and the realized value of a random error term—but does not depend by assumption on the treatment assignment of units $j \neq i$. Thus, while interference is a regrettable feature of the social world from the point of view of drawing successful causal inferences, it also bedevils various other models of causal process. I will return in later chapters to further discussion of the strengths and limitations of the Neyman model.

The Neyman model also often implies a final important assumption: treatment assignment only affects outcomes through its effect on treatment receipt. Consider again the Argentina land-titling study. We assume that being assigned to a property right title does not affect outcomes—such as beliefs in individual efficacy—through channels other than actually being granted a title. But what if being in the special status group—the group that gets land titles offered, by virtue of no court challenges—affects individual attitudes in other ways? For instance, what if changes in attitudes or beliefs are due to the fact of having won an apparent lottery, and not to the presence of a property title per se? If all situations in which property titles are granted feature similar assignment processes, this might not be a big stumbling block for inferences about the effect of titling. Yet, this could be cause for concern if other ways in which citizens might obtain land titles (for instance, by purchasing title) differ in this regard. Thus, the potential-outcomes model we have discussed implicitly defines what is known as an "exclusion restriction":

> Exclusion restriction: treatment assignment affects potential outcomes only through its effect on treatment receipt.

We will return to further discussion of this key assumption below, especially in connection with instrumental-variables analysis.

5.1.5 Analyzing standard natural experiments

Summing up, we can say that the Neyman model often (though not always) provides the right starting point for standard natural experiments; and if it does, a simple difference of means may be just the right estimator for the average causal effect. Analysis of standard natural experiments can thus be simple and transparent, and founded on a credible model of the data-generating process.

This setup applies to many, though not all, standard natural experiments. In later chapters (especially Chapter 9), I consider alternatives and discuss issues such as the inclusion of control variables through cross-tabulations or regression modeling. Special issues also arise in connection with both regression-discontinuity and instrumental-variables designs, topics to which I now turn. As we shall see, however, in many of these designs analysis may be simple and transparent as well, and simple differences of means across treatment and control groups continue to play a key role in estimation of causal effects.

5.2 Analyzing regression-discontinuity designs

Many of the principles discussed above for the analysis of standard natural experiments extend straightforwardly to regression-discontinuity designs. In these designs, as discussed in Chapter 3, individuals, municipalities, or other units are assigned to treatment or control groups according to their values on some pre-treatment covariate, such as an entrance exam score or a municipal poverty index. The key feature of the design is that there is a threshold or cutoff value, above or below which units may be assigned to a treatment condition; units on the other side of this threshold are assigned to the control group (or a different treatment condition).[20] Those units located just above and just below the key threshold constitute the study group in the regression-discontinuity design.

The central assumption in natural experiments using a regression-discontinuity design is that for units just on either side of this threshold—that is, for units whose pre-treatment covariate values place them in the neighborhood of the threshold—assignment to the treatment and control groups is as good as random. I will discuss below and in Chapter 8 how to evaluate the credibility of this assumption—and other crucial issues, such as how to define the size of the "neighborhood" of the threshold that defines the study group. Let us assume for the moment that this assertion holds: that is, for a group of units located "near" the threshold, assignment to treatment and control is as-if random.

Then, the simple and transparent analytic strategies discussed above for standard natural experiments are sensible for regression-discontinuity designs as well. In particular, the average causal effect can be defined and evaluated in regression-discontinuity designs in the same way as in standard natural experiments. For units located near the regression-discontinuity threshold, the average causal effect is the mean outcome if all of these units were assigned to treatment, minus the mean outcome if all of these units were assigned to control.

Moreover, Neyman's urn model then applies to the sampling process, as in Figure 5.1. According to the model, units are as-if randomly sampled into treatment and control groups, by virtue of their position above or below the key regression-discontinuity threshold. The average response among subjects assigned to the treatment group estimates the average response, if all subjects in the regression-discontinuity study group were assigned to treatment. The average response among subjects assigned to the control group estimates the average response, if all subjects were assigned to control. Finally, the difference of means in the assigned-to-treatment and assigned-to-control groups is an

---

[20] In some regression-discontinuity designs, as discussed in Chapter 3, there may be multiple such thresholds, with different associated treatment conditions. The Neyman model may be extended to include many finite-valued treatments, as discussed above, or may apply to various study groups defined by the different thresholds.

unbiased estimator for the average causal effect, for units in the regression-discontinuity study group.[21]

5.2.1 Two examples: Certificates of Merit and digital democratization

Two examples—one hypothetical and the other real—help to make this logic clear. First, in the Thistlethwaite and Campbell (1960) study discussed in Chapter 3, students who scored above a particular cutoff score on a qualifying exam received Certificates of Merit, which confer public recognition of their scholastic abilities. Students who scored below this cutoff merely received commendations, which do not confer public recognition. The goal of the analysis is to assess whether public recognition in the form of a Certificate of Merit had a causal effect on later educational and career outcomes.

Figure 5.2 shows a scatter plot, using the same hypothetical data that produced Series A at the top of Figure 3.1 in Chapter 3. The scores are again arbitrarily scaled so that 11 and above qualifies students for public recognition. The figure plots the outcome variable against scores on the pre-treatment entrance examination; here, the outcome variable is continuous rather than categorical (say, scores on an index measuring students' interest in intellectual careers). As in Chapter 3, the larger diamonds mark the average value of the dependent variable given each range of test scores (e.g., 12 to 13, 13 to 14, and so forth); however, here the data points for each individual student taking the qualifying exam are also shown. The vertical dotted line is drawn at the threshold score above which students are extended public recognition in the form of Certificates of Merit.

In many ways, Figure 5.2 represents an ideal setting for drawing a credible causal inference from a regression-discontinuity design. First of all, there is a large difference of average outcomes among units located near the threshold. On average, the outcome for students just to the left of the key regression-discontinuity threshold—that is, those who scored between 10 and 11 on the qualifying exam and thus did not receive public recognition—is 19.6, while it is 25.1 for students who scored between 11 and 12 on the exam and therefore received recognition. Given the role of luck in performance on any given exam, there is likely to be a strong a priori case that students who scored a 10 are, on average, a lot like students who scored an 11. Moreover, any potential confounders associated with having an exam score of 11 rather than 10 would have to have a rather powerful influence to explain such a large difference in average outcomes on either side of the regression-discontinuity threshold.

---

[21] Not all analysts agree with this conclusion; see, e.g., Hahn, Todd, and Van Der Klaauw (2001), Imbens and Lemieux (2007), or Porter (2003). I will discuss this alternative perspective below.

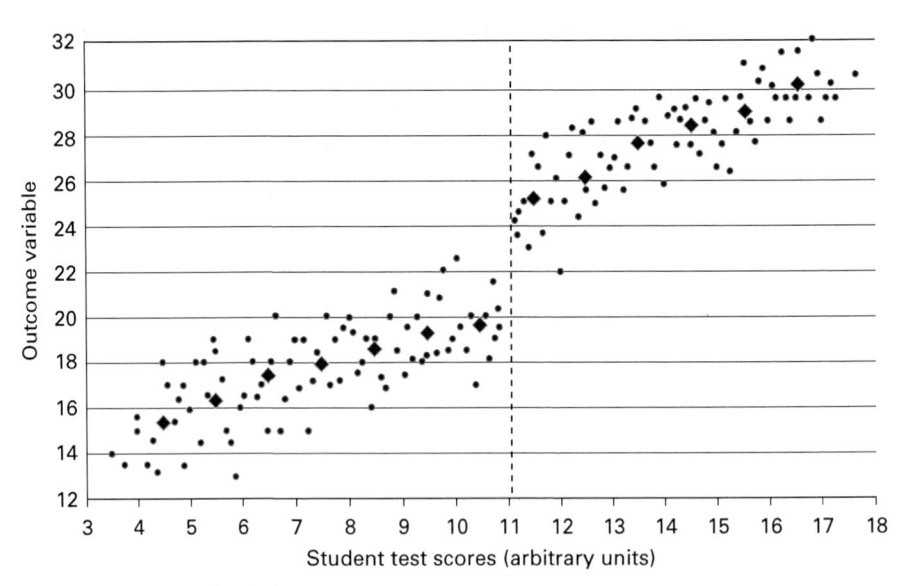

Figure 5.2 A regression-discontinuity design.
The figure plots an outcome variable (such as measured interest in an intellectual career) against student scores on a qualifying exam. Students who received a score of 11 and above received public recognition of their scholastic achievement, in the form of Certificates of Merit, while those below the key threshold merely receive commendations (see Thistlethwaite and Campbell 1960). The large diamonds mark the average outcome within each unit bin of test scores (e.g., 10 to 11, 11 to 12, and so forth).

Next, along with the large difference in mean outcomes on either side of the threshold, here there is barely any overlap in the *distribution* of outcome values on either side of the key threshold. The clear graphical evidence of an effect suggests that statistical adjustment or other corrections will not matter qualitatively or probably even quantitatively for the inferences about the causal effect. Here, data are relatively sparse in the neighborhood of the threshold: only 12 students scored between 10 and 11 on the qualifying exam, while 11 students scored between 11 and 12. Yet the size of effect—a difference of means of 5.5 points—implies that the estimated causal effect is still significantly distinguishable from zero, i.e., unlikely to have arisen by chance if the true effect is zero (as discussed in Chapter 6).[22]

Finally, the finding of a causal effect also appears robust, even given different choices for the size of the bandwidth around the key regression-discontinuity threshold. For example, widening the bin by one exam-score

---

[22] Here, the size of the estimated effect will be compared to the empirical variability in the treatment and control groups (Chapter 6), which is relatively small in this example.

interval on each side of the threshold, we find that the average outcome for students scoring between 9 and 11 is 19.4, while the average outcome for students scoring between 11 and 13 is 25.6, giving a difference of means of 6.2 points. Widening again to create a bandwidth of three exam-score intervals on each side of the threshold, we find that the average outcome for students scoring between 8 and 11 is 19.1, while the average outcome for those scoring between 11 and 14 is 26.2, for a difference of 7.1 points.[23] This stability of outcomes near the key regression-discontinuity threshold is reassuring: across several different ways of defining the width of the "bins" on either side of the regression-discontinuity threshold, we see strong evidence for an effect of public recognition of scholarly achievement.[24] In sum, Figure 5.2 presents a setting in which simple and transparent analysis of a regression-discontinuity design is highly compelling: a simple difference of means should suffice to estimate the causal effect.

A real-world example that shares many of these desirable characteristics can be found in Hidalgo (2010). As discussed in Chapter 3, this study focuses on the effects of the introduction of electronic voting machines in Brazil. The study asks two important causal questions: did easy-to-use electronic voting machines broaden the effective franchise, by allowing poorer and less well-educated voters to more accurately record their choices in the ballot box? And did this de facto extension of the suffrage have political and policy consequences? In the 1998 legislative elections in Brazil, electronic voting machines were introduced in municipalities with more than 40,500 registered voters, while municipalities with fewer than 40,500 voters continued to use traditional paper ballots. Hidalgo (2010) finds that among municipalities with 1996 populations located within 5,000 voters of this threshold, the introduction of electronic voting lowered "null"-vote rates by an estimated 13.5 percentage points and "blank" votes by an estimated 10 percentage points. In total, the technology increased the number of votes affecting political outcomes by about 23 percentage points, or about 34 percent—a massive de facto enfranchisement that appears more pronounced in poorer municipalities with higher

---

[23] Notice also that the variance in average outcomes in the several bins on either side of the key threshold (e.g., 19.6, 19.2, and 18.6 to the left of the threshold and 25.1, 26.0, and 27.6 to the right of the threshold) is low, relative to the variance in average outcomes *across* the regression-discontinuity cutoff.

[24] This is due also to the fact that the pre-treatment covariate—exam score—is not all that strongly related to the outcome variable in this figure, i.e., the slope is fairly flat. In general, as discussed below, widening the width of the bin around the regression-discontinuity threshold can raise some difficult issues of interpretation: depending on the original scale of exam scores, students who score 8 on average may be quite different than those who score, say 14, opening the door to potential confounding by unobserved variables.

illiteracy rates (see also Fujiwara 2011). Moreover, the introduction of voting machines led to substantial declines in the vote shares of incumbent "machine" parties in several Northeastern states.

Like the hypothetical results discussed above in the case of the Thistlethwaite and Campbell (1960) study, several factors make Hidalgo's (2010) study a convincing illustration of regression-discontinuity analysis. First, there is a strong a priori case that the population threshold of 40,500, which was applied uniformly throughout most of the country, generated a regression-discontinuity study group in which assignment to treatment is as good as random. (As discussed further in Chapters 7 and 8, qualitative and quantitative evidence is also consistent with this assertion.) Next, not only is there clear graphical evidence of an effect at the regression-discontinuity threshold—from a scatter plot of percentage of null and blank votes in 1998 against municipal population—but the distribution of outcomes to the left of the 40,500 threshold barely overlaps with the distribution of outcomes to its right (see Hidalgo 2010). Finally, clear evidence for a sizeable difference of means appears for municipalities very close to the key threshold as well as those slightly further away, so results are not sensitive to the choice of bandwidth. Results are also very similar using local-linear regression and the cross-validation procedure advocated by Imbens and Lemieux (2007) to choose the bandwidth and thus select units for the study group (discussed below). While the difference-of-means test is in many ways better motivated (and is more consistent with the Neyman urn approach), the similarity of results across choices of bandwidth and analytic procedures may be reassuring.

In these settings, then, the difference of means is a reliable and convincing estimator for the average causal effect.[25] One may certainly elaborate various somewhat more complicated tests, as discussed later in this book. Yet, the Neyman urn model seems highly credible in this context, and so the most important comparisons are simple, transparent, and highly compelling. The research design and the size of the effect—not the elaboration of complicated statistical methodology—should compel the conviction. In regression-discontinuity designs, as in standard natural experiments, differences of means provide the key estimator of the average causal effect for the study group.

---

[25] Below I consider the issue of possible bias in the difference-of-means estimator, as raised by Imbens and Lemieux (2007) among others.

5.2.2 Defining the study group: the question of bandwidth

Not every regression-discontinuity design gives rise to such straightforward procedures, however. Probably the most important issue relates to how to define the regression-discontinuity study group—that is, how big the window or "bandwidth" around the key regression-discontinuity threshold should be—and what to do when results conflict with different choices of bandwidth.

There is a central trade-off involved in the issue of how large the bandwidth should be. By enlarging the bandwidth, one typically gains precision; that is, because the study group is typically larger, treatment effect estimators will have lower variance. However, enlarging the bandwidth opens up the risk of bias, because units located further from a key regression-discontinuity threshold may not provide valid counterfactuals for each other. Thus, in the example from Thistlethwaite and Campbell (1960) in which the key regression-discontinuity threshold was an entrance exam score of 11, students who score a 5 on the exam may have quite different potential outcomes under treatment and control than students who score, say, 17. Put differently, *ex post* differences between units exposed to treatment (due to their position above the regression-discontinuity threshold) and those not exposed to treatment (due to their position below the threshold) could be due to confounding factors, rather than to the effect of treatment.

There have been a number of attempts to implement the "optimal" bandwidth size through algorithms that seek to balance the trade-off in the gain in precision from expanding the bandwidth against the risk of bias that this incurs. For example, Imbens and Lemieux (2007) discuss an increasingly utilized cross-validation procedure. Ultimately, however, the bias comes from unobservables, and so it is quite difficult to develop reliable hard-and-fast rules for how to optimize the trade-off between bias and precision.

The issue comes down to whether analysts can credibly posit as-if randomization for a chosen bandwidth. As in other natural experiments, the assumption of as-if randomization is ultimately just that: an assumption. However, this assertion can be bolstered by a priori reasoning and by appealing to the quantitative and qualitative tools discussed elsewhere in the book. Quantitative and graphical evidence showing balance on observable pre-treatment covariates in the treatment and control groups, supplemented by various forms of qualitative evidence, is generally most important (see Chapters 7 and 8).

As a rule of thumb, analysts might present the analysis with several different choices of bandwidth, including often the smallest feasible bandwidth. For example, in the Thistlethwaite and Campbell study, analysts might present analysis for several bandwidths but include analysis that compares students who scored in the interval from 10 to 11 to those who scored in the interval from 11 to 12. Data may be sparse in this bandwidth, which may be an issue, but that would counsel gathering more data, not necessarily expanding the bandwidth.

If results do not persist in the smaller bandwidth, this may caution against drawing strong conclusions from the analysis. Ultimately, the inference should rest on the research design and the size of the estimated effect. With a strong design and a strong true effect, results should not be highly sensitive to the choice of bandwidth.

5.2.3 Is the difference-of-means estimator biased in regression-discontinuity designs?

The difference-of-means estimator, as applied to data from regression-discontinuity designs, has recently acquired an undeservedly bad reputation. Drawing on Hahn, Todd, and Van Der Klaauw (2001) and Porter (2003), for example, Imbens and Lemieux (2007) describe the difference-of-means estimator as "not very attractive" for regression-discontinuity designs (see also Lee and Lemieux 2010). Indeed, these authors suggest that the difference-of-means estimator is biased in regression-discontinuity designs, and they derive an expression for the large-sample bias in the difference-of-means estimator under particular assumptions about the nature of the estimand. These authors typically recommend instead the use of local-linear or global polynomial regressions.[26]

In this section, I briefly describe this argument, which is elaborated in Appendix 5.2. However, I suggest that this scepticism of difference-of-means analysis is ultimately misguided, and it leads us away from the potential for simple and transparent design-based inferences in strong regression-discontinuity designs. In brief, the key issue is whether the Neyman urn model (Figure 5.1) applies, in a given regression-discontinuity design with a given choice of bandwidth around the key regression-discontinuity threshold. When it does, the difference of means is not a biased estimator for the average causal effect for the study group. When it does not, the design does not very

---

[26] These techniques are further described in Chapter 9, where I discuss some the interpretive issues that can arise when such regressions are fitted to the data from regression-discontinuity designs, with or without covariates.

Simplicity and transparency: keys to quantitative analysis

plausibly involve a strong natural experiment—and the inferential power of the regression-discontinuity design is in consequence substantially mitigated.

The central issue relates to the definition of the key causal parameters in the regression-discontinuity design. Much theoretical work on regression-discontinuity designs has defined the causal quantity of interest as the limit of a regression function at the regression-discontinuity threshold. Consider, for example, Figure 5.3, which shows hypothetical average observed and potential outcomes at each level of a pre-treatment covariate. The figure continues the example from Thistlethwaite and Campbell, so that the forcing covariate is students' pre-test scores; students scoring 11 and above on the exam are assigned to the treatment group, i.e., public recognition in the form of Certificates of Merit. Here, observed outcomes are darkened, with squares indicating the assigned-to-treatment group and circles indicating the assigned-to-control group. Light squares and circles indicate the counterfactual, unobserved average potential outcomes at each level of test scores. For example, the light squares to the left of the dotted vertical line over 11 indicate the average test scores that students assigned to the control group

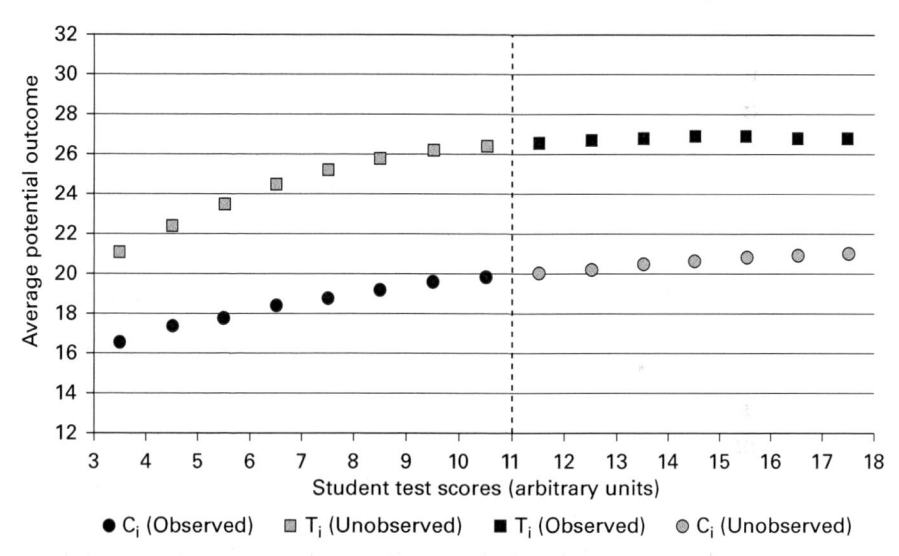

Figure 5.3 Potential and observed outcomes in a regression-discontinuity design.
The figure plots the average potential outcomes for all test-takers, at each unit bin of student test scores. Squares indicate the potential outcomes under treatment, and circles indicate potential outcomes under control. Darkened markers indicate outcomes that are observed. Only students who score higher than 11 receive the treatment: public recognition in the form of Certificates of Merit.

would have obtained, had they been assigned to treatment; the light circles to the right of the dotted vertical line indicate the average test scores that students assigned to the treatment group would have obtained, had they been assigned to the control group. Because the figure plots the average value of (potential) outcomes at each level of exam scores, for both the treatment and control groups, these plotted functions are known as regression functions.

Many authors then define the causal parameter of interest in regression-discontinuity designs as the difference between two quantities: the value of the regression function of potential outcomes under treatment at the key threshold (here, an exam score of exactly 11), and the value of the regression function of potential outcomes under control at this same threshold. These values provide valid counterfactuals, as long as the potential outcome regression functions are "smooth" (i.e., do not jump discontinuously) at the regression-discontinuity threshold. Of course, average outcomes can only be observed at the threshold for one of the treatment conditions, at most.[27] In consequence, at least one of these two quantities is defined as the (unobserved) limit of the potential-outcomes regression function at the point of discontinuity. For instance, by extending the regression function for potential outcomes under control (light circles in Figure 5.3) to the vertical dotted line over 11, we would obtain the counterfactual outcomes under control for units that will in fact be assigned to the treatment group. Many authors thus emphasize that the regression-discontinuity design identifies the average causal effect only at this point of discontinuity.

As Appendix 5.2 shows, this way of defining the causal effect as the limit of a regression function leads to the definition of bias in the difference-of-means estimator. Essentially, the issue is that the limit must be approximated by the derivative of observed outcomes at the boundary point, i.e., the point of discontinuity. If this derivative is non-zero, then there is asymptotic bias in the difference-of-means estimator; the size of the bias is a linear function of the size of the bandwidth h that is chosen around the regression-discontinuity threshold. Thus, consideration of the shape of potential outcome functions on either side of the key threshold is the central issue in evaluating the argument that the difference-of-means estimator is biased in regression-discontinuity designs. According to Imbens and Lemieux (2007: 10), "we typically do expect the regression function to have a non-zero derivative, even in cases where the treatment has no effect. In many applications the eligibility criterion is based

---

[27] This leaves aside for the moment the question of whether there are data for either the assigned-to-treatment group or the assigned-to-control group directly at the threshold.

on a covariate that does have some correlation with the outcome, so that, for example, those with poorest prospects in the absence of the program are in the eligible group."

Yet, why should units eligible for a program on the basis of having a qualification score that is, say, just above the regression-discontinuity threshold respond systematically differently to treatment than those just below the threshold? If the conditional expectation of the potential outcomes under treatment (or control) on either side of the regression discontinuity is much different, for units included in the study group, we would have to say that the natural experiment has failed—for it has not in fact generated locally as-if random assignment to treatment conditions. In this case, the assigned-to-control group is not a valid counterfactual for the assigned-to-treatment group. If, on the other hand, the natural experiment is successful—in that it generates groups just on either side of the regression-discontinuity threshold that are valid counterfactuals for one another—then the graph of the conditional expectations of the potential outcomes should look like those in Figure 5.3 at the key discontinuity. That is, the slopes of the two potential-outcomes regression functions should be approximately flat, at least in the neighborhood of the threshold. To be sure, over the range of the data, the pretreatment covariate may have some relationship to the outcome variable; yet, in the strongest regression-discontinuity designs, this relationship will be locally weak, and any discontinuity in the conditional mean of the potential-outcomes regression functions would need to be swamped by the discontinuity in actual outcomes on either side of the threshold, if valid and compelling causal inferences are to be made.

Indeed, the whole idea of the regression-discontinuity design *qua* natural experiment is that the distribution of potential outcomes in the assigned-to-treatment group is just like the distribution of potential outcomes in the assigned-to-treatment group, up to random error. At least near the threshold, the groups should be exchangeable.[28] Whether one happens to score 10 or 11 on an entrance exam—or even a 9 or a 12—should not much affect how one responds to public recognition of scholastic achievement. Yet, if the derivative—the slope—of the potential-outcomes regression function on either side of the key threshold is not approximately zero, how can one make a credible argument that subjects on either side of the threshold are exchangeable? To be sure, there might be regression-discontinuity designs in which this condition

---

[28] A sequence of random variables is exchangeable if any permutation of the sequence has the same joint probability distribution as the original sequence.

does not hold, i.e., in which the slope of the potential-outcomes regression function is locally steep and the groups on either side of the threshold do not provide valid counterfactuals for each other. Yet, such designs should not be considered valid natural experiments. By contrast, in those regression-discontinuity designs in which as-if random assignment does in fact apply for a study group located near the key threshold, the groups on either side of the threshold should be exchangeable. Then, simple comparisons such as differences of means in the treatment and control group suffice to estimate the average causal effect (see Appendix 5.2).

In sum, the spirit of the natural-experimental regression-discontinuity design—in which treatment assignment is locally as-if random—is not well captured by defining the causal effect only at the limit, that is, at the point of discontinuity. If the effect is only identified at the limit—and if the slope of the potential-outcomes regression function implies that the conditional expectation to the right of the threshold is very different from that to the left of the threshold—then the claim of as-if random is not going to be very plausible. Claiming that the difference of means does not suffice to estimate the average causal effect is tantamount to saying that units have been included in the study group that should not really be there.

Instead, in a strong regression-discontinuity design, the average of the potential outcomes under treatment and control should be about the same on both sides of the threshold, for units in the study group.[29] Thus, the slope (i.e., derivative) of the potential-outcomes regression function should be about zero at least locally. This is an important issue because, as I show in Appendix 5.2, the linear bias in the bandwidth size h disappears if average potential outcomes are the same on either side the discontinuity—that is, if the slopes of the two potential-outcomes regression functions are approximately flat in the neighborhood of the regression-discontinuity threshold. In this case, the core of Imbens and Lemieux's (2007) objection to the difference-of-means estimator disappears. The relevant point is thus whether the Neyman model, including its assumption of as-if random assignment, applies for the study group at hand. If as-if random holds, then simple and transparent tools for estimating the average causal effect are available. If it does not, analysts probably have a regression-discontinuity design that is something less than a natural experiment.

---

[29] Remember, these potential outcomes are only partially observed: we see the potential outcomes under treatment, for units assigned to treatment, and the potential outcomes under control, for units assigned to the control group.

Not all analysts agree that achieving as-if random assignment for the study group is the *sine qua non* of compelling regression-discontinuity designs. Many analysts simply invoke the smoothness (lack of discontinuity) of potential-outcome regression functions as the key identifying assumption of regression-discontinuity designs. This leads to a definition of causal effects in terms of the limits of potential outcome regression functions—rather than as the difference in average potential outcomes under treatment and control, for the whole study group. Yet, the latter estimand seems most relevant. Again, if as-if random assignment holds—and the Neyman urn model provides a good depiction of the data-generating process for the study group—then the difference of means is an unbiased estimator for the average causal effect. This discussion may remind us that the bias of an estimator depends on the definition of the estimand—which in turn depends on the assumed model in terms of which that causal parameter is formulated. See Appendix 5.2 and Chapter 9 for further discussion.

5.2.4 Modeling functional form

While values on the pre-treatment covariates may in general be associated with potential outcomes under treatment and control—and thus, covariate values could in general confound the effects of treatment assignment—potential outcomes of units just on either side of the threshold should not be very different. Thus, units located just on one side of the threshold may serve as valid counterfactuals for units just on the other, since these units are *ex ante* very similar—save for their differential assignment to treatment or control.

In sum, the simplicity, transparency, and credibility of quantitative data analysis can potentially be great in regression-discontinuity designs—just as in standard natural experiments. Difference-of-means tests using units just at the point of discontinuity should thus be seen as the best approach for analyzing data from regression-discontinuity designs—at least those that are valid natural experiments. Here, the causal model is a plausible depiction of the data-generating process, and statistical inference rests on a reasonable box model—in which tickets are drawn as-if at random from an urn and placed into treatment or control.

However, just as with standard natural experiments, this simplicity is not always realized in practice. Perhaps the major reason in real applications is a lack of sufficient data "near" the threshold, which raises concerns about statistical power (the ability to detect true causal effects).

This concern may lead researchers to include in the study group units that are located further from the regression-discontinuity threshold—for which, however, the assumption of as-if random assignment can be less plausible. When as-if random assignment may not hold, analysts may attempt to adjust for confounders by including pre-treatment covariates in a multiple regression model. However, the presence of such controls amounts to an admission that the research design is something less than a natural experiment.

Lack of data near the threshold may also lead analysts to fit local-linear or polynomial regressions to either side of the key regression-discontinuity threshold. These regressions draw power from observations further from the threshold. Green et al. (2009) demonstrate the difficulties that can be involved in using this approach to recover benchmark results from true experiments. However, these models may lack credibility as descriptions of the data-generating process. Analyses that are based on local-linear or polynomial regressions using data far from the regression-discontinuity threshold should be seen as more model based than design based. Inferences from such analysis are more dependent on the model, and the modeling record is mixed (e.g. Green et al. 2009). Lack of data near the threshold is a practical problem in many regression-discontinuity designs. Yet, if data are sparse at the threshold, the local-linear or global polynomial approach may not fix things much. Indeed, the cure can sometimes be worse than the disease. The difference of means therefore seems to be a sensible estimator and the right starting point in regression-discontinuity designs, as in other kinds of natural experiments.[30]

5.2.5 Fuzzy regression discontinuities

In the discussion of regression-discontinuity designs to this point, I have implicitly assumed that treatment receipt is a deterministic function of the running covariate. This assumption applies in many regression-discontinuity designs. For instance, in the setting studied by Thistlethwaite and Campbell (1960), students were awarded Certificates of Merit, and thus public recognition of scholastic achievement, if they scored above a (state-specific) threshold on a qualifying exam; all students who scored above the threshold were

---

[30] Using the replication data for Green et al. (2009), one finds that the simple difference-of-means estimator does a much better job of recovering experimental benchmarks than other estimators, especially when the bandwidth is narrow. See Exercise 5.4.

recognized, while none who scored below the threshold received certificates or recognition. In Hidalgo's (2010) study of enfranchisement in Brazil, electronic voting machines were used in all municipalities exceeding a given population threshold, and none were used in municipalities below that threshold.

In other regression-discontinuity designs, however, location above or below a threshold may only make units eligible for some treatment—but whether they opt into the program may be up to them. In this case, treatment receipt is not a deterministic function of the value of the running covariate. However, the probability of program participation is shaped by the value of the forcing variable. Campbell (1969) and Trochim (1984) referred to such designs as "fuzzy" regression-discontinuity designs—in contrast to the "sharp" regression-discontinuity designs in which treatment assignment is a deterministic function of the running covariate (Chapter 3).

Data from fuzzy regression-discontinuity designs may be analyzed according to the intention-to-treat principle (Box 4.1). Here, comparisons are made across the groups assigned to eligibility or lack of eligibility for a program, on the basis of their position relative to the regression-discontinuity threshold. That is, we simply ignore whether units actually choose to participate in the program and instead focus on the behavior of the two groups subject to the randomization. The intention-to-treat strategy is often relevant for policy-makers as well as social scientists. For instance, knowing how much eligibility for a municipal poverty program decreases poverty rates—regardless of who chooses actually to participate in the program—would tell researchers how much expanding the eligibility threshold would reduce poverty rates, on average.

However, fuzzy regression-discontinuity designs can also be analyzed in a way that adjusts for the imperfect correlation between eligibility and participation. This analysis closely parallels the logic of instrumental-variables analysis—in fact, such analysis of a fuzzy regression-discontinuity design is indistinguishable from standard instrumental-variables analysis. Thus, I return to this topic below, after introducing analytic techniques appropriate to the third variety of natural experiments: instrumental-variables designs.

5.3 Analyzing instrumental-variables designs

As we saw in Chapter 4, instrumental-variables designs have been used in a wide variety of substantive settings, and many different kinds of data-analytic strategies have been brought to bear, including linear multivariate regression models.[31] However, this is not necessarily the best setting in which to understand how instrumental-variables analysis actually works.

The first goal of this subsection is therefore to describe the logic for a simple and often highly credible form of instrumental-variables analysis: estimating the effect of treatment on Compliers, in natural experiments with "crossover." In many true experiments and natural experiments, some units assigned to treatment in fact receive the control, while some units assigned to the control group may receive the treatment. In this context, instrumental-variables analysis may be used to estimate the average causal effect for the subset of units that comply with the treatment condition to which they are assigned— that is, the average causal effect for "Compliers."

After introducing the use of instrumental variables to estimate this effect of treatment on Compliers, I then discuss the link from this setting to fuzzy regression-discontinuity designs as well as to linear regression models. As we get further from the clean estimation of effects of treatment on Compliers, in a bivariate setting, towards multivariate regression models, more complicated assumptions are involved—and results can in consequence be less credible. Discussion of some of these issues will be postponed for Chapter 9.

However, as will become clear, at its core successful instrumental-variables analysis centrally involves difference-of-means estimators. Thus, while there are some important caveats about analysis and estimation in instrumental-variables designs, successful instrumental-variables analysis can also rely on simple strategies, akin to those we encountered with standard natural experiments and sharp regression-discontinuity designs.

5.3.1 Natural experiments with noncompliance

To understand the logic of instrumental-variables analysis, it is useful to consider the problem of noncompliance or "crossover," which occurs in both true and natural experiments. In true experiments, random assignment to treatment and control groups is under the control of the experimenter. Yet, even in true experiments, subjects may not comply with the treatment condition to which they have been assigned. For example, Gerber and Green (2000) studied of the effect of door-to-door political canvassing on voter turnout. Yet, some voters who were assigned to receive a face-to-face

---

[31] Here, some variable typically serves as an "instrument" for a regressor thought to be endogenous, that is, statistically dependent on the error term in the regression model.

get-out-the-vote message did not answer the canvasser's knock on their door. Such subjects can be understood to have "crossed over" from the treatment to the control arm of the experiment, because they were assigned to treatment but instead received the control.

Crossover also arises frequently in medical trials. For instance, subjects assigned to the treatment arm of a pharmaceutical trial of a new drug may refuse to take the drug; or those assigned to the control group may seek it out. When all subjects assigned to control accept the control regime, but some subjects assigned to the treatment group decline the treatment (or vice versa), we have *single crossover*. By contrast, *double crossover* means that some subjects assigned to treatment cross over to the control arm, while some subjects assigned to the control arm also cross over to treatment (Freedman 2006).

This problem of imperfect compliance with treatment assignment arises in many natural experiments as well. In standard natural experiments involving lotteries, such as the Colombia voucher study (Angrist et al. 2002; Angrist, Bettinger, and Kremer 2006), not all subjects follow treatment assignment: for instance, students assigned to receive a voucher may not choose to use it to go to private schools. Similarly, in Angrist's (1990a) study of the earnings effects of being drafted for the Vietnam War (discussed in detail below), drafted soldiers may be disqualified by medical examinations, stay in college, or go to Canada.[32] With the fuzzy regression-discontinuity designs mentioned in the previous section, eligibility for a program—based on position just above or below the regression-discontinuity threshold—may not imply that units choose to opt into the program. And in many other natural experiments, analysts are interested in exposure to some treatment, such as economic growth, that is only imperfectly correlated with some as-if randomly assigned variable, such as weather—just as in experiments with crossover, treatment assignment is only imperfectly correlated with treatment receipt. As we will see, the basic logic of experimental crossover can be understood to apply in all of these cases, subject to suitable modification.

How should data from experiments or natural experiments with crossover be analyzed? In general, it is misleading to compare subjects according to whether they receive treatment or not—because there may be confounding. In Gerber and Green's (2000) study, subjects who open the door for politicsal canvassers are different than those who do not. For example, such subjects

---

[32] This voucher study was discussed in Chapter 2, where the focus was on intention-to-treat analysis—the effect of assignment to a voucher. Yet, such a study can also be analyzed as an instrumental-variables design, which suggests that the difference between instrumental-variables and other natural experiments depends on how the parameters of interest are defined.

may be more politically aware or politically active and thus more likely to turn out to vote, even absent a visit from a canvasser. Attributing differences in turnout between subjects who talked to a canvasser and those who did not will tend to overstate the causal impact of canvassing: this is selection bias at work.

Intention-to-treat analysis is a useful strategy in such settings (Box 4.1). The power of intention-to-treat analysis is that it focuses on the groups created by the randomization, not the groups created by self-selection. With random or as-if random assignment, intention-to-treat analysis is always available and is a credible option for analyzing the data. As I have argued elsewhere in this book, analyses of natural-experimental data should almost always present intention-to-treat analysis.

Yet, intention-to-treat analysis may lead to conservative estimates of the effect of treatment—for instance, if many subjects in the assigned-to-treatment group did not actually receive the treatment. The Neyman model can be extended to analyze the problem of noncompliance and to derive the basic instrumental-variable estimator—which, in a nutshell, estimates the effect of treatment on subjects who comply with the treatment condition to which they have been assigned.

To see this, imagine that there are three types of subjects in the study group:

Always-Treats. If assigned to the treatment group, these subjects accept treatment. If assigned to the control group, they insist on treatment. In other words, they are always treated, regardless of assignment.

Compliers. If assigned to the treatment group, these subjects accept treatment. If assigned to the control group, they accept the control regime. In other words, they follow treatment assignment faithfully.

Never-Treats. If assigned to the treatment group, these subjects decline treatment and follow the control regime. If assigned to the control group, they accept the control regime. In other words, these subjects never take the treatment.

Figure 5.4 depicts this model as a box of tickets. As in Figure 5.1, here the box represents the natural-experimental study group; there is one ticket in the box for each unit in the study group. Notice that in contrast to Figure 5.1, now there are three kinds of tickets. The first kind has only one value:

$$\boxed{T_i \mid T_i}$$

These tickets represent the Always-Treats. The reason there is only one value is that these subjects always receive the treatment, whether they are assigned to treatment or control. Thus, we can substitute the potential outcome under control for the potential outcome under treatment: $T_i = C_i$.[33] The second kind of ticket also has only one value:

$$\boxed{C_i \mid C_i}$$

These tickets represent the Never-Treats. These subjects always receive the control regime, whether assigned to treatment or control. Thus, again, we can substitute the potential outcome under control for the potential outcome under treatment: $T_i = C_i$.[34] For these first and second types, the average responses to assignment to treatment or control are assumed to be the same. Since Never-Treats always follow the control regime and Always-Treats always receive the treatment, this is a sensible assumption—as long as treatment assignment itself doesn't somehow affect their responses. Finally, the third type of ticket in Figure 5.4 is

$$\boxed{T_i \mid C_i}$$

These are the Compliers. If these subjects are assigned to treatment, we observe T_i; if they are assigned to control, we observe C_i.[35]

Now, suppose we sample some of the tickets at random from the box and place them in the assigned-to-treatment group. The remainder of tickets goes to the assigned-to-control group. Also assume for the moment that we can observe who complies with their treatment assignment. Then, given the model, partial information about subject type is available from the data. For example, subjects who are assigned to treatment but receive the control must be Never-Treats. (These are shown in the bottom of the assigned-to-treatment group on the left of Figure 5.4.) Similarly, subjects who are assigned to control

---

[33] Remember that the potential outcome under control is the outcome the unit would experience, if assigned to control. Since an Always-Treat always receives the treatment—and since we assume that the potential treatment response is not affected by treatment assignment—the potential outcome under control must be the same as the potential outcome under treatment.

[34] I copy C_i into both fields of the ticket, rather than T_i, to emphasize that this is indeed the potential outcome when subject to the control condition.

[35] I discuss below a fourth possible type—Defiers—who are here assumed not to exist.

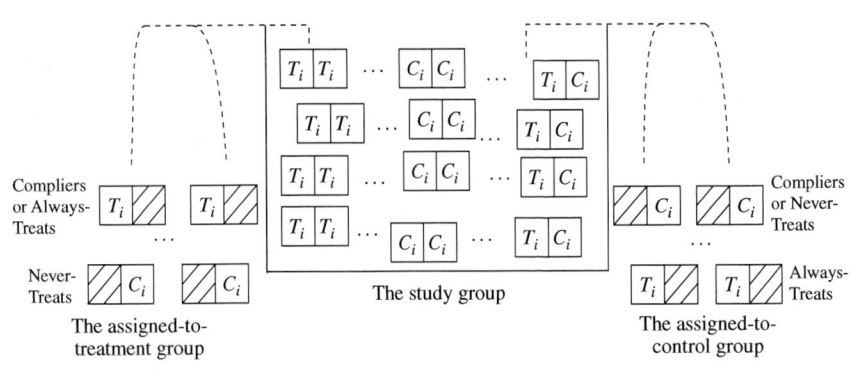

Figure 5.4 Noncompliance under the Neyman model.
A model of natural-experimental crossover. Each ticket in the box represents one unit in the natural-experimental study group. Every ticket has two fields, one representing potential outcomes under assignment to treatment and the other potential outcomes under assignment to control. Tickets with T_i in both fields are "Always-Treats." Tickets with C_i in both fields are "Never-Treats." Tickets with T_i in one field and C_i in the other are "Compliers." (Defiers are ruled out by assumption.) Here, we draw at random without replacement from a box with N tickets, placing $n < N$ tickets in the assigned-to-treatment group and $m = N - n$ tickets in the assigned-to-control group. The assigned-to-treatment groups and assigned-to-control groups contain a mixture of Always-Treats, Compliers, and Never-Treats; the mixture should be the same in both groups, up to random error, because both groups are random samples of the tickets in the box.

but receive the treatment must be Always-Treats (as shown in the bottom of the assigned-to-control group on the right of Figure 5.4).

Yet, certain detail on subject type at the individual level is not possible to obtain. For example, according to the model above, if nature assigns a subject to treatment and she takes the treatment, she could be an Always-Treat or a Complier. This is indicated at the top of the assigned-to-treatment group on the left of Figure 5.4. Similarly, a subject assigned to control who follows the control regime could be a Complier or Never-Treat, as indicated at the top of the assigned-to-control group on the right of Figure 5.4. In such cases, we can't readily tell which kind of subject is which—because we do not observe counterfactually whether a subject assigned to treatment would stay in the control condition if assigned to control, and vice versa for a subject assigned to control.

In an experiment or natural experiment with single crossover from the treatment to control, the study group must be comprised only of Never-Treats and Compliers: if there were any Always-Treats in the study group, some subjects assigned to control would take the treatment.[36] Still, among subjects in the assigned-to-control group, we cannot tell which are Compliers and which are Never-Treats. And if there is double crossover, we cannot separate the Never-Treats and Always-Treats from the Compliers.

This is akin to the fundamental problem of inference that arises for the unit causal effect. As noted above, however, other parameters—such as the average causal effect—are estimable. Instrumental-variables analysis defines and estimates a particular average causal effect—the causal effect for Compliers.

To see the intuition for instrumental-variables analysis, notice that the model described above implicitly defines the following parameters:

(A) the fraction of Compliers in the study group;
(B) the average response of Compliers to treatment;
(C) the average response of Compliers to the control regime;
(D) the difference between (B) and (C), which is the average causal effect for Compliers.

The model also defines other parameters, such the average responses of Never-Treats and Always-Treats to treatment and control.

Given the model in Figure 5.4, these parameters can all be estimated. Indeed, the goal of instrumental-variables analysis is to estimate (D), the *average causal effect for Compliers*. (This parameter is also known as the effect of treatment on Compliers, or the Complier average causal effect; in experiments with single crossover, it is sometimes called the effect of treatment on the treated, though that term is used to refer to other estimands and is thus ambiguous.)

Let us now investigate how the logic of random sampling allows estimation of this parameter. To simplify the exposition, assume that we have a study in which there is only single crossover from treatment to control—thus, there are no Always-Treats. Then, the fraction of Compliers in the assigned-to-treatment group—that is, the fraction of subjects who are assigned to treatment and who take the treatment—estimates the parameter (A), the fraction

---

[36] Single crossover often arises in both true experiments and natural experiments. For instance, in experimental studies on voter turnout such as Gerber and Green's (2000), canvassers do not visit any voters in the assigned-to-control group (unless researchers or canvassers make mistakes and visit households they were not assigned to receive canvassing). Thus, there are no "types" we would call Always-Treats.

in the whole study group. This is because of random assignment: the treatment group is a random sample from the small population comprised of the study group, and the average of a random sample is an unbiased estimator for the average of the population.

Similarly for parameter (B): the average response among Compliers in the assigned-to-treatment group—that is, the average outcome among the subjects assigned to treatment who accept treatment—estimates the average response to treatment of all Compliers in the study population. Note also that the average response among subjects in the treatment group who decline treatment—these are the Never-Treats—estimates the average response of all Never-Treat subjects, because Never-Treats in the assigned-to-treatment group are a random sample of the Never-Treats.

What about parameter (C)? The average response in the control group is a mix of the average response for Compliers in the control condition (which is unknown, because we cannot distinguish Compliers from Never-Treats in the control group), and the average response for Never-Treat subjects (which has already been estimated from the treatment group). Due to random assignment, the mix of subjects in the control group is the same as the mix in the treatment group, up to random error. That sets up an algebraic equation, which can be solved to get an estimate for (C), the average response of Compliers to the control regime. Once we have (C) and (B), parameter (D) is estimated by subtraction.

Standard instrumental-variables analysis involves a formula that mechanizes these comparisons. In essence, the intention-to-treat estimator—that is, the difference of average outcomes in the assigned-to-treatment and assigned-to-control groups—is divided by what might be called the "net crossover rate": the proportion of units assigned to the treatment group who in fact received the treatment, minus the proportion of units assigned to the control group who in fact received the treatment. This "net crossover rate" estimates the proportion of Compliers in the study group. The following subsection, "Estimating the average causal effect for Compliers," states the formula; Appendix 5.1 derives it more rigorously and discusses other important details related to instrumental-variables analysis.

Intuitively, instrumental-variables analysis simply adjusts outcome differences by treatment assignment for the fact that not all units assigned to the treatment group actually receive treatment, while some assigned to the control group cross over into treatment. As discussed elsewhere (see Chapters 4 and 9), an important justification for estimation of the effects of treatment in this manner is clear: it is assumed that nothing other than differences in the probability of actually receiving the treatment is responsible for differences in outcomes by treatment-assignment status. This "exclusion restriction" may be valid in some settings and substantially less plausible in others.

Estimating the average causal effect for Compliers

This subsection presents the instrumental-variables estimator for the average effect of treatment for Compliers; the estimator is derived and discussed fully in Appendix 5.1. Here, as in Figure 5.4, there are three types of subjects in the natural-experimental study group: Always-Treats, Never-Treats, and Compliers. The average causal effect for Always-Treats and Never-Treats is zero, because these subjects are assumed to respond the same whether assigned to treatment or to control. However, the average causal effect for Compliers may be different from zero, and this is the quantity we want to estimate.

The instrumental-variables estimator for the average causal effect for Compliers can be written as

$$\frac{Y^T - Y^C}{X^T - X^C}, \qquad (5.1)$$

where Y^T is the average outcome in the assigned-to-treatment sample and Y^C is the average outcome in the assigned-to-control sample. Thus, the numerator estimates the average causal effect for the whole study group, that is, the intention-to-treat parameter (see Boxes 5.1–5.2). Here, X^T is the fraction of people in the assigned-to-treatment group who accept treatment, and X^C is the fraction of people in the assigned-to-control group who cross over into treatment. The difference $X^T - X^C$ estimates the proportion of Compliers in the study group. See Appendix 5.1 for further details.

5.3.2 An example: the effect of military service

The study by Angrist (1990a) again provides a useful illustration of instrumental-variables analysis in the presence of crossover. How does military service affect labor-market earnings? The question is difficult to answer, since confounding factors may be responsible for any observed differences in the earnings of soldiers and nonsoldiers (Chapter 1).

Angrist (1990a) thus uses an instrumental-variables design to study the earnings effects of military service (Chapter 4). In the randomized draft lotteries of 1970, 1971, and 1972, cohorts of 19- and 20-year-old men were randomly assigned lottery numbers ranging from 1 to 366, according to their dates of birth.[37] All those with lottery numbers below the highest number called for induction each year were "draft eligible."[38] In 1970, the ceiling for draft-eligible lottery numbers was 195, while in 1971 and 1972 it was set at 125 and 95, respectively. (The military's manpower requirements apparently declined as the war went on.)

Records of the Social Security Administration provide data on the later earnings of men in each cohort. For a random sample of one percent of all Social Security numbers on file, the Administration also matched earnings records to birthdates, creating a dichotomous indicator for draft eligibility in the 1970s. This allows Angrist (1990a) to identify men in each tax year and each cohort who had been eligible and ineligible for each Vietnam draft. In 1981, for example, 5,657 white men in the data set had been eligible for the draft in 1971, while 10,858 such white men had been ineligible.[39] (Angrist's data are presented separately for whites and non-whites; it is customary in some studies of US labor markets to separate these groups, perhaps because of their quite different earnings outcomes.)

Table 5.2, adapted from Angrist (1990a) using his replication data set, shows average non-zero FICA (Federal Insurance Contributions Act) Social Security earnings in 1981 for both groups.[40] As discussed in Chapter 1, this intention-to-treat analysis shows a moderate effect in absolute and relative terms. In the draft-eligible group, average earnings were $15,813.93 in current US dollars, while in the ineligible group they were $16,172.25. Thus, assignment to draft eligibility in 1971 caused a decrease in average earnings of $358.32, or about a 2.2 percent drop from average earnings of the assigned-to-control group.[41]

---

[37] The 1970 lottery also drafted older men born between 1944 and 1949; Angrist (1990a) ignores these cohorts, for reasons discussed in that paper.

[38] There were subsequent physical and mental exams that disqualified some draft-eligible men from actual service; only draft eligibility was randomly assigned.

[39] This is a one-percent sample, so the number of eligible white men in the population, in this cohort and tax year, is about 565,700, while the number of ineligible white men is 1,085,800. The reason the draft-eligible number is about half the ineligible number is that in the 1971 draft, 125 birthdates were draft eligible and 231 were not.

[40] I follow Angrist (1990a) in reporting non-zero Social Security earnings, though those with zero earnings should perhaps be included—particularly because those in the draft-eligible group might be more likely to have zero earnings due to war-related mortality.

[41] My focus here is not on estimating variability in treatment effect estimators. However, this intention-to-treat estimator is statistically significant at standard levels, using the corrected standard errors included in Angrist (1990b).

Table 5.2 Social Security earnings in 1981 (white men born in 1951, current US$)

	Estimated proportion of types in each group	Estimated number of types in each group	Average earnings
Assigned to treatment (draft eligible)		5,657	$15,813.93
Volunteers (Always-Treats)	0.1468	831	
Served because drafted (Compliers)	0.1363	771	
Refused draft or disqualified (Never-Treats)	0.7169	4,055	
Assigned to control (draft ineligible)		10,858	$16,172.25
Volunteers (Always-Treats)	0.1468	1,594	
Would have served if drafted (Compliers)	0.1363	1,480	
Would have refused or been disqualified if drafted (Never-Treats)	0.7169	7,784	

However, intention-to-treat analysis does not actually estimate the effect of military service. After all, a substantial proportion of men who were draft eligible did not actually serve—either because they were disqualified by a physical or mental exam, went to college (which typically deferred induction during the Vietnam War), went to Canada, or for some other reason. Angrist (1990a: 315) notes that in 1970, fully half of all registrants from the draft-eligible pool failed pre-induction exams, and 20 percent of those who passed were eliminated after further physical inspections. By the same token, some men who were not draft eligible volunteered for service. Angrist (1990a) uses data from a household survey as well as military records to estimate the percentage of draft-eligible and draft-ineligible men who actually served. For the 1971 draft, these percentages are estimated at 28.31 and 14.68 percent, respectively.[42] Thus, the 1971 draft actually only increased the military participation of draft-eligible men by about 13.63 percentage points.

What was the effect of draft eligibility on men in the assigned-to-treatment group who actually served—but who would not have served had they not been drafted? Instrumental-variables analysis answers this question. Here, Compliers are men who accept service if they are assigned to the draft but

---

[42] One of the unusual features of Angrist's (1990a) study, which is driven by data availability, is that estimates of earnings for each cohort in each year come from a different sample—and thus, are calculated for different individuals—than the data on rates of service among draft-eligible and draft-ineligible men.

do not serve if they are not drafted. Always-Treats are men who serve in the military whether drafted or not (in ordinary language, these are called volunteers). Finally, Never-Treats are men who never serve whether drafted or not (these include people who refuse the draft or are disqualified in physical or mental exams).

As usual, by looking at the control group alone, we cannot tell Never-Treats from Compliers: neither type of subject serves in the military when assigned to the draft-ineligible group. However, since we know that 14.68 percent of draft-ineligible men in the 1971 cohort actually served, our best guess for the number of Always-Treats in the control group is $(0.1468)(10{,}858) \approx 1{,}594$. Moreover, due to random assignment, the proportion of Always-Treats in the draft-eligible group should also be about 0.1468. Thus, our best guess of the number of Always-Treats in the assigned-to-treatment group is $(0.1468)(5{,}657) \approx 831$. This is what is secured by random assignment: the mix of each type should be about the same in the assigned-to-treatment and assigned-to-control group.

By the same token, about 28.31 percent of the draft-eligible men actually served. Thus, about $(0.2831)(5{,}657) \approx 1{,}602$ draft-eligible men are Always-Treats or Compliers. But since around 831 men in the draft-eligible group are Always-Treats (as calculated above), this implies that about $1{,}602 - 831 = 771$ men in the draft-eligible group are Compliers—that is, 711 out of 5,657 or 13.63 percent of this group. Thus, about $5{,}657 - 831 - 771 = 4{,}055$ or 71.68 percent of the draft-eligible men are Never-Treats.

These data allow us to fill in Table 4.2 for the draft-ineligible group as well. For instance, the number of Compliers is about $(0.1363)(10{,}858) \approx 1{,}480$, while the number of Never-Treats is about $10{,}858 - 1{,}594 - 1{,}480 = 7{,}784$. Thus, the fact that randomization ensures that the mix of types is about the same in the assigned-to-treatment and assigned-to-control groups—the approximation gets better as the experiment gets larger—allows us to identify the proportions belonging to each type in each group (first column of Table 5.2) as well as their absolute number (second column of Table 5.2).

In many studies, we directly observe outcome data directly for some of these types in the treatment and control groups. For instance, if we observed earnings for draft-ineligible men who had volunteered for the military, we could directly fill in earnings for the Always-Treats in the control group—and thus the treatment group. Similarly, if we observed earnings for draft-eligible men who did not serve, we could fill in the earnings for Never-Treats in both groups. By subtraction, that would allow us to calculate the earnings of

Compliers in the treatment group and Compliers in the control group—and thereby estimate the effect of treatment on Compliers directly.

We cannot do that with Angrist's (1990a) data, because veteran status is not actually recorded in the same data set that records later earnings. (The estimated percentages of draft-eligible and non-eligible men who serve in the military come from a different sample survey, as discussed in note 42, above.) However, as Appendix 5.1 shows in more detail, we can set up a series of equations that can be solved for the conventional instrumental-variables estimator.

This estimator is simply a fraction. In the numerator, we have the intention-to-treat estimator—the difference of mean outcomes across the assigned-to-treatment and assigned-to-control groups. Thus, as in the analysis of standard natural experiments and regression-discontinuity designs, the difference of mean outcomes in the assigned-to-treatment and assigned-to-control groups plays a key role. In the denominator, we have the fraction of the assigned-to-treatment group that received treatment minus the fraction of the assigned-to-control group that received treatment. Notice that the denominator is an estimator of the proportion of Compliers in the study group: after all, the units that are assigned to treatment and receive treatment are Always-Treats or Compliers, while units that are assigned to control but receive the treatment are Always-Treats. Thus, the subtraction nets out Always-Treats and gives us an estimator of the proportion of Compliers in the study group.

Thus, for white men born in 1951, the instrumental-variables estimator of the effect of military service on Compliers is

$$\frac{\$15,813.93 - \$16,172.25}{.2831 - .1468} = -\$2,628.91.$$

This estimator suggests a large effect of military service on those men whose behavior was affected by draft eligibility, and a stronger effect than suggested by intention-to-treat analysis. Of course, this is an estimate for only one cohort, white men born in 1951, and only one year of earnings, 1981. Estimates should be computed separately for each cohort, because the probability of assignment to draft eligibility is different in each cohort: recall that the ceiling draft lottery number for induction was set at 195 in 1970, 125 in 1971, and 95 in 1972. Thus, pooling across cohorts would introduce a correlation between treatment assignment and year of birth (among other factors), which could in principle introduce bias (see Gerber and Green 2012). There are also different ways of measuring later earnings (for instance, using

Social Security wages or total income, filed after 1978 on IRS [Internal Revenue Service] Form W-2), with somewhat different implications for the results. In one specification, using mean W-2 earnings in 1981–84, Angrist (1990a, 1990b) estimates an effect of military service on earnings of about $2,384 dollars with a standard error of 778 dollars—or about 15 percent of average annual W-2 compensation for white men in 1981–84, certainly a nontrivial effect in substantive terms.

There are some important caveats here, however. Perhaps the most important is the assumption that draft eligibility only affects earnings through its effect on military service; this is sometimes known as an "exclusion restriction" (see Chapter 4). After all, some Vietnam-era students with low lottery numbers stayed in college to defer the draft. Thus, draft eligibility could plausibly have affected earnings through another channel—the accumulation of schooling and investments in human capital.[43] Another possible concern is attrition bias: mortality rates may be higher among draft-eligible men (due to greater exposure to combat in Vietnam), which is particularly a concern if propensity to die in combat is related to potential outcomes (i.e., potential future earnings).[44] Finally, and partially related to the first point above, it is not straightforward to formulate an explanation for why military service itself diminishes earnings. Angrist (1990a) attributes the finding to loss of labor-market experience, yet it seems just as plausible that psychological trauma induced by war experiences in Vietnam (not to mention simply the experience of being drafted) is to blame. I discuss potential pitfalls of this type in further detail below.

5.3.3 The no-Defiers assumption

The extension of the Neyman potential outcomes model depicted in Figure 5.4 posits Always-Treats, Compliers, and Never-Treats as theoretical types. Before using this model to construct instrumental-variables estimates in any substantive application, analysts should carefully consider the plausibility and

---

[43] If anything, this should presumably lead to a positive correlation between draft eligibility and later earnings, so the detrimental effects of Vietnam-era military service could be even larger than those captured here. Yet, it is difficult to know how big the bias may be, without making assumptions that might be equally implausible.

[44] This would not be an issue, if mortality were assigned more or less at random among soldiers. On the other hand, soldiers with special skills or education that are also rewarded in the labor market might be assigned office jobs rather than positions with combat battalions, so potential earnings could well be related to mortality rates. For an excellent discussion of threats to causal inference from attrition, see Green and Gerber (2012).

existence of these three types. For instance, in the Angrist (1990a) example above, military volunteers—aka Always Treats—are assumed to have the same military experience and thus the same *ex post* outcome, whether they were in fact drafted or not. This may be plausible; but one could also imagine that even a person who would have volunteered for the military regardless might feel anger at being drafted (or might perform with special pride if he can say that he volunteered *without* being drafted).[45] Analysts should thus always ask whether it is plausible to think that there are types who always respond to treatment the same whether they were assigned to receive it or not.

For instrumental-variables analysis, an additional assumption is also required—that there are no Defiers. This fourth type of subject is defined as follows:

> *Defiers*. If assigned to the treatment group, these subjects decline treatment; if assigned to the control group, they seek out the treatment. In other words, these subjects do the opposite of what they are assigned to do.

In the Angrist (1990a) study discussed above, for example, Defiers are subjects who would volunteer and be accepted for the military if they were not drafted but would refuse to serve if drafted. As this example suggests, the maintained assumption that there are no Defiers may be plausible in many contexts—but the possibility that it could be violated should always be considered. Notice that the no-Defier assumption is implicit in the model depicted in Figure 5.4.[46] Appendix 5.1 explains in further detail why the no-Defiers assumption is necessary.

5.3.4 Fuzzy regression-discontinuities as instrumental-variables designs

We can now return to our discussion of "fuzzy" regression-discontinuities in the previous section. Recall that in these designs, units' position relative to a key threshold value of a covariate only determines treatment receipt probabilistically, rather than deterministically. For instance, all subjects scoring below a given threshold on an entrance exam might be *invited* to join a

---

[45] The failure of this assumption can be seen as a failure of the "exclusion restriction," for here the instrumental variable—draft lottery number—may have a direct effect on outcomes, above and beyond its effect on military service.

[46] Imbens and Angrist (1994) define a related restriction called the *monotonicity* assumption: for each unit, the instrument only moves the probability of treatment receipt in one direction. This is analogous to the no-Defier condition.

remedial education program, but some might not choose to participate—while others scoring above the threshold might still seek out participation. However, those scoring just below the threshold may still be more likely to participate than those above the threshold—and assignment to the invitation to participate is plausibly as-if random in the neighborhood of the threshold. Thus, comparing average later outcomes for exam-takers located just above and below the key threshold validly estimates the causal effect of *invitation* to participate in the remedial education program, if not the effect of program participation itself. This is intention-to-treat analysis, which is valid in the regression-discontinuity context whether the key threshold determines treatment receipt deterministically or merely probabilistically.

However, just as in other settings, instrumental-variables analysis can be used to estimate the effect of treatment on Compliers. In this setting, Compliers are exam-takers who enter the remedial education program if invited to do so but otherwise do not. Because the invitation is issued as-if at random to exam-takers just below the key threshold—but not above it—assignment to the invitation should be a valid instrumental variable for program participation, as long as receiving an invitation does not have an independent impact on earnings, above and beyond its impact on participation.

An equation akin to Equation 5.1 in Section 5.3.1 (under "Estimating the average causal effect for Compliers") above will be the relevant instrumental-variables estimator in this case. Just as in Equation 5.1, the intention-to-treat estimator—the average outcome for test-takers just below the threshold, minus the average outcome for test-takers just above the threshold—will be divided by the "net crossover rate"—the proportion of exam takers located just below the threshold who elect to enter the program, minus the proportion of exam takers located just above the threshold who also elect to do so.

5.3.5 From the Complier average effect to linear regression

There is also a link from Equation 5.1 above to linear regression analysis. Analysts typically posit a regression model such as

$$Y_i = \alpha + \beta X_i + \varepsilon_i, \tag{5.2}$$

where Y_i is the response variable and ε_i is a random error term. The dichotomous variable X_i equals 1 when unit i receives the treatment, and otherwise equals 0. The parameter α is an intercept, while the parameter β describes the effect of treatment received. Here, X_i and ε_i are dependent—perhaps because unobserved factors that cause individual i to select into treatment status will also influence the outcome Y_i. Thus, the ordinary least squares (OLS) estimator for β will be biased and inconsistent.[47]

The solution is to find an instrument Z_i that is correlated with X_i but independent of ε_i. Treatment assignment—if it is randomized—will typically do the trick. The instrumental-variables least squares (IVLS) estimator for β in Equation 5.2 is usually written as

$$\hat{\beta}_{\text{IVLS}} = \frac{\text{Cov}(Z_i, Y_i)}{\text{Cov}(Z_i, X_i)}, \qquad (5.3)$$

where the covariances are taken over the sample data. Notice that Equation 5.3 is the slope coefficient from a regression of Y_i on Z_i—that is, $\frac{\text{Cov}(Z_i, Y_i)}{\text{Var}(Z_i)}$—divided by the slope coefficient of a regression of X_i on Z_i—that is, $\frac{\text{Cov}(Z_i, X_i)}{\text{Var}(Z_i)}$. Analysts sometimes refer to the regression of Y_i on Z_i as a "reduced form" regression: this is the intention-to-treat estimator.

Mechanically—at least in the bivariate regression model where X_i is dichotomous—the instrumental-variables least squares estimator in Equation 5.3 is equivalent to the estimator for the effect of treatment on Compliers in Equation 5.1, which is

$$\frac{Y^T - Y^C}{X^T - X^C}. \qquad (5.4)$$

Here, Y^T is the average outcome in the sample of units assigned to treatment, and Y^C is the average outcome in the sample of units assigned to control. In the denominator, X^T is the proportion of units assigned to treatment who receive treatment (that is, it is the mean of the 0–1 variable X_i among the assigned-to-treatment units), while X^C is the proportion of assigned-to-control units who receive treatment. The equivalence of the estimators, Equations 5.3 and 5.4, is simply a matter of algebra (see, e.g., Freedman 2006).

Yet, the model in Equation 5.2 is otherwise quite different from the Neyman model we have been considering so far. For instance, it posits that observed data are an additive function of treatment received and a random

---

[47] See an introduction to regression analysis such as Freedman (2009) for discussion.

error term. The effect of treatment received, β, is the same for every subject. The assumed statistical properties of the error term (considered in detail in the next chapter) usually do not follow from the design of a randomized natural experiment, and they are quite different from the Neyman urn model. With multiple levels of treatment or a continuous treatment variable, or the addition of covariates in Equation 5.2, the analogy to the Neyman model would break down further. I will return to these points in Chapter 9.

Several points might also be made in conclusion to this subsection. First, like other kinds of natural experiments, a central feature of successful instrumental-variables designs is random or as-if random assignment. After all, the random sampling of subject types and potential outcomes from the study group is what allows us to estimate parameters such as (A)–(D), defined in Section 5.3.1. Without random or as-if random sampling, the Neyman urn model does not apply, and estimators for the effect of treatment on Compliers in the model for natural-experimental crossover (Figure 5.4) break down.

Indeed, with many natural experiments, the sampling is not typically truly randomized, and this can raise important difficulties. Just as not all natural experiments are instrumental-variables designs, not all instrumental-variables analyses involve credible natural experiments—because the claim to as-if random assignment to the instrument is not very plausible. In applications, analysts often estimate multivariate instrumental-variables regression models, that is, linear models with controls. Yet, the more controls analysts feel they must add, the less valid is the instrument—and the natural experiment from which it comes—likely to be. After all, many included covariates are probably endogenous, that is, statistically dependent on the error term of the regression model (which violates a key assumption of the IVLS model). If the assignment is truly as-if random, then one instrumental variable should be sufficient—and control variables are not needed. Analysts should therefore be encouraged to present results from instrumental-variables regressions without control variables (Chapter 8).

Second, when we move beyond the simple extension to the Neyman model that considers natural-experimental crossover to linear regression models, many other assumptions come into play—and these may or may not be plausible (Chapter 9). Natural experiments often play a key role in generating instrumental variables. However, whether the ensuing analysis should be viewed as more design based or more model based depends on the techniques used to analyze the data. If multiple regression models are used, the assumptions behind the models are crucial, yet the assumptions may lack credibility—and they cannot be readily validated. Instrumental-variables analysis can therefore be positioned between the poles of design-based and model-based inference, depending on the application.

Finally, notice that instrumental-variables analysis estimates the causal effect of treatment assignment for a specific subset of experimental subjects, namely, Compliers. Since these are subjects who comply with assignment, this gives us the effect of treatment received for these units. However, this "local average treatment effect" may not in general be the same as the average causal effect of treatment (rather than treatment assignment) for all subjects in the experimental population. I return to this issue of generalizability later in the book (Chapter 10).

The difficulties and issues of interpretation associated with instrumental-variables analysis make intention-to-treat analysis the most robust way of analyzing the natural-experimental data. Instrumental-variables analysis has its place—since intention-to-treat analysis can make it difficult to discern why draft eligibility matters for future income, and it can lead to conservative estimates of the effect of treatment. Yet, analysts should usually present unadjusted difference-of-means estimators (or their analogue in studies with continuous instruments) as well, just as they should with standard natural experiments and regression-discontinuity designs.

5.4 Conclusion

The Neyman potential outcomes model often provides the right starting point for the quantitative analysis of natural-experimental data. It leads to natural definitions of interesting parameters, such as the average causal effect. And it defines estimators—such as the difference of means or difference of percentages—that are simple and transparent, and have the advantage of being built on a model of the data-generating process that is often credible for natural experiments. Thus, the difference of means is an important analytic tool, whether for standard natural experiments, regression-discontinuity designs, or instrumental-variables analysis.

Of course, if the natural experiment is not valid, simple techniques such as the difference of means may not provide the right tool. With weaker designs, analysts may seek to adjust the data to confront confounding. Yet successful adjustment is difficult to achieve, because it depends not only on identifying and measuring the relevant confounders but also on formulating a valid model of the data-generating process—that is, describing the way in which treatment assignment and confounders together determine response. This leads to many difficulties, as discussed later in the book (e.g., Chapter 9).

When confounding is obviated by the research design, however, analysts may sidestep such difficulties. At least in principle, this is a key advantage of design-based research. Again, whether natural experiments are more design based or more model based varies across studies. Yet, the potential of natural experiments to lead to credible and transparent causal inference is best realized on the more design-based end of the spectrum—a theme to which I will return later (e.g., Chapters 8–10).

The bottom line is that in strong natural experiments, the research design permits data analysis with weaker assumptions. When the design is strong, the analysis can be simple, transparent, and compelling. The techniques outlined in this chapter are most appropriate in that setting.

The discussion in this chapter has described parameters such as the average causal effect as well as estimators of those parameters, but it has largely ignored chance variability – for instance, how to think about the sampling processes that produce observed data and how to attach standard errors to estimators of causal effects. The next chapter turns to these topics.

Appendix 5.1 Instrumental-variables estimation of the Complier average causal effect

In this appendix, I derive in detail the instrumental-variables estimator for the average effect of treatment for Compliers that is presented in Section 5.3.1 (under "Estimating the average causal effect for Compliers"). As in Figure 5.4, there are three types of subjects in the natural-experimental study group: Always-Treats, Never-Treats, and Compliers. The average value of the potential outcomes under assignment to treatment, across all three types, is $\overline{T} = \frac{1}{N}\sum_{i=1}^{N} T_i$, where N is the size of the study group, while the average value of the control tickets is $\overline{C} = \frac{1}{N}\sum_{i=1}^{N} C_i$. The average causal effect—aka the intention-to-treat parameter—is defined as $\overline{T} - \overline{C}$.

However, the average effect for each of the three types may differ. For Always-Treats and Never-Treats, $T_i = C_i$: according to the model, their potential outcome under assignment to treatment is the same as their potential outcome under assignment to control. Thus, let A be the average response of Always-Treats under treatment and control, and let N be the average response of Never-Treats under both conditions. Note that $A - A = N - N = 0$: the average causal effect of treatment assignment, for both Always-Treats and Never-Treats, is zero. The proportion of Always-Treats, Never-Treats, and Compliers in the study group is denoted by α, γ, and β, respectively, with $\alpha + \gamma + \beta = 1$. These are parameters that describe the whole study group.

Now, let the average response of Compliers to treatment be T and the average response of Compliers to control be C. Note that these parameters do not appear with bars; they are distinct from $\bar{T}$ and $\bar{C}$, which are averages across all three subject types. Our goal is to estimate $T - C$, the average causal effect for Compliers. We sample tickets at random from the study group, as in Figure 5.4. Let Y^T be the average outcome in the assigned-to-treatment sample. Thus, the expected value of Y^T is

$$E(Y^T) = \alpha A + \gamma N + \beta T, \qquad (5.A1.1)$$

where E is the expectations operator. In other words, the expected value is a weighted average of the mean outcomes for each type of subject, where the weights are the proportions of each type in the natural-experimental study group. Equation 5.A1.1 is an expected value: if we drew an arbitrarily large number of samples from the study group and observed the average outcome under treatment assignment for each of these samples, the average of the Y^Ts across these samples would come arbitrarily close to $E(Y^T)$.[48] Of course, in any particular sample, Y^T will differ from $E(Y^T)$—because the actual fraction of Always-Treats, Never-Treats, and Compliers will differ from α, γ, and β, respectively.

We can define the expected value of the mean outcome in the assigned-to-control group, denoted Y^C, analogously:

$$E(Y^C) = \alpha A + \gamma N + \beta C. \qquad (5.A1.2)$$

Deriving an expression for $T - C$ therefore involves rearranging Equations 5.A1.1 and 5.A1.2. From Equation 5.A1.1, we have

---

[48] That is, the mean of the sampling distribution of the random variable Y^T is $E(Y^T)$.

$$T = \frac{E(Y^T) - \alpha A - \gamma N}{\beta}, \tag{5.A1.3}$$

and from Equation 5.A1.2,

$$C = \frac{E(Y^C) - \alpha A - \gamma N}{\beta}, \tag{5.A1.4}$$

Thus, we have

$$T - C = \frac{E(Y^T) - E(Y^C)}{\beta}, \tag{5.A1.5}$$

How should we estimate $T - C$? We first need unbiased estimators for $E(Y^T)$, $E(Y^C)$, and β. The first two are easy: the sample means $\overline{Y}^T$ and $\overline{Y}^C$ are unbiased estimators for the corresponding population (i.e., study group) averages, because the assigned-to-treatment and assigned-to-control groups are random samples from the study group. Notice that $E(Y^T) - E(Y^C) = \overline{T} - \overline{C}$; this is the intention-to-treat parameter. Thus, $\overline{Y}^T - \overline{Y}^C$ estimates this parameter.

What about an estimator for β, the fraction of Compliers in the whole study group? The proportion of people in the assigned-to-treatment group who accept treatment is approximately $\alpha + \beta$, because the mix of Always-Treats and Compliers in the sample—that is, the assigned-to-treatment group—will be about the same as the mix in the population—that is, the whole study group. The approximation gets better as the number of units in the sample gets bigger. Similarly, since those who cross over from control to treatment are Always-Treats, the proportion of people in the assigned-to-control group who receive the treatment will be approximately α.

This suggests a natural estimator for β. Let X^T be the fraction of people in the assigned-to-treatment group who accept treatment, and let X^C be the fraction of people in the assigned-to-control group who cross over into treatment. These are both random variables, because the exact mix of Always-Treats and Compliers will depend on the randomization and so will vary from sample to sample. Then, we have

$$E(X^T) = \alpha + \beta,$$

$$E(X^C) = \alpha$$

and
$$E(X^T - X^C) = \beta. \qquad (5.A1.6)$$
Thus, by Equation 5A.1.6, $X^T - X^C$ is an unbiased estimator for β.

To form an estimator for $T - C$, the average causal effect for Compliers, we should therefore replace the right-hand side of equation (5.A1.5) with the unbiased estimators for $E(Y^T)$, $E(Y^C)$, and β. Thus, the usual estimator for $T - C$ in (5.A1.5) is

$$\frac{Y^T - Y^C}{X^T - X^C}. \qquad (5.A1.7)$$

Equation 5.A1.7 is equivalent to the usual instrumental-variables estimator with a dichotomous treatment variable, with assignment to treatment as the instrumental variable (Freedman 2006).

The estimator in Equation 5.A1.7 is not unbiased, even though Y^T, Y^C, and $X^T - X^C$ are unbiased estimators for $E(Y^T)$, $E(Y^C)$, and β in (5.A1.5), respectively. This is due to ratio-estimator bias: we have random variables in both the numerator and the denominator of (5.A1.7). However, the estimator is consistent, that is,

$$\text{plim}\frac{Y^T - Y^C}{X^T - X^C} = \frac{\text{plim}(Y^T - Y^C)}{\text{plim}(X^T - X^C)} = \frac{\overline{T} - \overline{C}}{\beta} = T - C. \qquad (5.A1.8)$$

The first equality in Equation 5.A1.8 follows from the Slutsky theorem;[49] the second equality follows because $Y^T - Y^C$ and $X^T - X^C$ are consistent estimators for $\overline{T} - \overline{C}$ and β;[50] and the final equality follows from (5.A1.5) with $\overline{T} - \overline{C}$ substituted for $E(Y^T) - E(Y^C)$. Here, "plim" indicates the "probability limit." In sum, the instrumental-variables estimator in Equation 5.A1.7 suffers from *small-sample bias*, but it should provide a good approximation to $T - C$ in a large study. Further references on instrumental-variables estimation can be found in Imbens and Angrist (1994), and Angrist, Imbens, and Rubin (1996); the discussion above draws especially on Freedman (2006).

---

[49] The Slutsky theorem says that for a continuous function g that is not a function of N, plim $g(x_N)$ = g(plim x_N).

[50] Both estimators are unbiased. Moreover, the variances of Y^T-Y^C and X^T-X^C vanish as the treatment and control groups go to infinity in size. Thus, both estimators are consistent.

Appendix 5.2 Is the difference-of-means estimator biased in regression-discontinuity designs (further details)?

This appendix elaborates on several points made in the text about the appropriate causal estimand for the regression-discontinuity design, and about whether the simple difference of means is a biased estimator for that estimand. First, adapting the notation in Imbens and Lemieux (2007), let $\mu_1(x) = \lim_{z \uparrow x} E[C_i|X = z]$ and $\mu_\Gamma(x) = \lim_{z \downarrow x} E[T_i|X = z]$ be the limits from below and above of the regression function for potential outcomes under control and under treatment, respectively, at the point x. (The potential-outcomes regression function is simply the conditional expectation of potential outcomes given the level of the running covariate, as depicted in Figure 5.2.) Here, X is the running covariate (i.e., the forcing variable).

Imbens and Lemieux (2007) define the estimand of the (sharp) regression-discontinuity design as

$$\tau_{RD} = \mu_\Gamma(c) - \mu_1(c),$$

where c is the point of regression discontinuity, i.e., the value of the running covariate X that determines treatment assignment. Notice that the estimand is here defined at a single point—the point of the discontinuity. A rectangular kernel estimator for this parameter is

$$\hat{\tau}_{RD} = \frac{\sum_{i=1}^{N} Y_i \cdot 1\{c \leq X_i \leq c+h\}}{\sum_{i=1}^{N} 1\{c \leq X_i \leq c+h\}} - \frac{\sum_{i=1}^{N} Y_i \cdot 1\{c-h \leq X_i < c\}}{\sum_{i=1}^{N} 1\{c-h \leq X_i < c\}} = \overline{Y}_{h\Gamma} - \overline{Y}_{h1},$$

where $1\{\bullet\}$ is an indicator variable that takes the value 1 if the condition in the braces is satisfied and otherwise is zero. This estimator is just the simple difference of mean outcomes for units located within a bandwidth h above and below the regression-discontinuity threshold c.

Drawing on Hahn, Todd, and Van Der Klaauw (2001) and Porter (2003), Imbens and Lemieux (2007: 10) give an expression for asymptotic bias in this rectangular kernel estimator for this effect defined at the point of discontinuity:

$$p\lim[\hat{\mu}_r(c) - \hat{\mu}_1(c)] - [\mu_r(c) - \mu_1(c)] = \frac{h}{2}\left(\lim_{x \downarrow c}\frac{\partial}{\partial x}\mu(x) + \lim_{x \uparrow c}\frac{\partial}{\partial x}\mu(x)\right)$$
$$+ O(h^2),$$

where O is the order operator, and $\hat{\mu}_r(c) - \hat{\mu}_1(c) = \hat{\tau}_{RD}$ is the difference-of-means estimator. The core of their objection to the rectangular kernel—that is, to the simple difference-of-means estimator, which they refer to as "not very attractive"—is the linear bias in h due to non-zero derivatives of the potential-outcomes regression functions at the point of discontinuity. As noted in the text, Imbens and Lemieux (2007: 10) suggest that "we typically do expect the regression function to have a non-zero derivative, even in cases where the treatment has no effect. In many applications the eligibility criterion is based on a covariate that does have some correlation with the outcome, so that, for example, those with poorest prospects in the absence of the program are in the eligible group."

However, this statement appears to confuse the slope of a regression of actual outcomes on the running covariate across a wide range of values of X—which is not a causal quantity—with the derivative of the *potential*-outcomes regression functions on either side of the regression discontinuity. Why should units eligible for a program on the basis of having a qualification score that is, say, just above the regression-discontinuity threshold respond systematically differently to treatment than those just below the threshold? Again, if the conditional expectation of the potential outcomes under treatment (or control) on either side of the regression discontinuity is much different, for units included in the study group, the natural experiment has failed—for it has not in fact generated as-if random assignment to treatment conditions. In this case, the assigned-to-control group is not a valid counterfactual for the assigned-to-treatment group.

If, on the other hand, the natural experiment is successful—in that it generates groups just on either side of the regression-discontinuity threshold that are valid counterfactuals for one another—then the graph of the conditional expectations of the potential outcomes should look like those in Figure 5.3 at the key discontinuity. That is, the slopes of the two potential-outcomes regression functions should be approximately flat in the neighborhood of the threshold. Notice that the linear bias in h disappears if average potential outcomes are the same on either side the discontinuity. Then, the core of Imbens and Lemieux's (2007) objection to the difference-of-means estimator disappears.

Whereas the previous point concerned the estimator $\hat{\tau}_{RD}$, a second point to make here concerns the estimand τ_{RD}. It may be misleading to suggest that we are interested in the potential-outcome regression function only at the single point of discontinuity, as in the definition of the parameter τ_{RD}. While this is technically a valid way of thinking about the estimand of a regression-discontinuity design—and while smoothness of potential outcomes at the regression-discontinuity threshold may be sufficient in principle to identify this effect—this definition of the causal parameter does not lead to best practice in applications, nor does it allow us to take advantage of strong natural-experimental designs in which as-if random holds in the neighborhood of the threshold. It is instead more helpful to think about the estimand as the average causal effect for those units in the neighborhood of the threshold. Thus, if the Neyman urn model applies, we should instead be interested in comparing the conditional expectations of the potential outcomes $\mu(x|x \in [c, c+h])$ and $\mu(x|x \in [c-h, c])$, where c is the regression-discontinuity threshold and h is the bandwidth—which is chosen so that we are willing to posit as-if randomization for units with $x \in [c-h, c+h]$. Under Neyman's urn model, it is precisely these conditional expectations that estimate the average causal effect for the regression-discontinuity study group.

Of course, this discussion leaves aside the crucial questions of how to choose the bandwidth h and how to validate at least partially the assumption of as-if randomization—which I take up elsewhere. Given valid choices in this regard, however, the difference of means is an unbiased estimator for the most relevant causal quantity in the regression-discontinuity design.

Exercises

5.1) As discussed in Chapter 4, Iyer (2010) compares contemporary public goods provision in certain districts in India that were ruled directly by the British during the colonial period with districts where the British ruled indirectly, through native states. Districts in which the native ruler lacked a natural heir "lapsed" and were annexed by the British: Lord Dalhousie, Governor-General of India from 1848 to 1856, announced that

> On all occasions where heirs natural shall fail, the territory should be made to lapse and adoption should not be permitted, excepting in those cases in which some strong political reason may render it expedient to depart from this general rule.

Iyer argues that if the death of a natural heir is as-if random, this creates an instrumental variable for direct colonial rule.

(a) How plausible is the assumption of as-if random in this natural experiment? What are some methods you might use to evaluate its plausibility empirically?
(b) In this context, what are Compliers, Always-Treats, Never-Treats, and Defiers? How plausible is the assumption of no Defiers here? List other assumptions that must be satisfied for valid use of instrumental variables.

5.2) In the 1960s, the Health Insurance Plan of Greater New York clinical trial studied the effects of screening for breast cancer. Researchers invited about 31,000 women between the ages of 40 and 64 for annual clinical visits and mammographies, which are X-rays designed to detect breast cancer. About 20,200 women or two-thirds of these women accepted the invitation to be screened, while one-third refused. In the control group, 31,000 women received the status quo health care. (None of them received mammographies of their own initiative; screening for breast cancer was rare in the 1960s.) Among the 62,000 women in the study group, the invitation for screening was issued at random. Table 5.E2, adapted from Freedman (2009: 4–5, 15), shows numbers of deaths and death rates from breast cancer five years after the start of the trial. It also shows deaths from other causes, among women in the treatment group who accepted the invitation for screening and those who

Table 5.E2 Deaths from breast cancer and other causes (Health Insurance Plan of Greater New York study)

	Group size	Deaths from breast cancer	Death rate per 1,000 women	Deaths from other causes	Death rate from other causes, per 1,000 women
Assigned to treatment					
Accepted screening	20,200	23	1.14	428	21.19
Refused screening	10,800	16	1.48	409	37.87
Total	31,000	39	1.26	837	27.00
Assigned to control					
Would have accepted screening	—	—	—		
Would have refused screening	—	—	—		
Total	31,000	63	2.03	879	28.35

refused. (In the treatment group, these two types of women can be distinguished. Why?)

Now answer the following questions:

(a) Is this a natural experiment?

(b) It might seem natural to compare women who were screened with women who were not screened. Why, in general, is this a bad idea? Is there any specific evidence in the table that suggests this is in fact a bad idea?

(c) What is intention-to-treat analysis in this context? Calculate the intention-to-treat estimate. What is a potential limitation of intention-to-treat analysis?

(d) In this study, is there "single crossover" or "double crossover"? Explain the difference.

(e) In the first column of the table, the number of women who would have accepted screening and the number who would have refused, among women who were assigned to the control group, is unobserved (as indicated by the "__"). Why are these quantities unobserved? Find an unbiased estimate for each of these quantities and fill in the corresponding cells of the table with these estimates. What is the rationale for your estimates (i.e., why are they unbiased)?

(f) What is the proportion of Always-Treats, Never-Treats, and Compliers in the study group?

(g) What is the death rate among Compliers in the assigned-to-treatment group? (The death rate per 1,000 women is simply the number of deaths divided by the group size, times 1,000.)

(h) Now, estimate the death rate among Compliers and Never-Treats in the control group. To do this:
- First, estimate the number of Never-Treats in the control group who died from breast cancer. Why is this quantity unobserved? What is the rationale for your estimate?
- Now, use this information to estimate numbers of deaths from breast cancer among Compliers in the control group, and use these numbers to estimate the death rates per 1,000 women among Compliers and Never-Treats in the control group.

(i) Estimate the effect of treatment on Compliers in terms of death rates, using the information in (h).

(j) Formulate the instrumental-variables estimator in Equation 5.1 in Section 5.3.1 (under "Estimating the average causal effect for Compliers"), using several of the quantities you derived above. Show that this is identical to your answer in (i). Why are these equivalent?

(k) Bonus question: Note that the death rate from breast cancer among Compliers in the assigned-to-control group is higher than the death rate among Never-Treats. Why might this be so? (Hint: Child-bearing is protective against breast cancer. What do the final two columns suggest about Compliers, and how might their characteristics be related to fertility behavior?)

5.3) *Effect of treatment on Compliers.* Work exercise 21 in the discussion questions in Freedman (2009: chapter 4) and then look at the data in the "answers to exercises" section on p. 252 of Freedman (2009).

(a) Which subjects are the "Always-Treats" in the assigned-to-control group? Which subjects are the "Never-Treats" in the assigned-to-treatment group?

(b) Estimate the effect of treatment on Compliers. (Show your work.) Compare your results to the intention-to-treat analysis.

(c) If intention-to-treat analysis shows zero effect of treatment assignment, can the estimated effect of treatment on Compliers be non-zero? Why or why not?

5.4) Download the replication data set for Green et al. (2009). (Data and replication code are available through the data archive at the Institution for Social and Policy Studies at Yale University, http://isps.research.yale.edu/, though only R code is available for the program files [R Development Core Team 2008]. A Stata [StataCorp 2009] routine for the Imbens and Kalyanaraman [2009] bandwidth selection technique used by Green et al. [2009] is available at www.economics.harvard.edu/faculty/imbens/software_imbens.)

(a) Replicate the various results reported in Green et al., including the cross-validation procedure.

(b) Conduct a conditional density test at the regression-discontinuity threshold, of the sort proposed by McCrary (2007).

(c) Compare estimates from simple difference-of-means tests to the experimental benchmarks, using bandwidths suggested in the article. For which bandwidths does the difference-in-means estimator most successfully recover the experimental benchmarks?

How do the difference-of-means estimates compare to results from polynomial regressions?

5.5) As noted in Appendix 5.1, the instrumental-variables estimator suffers from ratio-estimator bias: the numerator and the denominator of Equation 5.A1.7 are both random variables. Why is the numerator a random variable? Why is the denominator a random variable?

6 Sampling processes and standard errors

The previous chapter introduced the Neyman causal model and described that model as a sensible starting point for many natural experiments. Parameters such as the average causal effect are defined in terms of this causal model. Yet, estimators of those parameters, such as the observed difference of means in treatment and control groups, also depend on the model of the chance—i.e., stochastic—process that gives rise to observed data. The Neyman urn model is one such model: it says that units are sampled at random from the study group and placed into treatment and control groups.

Because this sampling process is stochastic, estimators such as the difference of means will vary across different realizations of the data-generating process. Suppose Nature could run a given natural experiment over and over again, drawing units at random from an urn and assigning them to the treatment and control group. The data would likely turn out somewhat differently each time, due to chance error. Some units that went into the treatment group in one realization of the natural experiment would go the second time into control, and vice versa. Thus, the observed difference of means would differ across each hypothetical replication of the natural experiment. The spread or distribution of all the hypothetical differences of means is called the sampling distribution of the difference of means. A natural measure of the size of this spread is the standard deviation of this sampling distribution—the *standard error*. The standard error tells us how much the observed difference of means is likely to vary from the mean of the sampling distribution of the estimator, in any given replication.

Of course, Nature rarely cooperates by generating the same natural experiment twice. (Whether it is even reasonable to think of a given natural experiment in terms of such hypothetical stochastic replications is considered below.) We only observe the data at hand: the result of one realization of the data-generating process. If the model for the data-generating process is correct, however, statistical theory tells us how to use the data from one realization of a natural experiment to estimate parameters of the sampling distribution—such as the standard error. It turns out that under the Neyman model, a simple and transparent formula for the standard error is very often the right one to use. This means that not only is the appropriate estimator for the average causal effect often very simple—it is just a difference of means—so, too, is the estimator of the standard error. This chapter describes how to estimate the standard errors of the difference-of-means estimator, in terms of the Neyman model.

The chapter also discusses several additional topics that are especially important in many natural experiments. Many common natural-experimental designs feature clustered randomization, which occurs when groups of units, rather than the individual units themselves, are assigned to treatment and control groups. The Neyman model must then be adapted to this setting of clustered randomization. Assuming individual-level randomization when units have been assigned to clusters can lead to very misleading statistical inferences, as this chapter will show.

Finally, the chapter also considers hypothesis testing. When the natural experiment is large, with many units in the study group, standard techniques such as *t*-tests or *z*-tests are usually appropriate. When the study group is small, other techniques may be useful: for instance, Fisher's exact test (also called a randomization test, that is, the use of randomization inference) is a particularly powerful approach. This approach allows us to trace out the sampling distribution of the difference-of-means estimator exactly, without recourse to parametric assumptions about the distribution of potential outcomes, and to calculate *p*-values with reference to that distribution. However, this test is conducted under the strict null hypothesis of no unit-level effects, which may or may not be the most relevant null hypothesis depending on the natural-experimental application.

6.1 Standard errors under the Neyman urn model

As we saw in the previous chapter, the idea of sampling potential outcomes at random from an urn is central to the Neyman model (see Figure 5.1). Randomization or as-if randomization plays a key role in the model, for two reasons. First, it secures the claim that the group of units assigned to treatment is identical to the group of units assigned to control, up to random error and save for the presence or absence of the treatment. The importance of this definitional feature of natural experiments cannot be overstated. For example, this is what justifies the claim that the difference of average outcomes in the treatment and control groups is an unbiased estimator for the average causal effect. Thus, the value of the simple and transparent quantitative analysis of natural-experimental data depends on the veracity of this analogy to sampling potential outcomes at random from an urn.

Second, however, and more directly relevant to the questions considered in this chapter, *p*-values and test statistics can only legitimately be given their conventional interpretation because of the presence of a stochastic (chance) process—or something that is closely akin to a stochastic process. As Fisher ([1935] 1951: 19–21) put this point,

> The element in the experimental procedure which contains the essential safeguard is that . . . [the treatment and control conditions are administered] "in random order." This is in fact the only point in the experimental procedure in which the laws of chance, which are to be in exclusive control of our frequency distribution, have been explicitly introduced . . . it may be said that the simple precaution of randomisation will suffice to guarantee the validity of the test of significance, by which the result of the experiment is to be judged.[1]

The chance process that governs treatment assignment therefore allows for statistical inference—and without such a chance process, statistical inference does not make sense.

This raises an initial question, which must be addressed before one asks how to evaluate whether effects are due to chance. That question is: what do we mean by "chance" in natural experiments? In many natural experiments—barring those involving lotteries or other true randomizing devices—there is no true stochastic or chance process that determines treatment assignment. Because of this, analysts must take care to specify the precise way in which treatment assignment is *like* a lottery. Researchers should consider the question: what is the way in which the laws of chance—and thus the various procedures for statistical inference—enter into the data-generating process? The use of metaphors like as-if random assignment has risks, when there is in fact no real random procedure such as a lottery assigning units to treatment and control. The further the true assignment process is from a lottery, the less the validity of standard errors and tests of significance will be guaranteed.

---

[1] This discussion is presented in connection with the famous Lady Tasting Tea experiment (Fisher [1935] 1951).

There are also other important questions for practice. How should standard errors—that is, our estimates of uncertainty in the causal effect estimators—be calculated? And, how should hypothesis tests—for instance, tests of the null hypothesis that there is no average effect of treatment assignment—be conducted? Here, too, natural experiments offer simple and transparent options, with readily defensible interpretations.

Recall that in a natural experiment, the treatment group is viewed as a random (or as good as random) sample of the tickets in the box in Figure 5.1. Thus, the mean outcome in the treatment group is an unbiased estimator for the average potential outcomes under treatment—that is, the average of the treatment values for each ticket in the box. Similarly, the mean outcome in the control group is an unbiased estimator for the average potential outcomes under control. Thus, the difference in mean outcomes across the treatment and control samples is an *estimator* of the average causal effect—the idea being that things could have turned out differently under different (as-if) randomizations.

To estimate the role of sampling variability in producing the particular difference of means—that is, the estimated causal effect—that turned up in the data, the analyst therefore needs to attach a standard error to the difference. Recall that the mean of a random sample is itself a random variable: due to the luck of the draw, it will take on a particular value in one sample, while in a different sample it will take on some other value. The variance of the probability distribution of the mean is also known as the sampling variance of the mean; the sampling variance depends on the variance of the population from which the sample is drawn (that is, the variance of the numbers in the box of tickets) as well as the number of units in the sample. To estimate the sampling variance from a single sample, we can again appeal to statistical principle:

The sampling variance of the mean of an independent random sample is estimated by the variance of the sample, divided by the number of sampled units.

According to the Neyman model, the mean of the treatment group is the mean of a random sample of the treatment tickets in the box in Figure 5.1.[2] So the sampling variance of this mean is estimated by the empirical variance in the

---

[2] It is not, however, a simple random sample: we are sampling without replacement, so the probability distribution of each draw depends on previous draws. Why it is nonetheless valid to use the formula in the text is discussed below, and in Appendix 6.1.

treatment sample, divided by the number of units assigned to treatment. Similarly, the sampling variance of the mean of the control group is estimated by the variance of the control sample, divided by the number of units assigned to control.[3]

Thus, we have ready estimators of the sampling variance of the mean of the treatment and control groups. But what is the appropriate estimator of the variance of the difference of means—that is, the variance of our estimator of the average causal effect? Here, too, we can appeal to a final statistical principle: for the difference of means of two independent samples,

The variance of the difference of means is the sum of the sampling variances.

How, then, should the standard error for the average causal effect be calculated? First, the analysts should estimate the sampling variance of the treatment and control means using the usual formula: the empirical variance of the treatment or control sample, divided by the number of units assigned to treatment or control. (In taking the variance of the treatment or control samples, the sum of squared deviations from the mean should be divided by the number of units in the sample, minus one; see Box 6.1.) Next, the variances should be combined as if the treatment and control means were independent: the variance of the difference is the sum of the differences. Finally, recall that the standard error of an estimator is the square root of its variance. Thus, for the difference of treatment and control means—that is, the estimated average causal effect—we have the following:

The standard error is the square root of the sum of the variances.

In sum, to estimate the standard error, analysts should (i) compute the standard errors for the treatment and control group means as if the draws were made with replacement, and then (ii) combine the standard errors as if the samples were independent (Freedman, Pisani, and Purves 2007: 510). Box 6.1 presents this estimator formally.

---

[3] In calculating the empirical variance of the treatment or control samples, the sum of squared deviations from the mean should be divided by the number of units in each group, minus one. We subtract one from the number of units in the denominator because the sum of squared deviations is calculated in relation to the sample mean, rather than the true mean. With this degrees-of-freedom correction, the sample variance of observed outcomes is an unbiased estimator for the population variance of potential outcomes.

Box 6.1 Standard errors under the Neyman model

Let $\sigma^2 = \frac{1}{N}\sum_{i=1}^{N}(T_i - \overline{T})^2$ be the variance of the potential outcomes under treatment, for all the units in the study group, and $\delta^2 = \frac{1}{N}\sum_{i=1}^{N}(C_i - \overline{C})^2$ be the variance of the potential outcomes under control. A random subset of size n is assigned to the treatment group; without loss of generality, these units are indexed by $i = 1, \ldots, n$, while the remaining $m = N - n$ units are assigned to the control group. The mean outcome in the assigned to treatment group is denoted Y^T, while the mean outcome in the control group is Y^C. These are both estimators, with Y^T estimating $\overline{T}$ and Y^C estimating $\overline{C}$.

What is the estimated variance of these estimators? The sampling variance of the random variable Y^T is estimated by $\frac{\hat{\sigma}^2}{n}$, where $\hat{\sigma}^2 = \frac{1}{n-1}\sum_{i=1}^{n}(T_i - Y^T)^2$ is the empirical variance of the treatment sample and T_i is the observed outcome for units assigned to the treatment group. The sampling variance of the random variable Y^C is estimated by $\frac{\hat{\delta}^2}{m}$, where $\hat{\delta}^2 = \frac{1}{m-1}\sum_{i=n+1}^{N}(C_i - Y^C)^2$ is the empirical variance of the control sample. (These formulas hold under sampling with replacement; the reason for not using a finite population correction factor, even though we are sampling without replacement from the natural-experimental study group, is discussed in the text and Appendix 6.1.) In the formulas for $\hat{\sigma}^2$ and $\hat{\delta}^2$, we divide by $n - 1$ and $m - 1$ rather than n and m because the formulas use sample means, rather than the true average potential outcomes under treatment and control for the whole study group, which only leaves $n - 1$ and $m - 1$ degrees of freedom for the observed T_i s and C_i s in the treatment and control groups, respectively. With these adjustments, $\hat{\sigma}^2$ and $\hat{\delta}^2$ are unbiased estimators for σ^2 and δ^2.

The standard errors for each mean are then simply the square roots of these variances. And because the variance of the difference of means is very nearly the sum of the sampling variances (see Appendix 6.1), a conservative estimator for the standard error of the difference of means is simply

$$\widehat{SE} = \sqrt{\frac{\hat{\sigma}^2}{n} + \frac{\hat{\delta}^2}{m}}.$$

That is, the standard error for the difference of means is just the square root of the "sum of the variances": that is, the sum of the estimated sampling variance of the sample means. This formula for the standard error of the difference of means is used by standard statistical packages, for instance, by commands for t-tests where the variances in the two groups are allowed to differ (an example is found in Box 6.2).

Some readers will note a subtlety here: according to the Neyman model, we are not drawing independent samples. Indeed, there is dependence between the treatment and control groups: if one unit with large potential outcomes under treatment and control goes into the treatment group, it cannot go into control, so the means of both the treatment and control samples are affected by the assignment to treatment.[4] It is nonetheless generally valid to use variance calculations derived under the assumption of independent sampling (Freedman, Pisani, and Purves 2007: 508–11).

The reason, in brief, is that we are also drawing tickets from the box in Figure 5.1 at random without replacement—that is, we are not replacing the tickets into the box after each draw.[5] While the first feature (dependence between the treatment and control groups) tends to inflate the standard errors, the second feature cuts them down.[6] It turns out, as shown in Appendix 6.1, that these features just about balance each other out (Freedman, Pisani, and Purves 2007: A32–A34, n. 11). Assuming independent sampling typically leads to standard errors that are if anything a little conservative (that is, slightly too big), but that's a good thing if we want to be cautious about our causal claims. Thus, we can treat the treatment and control samples as independent for purposes of calculating standard errors.

The final topic to discuss here is hypothesis testing. To assess the presence or absence of an average causal effect, we need to answer the following question: could the difference between the treatment and control groups reasonably have arisen by chance? For moderately large experiments, due to the central limit theorem, the sampling distribution of the mean in the treatment and control groups will be nearly normally distributed, even if the potential outcomes are very non-normal; the approximation gets better as the number of units in treatment and control increases.[7] The normal approximation typically kicks

---

[4] In general, potential outcomes under treatment should be positively correlated with potential outcomes under control, across all subjects. For instance, in a get-out-the-vote experiment, unit i might be very likely to vote absent a get-out-the-vote message and slightly more likely to vote when given a get-out-the-vote message, while unit j may be very unlikely to vote, absent a get-out-the-vote message, and slightly less unlikely to vote when given a get-out-the-vote message. If many units with large potential outcomes are assigned to treatment, then fewer are left for the control group. Thus, we should expect the sample averages Y^T and Y^C to be *negatively* correlated. The dependence is obviously more severe in small samples.

[5] This implies that the draws are not independently and identically distributed (i.i.d.)—the first ticket drawn shapes the probability distribution of the second ticket, and so forth.

[6] That is, the estimated standard errors are bigger than the true standard errors, when drawing without replacement, if we don't use a correction factor. This is because when we draw without replacement, the box gets a bit smaller as we go, which reduces variability. On the other hand, if we don't account for dependence, the estimated standard error for the difference of means is smaller than the true standard error.

[7] The relevant central limit theorem is for sampling without replacement; see, e.g., Hájek (1960) or Höglund (1978).

in fairly rapidly, so use of the normal curve may be appropriate even for treatment or control groups of just 25 or 50 units each.[8]

Researchers often use *t*-tests instead of *z*-tests. The difference between the two is not important in a moderately large experiment, since Student's *t*-distribution converges to the normal distribution as the sample size grows. In small experiments, however, the assumption that potential outcomes are normally distributed—as required for the *t*-test—has more bite and may be problematic. In this case, randomization tests such as Fisher's ([1935] 1951) exact test (discussed below) may be useful. In larger experiments, however, results using Fisher's exact test will be virtually identical to those relying on normal approximations.[9]

In sum, analysts of strong natural experiments—in which the claim of as-if random is highly plausible—have simple and transparent options available for data analysis. In a moderately large natural experiment, and the simplest case in which there is one treatment condition and one control condition, there are four main steps involved:

(1) Calculate the average (or percentage) outcome in both the treatment and control groups.
(2) Find the difference between the two averages. This difference estimates the average causal effect.
(3) Attach a standard error to the difference: this is the square root of the sum of the estimated sampling variances of the two averages (Box 6.1).
(4) Conduct a hypothesis test using a *z*- or *t*-test. It is best to specify unequal variances in the treatment and control groups, especially when these groups are different sizes.

In small experiments, the hypothesis testing in step (4) might instead be conducted using Fisher's exact test, rather than a *z*- or *t*-test; this is discussed in more detail below.

This simple calculation can be contrasted with standard regression models. The difference-of-means test described above is *not* equivalent to a bivariate regression of the outcome on an intercept and a dummy variable for treatment assignment: for instance, if the Neyman model is assumed, the usual standard errors produced by regression analysis do not apply.[10] The situation is even

---

[8] For simulations, see e.g., Freedman, Pisani, and Purves (2007).
[9] That is to say, the permutation distributions also converge to the normal curve, due to the central limit theorems.
[10] See Exercise 6.6; also Chapter 9. For instance, the Neyman-based estimators adjust naturally for unequal sampling variances of the treatment and control group means; this may arise either because the treatment and control groups are unequal sizes or because the potential outcomes have greater variance

less satisfactory with multiple regression, when covariates are added to the regression model.[11]

In sum, the Neyman model justifies a simple procedure for estimating average causal effects by subtraction—the difference of mean outcomes in treatment and control. The variance of this difference can be estimated as the sum of the variances of the means, appealing to a well-defined and credible statistical model. Finally, hypothesis testing rests on well-known statistical principles—such as the central limit theorem—or else can be done using exact p-values in smaller natural experiments. The Neyman model can therefore motivate quantitative analysis of natural experiments that is simple, transparent, and highly credible.

6.1.1 Standard errors in regression-discontinuity and instrumental-variables designs

This discussion carries through to the case of regression-discontinuity designs. As discussed in the previous chapter, once an analyst has defined a "bandwidth" around the regression-discontinuity threshold for which he or she is willing to assume that assignment to treatment is as good as random, the Neyman urn model is likely to apply. The units in the regression-discontinuity study group are those located above or below the threshold, within this bandwidth. The average causal effect for these units is estimated as the average outcome in the assigned-to-treatment group, minus the average outcome in the assigned-to-control group. The variance of this estimator may be conservatively estimated as the estimated sampling variance of the treatment group mean, plus the estimated sampling variance of the control group mean. The square root of this sum is the standard error. Finally, hypothesis testing can proceed by dividing the mean difference by its standard error and referring this ratio to the standard normal or t-distributions. Fisher's exact test is again an alternative that may be useful when the number of units near the threshold is small.

Other analysts have not been as sanguine about such estimators of the variance for the difference-of-means and associated hypothesis tests. For instance, Thistlethwaite and Campbell (1960: 314) suggest that a t-test for

---

under treatment or control (for instance, if there is treatment effect heterogeneity, the potential outcomes under treatment may have greater variance). Adjustments for heteroskedasticity in the treatment and control groups can recover the Neyman-based estimators, in the bivariate regression case (see inter alia Samii and Aronow 2012). The relevance of these points of convergence seems limited, as there are also many other sources of error if the regression model doesn't describe the true data-generating process.

[11] As I discuss below, the treatment effect estimator then exhibits moderate bias, particularly in small experiments; variance may be smaller or greater after adjustment; and the standard errors again do not apply (Freedman 2008a, 2008b; D. Green 2009).

difference of means, for points directly on either side of a regression discontinuity, is "ruled out on the consideration that even if significant in itself, it is uninterpretable if a part of a very jagged line in which jumps of equal significance occur at numerous other places where *not* expected." Yet, this seems to misstate the role of chance variation. If assignment is truly as good as random at the regression-discontinuity threshold, we still expect significant discontinuities—that is, significant differences in means on either side of the threshold—to arise in 1 out of 20 assignments. As far as the variance is concerned, what happens at other thresholds (those where jumps are *not* expected) is not relevant for significance testing at the threshold.[12] The bottom line is that in the study group defined by its location near the key regression-discontinuity threshold, the Neyman urn model should apply; if it does not, then the status of the natural experiment itself may be called into question. And if the model applies, then the simple formulas for the variance of causal-effect estimators should apply.

For instrumental-variables analysis, including "fuzzy" regression-discontinuity designs in which treatment receipt is not a deterministic function of treatment assignment, things are somewhat more complicated.[13] As noted in the previous chapter, when there are two treatment conditions (e.g., one treatment group and one control group), and the instrumental variable is also dichotomous, the instrumental-variables estimator is a ratio, with the intention-to-treat estimator (i.e., the difference of means) in the numerator and the net crossover rate (the proportion of the assigned-to-treatment group that receives treatment, minus the proportion of the assigned-to-control group that receives treatment) in the denominator (see Section 5.3.1, under "Estimating the average causal effect for Compliers"). Thus, this estimator is the ratio of two random variables: the intention-to-treat estimator in the numerator depends on the realization of the treatment-assignment vectors, and the proportion of Compliers, Always-Treats, and Never-Treats in the treatment and control groups—which defines the estimator in the denominator—is also a random variable. This not only leads to small-sample bias in the estimation of the effect of treatment on Compliers (Appendix 5.1)—recall that the instrumental-variables estimator is consistent but biased—it also

---

[12] However, so-called "placebo" tests—discussed in Chapter 8—involve estimating causal effects at thresholds other than the key threshold, and these have a different and very useful role in some regression-discontinuity designs.

[13] For fuzzy regression-discontinuity designs as well as other instrumental-variables designs, the simple variance estimator for the difference of means is still relevant: the difference of means estimates the intention-to-treat parameter, and intention-to-treat analysis is important to conduct in instrumental-variables and fuzzy regression-discontinuity designs.

creates complications for estimating the variance of the estimator. Some standard statistical packages use the delta method, which employs a linear approximation (based on a Taylor-series expansion) to estimate nonlinear statistics such as the ratio of two variances. Bootstrapping and other methods may also be useful here; discussion of those methods goes beyond the scope of this chapter.[14] In practice, analysts often report the standard errors from an instrumental-variables regression of the outcome on treatment receipt, with treatment assignment as an instrumental variable.[15]

6.2 Handling clustered randomization

In the simplest version of the Neyman model, individual tickets are sampled at random from a box and placed into the treatment or control groups (Figure 5.1). For each ticket, we observe the potential outcome under treatment or the potential outcome under control, according to the treatment assignment of the unit that ticket represents. For many natural experiments, such as the Argentina land-titling study or John Snow's studies of cholera transmission, this model may be a credible depiction of the data-generating process.[16]

In other natural experiments involving assignment to treatment in *clusters*, however, this model may be quite misleading. Consider, for instance, natural experiments that exploit jurisdictional borders, such as Posner's (2004) study of Zambia and Malawi (see Chapter 2). Posner's study explores the interethnic attitudes of individuals living in communities on each side of the border between these countries; the goal is to assess the effects of location on one side or the other of the border (and, thus, exposure to disparate political institutions and practices) on individual political preferences, for instance, willingness to vote for a candidate from a different tribe.[17] Notice that here, all units on one side of the border are exposed to the same electoral rules and other institutions: the natural-experimental treatment is assigned to clusters of individuals who all receive the same treatment. This kind of clustered assignment also occurs in many such studies using jurisdictional boundaries—such as Miguel's (2004)

---

[14] Angrist and Pischke (2008) and Freedman (2009) both provide introductions to such techniques, as well as suggestions for further reading.
[15] The syntax in Stata 11 is *ivregress outcome (treatment_receipt=treatment_assignment)*, where *outcome* is the response variable, *treatment_receipt* is the endogenous independent variable, and *treatment_assignment* is the instrument (StataCorp 2009).
[16] However, potential threats to the standard Neyman model in these settings—such as possible SUTVA violations—are discussed below and in Chapters 7 and 9.
[17] In Posner's (2004) case, the hypothesis concerns the effects of relative group size and resulting patterns of electoral competition on intergroup ethnic relations.

study of Kenya and Tanzania, which assesses the effects of nation-building strategies common to all units on either side of the border, or Card and Krueger's (1994) study of the effects of state-level minimum-wage laws on employment in fast-food restaurants located on either side of the border between New Jersey and Pennsylvania. In other natural experiments, clustering may arise due to investigators' choices about data-collection strategies. For instance, treatment may be assigned at the level of villages, municipalities, states, or other aggregate units but outcomes are measured for multiple individuals within each cluster—perhaps for reasons of minimizing cost.[18] In sum, clustered randomization or as-if randomization fairly frequently arises in natural experiments, which are, after all, defined by the inability of the researcher to plan and implement the randomization.[19]

The problem is that analyzing the data as if the units had been individually randomized to treatment and control, rather than randomized as groups, can be seriously misleading. As Cornfield (1978: 101–2) puts it in a discussion of the epidemiological literature, "randomization by cluster accompanied by an analysis appropriate to randomization by individual is an exercise in self-deception ... and should be discouraged." In cluster-randomized studies, the unit of randomization is different from the unit of analysis. Rather than being individually "sampled" into the treatment or control groups, entire groups of units are assigned en masse to treatment or control. Yet, we are often interested in outcomes at the individual/unit level.

In the context of clustered as-if randomization, a better model than Figure 5.1 is one in which there are many *groups* of individual tickets—one for each cluster, as in Figure 6.1. Tickets will be sampled at random from each box, as before. Here, however, tickets are sampled in bunches—clusters—and all tickets in a single cluster are sent to either treatment or control. For instance, in Figure 6.1, there are K clusters in the natural-experimental study group; A of these clusters will be sampled at random for the treatment group, while $B = K - A$ clusters will go into the control group. Potential outcomes under treatment are observed for all units in a cluster that is assigned to treatment; potential outcomes under control are observed for all units in a cluster that is assigned to the control group.

---

[18] In Dunning's (2010b) natural-experimental study of caste-based quotas in India, the residents of each council constituency were exposed to the same electoral institution—that is, the presence or absence of a quota for a lower-caste village council president. By interviewing 10 residents in each village assigned to treatment or control, survey costs were substantially reduced, as villages were scattered throughout six far-flung districts in the Indian state of Karnataka (see also Dunning and Nilekani 2010).

[19] See also Card and Lee (2007) for discussion of regression-discontinuity designs.

Sampling processes and standard errors

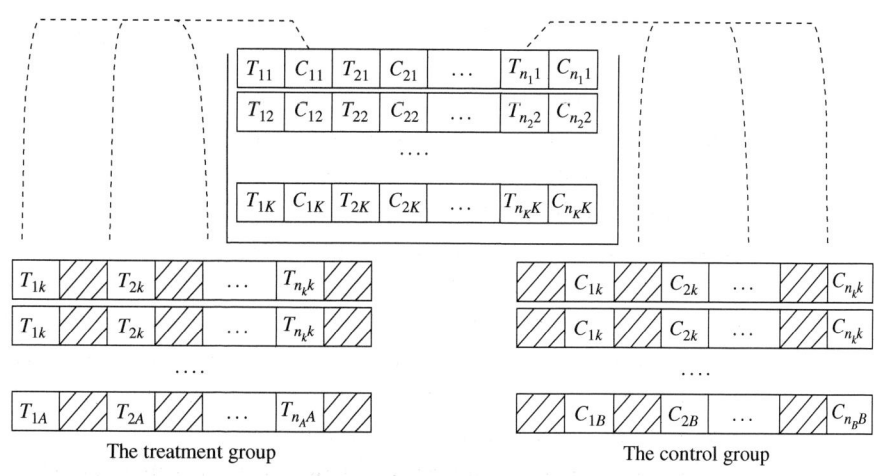

Figure 6.1 Clustered randomization under the Neyman model

The figure depicts clustered randomization as a box model. Here, there are K clusters of tickets—each with n_k individual units—in the natural-experimental study group; A of the K clusters are sampled at random and assigned to the treatment group, while B = K–A clusters go into the control group. If a cluster k is sampled at random into the treatment group, we observe the value of the potential outcome under treatment, T_{ik}, for every one of the i units in that cluster. If a cluster is instead assigned to the control group, we observe each potential outcome under control, C_{ik}, for each unit. If potential outcomes are more similar within clusters than across them, sampling clusters instead of individual tickets leads to more variability in treatment effect estimators than random samples of individual tickets. Data from a cluster-randomized natural experiment should not be analyzed as if they were from an individually randomized natural experiment.

The concern that arises with clustered randomization is that the potential outcomes within each cluster—that is, each group of tickets—may tend to be less variable within each group (cluster) than they are across groups. For example, individuals who live in the same communities, states, or countries may have similar baseline potential outcomes under control, and/or they may respond similarly to treatment assignment. This may be because individuals in the same communities share common influences that affect the outcome.[20] For instance, people living in the same village are exposed to the same village-level politicians, and this may affect their baseline political attitudes or engagement with local politics. Their responses to the introduction of a new local-level political institution may also tend to be similar. In sum, there are various reasons that clusters may exhibit such homogeneity of potential outcomes; however, the severity of this tendency may vary in different substantive contexts.

---

[20] This is not the same concept as confounding, because these cluster-specific factors are not systematically associated with assignment to treatment or control, due to randomization across all clusters.

If potential outcomes are less variable within groups than across them, draws of 10 treatment tickets from a single group or cluster provides less information about the overall variability of potential outcomes under treatment than would a simple random sample of 10 treatment tickets from the study group as a whole. To depict this most starkly, suppose that there are only two clusters in the study group, and that the potential outcomes under treatment and control are invariant within clusters. If one cluster is assigned to treatment and the other to control, then it is as if we are really just drawing two tickets, each with a single value, from a box (even though each value has been copied into many fields). Here, all of the variation in potential outcomes is between clusters, rather than within them; in fact, there is a perfect empirical correlation between treatment assignment and potential outcomes.

Moreover, when potential outcomes are homogeneous within clusters, assigning clusters rather than individual units to treatment and control groups will increase the variability of the treatment effect estimators. To see this, imagine that in one of the K clusters, all units have very large positive potential outcomes under both treatment and control. Assigning this cluster to the treatment group may thus substantially increase the overall treatment group mean; assigning it to the control group will increase the control group mean. Since this cluster will sometimes end up in treatment and sometimes end up in control—depending on the randomization—the sampling variance of the difference of means across different hypothetical natural experiments will tend to be large. In particular, it will be greater than if the units had been individually assigned to treatment and control groups: in the latter case, some of the units from the cluster with large potential outcomes would go into the treatment group in any given natural experiment, while others would go into the control group. This will make the difference of means more stable, across hypothetical replications of the natural experiment.

In sum, subjects' potential outcomes within a cluster may tend to be related. These dependencies increase the ratio of between-cluster to within-cluster variability, reducing the effective sample size and increasing the variance of the estimated effect of treatment. If an analyst fails to take the increase of sampling variability into account—for example, if she assumes a sampling process such as Figure 5.1, rather than clustered randomization as in Figure 6.1—then the estimated standard errors can be quite misleading. In particular, they will tend to understate the true variability of the treatment and control group means, leading to overconfidence in conclusions about causal effects.[21]

---

[21] That is, failure to account for clustering may produce a tendency to reject the null hypothesis, even when there is no true effect. This is sometimes called a "Type I" error in the statistical literature.

6.2.1 Analysis by cluster mean: a design-based approach

How should analysts approach natural-experimental data in which the treatment has been assigned in clusters? One very sensible possibility is simply to analyze the data at the level of randomization—that is, by comparing mean outcomes at the group/cluster level.[22] For instance, the average of the cluster means in the assigned-to-treatment group can be compared to the average of the mean outcomes in the clusters assigned to control. The variance of this difference-of-means estimator is then estimated by a formula similar to the case of individual-level randomization—except that the clusters are the units of analysis (Appendix 6.2). Thus, the variance is given by the sum of the variance of the average of cluster-mean outcomes in the treatment and control groups. Notice that we are still looking here at individual-level outcomes, but these outcomes are aggregated up to the cluster level for purposes of analysis. This is a design-based approach to handling clustered randomization—because the analysis based on the Neyman model follows the design of the randomization.

This procedure might strike some observers—incorrectly—as unduly conservative. After all, they might suggest, are we not throwing away information from individual-level observations, by aggregating the data and calculating means and variances at the cluster level? The answer is: not really. Note that each of the cluster means will tend to be more stable (have lower variance) than would a single observation drawn from a particular cluster. Were we to draw a single observation from each cluster, the variance of the resulting observations could be quite high. By first calculating cluster means, however, and then calculating the variance of the cluster means, we incorporate the information provided by the additional individual-level observations. Moreover, the more that clusters are alike—that is, the greater the intercluster homogeneity of potential outcomes—the lower the variance of the cluster means themselves. Thus, the variance of the cluster means—the variance *across* all the clusters—should be stable as well, when intercluster heterogeneity is low; when intercluster heterogeneity is high, the cluster-mean analysis also takes this heterogeneity into account.

---

[22] In an early contribution on clustered randomization, Lindquist (1940) recommended this approach, in his discussion of Fisher ([1935] 1951); see, e.g., Donner and Klar (1994). Similarly, Hansen and Bowers (2009: 879), in their discussion of a political science study in which households were randomized to receive get-out-the-vote messages (Gerber and Green 2000; Imai 2005), recommend analyzing effects with households, rather than individuals, as the unit of analysis.

In fact, analysis by cluster mean often turns out to be equivalent, or nearly equivalent, to analyses that take account of within-cluster correlations in other ways, for instance, adjusting individual-level data by an intraclass correlation coefficient. When the number of observations in each cluster is the same, the equivalence is exact. Cluster-mean analysis, however, has the virtue of simplicity and transparency, and it is the analytic strategy most directly tied to the sampling model in Figure 6.1. Thus, it is a design-based approach, in which analysis hews closely to the process that generated the data. Analysis by cluster-mean is thus often the best approach.

Thus, the procedure recommended for the analysis of individual-level randomization is simply adapted to the analysis of group means. Note that this procedure is advised when the number of units in each cluster is equal or about equal; otherwise, see the further discussion below:

(1) Take the mean of the outcomes in each cluster.
(2) Calculate the average of the cluster means, in both the treatment and control groups. To find the average of the cluster means, one simply sums across the cluster means and divides by the number of clusters.
(3) Find the difference between the two averages, that is, the average of the cluster means in the assigned-to-treatment group minus the average of the cluster means in the assigned-to-control group. This difference estimates the average causal effect.
(4) Attach a standard error to the difference. This is the square root of the sum of the estimated sampling variances of the average of the cluster means.
(5) Conduct a hypothesis test using a t-test.[23]

As before, the error from assuming sampling with replacement—which inflates the estimated standard errors, relative to the true standard errors—just about cancels the error from assuming independence between the cluster means in the treatment and control groups—which reduces the estimated standard errors, relative to the true standard errors. Thus, the standard error for the difference of the averages of the cluster means in the treatment and control groups can be calculated as if these averages were independent. Box 6.2 gives some simple Stata (StataCorp 2009) code for implementing such an analysis; the first four lines of code in the box implement step (1) above, while the fifth line implements steps (2)–(5). Appendix 6.2 describes the foundations of this analysis in more detail.

---

[23] As discussed below, the t-test is justified because, by the central limit theorem, the cluster means should be approximately normal, at least when the number of units in each cluster is moderately large; this is true when the means are themselves sampled from each cluster. Other approaches might instead be used for hypothesis testing, such as Fisher's exact test. The block bootstrap is another possibility (Angrist and Pischke 2008).

Box 6.2 Code for analysis by cluster means

Suppose that treatment assignment is by cluster or group, as in Figure 6.2. How can you implement an analysis by cluster or group mean, when the data are organized at the individual level? This section shows some simple Stata (StataCorp 2009) code that does the trick.

First, suppose you have a cluster or group identifier called *group*. You want to do analysis on an outcome variable called *income*, and you will compare incomes across the treatment and control groups using a dichotomous variable called *treatment*. After loading your data set into memory, type

sort *group*

This will sort the data by the group variable. Next, type the command below, which returns the average income within each group and stores it in a variable called ave_income:

by *group*: egen ave_income=mean(*income*)

Note that this variable ("ave_income") has the same value for every observation in each cluster. Now, we want to drop all but the first observation in each group. The syntax is

by *group*: generate obs_num=_n
drop if obs_num~=1

The first line above uses Stata's "_n" counter to identify the first observation, while the second line then drops all but the first observation. Now we can do a *t*-test, using the cluster averages:

ttest ave_income, by(*treatment*) unequal

Here, for example, *treatment=1* indicates that a unit was assigned to treatment and *treatment=0* indicates the unit was assigned to control. The unequal option specifies that variances are allowed to differ across the treatment and control groups.

The difference in the average of the cluster means will be the same as the difference in the simple averages across the treatment and control groups, as long as the clusters are the same size. But the estimated standard errors will reflect the clustering.

Analysis by cluster mean has several desirable characteristics. First, note that just as with the analysis appropriate to individual-level randomization (Section 6.1), the method naturally takes heteroskedasticity (unequal sampling variances of the sample means) into account: the sampling variances of the treatment and control groups means are estimated separately.[24] Second, even when the number of clusters is small, the sampling distribution of the average of the cluster means in the treatment and control groups—and thus their difference—should be approximately normally distributed: this is because the cluster means should themselves tend towards normality, so any linear combination of these mean outcomes (such as their average) will also be normally distributed.[25] Thus, a key assumption of the *t*-test may be approximately met when conducting analysis of cluster means (see Appendix 6.2).

Finally and most importantly, however, this approach is faithful to the actual process of as-if randomization, and it rests on quite credible (and conservative) assumptions about the data-generating process. Note that unless units in each cluster are exact replicates (with respect to potential outcomes), then taking data from multiple units in each cluster and conducting the analysis by cluster mean *does* decrease the variance of the overall treatment effect estimator. If means are homogeneous across clusters—that is, the within-cluster correlation of potential outcomes is weak—then the variance of the cluster means will also be low. In this case, we get about as much statistical power from cluster-mean analysis as we would when conducting the analysis at the individual level. Appendix 6.2 shows how the variance of the cluster-mean estimator depends on the stability of the means across clusters.

It is useful to compare this strategy of analyzing group or cluster means to other possible procedures for taking account of clustering. Methodologists from a variety of disciplines recommend a standard correction formula that is based on an intraclass correlation coefficient.[26] According to these authors (e.g., Donner and Klar 2000 in biostatistics, Angrist and Pischke 2008 in economics), the standard errors obtained from the conventional formulas assuming individual-level randomization should be multiplied by a correction factor, which is the square root of

one plus (the size of the clusters minus one)*ρ,

---

[24] This can be compared to the parametric regression approach, in which group means may be regressed on an indicator for treatment assignment (which does not vary at the group level). Some analysts recommend estimating grouped regressions using weighted least squares, with the group size as weights (e.g., Angrist and Pischke 2009: chapter 8).

[25] The average is a linear combination if the number of clusters in treatment and control is fixed, not random; otherwise, the average is a ratio estimator (the ratio of two random variables). Whether it is reasonable to view the number of clusters as fixed may depend on the details of the design.

[26] This is also referred to as the within-cluster correlation coefficient.

where ρ is the intraclass correlation coefficient, and "size of the clusters" refers to the number of individual units in each cluster.[27] In other words, the data are analyzed as if they were generated by unit- or individual-level randomization rather than clustered randomization—where the analysis may involve a simple comparison of mean outcomes and the associated variance formulas given above, or an estimation of a (possibly multivariate) regression model. Then, the estimated standard errors from the formulas appropriate to individual-level randomization are multiplied by the correction factor to obtain valid estimates of the true standard errors, before hypothesis testing is undertaken. In the survey-sampling context, the correction factor is called the *design effect* (Kish 1965: chapter 5), because it compares the estimated variance due to survey designs that involve clustering to the estimated variance that would obtain under simple random sampling. Note that this formula for the correction factor compares the estimated variance using the clustered randomization to unit-level randomization, for a fixed study group size; the reason the *number* of clusters is in the formula is that the overall size enters into both variances and thus is held constant. The formula holds when the clusters are of equal sizes and all units in the same cluster are assigned to the same treatment; a related but more complicated formula holds when clusters are of unequal sizes, though it is often approximately equivalent to use the average cluster size as a measure of the size of each cluster (Kish 1965: chapter 5; Angrist and Pischke 2008: chapter 8).[28]

The analysis by cluster means recommended above seems preferable to using this alternative method, however, for two reasons. First, the calculation of the correlation coefficient may depend on a particular parametric model of variance components, which may be undesirable. The procedure described above based on group means does not make parametric assumptions about the variance of the potential outcomes in treatment and control clusters,

---

[27] Economists refer to this formula as the Moulton correction factor (e.g., Angrist and Pischke 2008: chapter 8), though it was well-known in biostatistics, epidemiology, psychology, and other fields before Moulton's (1986) article; see, e.g., Donner, Birkett, and Buck (1981) or Cornfield (1978). The formula is an adaptation of standard corrections used in clustered survey sampling to the problem of clustered random assignment (see Kish 1965: chapter 5).

[28] Some natural experiments will naturally tend to have unequal cluster sizes—e.g., in regression-discontinuity designs where municipalities are the unit of assignment (though in expectation cluster sizes will be equal on average across treatment and control groups). If the size of the clusters is unequal, estimators suffer from small-sample bias, as discussed in the text below; unequal sample sizes must also be taken into account in the variance calculations, though it may suffice to use the average cluster size and/or to assume that cluster sizes are fixed. In other designs, such as where samples are taken within clusters (e.g., Dunning 2010b), the choice can be made to draw an equal sample size from each cluster.

beyond what is stipulated in the Neyman model. Moreover, there are different measures of the intraclass correlation coefficient ρ, which depend on somewhat different parametric models of the variance components, so it is necessary to commit to such a model before using the parametric correction.

Second, and in partial moderation of the previous point, these techniques are in fact often nearly equivalent, especially when the individual-level analysis is based on a simple difference of means and the associated variance estimator. That is, the correction that is calculated using (some measure of) the intra-class correlation coefficient is often very closely approximated by the ratio of the estimated variance using the cluster-mean procedure to the estimated variance assuming individual-level randomization. Indeed, in the survey-sampling context, Kish (1965: 162) presents these alternative definitions of the "design effect" as roughly equivalent. (They may not be closely related, however, when the parametric Moulton correction is applied to standard errors that are estimated from regression models.)[29] See Appendix 6.2 for further discussion.

It therefore seems most direct and transparent simply to conduct the analysis by group (cluster) means, using the procedure outlined above. This approach obviates the need to choose a method for calculating the intra-class correlation coefficient, and it rests on credible assumptions about the data- generating process. In contrast, correction factors such as Moulton's (1986) are often applied to bivariate or multivariate statistical models, which do not follow from the design of the natural experiment and may lack credibility as depictions of the data-generating process. With the simple cluster-mean approach, the analysis naturally takes account of any threats to valid statistical inference that arise from clustering—yet analysis by cluster means does not reduce statistical power (that is, the design effect is 1) if clusters are as heterogeneous with respect to potential outcomes as the study group as a whole. This can thus be considered the design-based approach, because it does not commit us to a particular model of variance or measure of intraclass correlation beyond what is implied by the Neyman model.

The picture is somewhat more complicated if clusters vary in size. Then, analysis by cluster mean suffers from ratio-estimator bias, because the sizes of the treatment and control groups are random variables (Appendix 6.2). The bias

---

[29] However, Angrist and Pischke (2008) present several closely related ways of accounting for clustering, including regressions based on group means, which in the data example they analyze give very similar estimated standard errors—all of which differ by large factors from the standard errors assuming unit-level randomization. They also recommend adjusting standard errors for clustering using so-called biased-reduced linearization (Bell and McCaffrey 2002).

goes away as the number of clusters increases. (This is akin to small-sample bias in instrumental-variables analysis, discussed in Appendix 5.1.) If the number of clusters is moderately large, and cluster sizes do not vary much, analysis by cluster mean is still a sensible procedure; clusters may be weighted by their size in calculating the treatment and control group means. An alternative is analysis by cluster *totals* rather than cluster means (Horvitz and Thompson 1952; Middleton and Aronow 2011), though estimators based on this approach will have larger variance than estimators based on cluster means.

In sum, analysts of cluster-randomized natural experiments should present results by cluster mean, along with any auxiliary analyses. As Angrist and Pischke (2008: 167) also put it, "At a minimum, you'd like to show that your conclusions are consistent with the inferences that arise from an analysis of group averages since this is a conservative and transparent approach."

Note that analysis by cluster mean does not obviate the potential problem that clustered randomization poses for some natural-experimental studies in which the number of clusters is small, such as Posner's (2004) study of Zambia and Malawi. When exactly one (or just a few) clusters are assigned to each treatment condition—as in natural experiments where communities are compared on each side of a jurisdictional border—it is sometimes impossible to distinguish two sources of variation: the variation in outcomes due to the effect of the treatment, and the natural variation that exists between the communities even in the absence of a treatment effect. Moreover, with just two clusters, the cluster-mean estimator of the standard error of the difference of means is undefined (not calculable).[30] Analysis of variance is then possible only under the improbable assumption that there is no clustering of individual-level potential outcomes within communities. In Posner's (2004) study, for instance, the data are analyzed as if the assignment were not clustered; if analysis were by cluster mean, the empirical results (that is, the finding of a significant difference between responses in Zambia and Malawi) would almost certainly not survive. Such cases present difficult dilemmas because it is not possible, given the design, to increase the number of clusters (after all, there is only one Zambia and one Malawi).

This may simply be a regrettable feature of the world. If potential outcomes are in fact much less variable within clusters than across clusters, then pretending that units were individually randomized to treatment may not be

---

[30] This is because, to calculate the standard error for each sample mean, the empirical standard deviation is divided by the number of cluster means, minus one. The denominator is zero—and thus the estimated standard error is undefined—when there is only one cluster in treatment and one cluster in control.

helpful. In other settings, it may be possible to pick more clusters (and perhaps survey fewer individuals within each cluster, if that is necessary for reasons of cost). For example, when the clustering is due to investigator choice—as when, for instance, a sample of villages exposed to treatment and control is taken and 10 citizens are surveyed in every treatment and control village—it may be possible to reduce the number of citizens interviewed in each village and increase the number of villages in the study group, by enlarging the sample of villages.[31] Greater gains in statistical power are typically obtained from increasing the number of clusters in a study, as opposed to increasing the average cluster size.

6.3 Randomization inference: Fisher's exact test

In the discussion of hypothesis testing in Section 6.1, I noted that the treatment and control means are approximately normally distributed (as random variables) in moderately large experiments, due to the central limit theorem. Analysts often appeal to this property when analyzing true experiments and natural experiments: for instance, they calculate z-scores based on the normal approximation, or else they assume normality of the potential outcomes and use the t-test. This approach is usually fine with moderately large natural experiments (since the t-distribution converges fairly rapidly to the normal as the sample size increases), but it may be inappropriate in small ones. Often, there is little basis for assuming that the potential outcomes are normally distributed. An alternative is to assume the strict null hypothesis and calculate p-values using an alternative procedure known as Fisher's exact test (Fisher [1935] 1951); this is also sometimes known as "randomization inference." (Scholars typically use the term Fisher's exact test when the outcome variable is dichotomous, but it may be used more generally to refer to the class of randomization tests described in this section.)

The object of this section is to describe this alternative procedure. To conduct the exact test, it is necessary to assume the strict (sometimes called sharp) null hypothesis. This is sometimes appropriate, though as discussed below it is not innocuous in every setting. Under the strict null hypothesis, there are no unit-level effects: that is, for each unit, the potential outcome

---

[31] For example, in the studies by Dunning (2010b) and Dunning and Nilekani (2010), many villages were located at the key regression-discontinuity threshold determining assignment to treatment and control, and so more than $N = 200$ villages could have been included in the study group.

Table 6.1 Potential outcomes under the strict null hypothesis

Unit	Outcome under treatment	Outcome under control
1	**3**	3
2	1	**1**
3	5	**5**
4	**−2**	−2

Note: **Boldface type** indicates that the outcome was observed in the experiment. In this case, units 1 and 4 were assigned to treatment, while units 2 and 3 were assigned to control. Under the strict null hypothesis, potential outcomes under treatment are the same as potential outcomes under control, so the boldfaced value is simply copied to the next cell. Here, the estimated average causal effect is (3 − 2)/2 − (1+5)/2 = −5/2.

under treatment equals the potential outcome under control. Thus, the two values on each of the tickets in the box in Figure 5.1 are assumed to be the same, under the null hypothesis. For each unit, we can therefore copy the value we happen to observe (the outcome under treatment or the outcome under control) into the field of the ticket we do not observe. The object of hypothesis testing is to use the data to assess how likely we would be to observe the data we do, if this strict null hypothesis were true.

As an example, consider a natural experiment with just four units, two of which are assigned to treatment and two of which are assigned to control. Table 6.1 shows one possible randomization, in which units 1 and 4 are assigned to treatment and units 2 and 3 are assigned to control; for each unit, the table also lists the outcome (which is the same under treatment and under control—that's by the strict null hypothesis). Boldfaced values indicate the outcomes we actually observe, given the randomized allocation. Here, the average outcome in the treatment group is (3 − 2)/2 = 1/2, while the average outcome in the control group is (1 + 5)/2 = 6/2, for an estimated average causal effect of −5/2.

The question now becomes, could such a large difference between the treatment and control groups reasonably arise by chance, if the strict null hypothesis of no unit-level effects were true? To answer this question, we first calculate the outcomes we would observe in the treatment and control groups under all six possible ways to randomize the four units to treatment and control.[32] This calculation can be done because under the null hypothesis,

---

[32] Here, there are $\binom{4}{2}$ possible randomizations, that is, $\frac{4!}{2!2!} = 6$ ways of choosing two units out of four for assignment to treatment.

Table 6.2 Outcomes under all randomizations, under the strict null hypothesis

Unit	Treatment or control	Observed outcome	Treatment or control	Observed outcome
	Natural experiment 1		Natural experiment 2	
1	T	3	T	3
2	T	1	C	1
3	C	5	T	5
4	C	−2	C	−2
Estimated effect	(3+1)/2 − (5−2)/2= **1/2**		(3+5)/2 − (1−2)/2= **9/2**	
	Natural experiment 3		Natural experiment 4	
1	T	3	C	3
2	C	1	T	1
3	C	5	T	5
4	T	−2	C	−2
Estimated effect	(3 − 2)/2 − (1 + 5)/2 = **−5/2**		(1 + 5)/2 − (3 − 2)/2 = **5/2**	
	Natural experiment 5		Natural experiment 6	
1	C	3	C	3
2	T	1	C	1
3	C	5	T	5
4	T	−2	T	−2
Estimated effect	(1 − 2)/2 − (3 + 5)/2 = **−9/2**		(5 − 2)/2 − (3 + 1)/2 = **−1/2**	

Note: The table shows observed outcomes for each unit for each of six possible randomizations, under the strict null hypothesis of no unit-level effects. Estimators of the average causal effect under each of the randomizations are in bold.

each unit has the same outcome whether randomized to treatment or to control. Table 6.2 shows the outcomes under the six possible randomizations and then calculates the estimated average causal effect, which is the average outcome in the assigned-to-treatment group minus the average outcome in the assigned-to-control group.

As Table 6.2 shows, there are six estimated effects, one for each of the six possible randomizations: 1/2, 9/2, −5/2, 5/2, −9/2, and −1/2. Each of these outcomes is equally likely, due to randomization. We can now answer the question, how likely is it that we would observe an outcome as large in absolute value as −5/2 under the strict null hypothesis, simply due to chance? (This procedure is the equivalent of a "two-tailed" test because here we ask about absolute values.) The answer is straightforward. In four out of the six experiments—numbers 2, 3, 4, and 5—the estimated effect is as large or larger in absolute value than −5/2: the estimated effects are 9/2, 5/2, −5/2, and −9/2, respectively. In the other two experiments—numbers 1 and 6—the estimated effects are 1/2 and −1/2, which are smaller in absolute value than the observed estimated effect of −5/2. Thus, the probability of observing an effect as large in absolute value as the observed effect, if the strict null hypothesis is true, is 4/6. So the p-value is approximately 0.66. The evidence against the null hypothesis is weak: the difference of −5/2 could easily have arisen by chance.

It is also possible to conduct the equivalent of a one-tailed test, which might be useful in settings in which there are strong hypotheses about the direction of the effect. Thus, instead of using the absolute value, we ask: what is the probability of observing an outcome as small or smaller than −5/2, if the strict null hypothesis is true?[33] As Table 6.2 shows, there are two experiments (3 and 5) in which the outcome is as small as −5/2, so the probability is $p = 2/6$, or about 0.33. Here, the p-value is smaller, but it is still not grounds for rejecting the null hypothesis.[34]

The logic extends to larger experiments and more complicated examples, but the calculations quickly become more intensive—which is where programming on the computer comes in.[35] Standard routines in Stata (StataCorp 2009) or R (R Development Core Team 2008) will implement versions of Fisher's exact test.[36] However, numerical complications can arise with large numbers of subjects, so the p-values are sometimes calculated by simulation rather than "exactly"—which is somewhat ironic, given the name of the test.[37]

---

[33] Rather than use the absolute value to define the two-tailed test, some analysts prefer to use the minimum of two probabilities: the probability that a random draw from the distribution is least as large as the value of the observed statistic, and the probability that a random draw from the distribution is at least as small as the observed statistic. This may be a better definition, when the measured effects under all permutations are nonsymmetric around zero.

[34] Standard significance levels can be used with these permutation tests. For instance, we reject the null hypothesis at $p < 0.05$ and then call the estimated effect *statistically significant*. If we reject at $p < 0.01$, the estimated effect is *highly significant*. As with conventional hypothesis testing, these thresholds hold by convention, but they are otherwise arbitrary.

[35] In the above experiment with four units, it is easy to do the exact calculations because the study group is so small. In general, with a study group of size N and with n units assigned to treatment and $m = N - n$ units assigned to control, there will be $\binom{N}{n}$ distinct values of the assignment vector. Numerical difficulties may result when N and n are large, due to the large values taken by the factorials, so it may not be easy to calculate the test statistic for every value of the assignment vector, even by computation. Standard statistical packages typically approximate the p-value by randomly choosing values of the assignment vector, rather than calculating the statistic for every possible value of the vector.

[36] For example, the "tabulate twoway" command in Stata (StataCorp 2009), using the "exact" option, will calculate Fisher's exact test for a 2×2 contingency table. So will the "> fisher.test(matrix)" command in R (R Development Core Team 2008), where "matrix" is the name given to the contingency table (which need not be 2×2).

[37] For example, the statistical package might draw an N-dimensional vector with $N - n$ zeros and n ones. Since there are $\binom{N}{n}$ ways of choosing a vector with n ones, the probability of drawing each vector is then $1/\binom{N}{n}$. The package will calculate the relevant statistic (say, the estimated average causal effect) for this draw and then repeat the process $T - 1$ times, each time drawing another vector of assignments with or without replacement. Then, p-values will be approximated by the fraction of these T statistics that are

When should Fisher's test be used? It appears most useful in quite small natural experiments: when the number of units is moderately large, the difference between the exact test and normal approximations will be negligible.[38] In many of the natural experiments surveyed in the first three chapters, the number of units assigned to treatment and control exceeds 50 or 100 for each group—in which case, results using the exact test are likely to differ only very marginally from those using z-tests or t-tests.[39] Moreover, as discussed above, when the exact test is computed in larger experiments, computational approximations and simulations are typically used, which raises some additional issues. This suggests that for many natural experiments, the exact test may not be necessary. (Of course, the exact test could certainly be reported even in larger experiments, alongside other test statistics.)

Yet, in many natural experiments, the number of units may be substantially smaller—particularly in natural experiments with clustered as-if random assignment, where the number of clusters is small. Regression-discontinuity designs—where only a small number of units may be located sufficiently near the critical regression-discontinuity threshold for the assertion of as-if random to be plausible—provide another example. In such cases, normal approximations may not be reliable, and the exact test may be quite convenient. Thus, it may be useful for analysts to be aware of Fisher's procedure.

Before relying on the exact test, however, researchers should ask whether assuming the strict null hypothesis is sensible. This hypothesis may not make sense in contexts with heterogeneity of treatment effects—for instance, when the unit-level causal effect may be positive for some units and negative for others. In this case, the more typically invoked weak form of the null hypothesis, which stipulates that the average potential outcome under treatment is the same as the average potential outcome under control (that is, the average causal effect is zero), might be more appropriate.

---

larger than the observed statistic in absolute value. The accuracy of the approximation is determined by the researcher's choice of T, and one can attach a standard error to the point estimate of the p-value as the square root of $p(1-p)/T$. However, this may encourage data mining, since researchers might increase T until confidence intervals suggest that the null hypothesis is rejected.

[38] When the number of units is moderately large, the normal curve closely approximates the hypergeometric distribution that is followed by the test statistics in permutation-based inference. For evidence and discussion, see, e.g., Hansen and Bowers (2009: 876).

[39] For example, in an experiment by Amos Tversky and others (McNeil et al. 1982), 167 doctors were assigned to one of two ways of receiving information about the effectiveness of surgery or radiation as therapies for lung cancer. Here, 80 were assigned to one form and 87 to the other. Computing probabilities based on the strict null hypothesis gives p-values that are nearly identical to the normal tail probabilities (Freedman, Pisani, and Purves 2007: A34–A35, n. 14).

6.4 Conclusion

Like the estimators of average causal effects discussed in the previous chapter, the standard errors of those estimators may be estimated through quite straightforward formulas. Doing so, however, depends on formulating and defending a sensible model of the chance process that gave rise to observed data—that is, a statistical model for the data-generating process. In many natural experiments, the standard Neyman urn model provides the right starting point. Then, the variance of the causal-effect estimators may be estimated as the sum of the estimated sampling variances of the means in the treatment and control groups; the square root of this quantity is the standard error for the difference of means. This approach may be slightly conservative, which is not a bad thing if we want to be appropriately cautious about our causal claims. The simplicity and transparency of the formulas also reduces the scope for discretion on the part of the researcher and helps to focus analysis on the credibility of the research design and the substantive size of the effect.

Other natural experiments may require some extensions to the basic Neyman model. One topic of particular importance to many natural experiments is clustered random assignment. Here, the appropriate statistical model for the data-generating process will be akin to Figure 6.1, not Figure 5.1. When treatment assignment takes place in groups or clusters, analysis based on the assumption of individual-level randomization, as in Figure 5.1, can lead to serious underestimates of the variability of treatment effect estimators and thus to overconfidence in statements about the presence of causal effects. A simple fix is available for this problem: the data should be analyzed at the level of cluster means, for example, the difference between the average of the cluster means in the treatment group and the average of the cluster means in the control group should be used to estimate the average causal effect. The estimated variance of this causal effect estimator is then the sum of the estimated sampling variances of the cluster means in the treatment group and the control group. In other words, the simple formula for the variance is simply adapted to analysis by cluster mean, with the N being given by the number of clusters, not the number of individual units. Of course, this formula highlights the inferential issues that arise when only one or a few clusters are assigned en masse to the treatment and control groups.

In sum, the quantitative analysis of natural experiments may be simple, transparent, and based on persuasive depictions of the underlying data-generating process. At least in principle, this underscores an important advantage of natural experiments, relative for example to many conventional observational studies. The simplicity of the analysis also leaves more scope in research articles for discussion of the research context and validation of the research design—both topics that centrally involve the qualitative methods discussed in the next chapter.

Appendix 6.1 Conservative standard errors under the Neyman model

This explanation follows Freedman, Pisani, and Purves (2007: A32–A34, n. 11). I use the weak form of the null hypothesis, which says that $\overline{T} = \overline{C}$: that is, the average potential outcome under treatment is the same as the average potential outcome under control. This is contrasted with the strict null hypothesis, which says that $T_i = C_i$ for all i: that is, the unit-level causal effect is zero for each unit. Let σ^2 and δ^2 denote the variances of potential outcomes under treatment and control, as in Box 6.1, while

$$\text{Cov}(T, C) = \frac{1}{N} \sum_{i=1}^{N} \left(T_i - \overline{T}\right)\left(C_i - \overline{C}\right) \qquad (6.A1.1)$$

is the unit-level covariance between potential outcomes under treatment and control. Here, σ^2, δ^2, and $\text{Cov}(T, C)$ are all parameters, defined for the entire study group.

As before, the sample mean in the treatment group is Y^T and the sample mean in the control group is Y^C. These are both observable random variables. Here, $Y^T - Y^C$ estimates the average causal effect $\overline{T} - \overline{C}$. Notice that unlike $\overline{T}$, $\overline{C}$, σ^2, δ^2, and the average causal effect $\overline{T} - \overline{C}$, which are all estimable from sample data, $\text{Cov}(T, C)$ is not estimable by a sample covariance—because we cannot observe both T_i and C_i for any single unit i.

What is the variance of $Y^T - Y^C$? It is the sum of the variances of Y^T and Y^C, minus two times the covariance of these random variables; we need the covariance term because these variables are not independent. For the variances of both Y^T and Y^C, we need a correction factor because we are drawing potential outcomes without replacement from a small population (the natural-experimental study group). Thus,

$$\text{Var}\left(Y^T\right) = \frac{N - n}{N - 1} \frac{\sigma^2}{n}, \qquad (6.A1.2)$$

where $\frac{N-n}{N-1}$ is the finite-sample correction factor (Freedman, Pisani, and Purves 2007: 368; Kish 1965: 62–63). Similarly,

$$\text{Var}(Y^C) = \frac{N-m}{N-1}\frac{\delta^2}{m}. \qquad (6.\text{A}1.3)$$

Next, the covariance term reflects the dependence between the treatment and control samples. By combinatorial calculations,

$$\text{Cov}(Y^T, Y^C) = -\frac{1}{N-1}\text{Cov}(T, C). \qquad (6.\text{A}1.4)$$

In sum, we have:

$$\begin{aligned}\text{Var}(Y^T - Y^C) &= \frac{N-n}{N-1}\frac{\sigma^2}{n} + \frac{N-m}{N-1}\frac{\delta^2}{m} + \frac{2}{N-1}\text{Cov}(T, C) \\ &= \frac{N}{N-1}\left(\frac{\sigma^2}{n} + \frac{\delta^2}{m}\right) + \frac{1}{N-1}\left[2\text{Cov}(T, C) - \sigma^2 - \delta^2\right] \\ &\leq \frac{N}{N-1}\left(\frac{\sigma^2}{n} + \frac{\delta^2}{m}\right). \end{aligned}$$

$$(6.\text{A}1.5)$$

The final weak inequality follows from $2\sigma\delta - \sigma^2 - \delta^2 \leq 0$, because $(\sigma - \delta)^2 \geq 0$; moreover, $\text{Cov}(T, C) \leq \sigma\delta$, where σ and δ are the standard deviations of the potential outcomes under treatment and control, respectively. This follows because $\rho = \frac{\text{Cov}(T,C)}{\sigma\delta}$, that is, the correlation between T and C, is bounded above by 1; thus, $\text{Cov}(T, C) = \sigma\delta$ only when $\rho = 1$ and otherwise $\text{Cov}(T, C) < \sigma\delta$. When $\rho = 1$, $\text{Var}(Y^T - Y^C)$ reaches its upper bound.

The equality on the second line of Equation 6.A1.5 suggests why the errors from dependence between the averages and sampling without replacement may balance each other out (Freedman, Pisani, and Purves 2007: A33–A35, nn. 11 and 14). Notice that the first term in the second line is

$$\frac{N}{N-1}\left(\frac{\sigma^2}{n} + \frac{\delta^2}{m}\right). \qquad (6.\text{A}1.6)$$

This is nearly the formula for the variance of the difference of two independent means when N is large. The second, positive term reflects the dependence between the treatment and control means—that is

$$\frac{2\text{Cov}(T, C)}{N-1}, \qquad (6.\text{A}1.7)$$

which drives up the variance (as long as the within-subject covariance of potential outcomes is positive, which is typically the case). Finally, the final two negative terms reflect the correction factor for sampling without replacement—that is,

$$\frac{-\sigma^2 - \delta^2}{N - 1}, \tag{6.A1.8}$$

which cuts the variance back down. If ρ is near its upper limit of 1—which is often reasonable, considering that potential outcomes under treatment and control should be highly correlated across subjects—then the errors from dependence and sampling without replacement will nearly cancel. For these reasons,

$$\operatorname{Var}(Y^T - Y^C) \approx \frac{N}{N-1}\left(\frac{\sigma^2}{n} + \frac{\delta^2}{m}\right) \tag{6.A1.9}$$

is a very serviceable approximation to the true variance. Moreover, even with moderate N, the difference between 1 and $\frac{N}{N-1}$ is negligible, so we can use the estimator

$$\widehat{\operatorname{Var}}(Y^T - Y^C) = \frac{\hat{\sigma}^2}{n} + \frac{\hat{\delta}^2}{m}, \tag{6.A1.10}$$

where $\hat{\sigma}$ and $\hat{\delta}$ are the sample estimators of σ^2 and δ^2 discussed in Box 6.1. Note that Equation 6.A1.10 is simply the standard estimator for the sampling variance of the difference of means for two independent samples. This is the justification for combining the variances of the treatment and control group means as if they were independent.

Under the weak form of the null hypothesis, this produces a conservative estimate of the variance of the difference of means, because the true variance may be less than the right-hand side of Equation 6.A1.9. Under the strict null hypothesis, however, Equation 6.A1.9 is exact. This is because under the strict null, $T_i = C_i$, and so $\sigma = \delta$; thus, $\operatorname{cov}(T, C) = \sigma\delta = \sigma^2$, because the correlation of T_i and C_i across subjects is 1. Moreover, $2\sigma\delta - \sigma^2 - \delta^2 = 0$, because $(\sigma - \delta)^2 = 0$.

There are other special cases in which Equation 6.A1.9 is exact as well. For instance, if assignment to treatment shifts outcomes by the same amount for every subject—i.e., if $T_i = C_i + \alpha$ for all i, where α is a real number—then the correlation of T_i and C_i across subjects remains 1. This holds for any affine transformation of C_i. Of course, this is the special case of the linear regression model, with a dichotomous variable for treatment assignment and no control variables. Note that Equation 6.A1.10 is not the formula that produces the usual nominal standard errors from regression analysis; this is why the regression standard errors do not apply.

Appendix 6.2 Analysis by cluster mean

Many natural experiments feature clustered assignment to treatment and control groups, as depicted in Figure 6.1. In the text, I recommend analysis by cluster mean as a simple and transparent procedure for such natural experiments. Here, the outcome data are aggregated to the mean value within each cluster. The difference-of-means estimator is the average of the cluster means in the assigned-to-treatment group, minus the average of the cluster means in the assigned-to-control group. The estimated variance of this difference-of-means estimator is then the estimated sampling variance of the average of the cluster means in the treatment group plus the estimated sampling variance of the average of the cluster means in the control group. Thus, the analytic principles are the same as in the case of individual-level variance, except that the unit of analysis is the cluster. The goal of this appendix is to describe this procedure in greater technical detail than in the text.

The appendix has another objective as well, which is to compare analysis by cluster mean to other procedures. For example, many scholars have suggested analyzing data from a cluster-randomized experiment or natural experiment at the individual- or unit-level but adjusting the variances by the intraclass correlation coefficient (what economists such as Angrist and Pischke 2008 call the Moulton correction factor). The appendix shows that when clusters are of equal size, analysis by cluster mean is equivalent to procedures based on the intraclass (within-cluster) correlation coefficient. Yet analysis by cluster mean is generally to be preferred, as it results in a simpler and more transparent procedure and can sometimes involve fewer parametric assumptions.

The average causal effect as the average of cluster means

Suppose there are K clusters in the natural-experimental study group. The size of the kth cluster is n_k, and individual units within each cluster are indexed by

$i = 1, \ldots, n_k$; for now, assume that the clusters are equally sized, so $n_k = n$. Thus, $\sum_{k=1}^{K} n = Kn = N$ is the total number of individual units in the study group.

As elsewhere in this book, let T_i denote the potential outcome under treatment of unit i. Now, however, let T_{ik} describe the potential outcome under treatment for the ith unit in the kth cluster. Then, $\overline{T}_k$ is the average potential outcome under treatment in the kth cluster, that is,

$$\overline{T}_k = \frac{1}{n} \sum_{i=1}^{n} T_{ik}. \tag{6.A2.1}$$

The average value of all the potential outcomes under treatment is then

$$\overline{T} = \frac{1}{K} \sum_{k=1}^{K} \overline{T}_k. \tag{6.A2.2}$$

Similarly, we can define C_i as the potential outcome under control of generic unit i, C_{ik} as the potential outcome under control of unit i in cluster k, $\overline{C}_k = \frac{1}{n} \sum_{i=1}^{n} C_{ik}$ as the average potential outcome under control in the kth cluster, and

$$\overline{C} = \frac{1}{K} \sum_{k=1}^{K} \overline{C}_k \tag{6.A2.3}$$

as the average value of all potential outcomes under control.

The average causal effect is $\overline{T} - \overline{C}$. Thus, we have defined the effect as the average of the cluster means. Notice that this definition of the average causal effect is equivalent to that given earlier. For example, in Box 5.1, we defined $\overline{T} = \frac{1}{N} \sum_{i=1}^{N} T_i$. Here, we have

$$\overline{T} = \frac{1}{K} \sum_{k=1}^{K} \overline{T}_k = \frac{1}{K} \sum_{k=1}^{K} \left[\frac{1}{n} \sum_{i=1}^{n} T_{ik} \right] = \frac{1}{Kn} \sum_{k=1}^{K} \sum_{i=1}^{n} T_{ik} = \frac{1}{N} \sum_{i=1}^{N} T_i, \tag{6.A2.4}$$

so $\overline{T}$ can be defined as the average of the mean potential outcome in each cluster (the right-hand side of the first equality) or the average of potential outcomes under treatment for all units in the study group (the right-hand side of the final equality). A similar expression applies for $\overline{C}$. Thus, the average causal effect $\overline{T} - \overline{C}$ can be equivalently described either in terms of the potential outcomes for the whole study group or the average of each cluster-specific average.

If clusters were of unequal size, parameters such as $\overline{T}$ and $\overline{C}$, and thus the average causal effect $\overline{T} - \overline{C}$, would be described as weighted averages; the weights would be the cluster sizes, for example,

$$\overline{T} = \frac{\sum_{k=1}^{K} n_k \overline{T}_k}{\sum_{k=1}^{K} n_k}. \qquad (6.A2.5)$$

Estimator of the average causal effect

Here, $\overline{T}$ and $\overline{C}$ are parameters, defined at the level of potential outcomes. As always, these parameters cannot both be observed simultaneously, because each unit is either assigned to treatment or to control. How does analysis of sample means allow us to estimate these parameters?

Suppose that the natural experiment assigns a random subset of size A of the K clusters to treatment and $B = K - A$ clusters to control. (Here I abuse notation slightly, because A denotes the random subset and is also the number of clusters assigned to treatment.) Without loss of generality, order the clusters assigned to treatment by $k = 1, \ldots, A$; the $B = K - A$ clusters assigned to control are then ordered $k = A + 1, \ldots, K$. We treat A and B as fixed, i.e., nonrandom numbers. I will assume for now that the potential outcomes under treatment are observed for each unit in every cluster assigned to treatment (and similarly, potential outcomes under control are observed for each unit in every cluster assigned to the control group). In other words, we have a census of units in each cluster, rather than (say) a random sample of those units.

Denote the average outcome in the A clusters assigned to treatment as

$$\tilde{Y}^T = \frac{1}{A} \sum_{k \in A} \overline{T}_k, \qquad (6.A2.6)$$

where we use the fact that for every k in the random subset of clusters A assigned to treatment, we observe the average potential outcome under treatment in that cluster. Here, I use the notation $\tilde{Y}^T$ to distinguish this variable from the simple mean outcome in the treatment group defined earlier. Note that $\tilde{Y}^T$ is a random variable; the realization of this random variable depends on which particular clusters $k = 1, \ldots, K$ are assigned to the treatment group. Moreover, because the clusters assigned to the treatment group are a random sample from the population of clusters in the study group, we have

$$E(\tilde{Y}^T) = \overline{T}. \tag{6.A2.7}$$

Similarly,

$$\tilde{Y}^C = \frac{1}{B}\sum_{k \in B} \overline{C}_k \tag{6.A2.8}$$

is the average outcome in the B clusters assigned to the control group, with

$$E(\tilde{Y}^C) = \overline{C}. \tag{6.A2.9}$$

Thus, the average of the cluster means in the clusters assigned to treatment, minus the average of the cluster means in the clusters assigned to control, is an unbiased estimator for the average causal effect. That is,

$$E(\tilde{Y}^T - \tilde{Y}^C) = \overline{T} - \overline{C}. \tag{6.A2.10}$$

Variance of the estimator

What is the variance of the estimator $\tilde{Y}^T - \tilde{Y}^C$? If these two random variables were independent, the formula would be simple:

$$\mathrm{Var}(\tilde{Y}^T - \tilde{Y}^C) = \mathrm{Var}(\tilde{Y}^T) + \mathrm{Var}(\tilde{Y}^C). \tag{6.A2.11}$$

Moreover, if the $\overline{T}_k$s and the $\overline{C}_k$s were drawn with replacement from the natural-experimental population, the formulas for each of the variance components would be straightforward. For example, we would have

$$\mathrm{Var}(\tilde{Y}^T) = \mathrm{Var}\left(\frac{1}{A}\sum_{k \in A} \overline{T}_k\right) = \frac{1}{A^2}\sum_{k \in A} \mathrm{Var}(\overline{T}_k) = \frac{\mathrm{Var}(\overline{T}_k)}{A}. \tag{6.A2.12}$$

The final two equalities in Equation 6.A2.12 follow from having a simple random sample of size A from the K clusters in the natural-experimental study group: this implies that the $\overline{T}_k$s are independent and identically distributed. Thus, we can distribute the variance across the sum in the penultimate equality, using independence; moreover, $\sum_{k \in A} \mathrm{Var}(\overline{T}_k) = A\mathrm{Var}(\overline{T}_k)$ follows from identical distributions, and this gives us the final equality. We can derive a similar expression for $\text{Var}(\tilde{Y}^C)$.

Since $\overline{T}$ is the average of the K cluster means (see Equation 6.A2.4), the variance of the cluster means is simply

$$\text{Var}(\overline{T}_k) = \frac{\sum_{i=1}^{K}(\overline{T}_k - \overline{T})^2}{K}, \quad (6.A2.13)$$

that is, the sum of the squared differences between each cluster mean and the overall average of the cluster means, divided by the number of clusters. Notice that this is a parameter, defined at the level of the population cluster means. (It could be denoted, say, σ^2, following notation often used for population-level variances.)

Here lies the beauty of analysis by cluster mean. Because the $\overline{T}_k$s are aggregates of the unit-level data from multiple units within each cluster, they are likely to be quite stable. In fact, if clusters are perfectly heterogeneous, so that potential outcomes under treatment are just as varied within clusters as across clusters, the variance of $\overline{T}_k$ is going to be small. Imagine if the distribution of each cluster were identical: then the difference between each cluster mean and the overall average of the cluster means would be zero. Therein lies the intuition for why the degree of within-cluster homogeneity, relative to across-cluster homogeneity, matters for the cost of clustering in terms of driving up the variance of treatment-effect estimators. If there is little homogeneity within clusters (equivalently, little heterogeneity across clusters), there is little cost from clustering. Conversely, if the means of the potential outcomes are very different from one cluster to another, then the expression for the variance in Equation 6.A2.13 will be large. I return to this topic below, when I compare analysis by cluster mean to strategies that use individual-level data and adjust them by a measure of the within-cluster (intraclass) correlation coefficient.

Equations 6.A2.12 and 6.A2.13 also suggest natural estimators for the variance of $\tilde{Y}^T$. Let $\tilde{Y}_k^T$ be the mean outcome in the kth cluster assigned to the treatment group, that is,

$$\tilde{Y}_k^T = \frac{\sum_{i \in k, A} T_{ik}}{n}. \quad (6.A2.14)$$

Then, the natural estimator for Equation 6.A2.12 is

$$\widehat{\mathrm{Var}}(\tilde{Y}^T) = \frac{\widehat{\mathrm{Var}}(\overline{T}_k)}{A}, \tag{6.A2.15}$$

where

$$\widehat{\mathrm{Var}}(\overline{T}_k) = \frac{\sum_{k \in A}(\tilde{Y}_k^T - \tilde{Y}^T)^2}{A - 1}. \tag{6.A2.16}$$

Equation 6.A2.16 is very nearly the empirical variance of the cluster means in the treatment group (that is, the mean squared deviation of the cluster means from their overall average), while Equation 6.A2.15 divides this empirical variance by the number of clusters in the treatment group. However, in the denominator of Equation 6.A2.16, we divide by the number of clusters in the treatment group minus one, because we have only $A - 1$ degrees of freedom in calculating the cluster means. (This degrees-of-freedom adjustment makes Equation 6.A2.16 an unbiased estimator for the population variance of the cluster means given in 6.A2.13). Similarly, the estimated variance of the average of the cluster means in the control group is

$$\widehat{\mathrm{Var}}(\tilde{Y}^C) = \frac{\widehat{\mathrm{Var}}(\overline{C}_k)}{B}, \tag{6.A2.17}$$

where

$$\widehat{\mathrm{Var}}(\overline{C}_k) = \frac{\sum_{k \in B}(\tilde{Y}_k^C - \tilde{Y}^C)^2}{B - 1}. \tag{6.A2.18}$$

Here, $\tilde{Y}_k^C$ is the mean outcome in the kth cluster assigned to the control group, and B is again the number of clusters assigned to control.

Thus, the estimated variance of our estimator of the average causal effect, in the cluster-randomized natural experiment, is

$$\widehat{\mathrm{Var}}(\tilde{Y}^T - \tilde{Y}^C) = \widehat{\mathrm{Var}}(\tilde{Y}^T) + \widehat{\mathrm{Var}}(\tilde{Y}^C). \tag{6.A2.19}$$

This variance estimator is very simple: it is the sum of the estimated variances of the cluster means in the treatment group and the cluster means in the control group. The standard error is the square root of Equation 6.A2.19.

Notice that the derivation above began in the subjunctive tense, because we do not in fact have a simple random sample from the K clusters in the natural-experimental study group: the draws are dependent (if one cluster goes into treatment, it cannot go into control), and they are made without replacement and so are not identically distributed. Yet, by the same argument given in Appendix 6.1, we may treat the data as if they were produced by such a simple random sample. The expression in Equation 6.A2.19 is a conservative estimator for the variance of the causal effect estimator under the weak null hypothesis (and is an exact estimator under the sharp null of no cluster-level effects).

What if we have a sample within each cluster, rather than a census of outcomes? As long as the number of units sampled in each cluster is small, relative to the size of the clusters, the variance formulas given above will remain valid. If not, a finite-sample correction factor may be needed.

If clusters are of unequal size, things are also more complicated: the denominator of the sample analogue to formulas such as Equation 6.A2.5 will be random variables, the realization of which will depend on treatment assignment. Unless clusters are of widely varying sizes, however—and particularly if the number of clusters is large—analysis by cluster mean generally provides an accurate approximation. It may be advisable to use the average cluster size as the measure of n in the formulas above. See Kish (1965: chapter 6) for further discussion of cluster sampling with unequal cluster sizes.

Exercises

In the exercises below, n is the number of units assigned to treatment, and m is the number of units assigned to control.

6.1) Which of the following is a parameter, and which is an estimator? If the latter, what does it estimate?
  (a) The average causal effect.
  (b) The mean outcome in the assigned-to-treatment group.
  (c) The average outcome if every unit were assigned to control.
  (d) The variance of the potential outcomes under treatment.
  (e) The empirical variance of the outcome in the control group, divided by m.

6.2) Match the word in the first column of Table 6.E2 with its synonym in the second column.

6.3) One ticket is drawn at random from a box containing six tickets: {1,2,3,4,5,6}. Then a second ticket is drawn, without replacement of the first ticket.

Table 6.E2: Matching concepts

(a) The intention-to-treat parameter	(1) The square root of the variance of the potential outcomes under treatment, divided by the square root of n
(b) The standard error of the mean in the assigned-to-treatment group	(2) The average causal effect of treatment assignment
(c) The estimated standard error of the mean outcome in the treatment group	(3) The standard deviation of observed outcomes in the treatment group, divided by the square root of n
(d) The average observed outcome in the assigned-to-treatment group, minus the average observed outcome in the assigned-to-control group	(4) An estimator of the effect of treatment assignment

(a) What is the probability that the second ticket is 3?
(b) What is the probability that the second ticket is 3, given that the first ticket is 2?
(c) Is the unconditional probability the same as the conditional probability?
(d) Is the value of the second ticket dependent or independent of the value of the first ticket?
(e) What is the probability that the first ticket is 2 and the second ticket is 3?
(f) What is the probability that the first or the second ticket is 3?
Explain your answers. If this material is unfamiliar, read chapters 13 and 14 of Freedman, Pisani, and Purves (2007).

6.4) Two tickets are drawn at random with replacement from a box containing two tickets: {0,1}.
(a) Construct a box model for this process, in which you draw once at random from a single box. (Hint: each ticket in the box should have two values.)
(b) What is the probability that at least one of the two tickets is 1?
(c) Now suppose this experiment of drawing twice at random with replacement from the original box is repeated 50 times. What is the expected value of the sum of the tickets?
(d) What is the standard error of the sum?
(e) Use the normal approximation to find the probability that the sum of the tickets is less than 60.

(f) Why does the normal approximation apply?

Explain your answers. If this material is unfamiliar, read chapters 16 and 1717 of Freedman, Pisani, and Purves (2007).

6.5) A sample of citizens is drawn from a large population for a public opinion survey. Citizens are asked whether they support Candidate A or Candidate B. A news organization reports the "margin of error" of the survey. (A little background: the margin of error is typically reported as plus or minus 2 standard errors, assuming that 50 percent of citizens support Candidate A and 50 percent support Candidate B.) Now:

(a) Construct a box model for the sampling process, assuming that 50 percent of citizens support Candidate A and 50 percent support Candidate B.

(b) What is the expected percentage of survey respondents who support Candidate A?

(c) What is the margin of error for this percentage, for a sample of size 100? What about for samples of size 200, 400, and 800?

(d) By about how much does doubling the sample size from 100 to 200 cut down the margin of error? How about from 400 to 800? Comment.

(e) What is the coverage of the confidence interval implied by a margin of error of plus or minus 2 standard errors? Give an interpretation of this confidence interval. (That is, say what it means.)

Table 6.E6 Observed outcomes in a small experiment

Assigned to treatment	Assigned to control
3	–
2	–
5	–
6	–
3	–
4	–
5	–
–	2
–	4
–	3

Explain your answers. If this material is unfamiliar, read chapters 20 and 21 of Freedman, Pisani, and Purves (2007).

6.6) There is a study group of 10 subjects in a randomized controlled experiment; 7 of the subjects are assigned at random to treatment and 3 are assigned to the control group. Observed data on the response variable look as in Table 6.E6.

Here, "—" indicates that the response to treatment or control was not observed for this subject (due to realized treatment assignment).

(a) Construct a box model for this experiment, drawing on the discussion of the Neyman model in this chapter. What is in the box?

(b) Define the intention-to-treat parameter in terms of the model you constructed in (a).

(c) Estimate the intention-to-treat parameter, using the data in the table.

(d) Attach a standard error to your estimate in (c). To do this, use the formula for the variance of a difference of means of two independent samples. (To estimate the variance of tickets in the box, you should divide by the number of tickets in the sample, minus one.)

(e) Now, suppose an investigator assumes the OLS (ordinary least squares) regression model:

$$Y_i = \alpha + \beta A_i + \varepsilon_i$$

where A_i is a 0–1 variable, with 1 indicating that subject i was assigned to treatment. (Here, to avoid confusion with the notation used for the potential outcome under treatment in the exposition of the Neyman model, I use the notation A_i rather than, say, T_i.) Make a list of the assumptions of the OLS model. How does this model differ from the box model you described in (a)?

(f) Under the OLS model, what is $E(Y_i|A_i = 1)$? How about $E(Y_i|A_i = 0)$?

(g) Denote the design matrix as X. What is a typical row of this matrix? What size is the matrix X? Denote the response variable as Y. What size is Y?

(h) Calculate $X'X$, $(X'X)^{-1}$, $X'Y$, and $(X'X)^{-1}X'Y$. Then, use $(X'X)^{-1}X'Y$ to estimate α and β.

(i) Express $(\hat{Y}|A_i = 1) - (\hat{Y}|A_i = 0)$ in terms of your estimates $\hat{\alpha}$ and/or $\hat{\beta}$. How does this difference compare to your answer in (c)? Comment briefly.

(j) Calculate the OLS residual for each subject, and calculate the sum of squared residuals. (Reminder: the OLS residual for each unit i is $e_i = Y_i - \hat{\alpha} - \hat{\beta}A_i$.)

(k) Now use the usual OLS formula to attach estimated standard errors to α and β. (Reminder: the usual formula is $\text{var}(\hat{\beta}|X) = \sigma^2(X'X)^{-1}$, and the standard errors are given by the square root of the diagonal elements of this matrix. Here, the true variance σ^2 will be estimated by the sample variance of the residuals, where the denominator gives the degrees of freedom.)

(l) Attach a standard error to the difference $(\hat{Y}|A_i = 1) - (\hat{Y}|A_i = 0)$ you found in (i). How does this compare to your estimated standard error in (d)?

(m) Do you think the usual OLS assumptions are satisfied here? Why or why not? Which assumptions are the most plausible? What assumptions might be less plausible? Explain your answers carefully.

NB, parts (e)–(m) of this question require knowledge of linear regression at the level of Freedman (2009). A calculator may come in handy, but it is best to work out the relevant matrices by hand (e.g., don't use statistical software).

6.7) What is the relationship, if any, between causal inference and statistical hypothesis testing? Are box models needed for both? How do these models differ?

6.8) In one natural experiment, a researcher compares 10 villages spread along one side of an African border with 10 villages spread along the other side of the border. The treatment and control villages are "matched" in pairs, so that each treatment village has a control village that is about the same distance from the border on the other side. The border was laid down during colonial times in an apparently arbitrary manner; the analyst posits that the location of individuals on one or the other side of the border is as-if random. In each village, the researcher samples 20 citizens at random for interviews, so that the total number of individuals surveyed is $20 \times 20 = 400$.

(a) Is this an example of a cluster-randomized natural experiment?
(b) How many clusters are there?
(c) What analytic strategies are available to the researcher, and how should he or she analyze data from this natural experiment? What problems or limitations do you see?

6.9) There is a small experiment with four units. Units A and D are assigned at random to a treatment group; units B and C are assigned to control. The observed outcomes for each unit are as follows. Unit A: 6; unit B: 2; unit C: −1; unit D: −3. Define and then estimate the average causal effect. Then use Fisher's exact test (aka randomization inference) to compute the probability, under the sharp null hypothesis, of observing an effect as large in absolute value as your estimated average causal effect.

6.10) In this exercise, you will use the data from the study of Miguel, Satyanath, and Sergenti (2004), "Economic Shocks and Civil Conflict: An Instrumental Variables Approach." These are available at: http://elsa.berkeley.edu/~emiguel/data.shtml. You should download the "Main Dataset" and "Results Do-file" along with any other files that may be of interest to you.

(a) Replicate tables 1–4 in Miguel, Satyanath, and Sergenti (2004), using the code in the file called "Results Do-file."
(b) Is rainfall growth independent of pre-treatment covariates in the data set? To investigate this question, you should decide which variables are "pre-treatment covariates." Then, conduct tests of the independence of these variables and rainfall growth. You can do this variable-by-variable or using other methods. (What methods? Which technique is preferable?)
(c) Run the reduced-form regression—that is, the regression of the incidence of civil conflict on rainfall growth. (Remember—these are linear probability models.)
(d) Now run the instrumental-variables regression of civil conflict on economic growth, instrumenting with rainfall growth—without covariates.
(e) Does rainfall growth at time t appear to be independent of rainfall growth at time $t + 1$? Comment on your results.

(f) Now regress NCEP_g on gdp_g_l, that is, regress current rainfall growth on lagged GDP growth. Are your results surprising? Why or why not?

(g) What are some possible violations of the exclusion restriction in Miguel, Satyanath, and Sergenti's study? Can you think of any possible ways to evaluate these potential violations empirically?

6.11) *Data snooping.* Using a standard statistical software package,

(a) Generate 1,000 observations of a standard normal random variable y.

(b) Generate 1,000 observations each of 50 standard normal random variables $x1$ through $x50$.

(c) Regress y on a constant and the 50 variables $x1$ through $x50$. Report your output.

(d) Keep the variables for which the estimated coefficients are significant at the 0.10 level. Regress y on these variables. Report your output. Comment.

(e) Repeat steps (a)–(d), this time screening at the 0.25 level in part (d). Report your output, and compare your results to your results screening at the 0.10 level. What differences do you observe, and why?

In working this exercise, the following loop syntax in Stata may be useful:
forvalues i=1/50{
gen x'i'=invnorm(uniform())
}

In the newer versions of Stata, you should replace

invnorm(uniform()) with rnormal().

7 The central role of qualitative evidence

Qualitative methods play a crucial role in natural experiments. Indeed, I argue that the knowledge of context and detailed information on process that qualitative methods often facilitate is crucial for the method's persuasive use. The goal of this chapter is to develop this idea systematically, by providing a framework for thinking about the general utility of qualitative evidence in natural experiments while also providing several examples from recent social-scientific research. This in turn may help provide the foundation for better use of qualitative methods in future natural-experimental research.

The topics discussed in this chapter relate not just to analysis—the focus of this Part II of the book—but also to the discovery and evaluation of natural experiments (the focus of Parts I and III, respectively). However, the central interplay between qualitative and quantitative analysis in many successful natural experiments suggests that this material is best presented in conjunction with the previous two chapters on quantitative analysis.

Many scholars have previously stressed the importance of qualitative methods and deep substantive knowledge for successful use of natural experiments. As Angrist and Krueger (2001: 83) nicely put it in their discussion of instrumental-variables designs,

> Our view is that progress in the application of instrumental variables methods depends mostly on the gritty work of finding or creating plausible experiments that can be used to measure important economic relationships—what statistician David Freedman (1991) has called "shoe-leather" research. Here the challenges are not primarily technical in the sense of requiring new theorems or estimators. *Rather, progress comes from detailed institutional knowledge and the careful investigation and quantification of the forces at work in a particular setting.* Of course, such endeavors are not really new. They have always been at the heart of good empirical research [emphasis added].

This chapter seeks to put this insight on more systematic foundations. For example, what kind of "detailed institutional knowledge" is most useful for natural experiments, and how can this knowledge best be acquired? How does "careful investigation" of information about causal process help inform specific aspects of the discovery and validation of natural experiments—and what distinctive contributions does this kind of information provide to the achievement of strong research designs?

In answering these questions, I also seek to bring the discussion into closer dialogue with recent research on qualitative methods in political science. In particular, I build on Collier, Brady, and Seawright's (2010) work on the contribution of "causal-process observations" to causal inference, highlighting the crucial role of this kind of evidence in testing theories, interpreting outcomes, and bolstering understanding of causal mechanisms in natural-experimental work. I then construct a typology that seeks to clarify the distinctive forms of inferential leverage that causal-process observations can provide in natural experiments. Drawing on Mahoney's (2010) framework, I distinguish several types of causal-process observations:

- *Treatment-assignment CPOs.* In brief, these are pieces or nuggets of information about the process by which units were assigned to treatment and control conditions in a natural experiment; they are especially useful for supporting or invalidating the claim of as-if random assignment.
- *Independent-variable CPOs.* These nuggets of information provide information about the presence or values of an independent variable (a treatment); they can contribute both to natural experiments and in exploratory or confirmatory research undertaken in conjunction with a natural experiment. They can also sometimes be useful for investigating what aspect or component of a treatment is plausibly responsible for an estimated causal effect.
- *Mechanism CPOs.* These types of causal-process observations provide information not just about whether an intervening event posited by a theory is present or absent but also about the kinds of causal *processes* that may produce an observed effect.
- *Auxiliary-outcome CPOs.* These provide data about auxiliary outcomes posited by a theory, that is, expectations about an outcome besides the main one of interest that should be present if a cause really affects the outcome. Auxiliary outcomes can especially be useful for generating plausible explanations for surprising natural-experimental findings.
- *Model-validation CPOs.* These are insights and sources of knowledge about causal process that support or invalidate core assumptions of causal

models, such as the Neyman potential-outcomes model or standard multivariate regression models.[1]

I take from Mahoney (2010) the idea of "independent-variable CPOs," "mechanism CPOs," and "auxiliary-outcome CPOs," though here I develop these concepts to discuss their utility in connection with natural-experimental research. The first and final types of causal-process observations—treatment assignment and model-validation CPOs—are original to this discussion. While these latter types of causal-process observations may be important in many kinds of mixed-method research, they are especially central in the case of natural experiments. After a brief general discussion of causal-process observations, I turn to each of these types, illustrating their use in a variety of natural experiments. In the Conclusion to the chapter, I turn to an important topic for further research: distinguishing more productive and less productive uses of causal-process observations in natural experiments.

7.1 Causal-process observations in natural experiments

To begin, it is useful to draw on several concepts developed in the burgeoning recent literature on qualitative and multi-method research. Central to these discussions is the idea of a "causal-process observation." Collier, Brady, and Seawright (2010: 184) describe a causal-process observation as "an insight or piece of data that provides information about context, process, or mechanism." They contrast causal-process observations with what they call the "data-set observations" discussed by King, Keohane, and Verba (1994), among others. A data-set observation is the collection of values on the dependent and independent variables for a single case.[2] In a natural experiment, for instance, a data-set observation might record, for each unit: the value of the outcome variable, the treatment condition to which the unit was assigned, and perhaps information on whether treatment was actually received or the values on a series of pre-treatment covariates.

---

[1] Treatment-assignment CPOs can be seen as a subtype of model-validation CPOs: the presumption of as-if random sampling is a core part of (for instance) the Neyman model. Still, since model-validation CPOs involve a broader range of issues regarding the stipulation of the model, beyond a natural experiment's definitional requirement of as-if random, it is useful to discuss treatment-assignment CPOs separately.

[2] For example, a data-set observation is a single row in the "rectangular data set" used in regression analysis, in which the columns give the values for each variable.

The central role of qualitative evidence

In contrast to data-set observations, the information contained within a causal-process observation typically reflects in-depth knowledge of one or more units or, perhaps, the broader context in which these data-set observations were generated. Thus, causal-process observations need not include data collected as part of a "rectangular data set." As Collier, Brady, and Seawright (2010: 185) say, "A causal-process observation may be like a 'smoking gun.' It gives insight into causal mechanisms, insight that is essential to causal assessment and is an indispensable alternative and/or supplement to correlation-based causal inference."[3] Following this "smoking gun" analogy, causal-process observations often function like clues in detective work.[4]

In sum, causal-process observations are insights or pieces of data that provide information about context, process, or mechanism and that are not expressed in the form of a rectangular data set. In some instances, systematically gathered causal-process observations could be recorded in the form of values of independent and dependent variables for each of the units (cases) in a study. Indeed, causal-process observations can sometimes lead to the generation of data-set observations, as Collier, Brady, and Seawright (2010: 185) have emphasized. Yet in other instances, the logic of causal-process observations appears fundamentally different from the logic of data-set observations, because crucial information about context or process cannot readily be expressed as a data matrix, that is, as a collection of values on independent and dependent variables for each of the units in a study.

Much qualitative research that is oriented towards causal inference consists of the generation of causal-process observations. For example, "process tracing," a technique long privileged in discussions of qualitative and case-study methodology (George and Bennett 2005; Van Evera 1997), is seen as a method for generating causal-process observations. As Mahoney (2010: 124) puts it, "Process tracing contributes to causal inference primarily through the discovery of CPOs." Freedman (2010a) also discusses the important role of causal-process observations in medical and epidemiological research.

Yet, what role do causal-process observations play in bolstering causal inference using natural experiments? I argue here that causal-process observations can be usefully conceptualized in terms of several different types, each

---

[3] Bennett (2010), drawing on Van Evera (1997), has discussed several kinds of hypothesis tests to which causal-process observations can contribute distinctive leverage: these include "hoop" tests, "straw-in-the-wind" tests, "smoking-gun" tests, and "doubly decisive" tests. These are classified according to whether passing these tests is necessary and/or sufficient for validating the cause of an effect.

[4] In his online addendum on teaching process tracing, David Collier uses the Sherlock Holmes detective story "Silver Blaze" to clarify the varied uses of causal-process observations in causal inference. See Collier 2011: 243).

with particular relevance to natural experiments as well as to other research designs.

7.1.1 Validating as-if random: treatment-assignment CPOs

One of the core challenges of using natural experiments, as discussed in previous chapters, is validating the claim that assignment to treatment is random or as-if random—which, after all, is the method's definitional criterion.

Since many statistical models invoked by analysts of natural experiments, such as the Neyman urn model, assume random assignment, validating as-if random is also a part of validating the broader model. Again, however, because of the core definitional importance of as-if random for natural experiments, it is useful to separate discussion of the validation of as-if random in this subsection from other aspects of model validation, discussed in Section 7.1.5.

Many different techniques are useful for validating as-if random. In the next chapter, I discuss several quantitative techniques that are useful in this regard. For instance, a necessary condition for a valid natural experiment may be that the treatment and control groups pass statistical balance tests: that is, the data should be consistent with the claim that treatment assignment is independent of pre-treatment covariates, just as they typically would be if treatment were really assigned at random. As I will discuss in Chapter 8, other quantitative techniques may be useful in specific kinds of natural experiments, such as regression-discontinuity designs. For instance, analysts using a regression-discontinuity design should seek to show that cases do not "bunch" on one side or the other of the critical regression-discontinuity threshold, as they might if there were strategic sorting around the threshold (rather than as-good-as-random assignment).

My aim in this section is different. Here, I discuss the ways in which qualitative information—especially, causal-process observations—can be used to validate the claim that treatment assignment is as good as random. In particular, I show how insights or pieces of data that provide information about the process by which cases ended up in the treatment or the control group can provide distinctive leverage in evaluating the claim of as-if random— and thus contribute central leverage to causal inference.

I call these pieces of information "treatment-assignment CPOs." I begin my discussion with these causal-process observations, because they play such a distinctive and important role in the discovery, analysis, and evaluation of natural experiments. Analysts who claim to use a natural experiment should be able to point to such information about the process of treatment assignment. Conversely, without such corroborating information, readers should approach alleged natural experiments with skepticism.

As a first example, consider again the Argentina land-titling study discussed in the introduction. Recall that here, the claim was that squatters in the province of Buenos Aires were allocated titles as-if at random, because some landowners challenged the expropriation of their land in court, while others did not—leading to the creation of a treatment group in which titles were ceded immediately to squatters, and a control group in which squatters did not obtain titles due to the legal challenges. Galiani and Schargrodsky (2004, 2010) argue that the decisions of owners to challenge expropriation were unrelated to the characteristics of their parcels or the squatters who occupied them, an assertion that is borne out by their quantitative analysis.[5]

Yet, qualitative evidence on the process by which squatting took place is also central to validating the natural experiment. Recall that squatters invaded the land prior to the return to democracy in 1983 and that they were organized by activists from the Catholic Church. According to Galiani and Schargrodsky, both the church organizers and the squatters themselves apparently believed that the abandoned land was owned by the state, not by private owners. The invaded land was then divided into equally sized plots and allocated to squatters. Thus, it is credible that neither squatters nor Catholic Church organizers could have successfully predicted in 1981 which *particular* parcels would eventually have their titles transferred in 1984 and which would not.

Notice that this qualitative information does *not* come in the form of systematic variable values for each of the units of analysis (the squatters)—that is, what Collier, Brady, and Seawright (2010) have called data-set observations. Instead, these causal-process observations come in the form of disparate contextual information that helps validate the claim that the treatment assignment is as good as random. Consider the fact that Catholic Church organizers (and squatters themselves) apparently did not know that the land was owned by private owners and also could not predict that the land would one day be expropriated. Such pieces of information help rule out alternative explanations whereby, for instance, organizers allocated parcels to certain squatters, anticipating that these squatters would one day receive title to

---

[5] Not only are characteristics of the parcels similar across the treatment and control groups, but the government also offered very similar compensation in per-meter terms to the original owners in both the treatment and the control groups.

their property. Thus, these causal-process observations are quite distinct in character from data-set observations (such as the values of pre-treatment covariates for each of the squatters).

On the basis of interviews and other qualitative fieldwork, Galiani and Schargrodsky also argue convincingly that idiosyncratic factors explain the decision of some owners to challenge expropriation. Here, too, qualitative information on the process by which squatting took place and by which legal challenges to expropriation and thus allocation of land titles arose suggests that systematic differences between squatters who eventually got titles and those who did not are unlikely to explain the *ex post* differences across these groups. Instead, the causal effect of land titles is most plausibly responsible for the differences.

Qualitative evidence on the process of treatment assignment plays a key role in other standard natural experiments as well. Consider the paradigmatic study by Snow on cholera (Chapter 1). Here, information both on the move of the water supply source and, especially, the nature of water markets helped to substantiate the claim of as-if random. For example, the decision of Lambeth Waterworks to move its intake pipe upstream on the Thames was taken before the cholera outbreak of 1853–54, and existing scientific knowledge did not clearly link water source to cholera risk.[6] In fact, there were some subtleties here. The Metropolis Water Act of 1852, which was enacted in order to "make provision for securing the supply to the Metropolis of pure and wholesome water," made it unlawful for any water company to supply houses with water from the tidal reaches of the Thames after August 31, 1855. Yet, while the Lambeth's move was completed in 1852, the Southwark and Vauxhall company did not move its pipe until 1855.[7] In principle, then, there could have been confounding variables associated with choice of water supply—for instance, if healthier, more adept customers noticed the Lambeth's move of its intake supply and switched water companies.

Here, qualitative knowledge on the nature of water markets becomes crucial. Snow emphasizes that many residents in the areas of London that he analyzed were renters; also, absentee landlords had often taken decisions about water-supply source years prior to the move of the Lambeth intake pipe.

---

[6] The directors of the Lambeth company had apparently decided to move the intake for their reservoirs in 1847, but facilities at Seething Wells were only completed in 1852. See UCLA Department of Epidemiology (n.d.-a).

[7] In 1850, the microbiologist Arthur Hassall described the Southwark and Vauxhall company's water as "the most disgusting which I have ever examined." To comply with the legislation, the Southwark and Vauxhall Company built new waterworks in Hampton above Molesey Lock in 1855. See UCLA Department of Epidemiology (n.d.-b).

The way in which the water supply reached households—with heavy interlocking fixed pipes making their way through the city and serving customers in side-by-side houses—also implied a limited potential for customer mobility, since owners had signed up for one company or another when the pipes were first laid down. As Snow put it in the passage quoted in the Introduction,

A few houses are supplied by one Company and a few by the other, *according to the decision of the owner or occupier at that time when the Water Companies were in active competition.* (Snow [1855] 1965: 74–75, italics added)

This qualitative information on the nature of water markets thus suggests that residents largely did not self-select into their source of water supply—and especially not in ways that would be plausibly related to death risk from cholera. As reported in Chapter 1, Snow instead suggests that the move of Lambeth Waterworks' intake pipe implied that more than 300,000 people of all ages and social strata were "*divided into two groups without their choice, and, in most cases, without their knowledge*" (Snow [1855] 1965: 75, italics added). The key methodological point here is that causal-process observations are central to supporting the claim of as-good-as-random assignment—and causal-process observations would likely be needed to challenge Snow's account as well.[8] In many other "standard" natural experiments, qualitative evidence is also key for validating the assertion of as-if random (see Chapter 8 for further examples).

Qualitative evidence also plays a crucial role in validating regression-discontinuity designs. Recall that such designs often depend on some rule (often a regulation or law) that assigns units to treatment or control on the basis of their position relative to a threshold value on an assignment covariate. For example, in Thistlethwaite and Campbell's (1960) study, students who scored above a qualifying score on an achievement exam were given public recognition in the form of a Certificate of Merit, while those below the qualifying score were not. In Angrist and Lavy's (1999) study, the addition of a few students to the schoolwide enrollment triggers sharp reductions in average class size, for schools in which the enrollment is near the threshold of 40 students or its multiples (e.g., 80, 120, etc.). In Litschig and Morrison's (2009) study of Brazil as well as Manacorda, Miguel, and Vigorito's (2011)

---

[8] For instance, evidence that customers did switch companies after Lambeth's move, or that directors took into account the effects of water supply on deaths from cholera in ways that might be correlated with confounding characteristics of customers, might undercut the claim of as-if random. Some such evidence might come in the form of data-set observations, while other evidence may come in the form of causal-process observations.

study of Uruguay, municipalities that are just under a particular poverty-index score and therefore are eligible for federal transfers are compared to municipalities just above the threshold.

All such designs could in principle be subverted by strategic behavior, on the part of the units being studied or the officials making and implementing the rules. In studies such as Thistlethwaite and Campbell's, the relevant thresholds might be manipulated after the fact to honor particular students. In Angrist and Lavy's study, proactive parents might conceivably seek out schools just below one of the thresholds, knowing that the addition of their child to the school could trigger reductions in class sizes. Alternatively, school administrators might have discretion to refuse admission to a child who would push schoolwide enrollment over the threshold; they might not want to trigger the creation of smaller classes and thus the hiring of more teachers. In poverty-alleviation or conditional cash-transfer schemes, politicians might be tempted to send transfers to control units just ineligible for treatment, or they might seek to use political or other criteria to choose the relevant threshold in the first place. These and other actions on the part of subjects or officials could obviously undercut the claim of as-if random assignment, and they can bias inferences about causal effects if treatment assignment is related to potential outcomes. The quantitative tools discussed in the next chapter are certainly essential for evaluating such threats to validity.

Yet, qualitative methods provide a critical and often indispensable complement to such techniques. For instance, interviews with key officials or with the units being studied can help establish whether the rules are manipulated or respected. Often, knowledge of context helps analysts understand what incentives key actors might have to subvert the assignment rules and suggests qualitative strategies they can use to check whether such manipulation is evident. Lee and Lemieux (2010: 16) appear to reach a similar conclusion with respect to regression-discontinuity designs, writing that "A deeper investigation into the real-world details of how [treatment assignment] is determined can help assess whether it is plausible that individuals have precise or imprecise control over [their value on the running covariate]. By contrast, with most non-experimental evaluation contexts, learning about how the treatment variable is determined will rarely lead one to conclude that it is 'as good as' randomly assigned."

One example comes from the regression-discontinuity study of Dunning (2010b; see Dunning and Nilekani 2010) in the Indian state of Karnataka (Chapter 3). There, caste-based quotas for village council presidents are required to rotate across councils within given administrative units (subdistricts) according to a fairly complex rule, in which councils are ranked in descending order by the number of council members' seats that are reserved for lower castes. (This is determined in turn by the proportion of lower-caste residents in each village-council constituency.) District bureaucrats are supposed to implement the rotation of reservation by working their way down this list in subsequent elections, reserving the block of councils at the top of the list in one election and then rotating down the list in the next. Whenever there are more councils at a given seat threshold at the bottom of one block than the number required for reservation, the quotas are assigned to councils at random (by drawing lots).

One way to verify that this process has been faithfully implemented is to look at the history of past reservation and to compare the bureaucratic process that should have been followed in each subdistrict to the realized history of quotas (see Dunning and Nilekani 2010). Yet, qualitative methods play an important role as well. Interviews with election commissioners and other bureaucrats help researchers to understand how the process was implemented, while fieldwork can help evaluate the process of assignment in concrete instances. For instance, state regulations require district bureaucrats to hold meetings with council members and presidents in each subdistrict to announce the allocation of quotas and explain in greater or lesser detail how the allocation was arrived at; fieldwork helps to verify whether such meetings are actually held. An additional concern in this setting is whether local politicians lobby bureaucrats for quotas or their absence, and qualitative interviews can help provide evidence on this point. The incentives created by the system of rotation may limit the usefulness of lobbying: if a village council has a quota in the present electoral term, it won't have a quota in the next term. However, interviews with bureaucrats and politicians and close engagement in the field can help analysts assess whether politicians do understand their incentives in this manner.[9]

Treatment-assignment CPOs contribute markedly to other regression-discontinuity designs as well. Such causal-process observations can come from interviews, participant-observation research, or a range of other procedures. For instance, Meredith and Malhotra (2011) use a regression-discontinuity design to study the effects of voting by mail, taking advantage of

---

[9] As I discuss elsewhere in this book, in this context fieldwork can also help with evaluating potential violations of basic experimental assumptions—such as SUTVA discussed in Chapter 5—and with interpreting effects, for instance, how the predictability of rotation may undercut the distributive effects of quotas (see Dunning and Nilekani 2010).

a rule in California that allows county elections officials to institute voting by mail but only in precincts with fewer than 250 voters (Chapter 3). These authors usefully interview county election officials to seek explanations for several anomalies in the process of treatment assignment (e.g., why some precincts with more than 250 registered voters had voting by mail). These apparent anomalies often turn out to be due to previously unobserved factors (such as the growth in voter rolls since the date at which voting by mail was established prior to an election), and thus these causal-process observations help to bolster the authors' understanding of the treatment-assignment process.

Finally, treatment-assignment CPOs can play a valuable role in instrumental-variables designs as well. Here, the issue is not whether units have been as-if randomly assigned to treatment but rather to the instrumental variable. In the regression context, this comes down to the assertion that the instrument is independent of the error term in the main equation. (Note that qualitative methods can be important for evaluating other key assumptions of instrumental-variables regression models—such as the exclusion restriction, that is, the assertion that the instrument only affects the dependent variable through its effect on treatment receipt—but this issue is discussed below, in the section on model-validation CPOs; Section 7.1.5.) This is not to say that the conscious use of treatment-assignment CPOs is the norm in practice. In fact, it seems relatively rare that qualitative methods are explicitly deployed in quantitative instrumental-variables analysis, but this is not inherent in the technique. Indeed, better use of qualitative methods might make many instrumental-variables analyses more credible.

In sum, there is a key lesson here: qualitative information on the process by which treatment assignment takes place appears to be a near-*sine qua non* of successful natural experiments. This information is not expressed as a set of values on independent and dependent variables for each case, that is, as dataset observations. Instead, disparate insights or pieces of data provide information about the process by which cases end up in the treatment or the control group. These treatment-assignment CPOs can provide distinctive leverage in evaluating the claim of as-if random assignment and in fact they are virtually indispensable for the convincing use of natural experiments.

Another way to think about this lesson is as follows. In natural experiments, it is crucial to be able to point to a *process* that governs treatment assignment and to offer a convincing argument for why this process leads to an as-if random allocation of units to treatment and control. Notice that this is quite different from simply saying that one cannot think of any potential confounders, and thus assignment must be as good as random (or perhaps worse, saying that the analyst has "controlled" for all of the confounders he or she can think of, so conditional on those covariates, assignment must be as good as random). In a valid natural experiment, there should be a clear process that leads units to be allocated to the treatment or control conditions, and qualitative details on this process are crucial in validating the claim of as-if random. In convincing natural experiments, qualitative methods—especially treatment-assignment CPOs—are therefore typically required.

7.1.2 Verifying treatments: independent-variable CPOs

Causal-process observations may play an important role in natural experiments in other ways as well. According to Mahoney (2010: 125), one type of causal-process observation—the *independent-variable CPO*—"provides information about the presence of an independent variable (or about the presence of a particular range of values on an independent variable)."

Mahoney (2010: 125) suggests that the simple existence of a cause itself is often essential, and not uncontroversial, when testing theories: "in many domains of scientific research ... the key issue is whether a cause occurred in the manner and/or at the time posited by the theory." He gives as examples the meteorite/collision theory of the extinction of dinosaurs discussed by King, Keohane, and Verba (1994), in which the presence of iridium in a particular layer of the earth's crust helped substantiate the existence of the meteorite in the appropriate historical era; and the "nuclear taboo" discussed by Tannenwald (1999), who suggests that a normative prohibition against nuclear weapons is a cause of the nonuse of nuclear weapons by the United States since World War II. In both cases, independent-variable CPOs play a key role in validating the existence of these causes—iridium in the case of the dinosaurs and a nuclear taboo in the case of the non-use of nuclear weapons—in the manner and time posited by the theory. For instance, Tannenwald drew attention to specific conversations among key decision-makers to provide evidence that a nuclear taboo existed.[10]

In natural experiments, too, causal-process observations can play a useful role in confirming the existence and character of a cause. Consider, again, the Argentina land-titling study, in which verifying that squatters who were allocated titles actually possessed them—and, perhaps, also knew about and *valued* the possession of their titles—was obviously important. Independent-variable CPOs also had an important function in Snow's work on cholera (Chapter 1).

---

[10] See the recent debate between Beck and Brady, Collier, and Seawright in *Political Analysis*.

For example, a great variety of the deaths from cholera that Snow studied early in his research suggested that person-to-person transmission was responsible for cholera's spread—because he found that infected water or waste was present during these cases of transmission.[11]

Consider also Snow's study of the Broad Street pump, in which independent-variable CPOs played a crucial role. While not itself a natural experiment, this study helped to lay the ground for Snow's subsequent study comparing deaths from cholera by water supply source. During London's cholera outbreak of 1853–54, Snow drew a map showing the addresses of deceased cholera victims (see this book's cover image). These addresses clustered around the Broad Street water pump in Soho. Snow argued that contaminated water supply from the pump caused the cholera outbreak. However, there were several anomalous cases: for example, there were residences located near the pump where there had been no deaths from cholera, and there were also residences far from the pump with cholera deaths.

Snow visited many of these locations to see what he might learn (Snow [1855] 1965: 39–45). At one address, a brewery near the Broad Street pump, he was told by the proprietor that there was a fresh-water pump located on the premises of the brewery—and that in any case the brewers mostly tended to drink beer, not water (Snow [1855] 1965: 42). At other addresses, closer to another water pump than to Broad Street, Snow learned that the deceased residents had preferred, for one reason or another, to take water at the Broad Street pump.[12] Thus, in pursuing these anomalous cases using interviews and various other forms of qualitative research, the presence or absence of an infected water supply was the key issue. In this case, then, independent-variable CPOs played an important role in testing key implications of the hypothesis that infected water from the Broad Street pump was responsible for the spread of cholera.[13]

---

[11] See also Snow's ([1855] 1965) discussion of the index cases of cholera in Horsleydown.

[12] Snow writes, "There were only ten deaths in houses situated decidedly nearer to another street pump. In five of these cases the families of the deceased persons informed me that they always sent to the pump in Broad Street, as they preferred the water to that of the pump which was nearer. In three other cases, the deceased were children who went to school near the pump in Broad Street. Two of them were known to drink the water; and the parents of the third think it probable that it did so. The other two deaths, beyond the district which this pump supplies, represent only the amount of mortality from cholera that was occurring before the irruption took place" ([1855] 1965: 39–40). One victim, a widow who lived in the Hampstead district of London and had not been in the neighborhood of Broad Street for months, used to send for water from the Broad Street pump, and she drank this water in the two days before dying of cholera during the epidemic (Snow [1855] 1965: 44).

[13] The Broad Street pump study isn't a natural experiment, of course: there is no argument made that location of residence near and far from the pump, or tendency to draw water from the pump, is as-good-as-randomly assigned.

Of course, data-set observations can also validate the existence of causes. In Snow's natural experiment, for example, painstaking legwork using surveys of households in affected areas—drawing on what Freedman (1991) and others refer to as "shoe-leather" epidemiology—was crucial to discovering the sources of water supply in the different houses included in the natural-experimental study group. Water supply source was then related quantitatively to death rates from cholera, using the cross-tabulation methods discussed in Chapter 1 and 5. This combination of CSOs and data-set observations is very much in the spirit of multi-method research: different kinds of tools can provide leverage for causal inference, and they should all be brought to bear when appropriate.

Finally, Posner's (2004) study of the political salience of cultural cleavages in Zambia and Malawi provides a different sort of example of independent-variable CPOs. Recall that Posner suggests that interethnic attitudes vary markedly on the two sides of the Zambia–Malawi border due to the different sizes of these groups in each country, relative to the size of the national polities (see also Posner 2005). According to Posner, the different relative sizes of the groups change the dynamics of electoral competition and make Chewas and Tumbukus political allies in populous Zambia but adversaries in less populous Malawi. Yet in order to argue this, Posner has to confront a key question which, in fact, sometimes confronts randomized controlled experiments as well: what, exactly, is the treatment (Chapter 10)? Or, put another way, which aspect of being in Zambia as opposed to Malawi causes the difference in political and cultural attitudes? Posner provides historical and contemporary evidence that helps rule out the influence of electoral rules or the differential impact of missionaries on each side of the border. Rather, he suggests that in Zambia, Chewas and Tumbukus are politically mobilized as part of a coalition of "Easterners," since alone neither group has the size to contribute a substantial support base in national elections, whereas in smaller Malawi (where each group makes up a much larger proportion of the population), Chewas are mobilized as Chewas and Tumbukus as Tumbukus (see also Posner 2005). This example is discussed critically in, e.g., Chapter 10, where it is pointed out the natural experiment itself does not help answer the important question about what the treatment is. However, Posner's investigation of the plausibility of the relevant treatment variables provides a valuable example of the use of "shoe leather" in seeking to identify the key causal variable that explains the contrast between ethnic relations on either side of the border and therefore demonstrates persuasive use of independent-variable CPOs.

7.1.3 Explaining effects: mechanism CPOs

Along with several other authors, Mahoney (2010: 128) emphasizes that causal-process observations can also help to illuminate the mechanisms linking causes to effects. As he puts it, "A second kind of causal-process observation—a *mechanism CPO*—provides information about whether an intervening event posited by a theory is present. It is not primarily by expanding the size of the *N* that these causal-process observations increase leverage. Instead, the leverage they provide derives from the ability of individual observations to confirm or challenge a researcher's prior expectations about what should occur." For instance, drawing on Skocpol (1979), Mahoney gives the example of the role of vanguard movements in social revolution. Though all of the cases of revolution that Skocpol examined featured vanguard movements, while several cases of nonoccurrence did not, Skocpol suggests that vanguard movements—despite their name—tended to arrive on the revolutionary scene late, after key structural events had already sparked urban and/or rural lower-class revolts. Thus, vanguard movements are not plausibly a key intervening factor between structural conditions and lower-class revolts.

This account of how mechanism CPOs work, however, does not appear to clearly distinguish mechanisms from intervening variables, that is, attributes on which units (cases) may take on particular values—such as early or late entry of revolutionary vanguards in the case of social revolutions. Thus, data on intervening variables could readily be gathered as data-set observations in some contexts. This is of course not a bad thing, yet it may not help clarify the distinct contributions of causal-process observations. Moreover, thinking about mechanisms in terms of intervening variables leads to nontrivial empirical difficulties, as the recent literature on mediation analysis nicely illuminates (Bullock and Ha 2010, Green, Ha, and Bullock 2010, Imai et al. 2011). Even in a true experiment, a focus on intervening variables can be misleading: treatment and intervening variables might have heterogeneous effects on different types of subjects, and making inferences based on non-manipulated mediators—or even experimentally manipulated mediators—is subject to hazards of unexplored interactions between type and these heterogeneous effects.

Note that this characterization of mechanisms as intervening variables is not reflected in all treatments of the topic. Waldner (forthcoming), for instance, takes a contrasting view. In his discussion, mechanisms are not intervening variables but rather are names for invariant processes, such as "combustion"—the mechanism that links the turning of the key in a car's ignition to generation of the power that leads to movement of the car. If this is the view taken of mechanisms, then a range of qualitative methods may help to generate "mechanism CPOs" in natural experiments—as in other kinds of research designs.

For example, a study of the effect of police presence on crime—in a natural experiment in which police may be as-if randomly allocated to blocks with Jewish centers, after a terrorist attack in Argentina—might seek to determine whether "deterrence" is the mechanism that explains a reduction in crime in blocks allocated greater police presence (Di Tella and Schargrodsky 2004). Explanations for why political participation (especially voting) among former child soldiers who were allegedly as-if randomly abducted by the Lord's Resistance Army in Uganda might turn to abstract psychological concepts such as "empowerment" (Blattman 2008). Quotas for heterogeneous groups of subcastes in India, rather than engendering greater "competition" for benefits, might promote "solidarity" among members of the group defined by a larger caste category (Dunning 2010b). Of course, concepts like deterrence, empowerment, or solidarity have empirical referents, and these may take the form of both causal-process observations and data-set observations; a variety of sources of evidence, from conventional observation to true experiments, may be useful here. Yet causal-process observations may make an especially important contribution to the discovery and validation of mechanisms, where these are understood as abstract principles that link intervention to effect.

Note that a range of qualitative methods may be useful for generating such mechanism CPOs in natural experiments. For example, "natural-experimental ethnography" (see Sherman and Strang 2004; Paluck 2008), which may refer to the deep or extensive interviewing of selected subjects assigned to treatment and control groups, could be particularly valuable for illuminating the strategic, cognitive, or intentional aspects of behavior that help to produce effects from causes. Here, the focus may also be interpretive in nature, with the social *meaning* subjects attribute to the treatment (or its absence) being a central topic of concern. Fieldwork of various types may be especially useful for generating and validating mechanism CPOs. Indeed, the act of collecting the original data often used in natural experiments—rather than using off-the-shelf data, as is often the case in conventional quantitative analysis—virtually requires scholars to do fieldwork in some form, which may make them aware of disparate kinds of information on context and process that may (inter alia) be important for interpreting causal effects.

Causal-process observations can also be useful when treatment-effect heterogeneity is an interesting tool for helping to explain effects. Here, too, various kinds of qualitative information can be useful. In Hidalgo's (2010) research on de facto enfranchisement in Brazil, for instance, several interviewees suggested that the major problems with electoral fraud that new voting machines were partly intended to counter were concentrated in a few states in the country's Northeast (Chapter 3).[14] This then led to subsequent analysis that compared the effects of voting machines in that region with other regions and helped to produce a deeper understanding of the role of fraud reduction in producing the broader effects of the voting technology on reform.

7.1.4 Interpreting effects: auxiliary-outcome CPOs

Auxiliary-outcome CPOs provide "information about particular occurrences that should occur alongside (or perhaps as a result of) the main outcome of interest if in fact that outcome were caused in the way stipulated by the theory under investigation . . . they are separate occurrences that should be generated if the theory works in the posited fashion" (Mahoney 2010: 129). They may thus be closely linked to theory-testing; the metaphor of a criminal detective searching for clues is especially useful here (Collier, Brady, and Seawright 2010).

Natural experiments may not lay any special claim to a privileged role for auxiliary-outcome CPOs—these can be useful in many kinds of research—and the role of these causal-process observations may relate to how theory generates hypotheses to explain observed effects. Yet, auxiliary-outcome CPOs can be useful both for confirming the presence of an effect in natural-experimental designs and also helping to explain a surprising absence of such an effect. In the study by Dunning and Nilekani (2010) mentioned earlier, for instance, caste-based electoral quotas in village councils in India were found to have no discernible effect in elevating the distribution of material benefits to members of marginalized castes. Initial fieldwork suggested that patterns of party competition might undercut the distributive effects of caste-based quotas; data analysis confirmed the important association between partisan affiliation and benefit receipt (a kind of auxiliary-outcome data-set observation rather than CSO); and subsequent fieldwork provided information about the important role of party financing in local elections, in a way that was consistent with theory developed from initial stages of the natural-experimental research. Thus, information on auxiliary outcomes helped to contextualize and explain the main finding from the natural experiment.

---

[14] Hidalgo, personal correspondence, July 2011.

7.1.5 Bolstering credibility: model-validation CPOs

In Chapters 5 and 6, I discussed the causal and statistical models that undergird the quantitative analysis of natural experiments. While in practice analysts may rely on various representations of the data-generating process—including multivariate regression models—the Neyman potential outcomes model often provides a sensible approach. This model incorporates a counterfactual as well as a manipulationist view of causality that is often appropriate for natural experiments; it is not as restrictive as regression models, because it allows for heterogeneity of unit-level responses; and it leads to ready definition of interesting causal parameters, such as the average causal effect or the effect of treatment on Compliers. Moreover, the Neyman approach appeals to a statistical model—that of sampling potential outcomes at random from an urn—that is often sensible for strong natural experiments, even those in which no explicit stochastic randomization occurred.[15]

Yet, as I also emphasized in Chapter 5, the Neyman model does impose some restrictions. One of the most often-noted is the assumption of "no interference between units" (D. Cox 1958), also known as the "stable unit-treatment value assumption" or SUTVA (Rubin 1978): in particular, potential outcomes are assumed invariant to treatment assignment of other units.[16] Whether such assumptions are sensible in any given substantive context is only partially verifiable—but they can certainly be subject to some measure of empirical inquiry.

The point I wish to make here is that qualitative methods—including causal-process observations—can sometimes make a central contribution to evaluating the plausibility of these modeling assumptions. For example, contextual knowledge that is often gained through fieldwork can also help with evaluating potential violations of basic assumptions—such as SUTVA. This can occur in true experiments as well. For example, Mauldon et al. (2000: 17) describe a welfare experiment in which subjects in the control group became aware of the existence of the treatment, which involved rewards for good educational achievement, and this may have altered their behavior.

---

[15] This is in contrast to the classical regression case, where the posited existence of i.i.d. (independently and identically distributed) error terms is at odds with the actual stochastic process of randomization, even in true experiments.

[16] Of course, SUTVA-type restrictions are also built into the assumptions of canonical regression models—in which unit i's outcomes are assumed to depend on unit i's treatment assignment and covariate values, and not the treatment assignment and covariates of unit j.

In this case and others, interviews or other qualitative assessments of units assigned to treatment and control could play a key role in uncovering such potential SUTVA violations. In many natural experiments, contextual knowledge and various qualitative techniques can also play a role in evaluating such possibilities.

Suppose that in the Argentina land-titling study, for example, squatters who did not get property titles are affected by the behavior of those who did. For instance, observation of the extension of titles to squatters in the treatment group might cause those in the control group to anticipate receiving titles, and perhaps to alter their behavior in consequence. Alternatively, if squatters who get titles have fewer children—a proposition for which Galiani and Schargrodsky (2004) find some evidence (Chapter 5)—this may affect the fertility rates of their neighbors in the control group. This may weaken contrasts between the treatment and control group and thus lead us to underestimate the effect of titles on childbearing—that is, the difference between giving titles to all squatters and giving titles to no squatters. The key problem is that the model of the data-generating process is misspecified: in the basic Neyman model, potential outcomes only depend on each unit's assignment to treatment or control, while the true data-generating process features dependencies between potential outcomes and the treatment assignments of other units. I return to these points at greater length in Chapter 9.

Qualitative information in the form of model-validation CPOs can make a critical contribution to bolstering—or undermining—assumptions like noninterference. Various qualitative methods can be crucial for generating such causal-process observations. For instance, structured interviews and unstructured sustained engagement with squatters can help analysts assess the extent to which squatters in the control group have knowledge of the treatment assignment status of their neighbors, and whether they anticipate receiving titles in the future. Such methods might also give researchers insight into how decisions about fertility or other outcomes may or may not be connected across treatment and control groups, and also give them some sense of the structure of such dependencies. To be sure, the assumption of noninterference is just that—an assumption—and it can only be partially verified. But close engagement with the research setting is critical for bolstering such maintained hypotheses, and analysts should offer qualitative information drawn from such engagement that allows them to assess the validity of their causal models.

Dunning and Nilekani's (2010) study of the effect of caste-based quotas in India discussed above also suggests the potential utility of model-validation

CPOs. A key issue here is how predictable the rotation of quotas across village councils in fact is. If units in the control group know with certainty that they will be assigned to the treatment group in the next electoral period, or the one after that, this could clearly affect the political and distributive consequences of caste-based quotas. Qualitative interviews with council members and presidents in the study group did not suggest this kind of certainty: only in cases in which the relevant council presidency had not been reserved for lower castes for many electoral cycles did interviewees express confidence that a quota would exist in the next cycle. Nonetheless, interviews did suggest that the predictability of rotation may undercut the distributive effects of quotas (see Dunning and Nilekani 2010). In this case, equilibrium contrasts between villages with and without quotas in any particular term may well not capture the effects of a permanent shift to reservation for all village councils.[17] Again, fieldwork was critical for better understanding of how dynamic incentives embedded in the structure of rotating quotas shape expectations and behavior at the local level.

Finally, model-validation CPOs may also be useful in the analysis of instrumental-variables designs—both of the stripped-down variety recommended in Chapter 5 and of multivariate approaches. Consider Miguel, Satyanath, and Sergenti's (2004) study of the effect of economic growth on the probability of civil war in Africa (see Chapter 4). Recall that reciprocal causation poses a major problem in this research—civil war causes economies to grow more slowly—and many difficult-to-measure omitted variables may affect both economic growth and the likelihood of civil war. Miguel, Satyanath, and Sergenti (2004) argue that year-to-year variation in rainfall probabilistically "assigns" African countries to rates of economic growth in ways that are as-if random. Thus, they use annual changes in rainfall as an instrument, in a multivariate regression of the incidence of civil war on economic growth.

One key assumption here is that changes in rainfall influence conflict only through their effect on growth (Sovey and Green 2009). Qualitative evidence might provide some guide to the plausibility of this assumption—for example, by supporting or rejecting the idea that soldiers don't fight during floods, which if true might undermine the exclusion restriction in the instrumental-variables

---

[17] That is, we could be estimating something other than the average causal effect, defined as the average outcome if every council were defined to treatment, minus the average outcome if every council were assigned to control.

regressions.[18] Another assumption is that growth has a single effect on the probability of conflict (Dunning 2008c). Yet, the effect of agricultural growth on civil war may be quite different than the effects of growth in the urban sector (Dunning 2008c). This has important policy implications, because according to the model (and given the estimates from the data), interventions to boost agricultural or industrial growth would both reduce the likelihood of conflict. Here, too, model-validation CPOs might be useful. For instance, how do growth in industrial and agricultural sectors of the economy shape (perhaps differentially) patterns of rebel recruitment? While this question might be investigated quantitatively, a contextual understanding of modes of rebel recruitment might also shed light on it. The modeling issues that arise in this context are discussed further in Chapter 9; here, the key point is again that the plausibility of core assumptions—e.g., that rainfall only affects conflict through its influence on economic growth, or that growth in a sector influenced by variation in rainfall has the same impact on conflict as growth in a sector not influenced by variation in rainfall—can be bolstered or called into question by substantive knowledge and close engagement with the research setting.

7.2 Conclusion

Qualitative evidence plays a central role in the analysis of natural experiments. This chapter has sought to put this observation on a more systematic foundation by conceptualizing the types of contributions that causal-process observations can make. Such nuggets of information about context, process, and mechanism not only help to generate natural experiments—i.e., help analysts to recognize the opportunity for productive use of this type of research design—but also may allow analysts to validate the assertion of as-if random assignment as well as the underlying causal and statistical models used in quantitative analysis.

Throughout this chapter, I have described specific instances in which such qualitative methods have played an indispensable role in the discovery, validation, and analysis of specific natural experiments, drawing on several examples discussed in previous chapters. This strategy could have its drawbacks, however. We may risk "selecting on the dependent variable" by analyzing only those cases in which causal-process observations appear to

---

[18] Data-set observations could of course be useful here: one might systematically measure rebel/military activity during times of floods and times of drought, as well as under more typical weather conditions.

have played a productive inferential role—either by supporting successful natural experiments or invalidating others—rather than also discussing those in which poorly cast causal-process observations have instead thrown causal inference off the rails.[19] An important agenda for future research is thus to conceptualize a more fleshed-out framework—and perhaps a set of examples—that distinguish and perhaps predict when and what kinds of causal-process observations will provide the most useful leverage for causal inference in natural experiments.

One principle that may prove useful, when feasible, is *blindness* on the part of the researcher to treatment-assignment status. For instance, in the Argentina land-titling study, researchers might seek to interview squatters without verifying before the interview whether or not they are part of the group granted titles. While it is obviously important eventually to learn this information from the squatters (among other things, as a check on the existence of the manipulation, or as an independent-variable CPO), it might also be helpful for the researcher to glean information about attitudes towards reproductive behavior or individual self-efficacy without prior knowledge of whether the interviewee is a titled squatter or not. Mechanism CPOs drawn from a series of such interviews might then be compared across treatment conditions to learn about plausible channels through which titling impacts outcomes such as reproductive behavior or beliefs in individual self-efficacy. The larger point is that to bolster the power of causal-process observations, they must not be used merely as convenient anecdotes; rather, where possible they should be gathered in as disciplined a manner as possible, so as to maximize their potential to contribute to successful causal inference.

This closing question about more and less productive uses of causal-process observations, however, should not distract from a core message of the chapter: natural experiments are typically much less successful and compelling when various qualitative methods are not used or are underutilized. As scholars such as Freedman (1991) and Angrist and Krueger (2001) have emphasized, "shoe leather" is crucial for natural experiments. The fine-grained information that comes from shoe-leather research often takes the form of information on process and mechanism; and this information may not take the form of attributes or outcomes that are systematically measured for each unit or case in a data set. Such nuggets of information are in turn often crucial for

---

[19] It can be argued that this is a weakness of work such as Freedman's (2010a), who emphasizes the vital contribution of causal-process observations to many successful episodes of biomedical and epidemiological research but pays less attention to unsuccessful deployments of causal-process observations.

the discovery, analysis, and evaluation of natural experiments. Studies that are not built on a foundation of substantive expertise are ultimately unlikely to be compelling.

While this section of the book has focused on analysis, we saw in Part I that knowledge of context and process is also important for discovery—that is, for recognizing the opportunity for productive use of this style of research in connection with a particular substantive research agenda. The next Part III on evaluation also makes ample reference to the vital contributions of qualitative tools. Qualitative methods play an important role in evaluating as-if random (Chapter 8), as in the discussion of treatment-assignment CPOs in this chapter; and they can also support or undermine the broader credibility of statistical and causal models (Chapter 9), as in the model-validation CPOs discussed here. Finally, knowledge on context, process, and mechanism can also be important for bolstering (or undermining) the case for the substantive or theoretical relevance of treatment (Chapter 10). I will return to the role of qualitative methods in building strong, multi-method research designs in the concluding Chapter 11.

Exercises

7.1) Brady and McNulty (2011) use the consolidation of polling places in the 2003 special gubernatorial election in California as a natural experiment, to study how the costs of voting affect turnout (see Chapter 2). How is the assertion of as-if random probed in this study? What distinctive contributions do treatment-assignment CPOs make to supporting this assertion? Can you think of other ways that treatment-assignment CPOs could have been used in this regard, other than those described in Chapter 2? What sorts of treatment-assignment CPOs would undermine the claim of as-if random?

7.2) Horiuchi and Saito (2009) are interested in the effect of turnout on budgetary transfers to municipalities in Japan. They argue that turnout might reflect past budgetary transfers, which also influence current budgetary transfers; or that omitted variables might influence both turnout and transfers. Thus, they suggest that a regression of current transfers on turnout would lead to biased inferences about the impact of turnout. They therefore use election-day rainfall as an instrumental variable, in a regression of budgetary transfers on turnout. (Here, municipalities are the units of analysis.)

(a) Comment on this approach. What are its overall strengths and limitations? Why do these analysts use instrumental-variables regression?

(b) Horiuchi and Saito (2009) argue that in this context, the assumption of "homogeneous partial effects"—that is, the assumption that variation in an endogenous regressor related to an instrumental variable has the same effect as variation unrelated to the instrument (Dunning 2008c; see Chapter 10 of this book)—is likely to be valid. What does the assumption of homogeneous partial effects imply in this substantive context? What sorts of *model-validation CPOs* might validate the assumption? What model-validation CPOs would undermine it?

7.3) (This exercise continues Exercise 7.2.) Campaign consultants have some tools at their disposal—such as in-person get-out-the-vote contacting—that influence turnout. Consider a randomized controlled experiment, in which some municipalities will be selected at random for get-out-the-vote efforts and subsequent budgetary transfers to municipalities will be studied. What are the potential costs and benefits of this second research design, relative to the design used by Horiuchi and Saito (2009)? How should the data from this experiment be analyzed, and what are the strengths and limitations of different ways of analyzing the experimental data? Would instrumental-variables analysis be useful here?

7.4) Holland (1986) presents the slogan "No causation without manipulation." What does he mean by this? What is the relationship of this slogan to the Neyman model? How convincing do you find Holland's argument? In one or two paragraphs, discuss the merits and possible demerits of his argument about the status of individual attributes—such as race or gender—as causal variables.

7.5) In her study of the long-term effects of direct British rule in India, Iyer (2010) compares former native states in India in which the prince died without a natural heir during Lord Dalhousie's rule—and which were therefore eligible for annexation by the British—with native states that did not have an heirless death (see Chapter 4 and Exercise 4.1). She relies on a number of data-set observations to support the claim that assignment to death of a ruler without a natural heir was as-if random. What sorts of treatment-assignment CPOs would contribute to supporting or undermining this assumption? In answering this question, list specific pieces of information that would support or undermine the as-if random assumption.

Part III

Evaluating natural experiments

8 How plausible is as-if random?

This chapter begins to develop the framework for analyzing the success of particular natural experiments, focusing on the key definitional feature: the random or as-if random assignment of units to treatment, that is, to different categories of the independent variable. Chapters 9 and 10 will then discuss two other dimensions on which different natural experiments may vary: the credibility of statistical and causal models and the substantive or theoretical relevance of the intervention.

In an important sense, the plausibility of as-if random assignment stands logically prior to the analysis of data from a natural experiment. After all, if the claim of random or as-if random assignment is not compelling, then the simple and transparent techniques discussed in previous chapters may substantially lose their credibility. For example, if confounding is an issue, then simple differences of means may not suffice as compelling evidence of causal effects. The material in this chapter could thus be placed before the discussion in Chapters 5–7. This is also one reason why, in published research reports, quantitative and qualitative diagnostics for assessing as-if random should usually precede the reporting of results. However, because one goal is to place the discussion of as-if random specifically in relation to the two desiderata discussed in the next chapter—the credibility of statistical models and the substantive relevance of intervention—it is useful to discuss this issue in the final part of the book.

I therefore begin this chapter by discussing quantitative and qualitative techniques for evaluating the claim of as-if random, for standard natural experiments, regression-discontinuity designs, and instrumental-variables designs.[1] I then turn to an extensive discussion of the validity of as-if random in several specific studies, arraying the examples discussed elsewhere in the

---

[1] While these techniques may also be useful as a check on randomization when natural-experimental treatments are truly randomly assigned, for instance, through a lottery, they are most relevant in the case of as-if random, when analysts must rely on argumentation and supporting evidence to validate the claim.

book along a "continuum of plausibility" defined by the extent to which the claim of as-good-as random assignment is plausible (see also Dunning 2008a, 2010a). Thus, this chapter provides many examples of how both quantitative and qualitative evidence have been used to validate the definitional criterion of natural experiments. It also suggests the limitations of many alleged natural experiments in this regard.

8.1 Assessing as-if random

The claim that treatment assignment is as good as random is likely violated if units self-select into treatment conditions: the whole point of randomization is that subjects should not be able to choose whether they go into the treatment or control groups. The concern is that unobserved determinants of outcomes, other than the key treatment, will not be symmetric across the treatment and control groups. In other words, there will be statistical dependence between treatment assignment and potential outcomes. Similarly, if policy-makers or politicians assign the units using some other rule than randomization, they may have incentives to manipulate the assignment so that certain types of units (say, constituents or supporters) end up receiving a benefit or policy.

The importance of these concerns, in any study lacking true randomization, might be assessed by considering the *information*, *incentives*, and *capacities* of units in the study group, as well as other key actors who have control over assignment decisions.[2] Thus:

(1) *Information.* Do units have information that they will be exposed to a treatment, or do policy-makers know which units are assigned to treatment conditions? Do these actors know the condition to which units end up being exposed?
(2) *Incentives.* Do units have incentives to self-select into treatment and control groups, or do have policy-makers have incentives to allocate particular units to particular groups?
(3) *Capacities.* Do units have the capacity to self-select into treatment or control groups, or do policy-makers have ability to allocate particular units to particular groups?

---

[2] I am grateful to David Waldner for suggesting this formulation.

A conservative classification rule might require that the units and other key actors have neither information, incentives, nor capacities to manipulate treatment assignment; in other words, satisfaction of each criterion would be individually necessary if not necessarily jointly sufficient for the presence of a natural experiment. This seems quite restrictive, because there may certainly be settings in which, say, information and incentives to manipulate treatment assignment exist but capacity does not. On the other hand, it may seem unduly permissive to qualify a study as a natural experiment simply because the answer is "no" to one of the three sets of questions above.

To put these considerations into sharper relief, recall again the Argentina land-titling study. Here, consideration of (1) information, (2) incentives, and (3) capacities can help to clarify threats to the validity of as-if random. Poor squatters invaded apparently public land in greater Buenos Aires, and were later extended titles to their plots by the state, which, however, had to expropriate the lands from their owners to do so; some owners challenged the expropriation of their land in court, creating a significant delay in extension of titles to the "control group" of untitled squatters. Is assignment to land titles then really as good as random? If squatters or Catholic Church organizers had (1) information about which plots would eventually be titled, that might have allowed them in principle to manipulate assignment of plots to particular squatters: for instance, they might have opted to assign titles to squatters who were sure to keep their plots. Of course, they would have needed (2) an incentive and importantly (3) the capacity to do so. In the Argentine example, however, church organizers plausibly had neither the information nor the capacity, nor plausibly the incentives, to manipulate the assignment process so that certain types of squatters would eventually receive title to their land.

On the other hand, the owners whose lands were expropriated plausibly had (1) information about which squatters would receive title if they failed to challenge the expropriation in court—though they may not have had detailed information about the attributes of those squatters and particularly what the potential outcomes of different squatters would be with titles and without titles—and they also certainly had (2) the capacity to file lawsuits and thereby delay or prevent the granting of titles. As far as the owners are concerned, the claim that assignment to titles was as good as random for squatters in the study group therefore amounts to a claim either that (1) owners did not have sufficient information about the potential outcomes of the squatters, or (2) they lacked incentives to press or fail to press claims to their property in a way that is related to these potential outcomes. Here it is important to consider the nature of the outcomes being considered—for instance, future access to credit markets, household investments, or fertility decisions of the affected households. The claim that owners lacked the information or incentives necessary to press (or fail to press) claims in ways related to these outcomes is more plausible because the outcomes are most relevant to the squatters, not the owners.

The plausibility that actors lack the information, incentives, and capacities to influence treatment assignment in a way that is related to potential outcomes may vary across applications. In the regression-discontinuity study of the effect of class size using Maimonides' Rule in Israel (Angrist and Lavy 1999), it might well be that parents have strong incentives to send children to schools with 40 or 80 students, as the addition of their child would trigger the creation of new classes in these schools and thus reduce average class size. The key question is whether they have the information and capacity to do so. Thus, knowledge of the ease with which families can choose schools, rather than being assigned schools based on residential location, would be valuable for researchers and their readers. In other regression-discontinuity designs, the capacity and incentives of units to "sort" on one side or the other of the key threshold determining treatment assignment may vary as well.

There are also other important means of evaluating the plausibility of as-if random beyond the criteria mentioned above. Instead of investigating the information, incentives, capacities of key actors—a task for which the qualitative tools discussed in the previous chapter may be especially suitable—one could instead take a different tack. The logic of this alternative means of investigating empirically the plausibility of as-if random is based on the following observation: if treatment assignment were truly as good as random, then it should be statistically independent of potential outcomes, and also statistically independent of pre-treatment attributes that might be related to those potential outcomes. This independence implies that, on average across many randomizations, assignment to the treatment and control groups would be empirically uncorrelated with these attributes. Of course, in any particular randomization, too many units with one or another attribute might be assigned to the treatment and control groups. Therein lies the role of statistical hypothesis testing, which here can help distinguish confounding from chance variation (Chapter 6). As I discuss below, such "balance tests" are a crucial quantitative tool for investigating the plausibility of as-if random, along with other quantitative tools that are specific to different kinds of natural experiments.

Investigating the plausibility of as-if random therefore relies on a number of different kinds of tools. Indeed, this discussion suggests that one could instead pose a broader set of criterial questions, beyond the three elements of information, incentives, and capacities discussed above. For instance, analysts exploiting apparent natural experiments might ask:

- Do subjects plausibly self-select into treatment and control groups in ways that are unobserved or unmeasured by the analyst but that are correlated with the outcome of interest?
- Have policy-makers or other political actors possibly made interventions in anticipation of the behavioral responses of citizens in ways that are correlated with these potential behavioral responses?
- Are treatment and control groups unbalanced with respect to other variables that could plausibly explain differences in average outcomes across groups?

Affirmative answers to any such questions suggest that one is probably dealing with something less than a natural experiment.

8.1.1 The role of balance tests

I now turn to a more extensive discussion of the role of quantitative and qualitative tools in evaluating as-if random, beginning with the former, before moving to tests used in specific types of natural experiments such as regression-discontinuity and instrumental-variables designs. Perhaps the central quantitative tool used to validate natural experiments of all types involves so-called balance tests, also known as randomization or as-if randomization tests.[3] Here, analysts investigate the degree of balance on pre-treatment covariates across treatment and control groups. "Pre-treatment covariates" are those whose values are thought to have been determined before the notional treatment or intervention took place. For instance, in the Argentina land-titling study, the sex and age of squatters at the time of invasion should not be affected by whether they later received land titles. If the land titles were truly assigned at random, assignment to treatment or control would be statistically independent of such covariates.[4] Age and sex

---

[3] This usage of "randomization test" is to be distinguished from the tests discussed in connection with randomization inference and Fisher's exact test in Chapter 6. However, such tests can also be used to test whether observed differences between treatment and control groups on pre-treatment attributes could reasonably have arisen by chance. Here, one posits the strict null hypothesis that covariate values are the same for each unit under assignment to treatment or control, and uses the permutation distributions to assess whether the data are consistent with this hypothesis.

[4] Analysts should not conduct tests on post-treatment covariates, since these could have been shaped by the treatment (and thus lack of balance on these characteristics is not evidence against randomization). In

should also be only weakly correlated with treatment assignment in the data, unless something unusual happened due to the luck of the draw. This logic was at work as well in Snow's informal discussion of his natural experiment on cholera transmission—where the "condition and occupation" of occupiers of houses supplied by two water companies in nineteenth-century London were compared.

Statistical "balance tests" formalize such comparisons. Here, analysts assume that treatment assignment is independent of pre-treatment covariates and then look for evidence to the contrary. The sampling model is akin to the Neyman urn model presented in Chapter 5. Under the null hypothesis, the population means of the treatment and control groups are equal on covariates such as age and sex that should not be affected by treatment assignment. The simplest tests therefore subtract sample mean covariate values—such as the average age or percentage female—in the control group from the treatment group. Under the null hypothesis, these differences will be zero; in the data, they may be non-zero. (Perhaps a few too many old people or women got titles, by the luck of the draw.) Again, the goal of the hypothesis testing is to distinguish real differences from chance variation.

Typically, the difference of means will be divided by its standard error, and (if the number of units is reasonably big) the normal approximation will be used. Thus, a p-value of less than 0.05 (a z- or t-score of around 1.96 or about 2.00 in absolute value, respectively) will be taken as evidence against as-if randomization.[5] That is, the analyst would reject the null hypothesis of equal means, since the difference of means on the pre-treatment covariate is statistically significant. In the Argentina land-titling study, for example, characteristics of the squatters such as age and sex, and characteristics of their plots, such as distance from polluted creeks, were found to be insignificant predictors of treatment-assignment status—just as they would be (in expectation) if true randomization had occurred. Thus, difference-of-means tests failed to reject the null hypothesis of equal means across treatment and control groups, supporting the claim of as-if randomization.

In many studies, as in the Argentina study, multiple pre-treatment covariates are available. In this case, analysts might conduct a difference-of-means test on each covariate. The logic of hypothesis testing suggests that even if treatment assignment is independent of each covariate, we

---

the Argentina land-titling study, the average age of subjects at the time of data collection (rather than at the time titles were extended) may be a post-treatment covariate, if titling makes subjects live longer.

[5] For the t-test, the critical value of the test at the 0.05 level depends on the degrees of freedom, but for moderately large experiments it is around 2.00.

would expect to find a "significant" difference in 1 out of 20 (that is, 5 out of 100) tests.[6] Thus, with 20 pre-treatment covariates, we would expect to reject the null hypothesis of equality of means across the treatment and control groups for 1 of the 20 pre-treatment covariates. The appearance of a few significant t-statistics in balance tests is therefore not necessarily undue cause for alarm.

In general, analysts conducting many hypothesis tests may consider adjusting for these multiple statistical comparisons. One possibility is known as the Bonferroni correction. Here, the significance level required to reject the null hypothesis is adjusted by dividing by the number of tests. Thus, if there are 20 pre-treatment covariates, a nominal p-value of 0.05/20=0.0025 for any single test would be required to reject the null hypothesis of equal means at a true level of 0.05. Since the Bonferroni correction assumes independent statistical tests, analysts sometimes use other adjustments that correct for the correlation of the pre-treatment covariates.[7] Of course, such adjustments for multiple comparisons will make it harder to reject the null hypothesis of randomization—which is not necessarily a good thing with natural experiments, since the absence of true randomization may counsel caution.[8] Thus, it may be best to use the usual nominal p-values but to expect a few imbalances if there are many covariates. (In contrast, when testing causal hypotheses for multiple *outcome* variables rather than balance testing on pre-treatment covariates, corrections for multiple comparisons are often a very good idea.)

Analysts should also consider the statistical power of their tests—which is shaped by the number of units in the treatment and control groups, as well as the variance of the covariates and the size of any true covariate differences across these groups. Proposed natural experiments with very many units may reveal significant imbalances on pre-treatment covariates, even if these differences are substantively small. By contrast, even in the presence of substantively large imbalances, analysts may fail to reject the null hypothesis of equal means when the number of natural-experimental units is small. Failing to reject the null

---

[6] The expectation may differ, however, depending on the degree of correlation of covariates across subjects: the expectation of 1 out of 20 significant differences assumes independent tests.

[7] See, e.g., Benjamini and Yekutieli (2001) or Benjamini and Hochberg (1995).

[8] An alternative is to regress treatment assignment on all pre-treatment covariates and conduct an F-test, which compares two models: one in which the coefficients of the pre-treatment covariates are constrained to vary and one in which they are constrained to zero. This allows analysts to conduct a significance test for the joint hypothesis that all coefficients are zero. However, the F-test is perhaps less in the spirit of the Neyman model than adjustments for multiple statistical comparisons: treatment assignment is assumed to be a linear combination of the covariates, and normality of the error term in the two regression equations is assumed.

hypothesis clearly does not imply acceptance of as-if randomization, particularly in small natural experiments. Passing balance tests is less compelling as evidence for as-if random if the study group is small (Imai, King, and Stuart 2008).

The quality of the available pre-treatment covariates should also be considered: failure to reject the null hypothesis of equal means for a few badly measured or theoretically irrelevant variables does not constitute persuasive evidence in favor of as-if randomization. Measurement error in these variables will tend to reduce power to detect differences across the treatment and control groups. In addition, if analysts are unable to measure at least some important potential confounders to include in balance tests, failure to reject the equality of means across treatment and control groups is less compelling as supportive evidence for as-if randomization.

Finally, another crucial point is that balance tests must be conducted at the level of randomization. Consider, for example, studies in which as-if randomization occurs at the level of the cluster.[9] If covariate values are highly correlated within clusters, then balance tests assuming individual-level randomization may be highly misleading. For instance, the luck of the draw may allocate one cluster with very high or low average covariate values to the treatment or control group—but this "accident" of randomization is then multiplied by the number of units in the cluster, if analysts conduct analysis at the individual level. In this case, analysts using tests at the individual level for cluster-randomized data may erroneously reject the hypothesis of equal means across the treatment groups—and thus erroneously call into question the premise of as-if randomization (see, e.g., Hansen and Bowers 2009). Thus, balance on pre-treatment covariates should be evaluated at the level of randomization, not the level of observation or analysis (if these differ).

For instance, in Snow's study of cholera, households (not individuals) were randomized to source of water supply. Therefore, balance on pre-treatment covariates should be evaluated at the level of the household—for instance, by comparing average household wealth or average household age across the treatment and control groups—rather than at the level of individuals. The reason: wealth or age may be correlated within households, leading analyses at the individual level to exaggerate disparities across the treatment and control conditions. Snow may implicitly have recognized this point, since his discussion of parity across treatment and control groups focuses on household characteristics (see Chapters 1 and 5).

---

[9] See Chapter 6 for discussion and examples.

In sum, balance or as-if randomization tests are essential in natural experiments, as this is one of the best diagnostics for evaluating the claim of as-if random. Indeed, the simple quantitative estimators of the average causal effect discussed above are premised on an assumption of as-if random assignment—so this should be evaluated and reported prior to analysis and estimation of causal effects. Finding significant imbalances across the treatment and control group may suggest something less than a natural experiment—though the power, quality, and number of the tests should also be taken into consideration. By the same token, a lack of evidence of imbalance on pre-treatment covariates may only be necessary, not sufficient, for validating a natural experiment.

8.1.2 Qualitative diagnostics

The qualitative techniques discussed in the previous chapter are also essential. Nuggets of information on context, process, and mechanism, or what, as we have noted, Collier, Brady, and Seawright (2010) call causal-process observations (see also Freedman 2010; Mahoney 2010), illuminate the process by which assignment took place and thus help to validate the claim of as-if random. The previous chapter catalogued a number of instances of such treatment-assignment CPOs; thus, my discussion in this subsection is briefer.

Yet, as mentioned at the start of this chapter, the role of such qualitative diagnostics can helpfully be framed in terms of the three criteria of information, incentives, and capacities. Snow's study of cholera transmission again provides a paradigmatic example. To reiterate, Snow went to great lengths to gather evidence and to use a priori reasoning to argue that only the water supply distinguished houses in the treatment group from those in the control group, and thus the impressive difference in death rates from cholera was due to the effect of the water supply. While some of this evidence came in the form of informal balance tests, others came from disparate nuggets of information about the treatment assignment process. Consider, for instance, the issue of whether occupants of households had the (1) *information*, (2) *incentives*, and (3) *capacities* to self-select into water supply sources. As Snow makes clear, (1) renters may not have known which water supply company supplied them, as the decision had often been taken by absentee landlords years before, when the water companies were in active competition; (2) water supply source was not clearly linked to death risk from cholera, and in any case the death risk was to the occupiers of the households, not to the absentee landlords whose incentives may have been most germane to the issue of selection; and (3) the water-supply pipes were laid down in a way that limited the ability of households to switch between suppliers, as the fixed pipes serving their house were tied to one company or the other. While systematic data-set observations could in principle be useful for some of these points (for example, in principle one could survey households and ask them if they know which company supplies their water), others clearly come in the form of disparate nuggets of information about the treatment-assignment process—such as the observation that the water-supply pipes had been laid down years before the cholera outbreak of 1853–54. Thus, treatment-assignment CPOs thus play a key role in establishing how information, incentives, or capacities might have plausibly shaped selection into treatment and control groups, thereby violating as-if random.

It is important to emphasize that such qualitative tools are complementary to the quantitative balance tests discussed above, however. Just as balance tests are incomplete without knowledge of substance and context, qualitative tools such as treatment-assignment CPOs should be complements to—rather than substitutes for—quantitative diagnostics. Ideally, both should be marshaled to provide compelling evidence of as-if random, particular in those natural experiments in which the a priori case is not as strong. (In the Argentina land-titling study, for example, one would immediately expect that more energetic or determined squatters would find ways to obtain land titles, and that these effort differentials would be responsible for differences in outcomes, as compared to squatters who do not obtain titles.) Even then, quantitative tests and qualitative diagnostics may not be jointly sufficient for establishing as-good-as-random assignment, for reasons I discuss further below.

8.2 Evaluating as-if random in regression-discontinuity and instrumental-variables designs

These analytic tools available for assessing threats to the plausibility of as-if random remain relevant in regression-discontinuity and instrumental-variables designs. For instance, if as-if random assignment holds, then pre-treatment covariates should be balanced across treatment and control groups—for example, across units assigned to treatment or control by virtue of being just above or just below the regression-discontinuity threshold. Thus, difference-of-means tests on pre-treatment covariates should be conducted; if significant differences are found across the treatment and control groups, this is evidence against the plausibility of as-if random. Again, analysts should pay careful attention to the power of their tests: passing balance tests is less compelling as evidence for as-if random if the study group is small, as it sometimes can be in regression-discontinuity designs where data near the threshold are sparse. In instrumental-variables designs, the same holds: here, however, the comparisons should be made across categories or levels of the instrumental variable, e.g., treatment assignment (rather than the variable measuring treatment receipt). Various qualitative diagnostics are also essential for both kinds of designs.

Yet, some specific issues and special kinds of tests are especially useful in the case of regression-discontinuity and instrumental-variables designs, which I take up in this section. For regression-discontinuity designs, three kinds of tests are especially important: conditional density tests that evaluate the possibility of strategic or intentional sorting around the regression-discontinuity threshold; placebo tests that test for the presence of apparent causal effects at points other than the key regression-discontinuity threshold; and various kinds of treatment-assignment CPOs that evaluate the possibility of strategic or intentional manipulation of the key threshold.

8.2.1 Sorting at the regression-discontinuity threshold: conditional density tests

In regression-discontinuity designs, an important threat to the plausibility of as-if random assignment relates to the possibility that units "sort" at the key threshold. Evidence that they do so would undermine the claim of as-if random and could lead to substantial confounding. For instance, if students know that a key threshold determines their entrance to university and they are able to precisely manipulate their scores to place them on one side of the threshold, the assertion of as-if random may be undermined. A different kind of sorting could arise if admissions officials manipulate the key threshold to admit a particular clump of marginal students who were almost eligible for admission.

A quantitative technique for assessing the possibility of strategic sorting is to compare the conditional density of the forcing variable for units on either side of the regression-discontinuity threshold—that is, the number or proportion of units located "just above" and "just below" the key cutoff. For instance, a simple histogram of cases on either side of the threshold, within the regression-discontinuity study group, may provide graphical evidence for the presence or absence of sorting. McCrary (2007) discusses a statistical test based on this basic idea. Of course, a finding that the density of cases is similar on either side of the regression-discontinuity cutoff may not on its own suffice to establish lack of sorting, particularly in settings in which sorting could occur in both directions (some units may seek to obtain a score below the threshold in order to opt out of treatment, while others make seek to obtain a score just above it to opt into treatment).

This caveat notwithstanding, graphical evidence of this kind can be quite useful. Consider the hypothetical data discussed in connection with the Thistlethwaite and Campbell study earlier in the book (Figure 4.2). Here, there is no evidence that the density of units is different on either side of the key threshold. For instance, in Figure 4.2, twelve students scored between 10 and 11 on the qualifying exam, while 11 students scored between 11 and 12. Thus, a histogram plotting the distribution of students by pre-treatment test scores would not show a systematic break at the regression-discontinuity threshold.

It is useful to point out that in some regression-discontinuity designs, such conditional density tests will be mechanically satisfied—for example, in designs that compare "near-winners" and "near-losers" of elections in first-past-the-post elections. Here, since there is often one near-winner and one near-loser in each electoral district, and since these two candidates will have the same difference in absolute value from the cutoff vote margin of zero, conditional densities on either side of the regression-discontinuity threshold will tend to be mechanically equated. This is true of similar regression-discontinuity designs used to study incumbency advantage in electoral systems with proportional representation, for instance, when the difference in votes (or vote share) of the party lists of the first- and second-highest vote-getting parties are compared.

8.2.2 Placebo tests in regression-discontinuity designs

The regression-discontinuity design also suggests a natural way of implementing "placebo tests" by testing for large discontinuities in outcomes at non-threshold points. The logic of the regression-discontinuity design suggests that potential outcomes—that is, the outcomes units *would* experience in the presence and absence of treatment—should be smooth functions of the assignment covariate, at points other than the discontinuity determining treatment assignment. (As discussed in Chapter 5, moreover, potential outcomes should not be rapidly changing at the point of discontinuity: put more technically, the derivative of the potential-outcomes regression function should be close to zero.) Thus, according to the logic of the regression-discontinuity design, only the presence of the treatment itself, for units on one side of the regression-discontinuity threshold, and its absence for units on the other side should drive large discontinuities in observed outcomes.

One way to test this assumption is to look for discontinuities in outcomes at points *other* than the regression-discontinuity cutoff; following the medical literature, these are called placebo tests because they search for apparent "effects" where none should occur. In a study such as Thistlethwaite and Campbell's (1960), for example, large differences in outcomes such as obtaining college scholarships as a function of small differences in entrance exam scores would suggest that small differences in exam scores are related to large differences in potential outcomes—violating the spirit of the regression-discontinuity design and invalidating the idea of as-if random assignment among students with very similar exam scores. Imbens and Lemieux (2007) suggest testing for discontinuities at the empirical median of values to the left and to the right of the regression-discontinuity threshold: these may be high-powered tests if there are many units located near these medians (though whether that is true depends on the distribution of covariate values, of course).

Passing balance, placebo, or sorting tests does not necessarily mean that as-if random assignment holds, of course. Moreover, careful analysis can turn up evidence of imbalances and question the assertion of as-if random even when the a priori case appears strong. Reanalyzing Lee's (2008) data, Caughey and Sekhon (2011) provide compelling evidence of nonrandom assignment in close Congressional elections, where near-winners and near-losers are compared (Chapter 3). The imbalance is worsened very close to the thresholds, suggesting that the winner of the very closest elections may sometimes *not* be as-if randomly assigned.

One lesson here is that as-if random must be evaluated on a case-by-case basis. At times this claim will be compelling, whereas in other designs strategic behavior or manipulation of thresholds may undermine as-if random. This is true both for the specific "near-winner/near-loser" regression-discontinuity design and for other kinds of natural experiments.

8.2.3 Treatment-assignment CPOs in regression-discontinuity designs

Qualitative evidence on the process by which a regression-discontinuity threshold was put into place can also play a crucial role in evaluating the possibility for strategic sorting around the threshold. Consider again the study by Hidalgo (2010) on the impact of electronic voting machines in Brazil, in which the regression-discontinuity design is based on the fact that in the 1998 legislative elections in Brazil, electronic voting machines were introduced in municipalities with more than 40,500 registered voters, while municipalities with fewer than 40,500 voters continued to use traditional paper ballots. Here, it is important that the threshold was announced in May of 1998 and the number of registered voters was recorded in the municipal elections of 1996 (see also Fujiwara 2009)—this is a simple but surely important treatment-assignment CPO, since it implies that municipalities should not have been able to manipulate their position in relation to the threshold. One would also want to use causal-process observations to evaluate whether the particular threshold was chosen by municipalities to exclude or include particular municipalities, and here too the evidence is persuasive: for instance, the same population threshold of 40,500 was applied uniformly throughout Brazil (with the exception of four states, where electronic voting machines were introduced everywhere), so it would have been difficult for policy-makers to manipulate the threshold in favor of more than a few municipalities. Thus, knowledge of the context in which the policy rule was devised, the scope and nature of its application, and so forth can provide important evidence about whether strategic sorting could confound inferences.

As noted in Chapter 7, many researchers who mostly focus on the quantitative analysis of regression-discontinuity designs also recognize the important role of qualitative methods (Lee and Lemieux 2010: 16). The bottom line is that in persuasive regression-discontinuity designs, deep investigation into the details of treatment assignment can substantially bolster confidence in as-if randomness. Without such investigation, the claim is typically substantially less credible.

8.2.4 Diagnostics in instrumental-variables designs

Finally, a range of quantitative and qualitative tools are useful for evaluating as-if random in instrumental-variables designs. Balance tests comparing pretreatment covariates across levels or categories of the instrumental variable are especially useful.[10] If the instrument is truly assigned as-if at random, it should be statistically independent of pre-treatment covariates. This also suggests that the strategy of including control variables in instrumental-variables multivariate regressions—and assuming, presumably, that as-if random assignment of the instrumental variable(s) only holds "conditional on controls"—is less than optimal and does not rise to the standard of as-good-as-random assignment.

Standard regression diagnostics for the instrumental-variables linear regression model may be somewhat less useful. For example, in applications it is common to see reports of "overidentification" tests. Here, there must be more instruments than endogenous regressors, and the independence of instruments is assessed by assuming that at least one instrument is exogenous (Greene 2003: 413–15). Thus, here the "proof" proceeds in substantial measure by assumption (i.e., that at least one instrument is assigned as-if at random). Establishing as-if random is not a technical matter, and there is no single algorithm for making the claim of as-if random persuasive. The use of model diagnostics specific to instrumental-variables designs is discussed further in Chapter 9.

8.3 A continuum of plausibility

Natural experiments present an intermediate option between true experiments and the conventional strategy of controlling for measured confounders in observational data. In contrast to true experiments, there is no manipulation of treatment variables. Further, unlike many observational studies, strong natural experiments employ a design-based method to control for both known and unknown confounders. The key claim—and the definitional criterion—for this type of study is that assignment is as-if random. As we have seen, this attribute has the great advantage of permitting the use of simple analytic tools—for example, mean or percentage comparisons—in making causal inferences.

Given the importance of this claim to as-if randomness in natural experiments, we must carefully evaluate the extent to which assignment meets this criterion. Figure 8.1 evaluates several studies in terms of a continuum of plausibility, drawing on examples presented in Chapters 1–4 (see also

---

[10] In the case of continuous covariates, regression of the instrument on pre-treatment covariates could be used, and an *F*-test conducted; see the related note 8 above.

Part III Evaluating natural experiments

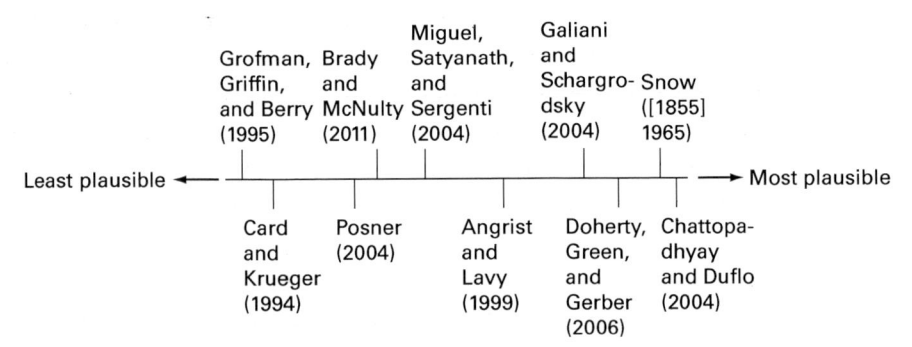

```
                            Miguel,     Galiani
       Grofman, Brady       Satyanath,  and
       Griffin,  and        and         Schargro- Snow
       and Berry McNulty    Sergenti    dsky      ([1855]
       (1995)   (2011)      (2004)      (2004)    1965)
            |       |          |           |         |
Least    ───┼───────┼──────────┼───────────┼─────────┼──→  Most plausible
plausible   |       |          |           |         |
         Card     Posner    Angrist    Doherty,  Chattopa-
         and      (2004)    and        Green,    dhyay
         Krueger            Lavy       and       and Duflo
         (1994)             (1999)     Gerber    (2004)
                                       (2006)
```

Figure 8.1 Plausibility of as-if random assignment

Dunning 2008a). The discussion is not intended as a definitive evaluation of these studies—and it is clearly not exhaustive of the studies surveyed in previous chapters. Readers should bear in mind that the rankings are inevitably somewhat subjective; the goal here is not to evaluate the overall quality of a particular study, but rather to assess the extent to which the natural experiment approximates an ideal of plausibility on this dimension of as-if random. Thus, the discussion has the heuristic goal of showing how useful it is to examine studies in terms of this dimension. Because these studies have been discussed extensively elsewhere in the book, the discussion here is fairly brief.

Our paradigmatic example, Snow's ([1855] 1965) study of cholera, is not surprisingly located on the far right side of this continuum. Given that the presumption of as-if random is highly plausible, Galiani and Schargrodsky's (2004) study of squatters in Argentina is also a good example where as-if random is plausible. Here, substantial evidence suggests that assignment to land titles met this standard—thus, confounders did not influence the relationship between the possession of titles and outcomes such as housing investment and self-perception of efficacy. In parallel, Angrist and Lavy (1999) argue convincingly that according to Maimonides' Rule, students near the thresholds are assigned as-if at random to smaller or larger classes.

Similarly, Chattopadhyay and Duflo (2004) study village council elections in which quotas for women presidents are assigned virtually at random (see also Dunning 2010b).[11] Among lottery players, lottery winnings are assigned at random given the kind and number of tickets bought, which

---

[11] A list of village council codes is used to do the assignment: councils are sorted by these codes and every third council is picked for a quota for a female president. This procedure seems unlikely to produce treatment assignments that are related to potential outcomes, yet treatment assignment is not strictly speaking due to a (quasi-)random number generator. See Gerber and Green (2012) for discussion.

may allow for inferences about the causal effects of winnings (Doherty, Green, and Gerber 2006). In close elections, electoral offices may be assigned nearly at random, due to the elements of luck and unpredictability in fair elections with narrow margins. This allows for comparisons between near-winners and near-losers (Lee 2008, though again see Caughey and Sekhon 2011). In such studies, the claim of as-if random is plausible, which implies that post-intervention differences across treatment and control groups should not be due to confounding.

In other examples, the plausibility of as-if random may vary considerably. Brady and McNulty (2011) study the effects on turnout of the consolidation of polling places during California's gubernatorial recall election of 2003. For some voters, the distances between their residences and their polling places had changed since the previous election; for others it remained the same. Here, the key question is whether assignment of voters to polling places in the 2003 election was as-if random with respect to other characteristics that affected their disposition to-vote, and it appears that this standard may not have been fully met. Brady and McNulty (2004, 2011) raise the possibility that the county elections supervisor closed polling places in ways that were correlated with potential turnout, finding some evidence for a small lack of pre-treatment equivalence on variables such as age. Thus, the assumption of as-if random may not completely stand up either to Brady and McNulty's careful data analysis or to a priori reasoning (after all, election supervisors may try to maximize turnout).

Posner (2004) argues that the border between Malawi and Zambia—the legacy of colonial-era borders—arbitrarily divided ethnic Chewas and Tumbukas. Of course, subsequent migration and other factors could have mitigated the as-if randomness of location on one side of the border or the other, though Posner argues against the importance of cross-border movements.

In another study, Card and Krueger (1994) analyzed similar fast-food restaurants on either side of the New Jersey—Pennsylvania border. Contrary to postulates from basic theories of labor economics, they found that an increase in the minimum wage in New Jersey did not increase—and perhaps even decreased—unemployment.[12] Yet do the owners of fast-food restaurants deliberately choose to locate on one or the other side of the border, thereby affecting the validity of inferences? A parallel concern might be that legislators

---

[12] In 1990, the New Jersey legislature passed a minimum-wage increase from $4.25 to $5.05 an hour, to be implemented in 1992, while Pennsylvania's minimum wage remained unchanged.

choose minimum-wage laws in ways that are correlated with characteristics of the units that will be exposed to this treatment.[13]

Finally, Grofman, Griffin, and Berry (1995) use roll-call data to study the voting behavior of congressional representatives who move from the US House of Representatives to the Senate. These authors ask whether new senators—who represent larger and generally more heterogeneous jurisdictions (i.e., states rather than congressional districts)—modify their voting behavior in the direction of the state's median voter.[14] Here, however, the treatment is the result of a representative's decision to switch from one chamber of Congress to another. Issues of self-selection make it much more difficult to claim that assignment of representatives to the Senate is as-if random.[15] Therefore, this study probably falls short of being a natural experiment in the framework of the present discussion.

A concluding point should be made about the array of studies in Figure 7.1. Research that is closer to the less plausible pole more closely resembles a standard observational study, rather than a natural experiment. Such studies may well reach valid and compelling conclusions. The point is merely that in this context, researchers have to worry all the more about the standard inferential problems of observational studies. On the other hand, natural experiments with true randomization are like true experiments, in that the plausibility of random assignment is very high.

8.4 Conclusion

In an alleged natural experiment, the assertion of as-if random assignment should be supported both by the available empirical evidence—for example, by showing equivalence on the relevant measured antecedent variables across treatment and control groups—and by a priori knowledge and reasoning about the causal question and substantive domain under investigation.

---

[13] Economic conditions deteriorated between 1990, when New Jersey's minimum-wage law was passed, and 1992, when it was to be implemented. New Jersey legislators then passed a bill revoking the minimum-wage increase, which the governor vetoed, allowing the wage increase to take effect (Deere, Murphy, and Welch 1995). Fast-food restaurants on the Pennsylvania side of the border were also exposed to worsened economic conditions, however.

[14] Grofman, Griffin, and Berry (1995) find that there is little evidence of movement towards the median voter in the state.

[15] As the authors themselves note, "extremely liberal Democratic candidates or extremely conservative Republican candidates, well suited to homogeneous congressional districts, should not be well suited to face the less ideologically skewed statewide electorate" (Grofman, Griffin, and Berry 1995: 514).

Qualitative tools, and especially various forms of treatment-assignment CPOs, play a critical role. By drawing on substantive knowledge of context and process and quantitative diagnostic tools, the assumption of as-if random can be at least partially validated in natural experiments.[16]

Yet, this claim is never completely testable. Even when a researcher demonstrates perfect empirical balance on observed characteristics of subjects across treatment and control groups, in observational settings there typically is the strong possibility that unobserved differences across groups may account for differences in average outcomes. This is the Achilles' heel of such studies as well as other forms of observational research, relative to randomized controlled experiments.[17] The problem is worsened because many of the interventions that might provide the basis for plausible natural experiments are the product of the interaction of actors in the social and political world. It can strain credulity to think that these interventions are independent of the characteristics of the actors involved, or that they do not encourage actors to "self-select" into treatment and control groups in ways that are correlated with the potential outcomes in question.

Still, strong regression-discontinuity designs, lottery studies, and other approaches can leverage random or as-if random to help eliminate the threat of confounding. After all, this is one of the strengths of successful natural experiments, relative to conventional observational studies. Perhaps the key point in this chapter is that the plausibility of as-if random will vary from application to application. It must therefore be assessed on a case-by-case basis, using a variety of quantitative and qualitative tools. When as-if random holds, inferences about the effects of treatments may be substantially more compelling.

However, as-if random is not the only key desideratum that matters in evaluating the success and utility of a given natural experiment. Other features

---

[16] A natural topic to discuss in relation to this issue is sensitivity tests. Here, analysts use a series of diagnostic tools to assess the sensitivity of conclusions to unobserved confounders. However, this typically involves making assumptions about nature and distribution of potential confounders, which may be more or less credible, and the resulting bounds may be more or less informative. Readers interested in such techniques are referred to, e.g., Manski (1995) or Gerber and Green (2012).

[17] In a thoughtful essay, Stokes (2009) suggests that critiques of standard observational designs—by those who advocate wider use of true experiments or natural experiments—reflect a kind of "radical skepticism" about the ability of theoretical reasoning to suggest which confounders should be controlled. Indeed, Stokes argues, if treatment effects are always heterogeneous across strata, and if the relevant strata are difficult for researchers to identify, then "radical skepticism" should undermine experimental and observational research to an equal degree. Her broader point is well taken, yet it also does not appear to belie the usefulness of random assignment for estimating average causal effects, in settings where the average effect is of interest and where random or *as-if* random assignment is feasible.

of different natural experiments may be just as important in contributing to the overall strength of the research design. The next chapters consider two other dimensions on which natural experiments may vary—credibility of the models and relevance of the intervention.

Exercises

8.1) An analyst proposes to study the diverse trajectories of the former Soviet bloc states in the wake of the end of the Cold War, arguing that the "common shock" experienced by these countries sets up a natural experiment. Is this a natural experiment? Why or why not?

8.2) Banerjee and Iyer (2005) study the effect of landlord power on development. They argue that land-tenure patterns instituted by the British in different parts of colonial India established two very different relationships between landlords and peasants, depending on whether landlords had the power to collect taxes. What argument must be made to establish that this is a natural experiment? How plausible do you find this assertion as an a priori matter, and what kind of empirical evidence would substantiate it?

8.3) Draws are being made at random with replacement from a box. The number of draws is getting larger and larger. Say whether each of the following statements is true or false, and explain. (Remember that "converges" means "gets closer and closer.")

(a) The probability histogram for the sum of the draws (when put in standard units) converges to the standard normal curve.

(b) The histogram for the numbers in the box (when put in standard units) converges to the standard normal curve.

(c) The histogram for the numbers drawn (when put in standard units) converges to the standard normal curve.

(d) The probability histogram for the product of the draws (when put in standard units) converges to the standard normal curve.

(e) The histogram for the numbers drawn converges to the histogram for the numbers in the box

(f) The variance of the numbers drawn converges to zero.

(g) The variance of the histogram for the numbers drawn converges to zero.

(h) The variance of the average of the draws converges to zero.

8.4) A team of political scientists conduct a true experiment, in which a relatively small number of subjects are randomly assigned to treatment and control conditions. They find a statistically significant difference between mean outcomes in the treatment and control groups. These scholars write that "covariates are balanced across the treatment and control groups in expectation but not necessarily in their realization. To check that our results are not driven by omitted-variable bias, we focus attention on two potential confounds." Can the difference in mean outcomes across the treatment and control groups be due to omitted-variable bias? Why or why not?

Comment. Sampling error is often confused with bias in discussions of experiments with small study groups. This is a natural error, but these are different concepts.

9 How credible is the model?

This chapter turns to the second of the three dimensions of the evaluative framework discussed in the Introduction: the credibility of the causal and statistical models that analysts employ. To make causal inferences, analysts must maintain some hypotheses about data-generating processes. These hypotheses are "maintained" because evidence does not permit researchers to verify all such a priori assumptions, at least not completely. Indeed, inferring causation requires a theory of how observed data are generated (that is, a *response schedule*; Freedman 2009: 85–95; Heckman 2000). This theory is a hypothetical account of how one variable would respond if the scholar intervened and manipulated other variables. In observational studies—including natural experiments—the researcher never actually intervenes to change any variables, so this theory remains, at least to some extent, hypothetical.

Yet, data produced by social and political processes can be used to estimate the expected magnitude of a change in one variable that would arise if one were to manipulate other variables—assuming that the researcher has a correct theory of the data-generating process. In quantitative analysis, this theory is usually expressed in the form of a formal statistical model; underlying causal assumptions may or may not be stated explicitly.[1] The key question is whether the maintained hypotheses implied by a given model are plausible depictions of the true data-generating process—and, especially, how that plausibility can be probed and, at least to some extent, validated.

In this chapter, I compare different approaches to model specification in natural-experimental research. I begin by further discussing the Neyman potential outcomes model (see Chapters 5–6). This model is flexible and general, and it often provides a credible representation of data-generating processes in natural experiments. For many natural experiments, this model

---

[1] For instance, the idea of a *response schedule* – which assumes the invariance of structural parameters to intervention – may or may not be mentioned.

therefore provides the appropriate starting point. Still, the model does impose some restrictions, which are also important to appreciate. For some true experiments and natural experiments—for instance, those in which treatment and control units routinely interact in ways that may violate the stability of potential outcomes under intervention or under different realized random assignments—the assumptions may be unrealistic. In each empirical application, researchers are therefore challenged to think about the ways in which the Neyman model does or does not provide a plausible depiction of the data-generating process at hand.

I then contrast the Neyman approach with typical linear regression models, especially the multivariate models used in much quantitative research using observational data. Analysis of such models often seems sophisticated. Yet, the analysis is sometimes high-tech only in appearance. The problem is that multivariate regression models linking alternative values of the independent variable to the dependent variable sometimes lack credibility as descriptions of the true data-generating process. As I discuss below, this can have practical consequences, even in settings where the consequences are not always recognized—for instance, when treatment assignment is plausibly independent of covariates included in the model. I also extensively discuss several issues related to model-specification in instrumental-variables regression.

What is the state of current practice in empirical applications? To gain a sense of this, I survey the data-analytic methods used in some of the natural experiments discussed in Chapters 2–4. As in the previous chapter, several exemplars are ranked along a continuum—this time, along the dimension of simplicity, transparency, and credibility of underlying causal and statistical models. This exercise gives further texture to the second evaluative dimension that is discussed in this chapter; and it underscores the idea that the credibility of models can vary across natural-experimental research.

As the examples I survey suggest, empirical results are only as good as the maintained assumptions about the data-generating process. When the assumptions are on shaky ground, so too are the conclusions. With strong natural experiments, in which the claim of as-if random is highly plausible—and in which the Neyman model provides a persuasive response schedule—simple difference-of-means (or difference-of-percentages) tests should be presented. Multivariate regression and its extensions should then be used for auxiliary analysis, if at all. Analysts working with instrumental-variables designs should usually present intention-to-treat analysis (also known as "reduced-form" regressions), as well as instrumental-variables regressions without control variables. Unfortunately, this analytic simplicity does not always follow in practice. While stronger research designs should permit data analysis with weaker assumptions, the causal models and statistical methods employed in many natural experiments are sometimes virtually indistinguishable from more conventional model-based approaches. I therefore conclude the chapter by suggesting several ways in which the credibility of models can be bolstered in applications.

9.1 The credibility of causal and statistical models

As I emphasized above, the definition of the causal model is critical to successful causal inference. After all, before an effect can be characterized or a causal hypothesis formulated and tested, a causal model must be defined, and the link from observable variables to the parameters of that model must be posited. Statistical inference, meanwhile—for instance, inferences about the value of causal parameters—depends on the validity of the sampling process envisioned by the model.

It is useful to distinguish in general terms between the causal and statistical assumptions of any model.[2] Causal assumptions involve maintained hypotheses about causal process—for instance, the ways in which responses are shaped by a given policy intervention. These hypotheses are not typically tested as part of a particular investigation. Such maintained hypotheses instead depend on unobservables, and in many settings they are not in fact amenable to empirical investigation.[3] Causal parameters such as the average causal effect are defined in terms of these causal assumptions.

Statistical assumptions, by contrast, involve assertions about the stochastic (chance) process that generates observable data. And statistical inference, which allows us to estimate unobserved parameters from data, relies on these assumptions about stochastic processes. Thus, we can separate the definition of parameters such as the average causal effect—which depends on the causal model—from the estimation of those parameters, which depends on a statistical model of the stochastic process that gives rise to observed data.[4] With these preliminaries, I turn to discussion of the

---

[2] Chapters 5 and 6.
[3] However, assumptions that are not tested in one setting could be tested in another context, with modifications to the research design. For instance, elegant experiments have been designed to detect the presence of spillovers and/or SUTVA violations (Nickerson 2008; Sinclair, McConnell, and Green 2011).
[4] Analysts usually present the Neyman potential-outcomes framework as a single model, and I largely follow this convention. Yet, it is useful to keep in mind the difference between causal and statistical assumptions.

Neyman model and its alternatives. The discussion in Section 9.1.1 reiterates several of the observations made in Chapters 5–6, yet it is useful for purposes of discussing the credibility of models to collect these observations in a single place.

9.1.1 Strengths and limitations of the Neyman model

The Neyman causal model has many virtues. The model is quite flexible and general. For instance, it does not impose common responses to treatment assignment across units—as in the standard regression models discussed below—but rather allows every unit's response to treatment to vary. This leads to the definition of structural parameters with intuitive appeal, such as the unit causal effect and the average causal effect.[5] Allowing each unit's response to treatment to vary across units also has the attraction of realism, and it leads to natural definitions of causal effects for particular subsets of the study group—such as the average causal effect for Compliers, as in instrumental-variables analysis based on the potential outcomes framework.[6]

At a more abstract level, the model also nicely formalizes important causal concepts. For example, it naturally emphasizes the problem of identifying the missing counterfactuals needed for causal inference. The idea of intervention or manipulation, and of invariance of the unit-specific effect to intervention, is also central to the model. Even for natural experiments—where the manipulation is by definition not carried out by an experimental researcher—the idea of the manipulability of the intervention is an important aspect of a cause (Holland 1986). Thus, the Neyman model privileges two critical ideas about causality: the importance of counterfactuals, and the role of manipulation.[7]

Yet, it is also important to reiterate that the Neyman causal model does impose some restrictions. For instance, responses to treatment are typically assumed to be deterministic at the level of the individual unit. This implies, for

---

[5] See Chapter 5. Analysis based on the Neyman potential outcomes model is sometimes called "nonparametric." This is contrasted with "parametric" regression analysis that makes stronger or more detailed assumptions, for example, about the functional form of relationships between treatments, covariates, and dependent variables. This terminology is somewhat misleading. After all, the Neyman model has many parameters – such as the unit causal effect $T_i - C_i$ or the average causal effect $\overline{T} - \overline{C}$. The point of data analysis is to use the data to estimate these parameters that are defined by the model. Thus, the key distinction between the potential outcomes model and its alternatives, such as multivariate regression, is not whether there are parameters. It is rather about whether the models, and the parameters the models define, make sense.

[6] See Chapter 5.

[7] Of course, nonmanipulationist and noncounterfactual accounts of causality exist (see, e.g., Goldthorpe 2001).

instance, that when and where treatment is assigned is not relevant: in the Argentina land-titling study, receiving a land title prompts a single deterministic response on the part of each poor squatter, as does failure to receive a title.[8] According to the model, details like the mode, manner, or timing of the offer of property rights are irrelevant: these vagaries are swept aside. This simplifying assumption may not come at great analytic cost, yet it likely does some violence to reality.

More restrictively, potential outcomes are also assumed invariant to the treatment assignment of other units in the study group. This assumption of "no interference" (D. Cox 1958), also known as the "stable unit-treatment value assumption" (SUTVA; Rubin 1978), may well be implausible in some settings. In the Argentina land-titling study (Introduction), for example, it is conceivable that the behavior of squatters who did not get property titles would have been affected by the behavior of those who did. For instance, if those who get titles have fewer children, and this affects the fertility rates of squatters in the control group, we would tend to underestimate the impact of titles on childbearing (Chapter 7). This causal assumption does not always hold, even when the design apparently is strong; for example, Mauldon et al. (2000: 17) describe a welfare experiment in which subjects in the control group became aware of the treatment, involving rewards for educational achievement, and this may have altered their behavior.[9]

This has nothing to do with a failure of randomization. Instead, examples such as the Argentina land-titling study or the Mauldon et al. (2000) welfare study may violate the assumption that potential outcomes are invariant to the treatment assignment of other units. If this violation holds, then, in the land-titling study, we are not necessarily estimating the impact of assigning titles to everyone, relative to the impact of leaving everyone in the control. This is because the model in terms of which that causal parameter has been defined is incorrectly specified. In particular, in contrast to the simple Neyman model, the true model features dependencies between the potential outcomes of one

---

[8] In principle, the model in Box 5.1 could be generalized so that T_i and C_i are random variables (Freedman 2006). For instance, the average potential outcome under treatment could be defined as the average of the expected values of T_i across all subjects. However, independence across subjects is needed to justify the usual variance calculations, and other complications may arise.

[9] Thus, Collier, Sekhon, and Stark (see Freedman 2010: xv) seem to go too far when they say that "causal inference from randomized controlled experiments using the intention-to-treat principle is not controversial – provided the inference is based on the actual probability model implicit in the randomization." Their caveat concerns inferences that depart from the appropriate statistical model implied by the randomization, but they do not address departures from the causal model on which the experimental analysis is based.

unit and the treatment assignments of others. Researchers should therefore consider the possibility of such violations of the potential-outcomes model in any given application. Of course, as we will see below, this restriction is not unique to the Neyman model; SUTVA-type restrictions are also built into the assumptions of canonical regression models—in which unit i's outcomes are assumed to depend on unit i's treatment assignment and covariate values, and not the treatment assignment and covariates of unit j. I will return below to further consideration of the ways in which empirical evidence can be used to probe the plausibility of such assumptions.

Beyond these causal postulates, what are the strengths and limitations of the statistical assumptions of the Neyman urn model—that is, the idea that units are sampled at random without replacement from the study group, like tickets from an urn, and placed into treatment or control groups? In some ways, the sampling model depicted in Figure 5.1 is simply the corollary of the definitional criterion of natural experiments: treatment assignment is as good as randomly assigned. With randomized natural experiments, the urn model appears particularly appropriate. After all, the model simply says that the treatment group can be considered as a random sample from the study group, with the remaining subjects going into control.

For strong natural experiments, this urn model has other strengths as well. Notice that under the Neyman model, we need not appeal to the presence of any (possibly ill-defined) population or super-population from which the study group is drawn.[10] In most natural experiments, as in many true experiments, the study group is not a probability sample from an underlying population. Often, it is even difficult to view the study group as a sample of convenience, because doing so would require defining a population from which the study group was drawn through some non-probability method. It is precisely for this reason that the Neyman urn model is appropriate for randomized natural experiments: the analogy to random sampling *from the study group* justifies statistical inferences under the Neyman model, and inferences are to the study group that is randomly assigned to treatment and control—though inferences about broader populations are also sometimes possible, as I discuss in Chapter 10.

Yet, if treatment is something less than randomly assigned, analysts may be working with something less than a natural experiment. Then, things become more complicated, for at least two reasons. First, the Neyman model (at least

---

[10] This is in contrast to some expositions of classical regression models, in which asymptotic inferences are justified by reference to sampling from populations (see, e.g., Wooldridge 2009).

in its simplest form) does not really consider the possibility of confounding.[11] That is why much of the discussion in this book focuses on ways to validate—or invalidate—the assertion that assignment to treatment is as good as randomly assigned.[12] Yet, the urn model in Figure 5.1 only applies when as-if random applies. Second, the analogy to "sampling" from an urn without replacement is more compelling in some natural experiments than others. For instance, the analogy may be stronger in, say, strong regression-discontinuity designs than in studies in which arbitrarily drawn jurisdictional borders lay the foundations for a natural experiment. In the latter research designs, it is sometimes hard to see where the "sampling" arises in the "sampling process."

In sum, the statistical assumptions of the Neyman model often appear suitable to the data-generating process—at least for strong natural experiments. With true randomization, the model is often most appropriate. Unlike classical regression models, the Neyman approach does not posit draws by Nature of independent and identically distributed error terms. Instead, the sampling of potential outcomes from an urn seems adequately to capture the way in which true randomization actually induces stochastic variation. This also provides a compelling analogy to the process of treatment assignment in many natural experiments with as-if randomization, rather than true randomization—though the quality of the analogy varies across different applications.

The Neyman model therefore provides a useful starting point and a credible approach in many natural-experimental settings. In the Neyman model, estimands such as the average causal effect have ready and defensible interpretations, and estimators often arise from well-defined sampling processes. Thus, many of the problems that Brady and Collier (2010: 15) identify with "mainstream quantitative methods," and which have been critiqued from the perspective of what Brady and Collier (2010: 16) call "statistical theory," need not arise in the analysis of natural experiments (see also Freedman 2008a, 2008b, 2009). With true experiments and strong natural experiments—where the research design minimizes confounding—the Neyman model and its associated simple and transparent data-analytic techniques are often highly credible.

---

[11] There are of course attempts to extend the model in this direction (see, e.g., Rosenbaum and Rubin 1983). Yet, in real applications the urn model sketched in Chapter 5 may apply to sampling within strata defined by the confounders only with some difficulty.
[12] See especially Chapter 8.

9.1.2 Linear regression models

Analysts of natural experiments do not always rely on simple and transparent analysis built on the Neyman potential outcomes model, for a number of different reasons. First, in less-than-perfect natural experiments—where the plausibility of as-if random assignment is not strong—researchers may feel compelled to control for observed confounders. Indeed, given the absence of true randomization in many natural experiments, it is not a bad idea to explore whether statistical adjustment (for example, the addition of covariates to a multivariate regression) makes a difference to estimated effects. Yet, the use of statistical controls raises some troubling issues as well. If adjustment does make a difference to point estimates, this may indicate a lack of as-if random assignment to treatment; and multiple regression can also lead to data-analysis and reporting practices that undermine the meaning of significance tests. As I discuss further below, reliance on statistical fixes—such as multivariate regression—should be viewed as an admission of less-than-ideal research designs. This does not imply that useful knowledge cannot be achieved through this route; but if the models are on shakier foundation, then so are the results.

Two other reasons that researchers routinely use regression models to analyze natural-experimental data should be mentioned: force of disciplinary habit, and the ease of implementing regression routines in standard software packages. Standard regression analysis, often involving the inclusion of various control variables, is a nearly universal reflex for many contemporary quantitative researchers. This is not a compelling rationale, however. If the underlying models are not credible depictions of the data-generating process, analysis can quickly go off track.

It is therefore useful to consider the nature of standard linear regression models in more detail. In typical models, the assumptions are more complicated than in Neyman-based approaches, and they may be even more contestable. Consider first the simplest case, in which the outcome for each unit is modeled as the sum of a constant (that is, an intercept), an unknown regression coefficient that multiplies a dichotomous indicator for treatment assignment, and a mean-zero random error term:

$$Y_i = \alpha + \beta X_i + \varepsilon_i. \tag{9.1}$$

The scalar Y_i is an observation on a dependent variable for unit i, and X_i is a scalar treatment variable. The parameter α is an intercept, β is a regression coefficient, and ε_i is an unobserved, mean-zero error term. Here, Y_i, X_i, and ε_i are random variables. The parameters α and β will be estimated from the data, typically by OLS (ordinary least squares). Here, the regression coefficient gives the causal effect of treatment, since the indicator variable is equal to zero for all units in the control regime. Without a valid natural experiment, treatment receipt may be statistically dependent on the error term in Equation 9.1—that is, endogenous. Given the model, however, random or as-if random assignment to X_i—as in some valid natural experiments—will ensure exogeneity.[13]

There are several important points to notice about this alternative model of the data-generating process, relative to the Neyman model. First, under the regression model, the causal effect is assumed to be constant for all units. Second, the additive error term is assumed to be drawn at random for each unit, as if from a box of tickets with mean zero; often, the tickets are assumed to be drawn independently and with replacement, that is, the draws are i.i.d. (independent and identically distributed). Finally, the realized value of this error term is added to the treatment effect. None of these assumptions follow from randomization or as-if randomization, and they are at odds with the Neyman model.

This can have practical consequences, even in the simplest bivariate case. For example, the nominal standard errors computed from the usual regression formulas do not apply, since they do not follow the design of the as-if randomization but rather appeal to independent draws from error terms posited in a regression model. The usual regression standard errors assume equal variances in the treatment and control groups (aka homoskedasticity). Yet, unequal variances are likely to arise, e.g., if treatment and control groups are of unequal size; or if treatment is effective for some units but not for others, which will typically cause the variance in the treatment group to be larger than the variance in the control group. Note that the Neyman-based estimator for the variance of a difference of means—the sum of the estimated sampling variances of the means—*does* account for unequal variances across the two groups (aka heteroskedasticity): the estimated sampling variance of the treatment-group mean is the estimated variance of potential outcomes under treatment, divided by the number of units in the treatment group, while the sampling variance of the control-group mean is the estimated variance of potential outcomes under control, divided by the number of

---

[13] Here, I do not distinguish between treatment assignment and treatment receipt: implicitly, assignment determines receipt, as in Chattopadhyay and Duflo's (2004) natural-experimental study of caste-based quotas for village council presidents in India.

units in that group (Chapter 6). Thus, if the variance of outcomes differs across the two groups, or the groups are of unequal sizes, the Neyman-based calculations will naturally take account of the resulting heteroskedasticity.[14] In sum, the assumption that a regression model governs the data-generating process—and not the model depicted in Figure 5.1—has some costs, even in this simplest case.

The situation is even less satisfactory when multiple regression models are used, for a number of reasons. Here, the regression equation in Equation 9.1 is amended, so that

$$Y_i = \alpha + \beta X_i + C_i \gamma + \varepsilon_i, \qquad (9.2)$$

where C_i is a row of covariate values for unit i and γ is a column vector of regression coefficients. As a description of the data-generating process, this multivariate extension of Equation 9.1 is likely to be even less compelling. The equation makes strong assumptions about the relationship of each covariate to the outcome. For example, why is the observed response a linear and additive function of the covariates? Why are coefficients like β and γ structural parameters, in the sense of being invariant to intervention, and why are they the same for every subject? Common statistical assumptions associated with models such as Equation 9.2 may muddy the waters further. For instance, why are random error terms drawn from independent and identically distributed distributions? In regression-discontinuity designs, scholars may include various polynomials or interaction terms in equations such as Equation 9.2; the same comments about model specification apply there (Chapter 5).

Scholars use such multivariate regression models for different reasons. In some cases, they are attempting to confront possible failures of as-if random assignment. For instance, Brady and McNulty's (2011) study controls for possible confounders such as age. Card and Krueger (1994) also include control variables associated with exposure to minimum-wage laws and with subsequent wages. Grofman, Brunell, and Koetzle (1998) use similar strategies, as do many other studies in which the assertion of as-if random assignment is not fully plausible.

---

[14] It is possible to adjust regression standard errors to account for heteroskedasticity; in the bivariate case, this can produce variance estimators for causal-effect estimators that are identical to those based on the Neyman model. However, this is not generally true in the case of multivariate regression. As a general matter, assuming a model that is at odds with the sampling process appears misguided, a point to which I return below.

Including measures of possible confounders on the right-hand side of an equation such as Equation 9.2 is thought to "control" for such confounders: after all, analysts reason, the measured confounders are in the equation, so that must control for the confounding. However, it is less common to justify the functional form of the posited relationship between the variables, or to defend the plausibility of a data-generating process such as Equation 9.2. One simple alternative might be cross-tabulations or stratification, that is, looking at the relationship between treatment and outcomes within each "cell" defined by the values of the covariates. Yet, with many controls or continuous covariates, the number of cells of the cross-tabulations would typically rapidly exceed the number of data points, which is one reason for using the models (Chapter 1).

In other cases, data limitations can also lead to more complicated modeling assumptions. In the prize lottery study by Doherty, Green, and Gerber (2006), for example, the level of lottery winnings is randomly assigned among lottery players. Thus, there are multiple treatment groups: the level of lottery winnings is conceptually a continuous variable, so (unlike, say, Snow's study of cholera) we cannot simply compare one group of subjects exposed to treatment to another group of subjects exposed to control. This raises issues that go beyond randomization: without imposing linearity or other assumptions on the response of subjects to different levels of treatment, for example, it may be misleading to speak of a single (marginal) effect of winnings. In principle, of course, we can compare people across narrower and narrower bins of lottery winnings, thus effectively using the natural-experimental data to trace out the true response schedule (Freedman 2009: 85–87) that links lottery winnings to political attitudes.[15] Again, in practice, the ability to do this is constrained by data availability: with only 342 lottery players in Doherty, Green, and Gerber's (2006) study, we have to substitute modeling assumptions such as linearity in place of cross-tabulations and stratification.[16]

Finally, researchers sometimes also use multivariate regression to reduce the variability of treatment effect estimators (D. Cox 1958; Gerber and Green

---

[15] In addition, note that levels of lottery winnings are only randomly assigned conditional on the number and type of tickets bought. Absent the data limitations, one nonparametric possibility would be to estimate treatment effects separately for groups of subjects who bought the same number and type of tickets. The alternative – including dummy variables for the number and type of tickets in a regression model with a common coefficient for winnings – involves additional assumptions.

[16] See Doherty, Green, and Gerber (2006), who estimate both linear and nonlinear models (where response to treatment is linear on the ordered probit scale), for further details.

2012). The idea, which is akin to blocking, has its place: within strata defined by regression controls, the variance in both the treatment and control groups may be smaller, leading to more precise estimation of treatment effects within each strata. However, whether variance is actually reduced depends on the strength of the empirical relationship between pre-treatment covariates and the outcome; variance may be higher or lower after adjustment (Freedman 2008a, 2008b; Gerber and Green 2012).[17]

Reliance on adjusted results—for example, those obtained from estimating multivariate models such as Equation 9.2—raises some difficult issues, however. If the study group is small, and if the Neyman model describes the true data-generating process, then multiple regression estimators may be biased, sometimes badly—even if the treatment is truly randomized (Freedman 2008a, 2008b).[18] Under the Neyman model, outcomes are deterministic functions of treatment assignment: if we know the vector of assignments (and the potential outcomes), we know the average outcomes in the treatment and control groups. The model in Equation 9.2 implies something different, however: given random assignment, outcomes are also a function of covariates, which are empirically correlated with treatment assignment (at least in small samples). In sum, the average estimate $\hat{\beta}$ across all possible randomizations may not equal β. The comments above about the nominal standard errors—those calculated from the usual regression formulas—also apply to multiple regression analysis.

The use of models such as Equation 9.2 may thus forego some of the key advantages of valid natural experiments, in terms of simplicity and transparency as well as credibility. Indeed, the crux of the matter seems to be this: why control for confounders, if the research design ensures that confounders are statistically independent of treatment? If treatment assignment is truly as-if random, then it is independent of potential outcomes, and a simple difference of means establishes credible evidence for the presence or absence of a causal effect. Of course, if treatment assignment is independent of covariates, point estimates of causal effects from fitting multivariate regression equations should be similar to estimates from difference-of-means tests, at least with large study groups. Yet, if treatment assignment is not in fact independent of covariates (or is at least not orthogonal in the sample data),

---

[17] Since the nominal standard errors do not apply (in either the multivariate or bivariate cases), analysts who fit multivariate models to natural-experimental data would do well to bootstrap the standard errors, rather than report the usual standard errors returned by statistical software.

[18] This is *small-sample bias*: it disappears as the study group grows larger, so the regression estimators are consistent (asymptotically unbiased).

the point estimates may differ substantially after adjustment. Below, I discuss examples in which unadjusted difference-of-means tests and multivariate regression models lead to different conclusions about the probable presence or absence of a causal effect. This raises some important issues of interpretation. For example, should we believe the adjusted or the unadjusted results, where they differ?

Moreover, and perhaps more importantly, the post hoc specification of regression models can lead to data mining, with only "significant" estimates of treatment effects making their way into published reports (Freedman 1983). This, of course, undermines the conventional interpretation of significance tests. Because of such concerns, analysts should report unadjusted difference-of-means tests, in addition to any auxiliary analysis. If an estimated treatment effect is insignificant in the absence of controls, this should clearly shape our interpretation of the effect being estimated.

These issues have important practical consequences. Consider the regression-discontinuity design in the study by Angrist and Lavy (1999), which the authors use to estimate the educational return to smaller class sizes in Israel. The logic of the regression-discontinuity design implies that treatment assignment is only as-if random near the threshold of the covariate determining assignment; units located near the threshold are thus assigned, as-if at random, into treatment or control. Thus, as emphasized in Chapter 5, the most defensible way to analyze data from a regression-discontinuity design is through a simple comparison of mean outcomes in the treatment and control groups, in the discontinuity sample of schools in the neighborhood of the relevant enrollments thresholds.

When estimating regression models with control variables such as the percentage of disadvantaged students, Angrist and Lavy (1999) find that a seven-student reduction in class size raises math test scores by about 1.75 points or about one-fifth of a standard deviation—an important apparent effect of class size. Yet, as Angrist and Pischke (2008: 267) note in discussing Angrist and Lavy (1999), estimated coefficients from regressions without controls are statistically insignificant. In other words, the significant results depend on estimation of a multivariate regression model.

Angrist and Lavy (1999) also present results using difference-of-means tests in a sample of schools that lie close to the relevant regression-discontinuity thresholds (that is, schools which have plus or minus 5 and plus or minus 3 students around the enrollment thresholds at which Maimonides' Rule kicks in, namely, 40, 80, or 120 students), but they do not find significant effects in this reduced sample.

This raises some difficult issues of interpretation. To be sure, the issue can be seen as one of data availability; as Angrist and Pischke (2008: 267) put it in discussing the latter findings, "these results are much less precise ... since they were estimated with only about one-quarter of the data used to construct the full-sample estimates." Thus, here again data limitations appear to lead to more complicated modeling assumptions: in the absence of adequate data near the regression-discontinuity threshold, the analysis moves closer to model-based inference and further from the ideal of design-based research. Yet, data points further from the threshold are subject to confounding; after all, it is only in the neighborhood of the threshold that treatment assignment is credibly as-if random. And the models make a variety of assumptions, e.g., about functional form, that do not follow from the research design. When estimated effects depend on the estimation of more complicated models—and do not appear robust to simple and transparent analytic strategies—this clearly should shape our interpretation of the results.

In sum, the inclusion of controls in a multivariate regression analysis may amount to an admission of less than fully random assignment. Of course, this does not necessarily undermine the analyses. The best advice for practice may be to start with simple and unadjusted comparisons, as Brady and McNulty (2011) and other scholars do, and then move to more complicated modeling strategies as appropriate. However, if adjusted and unadjusted results differ much, the adjusted results should be viewed with more hesitation. When the design is strong and the effects are substantively large, simple analysis based on the Neyman model should reveal the effects.

9.2. Model specification in instrumental-variables regression

I have discussed one setting in which instrumental-variables regression may be useful: natural experiments in which subjects are randomly assigned to treatments but comply only imperfectly with treatment assignment.[19] In the Angrist (1990a) study of the effects of military service on later earnings, for example, cohorts of men were assigned at random to the Vietnam War draft. Yet, the draft is not perfectly correlated with actual service: some drafted men fail physical or mental exams or simply refuse to serve in the military, while

---

[19] See Chapters 4 and 5.

other men volunteer for the military, even if they are not drafted. According to an extension of the Neyman potential-outcomes model, a soldier who would serve in the military if drafted—but otherwise would not—is known as a Complier. Instrumental-variables analysis estimates the average causal effect for Compliers (Chapter 5).[20]

Even in this simple setting, instrumental-variables analysis involves some key assumptions—and these may or may not be plausible. With a randomized lottery, the assumption that assignment to the instrument is as good as random is highly credible (barring failure of the randomization procedure). A second key assumption—that the draft lottery only affects outcomes through its influence on military service—is more debatable. If being drafted causes men to stay in college, and education is related to earnings, then this "exclusion restriction" is violated.

Using instrumental-variables analysis to estimate a linear regression model such as Equation 9.1 or 9.2 brings further issues to the fore, however.[21] Consider again Equation 9.1, repeated here for convenience:

$$Y_i = \alpha + \beta X_i + \varepsilon_i.$$

I focus here on the bivariate case, though the comments in this section apply to multivariate regression as well (Appendix 9.1 extends the discussion to the multivariate case). Here, let X_i denote actual treatment receipt, not treatment assignment. Unlike the classical regression model, here X_i is assumed to be statistically dependent on the error term. The OLS regression estimator will therefore be biased and inconsistent. Under additional assumptions, however, IVLS (instrumental-variables least squares) regression provides a way to obtain consistent parameter estimates. To use IVLS, we must find an instrumental variable, namely, a random variable Z_i that is statistically independent of the error term in Equation 9.1 (see Section 5.3.5).

Now, suppose we have a randomized natural experiment—for instance, the draft lottery studied by Angrist (1990a), or a study using prize lotteries (Doherty, Green, and Gerber 2006). Given the model in Equation 9.1, the statistical independence of Z_i and ε_i is secured by random assignment of Z_i. Without true randomization, exogeneity cannot be completely verified.[22] In applications, analysts may devote some attention to defending the assumption of exogeneity of the instruments—though, as discussed by Sovey and Green

---

[20] See Chapter 5. [21] This section draws in part on Dunning (2008c).
[22] Standard overidentification tests using multiple instrumental variables, for instance, assume that at least one instrument is exogenous (Greene 2003: 413–15).

(2009), explicit attention to this issue is not particularly common. In practice, X_i and Z_i must also be reasonably well correlated; this can be checked (Bound, Jaeger, and Baker 1995). In a randomized natural experiment with imperfect compliance, the assumptions are thus that (i) treatment assignment is randomized; and (ii) treatment assignment has a reasonably strong influence on actual treatment receipt.

Yet, it is not merely the exogeneity of the instrument that allows for estimation of the effect of treatment. The inference also depends on a causal model that can be expressed in a regression equation like Equation 9.1. Without the regression equation, there is no error term, no exogeneity and no causal inference by IVLS. Exogeneity, given the model, is therefore necessary but not sufficient for the instrumental-variables approach. The specification of the underlying causal model is at issue as well.[23]

In the instrumental-variables context, the differences between the causal model implied by Equation 9.1 and the Neyman model become even sharper. Notice, for instance, that here a single parameter β captures the effect of treatment receipt. Thus, the causal effect is posited to be the same for every unit: in particular, it is equivalent for Compliers, Always-Treats, and Never-Treats. Thus, what Imbens and Angrist (1994) call "local average treatment effects"—that is, average treatment effects for the subset of units whose participation in treatment is influenced by the instruments—are assumed to capture average causal effects for all units.[24] Yet, this assumption may not be plausible. In Angrist's (1990a) study, for instance, people who only serve in the military because they were drafted may be quite different from volunteers, in ways that matter for later earnings.[25]

Another important assumption is embedded in Equation 9.1: variation in the endogenous regressor related to the instrumental variable must have the same causal effect as variation unrelated to the instrument (Dunning 2008c). In Equation 9.1, for example, a single regression coefficient β applies to endogenous as well as exogenous components of X_i.[26] In many applications,

---

[23] This general point has been raised by, *inter alia*, Angrist, Imbens, and Rubin (1996), Freedman (2006), Heckman and Robb (1986), Heckman, Urzúa, and Vytlacil (2006), Imbens and Angrist (1994), and Rosenzweig and Wolpin (2000). There is a large literature that discusses other aspects of IVLS (see, e.g., Bartels 1991; Bound, Jaeger, and Baker 1995; Hanushek and Jackson 1977: 234–39, 244–45; and Kennedy 1985: 115).

[24] See also Angrist, Imbens, and Rubin (1996) and Heckman and Robb (1986, 2006).

[25] Also notice that according to Equation 9.1, subject i's response to treatment depends on the values of i's right-hand side variables; values for other subjects are irrelevant. The analog in Rubin's formulation of the Neyman model is SUTVA (Neyman et al. [1923] 1990; Rubin 1974, 1978, 1980; see also D. Cox 1958, Holland 1986) (Chapter 5).

[26] Dunning (2008c) calls this the assumption of "homogeneous partial effects."

this assumption may be quite strong, yet relaxing it can limit our ability to use instrumental variables to estimate structural parameters of interest.

To see this point, let X_i be a measure of income and Y_i be a measure of political attitudes, such as opinions about taxation.[27] In randomized lottery studies, the population of subjects is limited to participants in a prize lottery (e.g., Doherty, Green, and Gerber 2006).[28] Then, the overall income of subject i consists of $X_i \equiv X_{1i} + X_{2i}$, where X_{1i} measures lottery winnings and X_{2i} is ordinary income.[29] Overall income X_i is likely to be endogenous, because factors associated with family background influence both ordinary income and political attitudes. For example, rich parents may teach their children how to play the stock market and also influence their attitudes towards government intervention. Peer-group networks may influence both economic success and political values. Ideology may itself shape economic returns, perhaps through the channel of beliefs about the returns to hard work. Even if some of these variables could be measured and controlled, clearly there are many unobserved variables that could conceivably confound inferences about the causal impact of overall income on political attitudes.

Given a model such as Equation 9.1, randomized prize lotteries may supply an excellent instrument—that is, a variable that is both correlated with the overall income of person i and is independent of the error term in Equation 9.1.[30] This variable is the level of lottery winnings of subject i, among lottery players. After all, some lottery players win a lot of money and some win little. Moreover, conditional on the kind and number of lottery tickets they buy, how much each player wins is assigned at random. Winnings should therefore be statistically independent of other characteristics of the respondents, including characteristics that might influence political attitudes. In sum, lottery winnings randomly "assign" subjects to levels of overall income X_i.[31]

---

[27] For instance, Y_i might be a measure of the extent to which respondents favor the estate tax, or a measure of opinions about the appropriate size of government.
[28] These studies were discussed in Chapters 2 and 4.
[29] That is, X_{2i} is shorthand for the income of subject i, net of lottery winnings; this could include earned income from wages as well as rents, royalties, and so forth.
[30] Doherty, Green, and Gerber (2005) use instrumental variables.
[31] Here, X_{1i} will instrument for X_i in equation (9.1). The IVLS estimator is

$$\hat{\beta}_{\text{IVLS}} = \frac{\text{Cov}(X_{1i}, Y_i)}{\text{Cov}(X_{1i}, X_i)},$$

However, this approach requires the true data-generating process to be

$$Y_i = \alpha + \beta(X_{1i} + X_{2i}) + \varepsilon_i, \qquad (9.3)$$

as in Equation 9.1.[32] Notice that the model assumes that a marginal increment in lottery winnings has the same causal effect on political attitudes as a marginal increment in other kinds of income. As Doherty, Green, and Gerber (2005: 8–10, 2006: 446–7) carefully point out, the effect on political attitudes of "windfall" lottery winnings may be very different from other kinds of income—for example, income earned through work, interest on wealth inherited from a rich parent, and so on. Yet, according to the model, it does not matter whether income comes from lottery winnings or from other sources: a marginal increment in either lottery winnings or in ordinary income will be associated with the same expected marginal increment in political attitudes. This is because β is assumed to be constant for all forms of income.[33]

An alternative model to consider is

$$Y_i = \alpha + \beta_1 X_{1i} + \beta_2 X_{2i} + \varepsilon_i \qquad (9.4)$$

with $\beta_1 \neq \beta_2$. Here, the variable X_{1i}—that is, lottery winnings—is plausibly independent of the error term among lottery winners, due to the randomization provided by the natural experiment. However, ordinary income X_{2i} remains endogenous, perhaps because factors such as education or parental attitudes influence both ordinary income and political attitudes. We could again resort to the instrumental-variables approach; yet, since we need as many instruments as regressors in Equation 9.4, we will need some new instrument in addition to X_{1i}. If Equation 9.4 is the true model, assuming Equation 9.1 will produce misleading instrumental-variables estimates.[34]

where covariances are taken on the sample data; thus, the estimator is the sample covariance of lottery winnings and attitudes divided by the sample covariance of lottery winnings and overall income. Note that $\text{Cov}(X_{1i}, X_i) \neq 0$, since X_{1i} is a component of X_i; this assumes, eminently plausibly, that $\text{Cov}(X_{1i}, X_{2i}) \neq -\text{Var}(X_{2i})$. Given statistical independence of X_{1i} and ε_i, $\hat{\beta}_{\text{IVLS}}$ is therefore a consistent estimator for β in equation (9.1).

[32] Doherty, Green, and Gerber (2005, 2006) present a linear regression model similar to Equation 9.1, though they report estimates of ordered probit models. Their main equation includes various covariates, including a vector of variables to control for the kind of lottery tickets bought.

[33] Another issue is related to the restriction of the study group to lottery players. The causal effect of income for this group may not generalize to other populations; that is, the β defined by Equation 9.1 may not be equal to structural parameters for people who do not play lotteries. This is usually described as an issue of "external validity" (Campbell and Stanley 1966).

[34] For instance, if X_{1i} and X_{2i} are statistically independent (as when subjects are randomized to levels of lottery winnings), IVLS asymptotically estimates β_1, the coefficient of the exogenous portion of

Model specification matters: for IVLS to estimate the parameter of interest, the data must be generated according to Equation 9.1, not Equation 9.4. See Appendix 9.1 for further discussion of this issue.

The model must be specified before IVLS or another technique can be used to estimate it. Of course, the assumption of common effects across pieces of treatment variables is a general issue, whether or not X_i is endogenous. Applications of IVLS tend to bring the importance of this assumption to the fore, however. When analysts exploit natural experiments to construct an instrumental variable Z_i, variation in X_i that is related to Z_i may not have the same causal effect as variation unrelated to Z_i. Unfortunately, it is often the desire to estimate the effect of variation unrelated to the instrument that motivates us to use instrumental variables in the first place. Otherwise, we could simply regress Y_i on Z_i.[35]

Similar issues arise in many other social-scientific applications of instrumental-variables regression (Chapter 4). For instance, in a regression of civil conflict on economic growth, using data from sub-Saharan African countries, economic growth may be endogenous. However, annual changes in rainfall may be used as an instrumental variable for economic growth (see Chapter 4). Miguel, Satyanath, and Sergenti (2004) posit that the probability of civil conflict in a given country and year is given by

$$Pr(C_{it} = 1 | G_{it}, \varepsilon_{it}) = \alpha + \beta G_{it} + \varepsilon_{it}. \tag{9.5}$$

Here, C_{it} is a binary variable for conflict in country i in year t, with $C_{it} = 1$ indicating conflict. The economic growth rate of country i in year t is G_{it}, α is an intercept, β is a regression coefficient, and ε_{it} is a mean-zero random variable.[36] According to the model, if we intervene to increase the economic growth rate in country i and year t by one unit, the probability of conflict in that country–year is expected to increase by β units (or to decrease, if β is

---

treatment; see Dunning (2008c). In other cases, instrumental-variables regression may estimate a mixture of structural coefficients, but not necessarily a mixture of theoretical interest.

[35] That is, we would restrict attention to the "reduced-form" regression—the analogy in this context to intention-to-treat analysis.

[36] Equation 9.5 resembles the main equation found in Miguel, Satyanath, and Sergenti (2004: 737), though I ignore control variables as well as lagged growth values for ease of presentation. The specification in Miguel, Satyanath, and Sergenti is $C_{it} = \alpha + X_{it}\beta + \varepsilon_{it}$, where X_{it} gives the value of lagged economic growth and of covariates for unit i at time t. Thus, the dichotomous variable C_{it} is assumed to be a linear combination of continuous right-hand side covariates and a continuous error term. However, the authors clearly have in mind a linear probability model, so I use Equation 9.5 instead. The notation $Pr(C_{it} = 1|G_{it}, \varepsilon_{it})$ indicates that the probability of conflict is conditional on the growth rate and the realization of the random error term.

negative). The problem is that G_{it} and ε_{it} are not independent. The proposed solution is instrumental-variables regression.

Annual changes in rainfall provide the instrument for economic growth. In sub-Saharan Africa, as the authors demonstrate, there is a positive correlation between percentage change in rainfall over the previous year and economic growth, so the change in rainfall passes one requirement for a potential instrument. Another key requirement is that rainfall changes are independent of the error term—that is, that the assertion of as-if random is valid. An exclusion restriction is also necessary in this context: Z cannot appear in Equation 9.5. This restriction would be violated if rainfall had a direct effect on warfare, above and beyond its influence on the economy; for instance, soldiers may not fight when it rains (Chapter 4). This restriction is not fully testable, though Miguel, Satyanath, and Sergenti probe its plausibility at length (see also Sovey and Green 2009). The IVLS estimates presented by Miguel, Satyanath, and Sergenti suggest a strong negative relationship between economic growth and civil conflict.[37] This appears to be evidence of a causal relationship, and Miguel, Satyanath, and Sergenti also propose a plausible mechanism to explain the effect—namely, the impact of drought on the recruitment of rebel soldiers.

Yet, have Miguel, Satyanath, and Sergenti estimated the effect of economic growth on conflict? Making this assertion depends on how growth produces conflict. In particular, it depends on positing a model in which economic growth has a constant effect on civil conflict—constant, that is, across the components of growth. Notice, for instance, that Equation 9.5 is agnostic about the sector of the economy experiencing growth. According to the equation, if we want to influence the probability of conflict we can consider different interventions to boost growth: for example, we might target foreign aid with an eye to increasing industrial productivity, or we might subsidize farming inputs in order to boost agricultural productivity.

Suppose instead that growth in agriculture and growth in industry—which both influence overall economic growth—have different effects on conflict, as in the following model:

$$Pr(C_{it} = 1 | I_{it}, A_{it}, \varepsilon_{it}) = \alpha + \beta_1 I_{it} + \beta_2 A_{it} + \varepsilon_{it}. \qquad (9.6)$$

---

[37] "A five-percentage-point drop in annual economic growth increases the likelihood of a civil conflict... in the following year by over 12 percentage points—which amounts to an increase of more than one-half in the likelihood of civil war" (Miguel, Satyanath, and Sergenti 2004: 727). A civil conflict is coded as occurring if there are more than 25 (alternatively, 1,000) battle deaths in a given country in a given year.

Here, I_{it} and A_{it} are the annual growth rates of industry and agriculture, respectively, in country i and year t.[38] What might motivate such an alternative model? Decreases in agricultural productivity may increase the difference in returns to taking up arms and farming, making it more likely that the rebel force will grow and civil conflict will increase. Yet in a context in which many rebels are recruited from the countryside, as recent studies have emphasized, changes in (urban) industrial productivity may have no, or at least different, effects on the probability of conflict.[39] In this context, heterogenous effects on the probability of conflict across components of growth may be the conservative assumption.

If the true data-generating process is Equation 9.5, but economic growth is endogenous, instrumental-variables regression delivers the goods. On the other hand, if the data-generating process is Equation 9.6, another approach may be needed. If β_2 is the coefficient of theoretical interest, we might still use rainfall changes to instrument for agricultural growth in Equation 9.6. However, industrial growth and agricultural growth may both be dependent on the error term in this equation, in which case a different instrument for industrial growth would be required.[40]

The point for present purposes is not to try to specify the correct model for this substantive context. Nor is the point that there is necessarily a general failure in IVLS applications. Standard assumptions—like exclusion restrictions, or the assumption of homogeneous effects across pieces of treatment variables—may be innocuous in some settings, misleading in others. The objective is to point out that what IVLS estimates depends on the assumed model, and not just on the exogeneity or as-if randomness of the instrument in relation to the model. In the present context, there are important policy implications, of course: again, if growth reduces conflict no matter what the source, we might counsel more foreign aid for the urban industrial sector, while if only agricultural productivity matters, the policy recommendations would be quite different. Whether different pieces of treatment variables plausibly have the same effect in any given application is mostly a matter for a priori reasoning; supplementary evidence may help.[41]

---

[38] I present this alternative model for heuristic purposes. The similarity to Equation 9.4 is not meant to imply that overall economic growth is an additive function of growth in the industrial and agricultural sectors.

[39] Kocher (2007), for example, emphasizes the rural basis of contemporary civil wars.

[40] For instance, conflict may depress agricultural growth and harm urban productivity as well, thus inducing a correlation between the error term and the independent variables.

[41] Dunning (2008c) presents a statistical specification test that might be of some use for adjudicating between equations like Equation 9.3 and 9.4. The specification test requires at least one additional instrument, however, and therefore may be of limited practical utility. See also Appendix 9.1.

Ultimately, the question of model specification is a theoretical and not a technical one. Whether it is proper to specify constant coefficients across exogenous and endogenous portions of a treatment variable, in examples like those discussed here, is a matter for theoretical consideration, to be decided on theoretical grounds. Supplemental evidence may also provide insight into the appropriateness of the assumptions. The issues discussed in this chapter are not unique to natural experiments. Yet special issues are raised with natural experiments—and especially with instrumental-variables designs—because we often hope to use the technique to recover the causal impact of endogenous portions of treatment.

What about the potential problem of infinite regress? In the lottery example, for instance, it might well be that different kinds of ordinary income have different impacts on political attitudes; in the Africa example, different sources of agricultural productivity growth could have different effects on conflict. To test many permutations, given the endogeneity of the variables, we would need many instruments, and these are not usually available. This is exactly the point. Deciding when it is appropriate to assume homogeneous effects across pieces of a treatment variable is a crucial theoretical issue. That issue is sometimes given short shrift in applications of the instrumental-variables approach, where the focus is on exogeneity.

9.2.1 Control variables in instrumental-variables regression

A final important point should be made about instrumental-variables regression. Natural experiments may generate as-if random assignment of units to an instrumental variable (such as treatment assignment), which instruments for an endogenous variable in a linear regression model (such as treatment receipt). In applications, however, it is common to estimate instrumental-variables models with various controls, as in Equation 9.2. Here, various covariates are presumed exogenous and included in the matrix of instrumental variables (Greene 2003; Freedman 2009). Yet, if these covariates are themselves endogenous, substantial bias may result (especially in small samples). Indeed, the presumption should perhaps be that such variables are endogenous: in a regression of voter turnout on polling place location, a covariate such as age may be related to a number of unobserved voter characteristics (such as income) that help determine turnout choice (Brady and McNulty 2011).

It may therefore be advisable to exclude covariates from instrumental-variables regressions. If the instrumental variable is truly randomly assigned, covariates should be unnecessary: given the linear regression model, random assignment of the instrument implies that the instrumental variable is valid. At the least, analysts would do well to report unadjusted instrumental-variables estimates (those calculated without control variables), in addition to other analyses they may report.

9.3 A continuum of credibility

To summarize the discussion above, presence of a valid natural experiment does not guarantee valid models of the data-generating process. While the Neyman model has some limitations that should be carefully considered in any application, it is usually an appropriate starting point. In contrast, the source of much skepticism about widely used regression techniques is that the statistical models employed require many assumptions—often both implausible and numerous—that undermine their credibility. In strong natural experiments, as-if randomness should ensure that assignment is statistically independent of other factors that influence outcomes. This would seem to imply that elaborate statistical models that lack credibility may often not be required. The data analysis can be simple and transparent—as with the comparison of percentages or of means (Chapter 5).

Unfortunately, while this is true in principle, it is not always true in practice. In Chapters 2 and 3, I surveyed many standard natural experiments and regression-discontinuity designs and coded whether a simple, unadjusted difference-of-means test was reported (Tables 2.2, 2.3, and 3.2).[42] In Chapters 4 and 5, I also discussed the data analysis in a number of instrumental-variables designs. The survey of applications in those chapters does not pretend to provide a representative sample of natural experiments, yet it includes many of the best-known and widely cited recent examples. The survey therefore allows us some insight into the question: do analysts

[42] An unadjusted difference-of-means test subtracts the mean outcome for the control group from the mean outcome for the treatment group and attaches a standard error to the difference. Note that in deciding whether such a test has been applied in Tables 2.2, 2.3, and 3.2. I adopt the most permissive coding possible. For example, if an analyst reports results from a bivariate linear regression of the outcome on a constant and a dummy variable for treatment, *without control variables*, this is coded as a simple difference-of-means test (even though, as discussed below, estimated standard errors from such regressions can be misleading). More generally, the quality of the estimator of the standard errors—involving considerations such as whether the analyst took account of clustering in the *as-if* random assignment—is not considered here. All that is required for a coding of "yes" is that a difference-of-means test (or its bivariate regression analogue) be reported, along with any estimates of the coefficients of multivariate models or other, more complicated specifications.

routinely report unadjusted results, in addition to any auxiliary analyses they may perform?

In general, the results of the survey are not encouraging. As Table 2.3 shows, 9 out of the 19 surveyed standard natural experiments with as-if randomization present unadjusted difference-of-means tests, in addition to any auxiliary analysis; even among natural experiments with true randomization, only 7 out of 10 present the simple analysis (Table 2.2). The same low prevalence applies to regression-discontinuity designs: only 8 out of 20 in Table 3.2 report simple difference-of-means tests. My survey of instrumental-variables analyses also suggests great variance in the tendency of analysts to report intention-to-treat analyses and analyses without control variables. Particularly given that the coding scheme employed is highly permissive in favor of scoring studies as "yes" in terms of employing difference-of-means tests,[43] it is striking that the majority of these studies do not report simple difference-of-means or difference-of-proportions tests.[44] These are some of the best examples of natural experiments from political science, economics, and other disciplines. With more examples, the proportion of studies presenting unadjusted results might fall even further.

This suggests that in empirical applications, there may be considerable variability in the credibility of the underlying models, as well as in the simplicity and transparency of data analysis. Natural-experimental research can indeed be ranked along a "continuum of credibility"—defined by the extent to which causal and statistical models are simple, transparent, and credible. As in the previous chapter, such a ranking is inevitably somewhat subjective, and different readers might reach different conclusions about particular studies. Again, the idea is not to evaluate the overall quality of a particular study, but rather to assess the extent to which the natural experiment approximates an ideal of credibility on this dimension. The idea of evaluating specific studies here is to give texture to the idea that the credibility of models may vary, even in valid natural experiments.

How, then, do the studies discussed earlier in this book fare on this dimension? The construction of Figure 9.1 is parallel to that of Figure 8.1. At the far left side, the least credible statistical models correspond to those employed in model-based inference and mainstream quantitative methods.

---

[43] See the preceding footnote.
[44] Several of the studies in Tables 2.2, 2.3, and 3.2 have continuous treatments or use instrumental variables, which complicates the calculation of a difference of means; these studies are noted in the tables. Even excluding these studies, however, only about half of the studies report unadjusted difference-of-means tests.

Part III Evaluating natural experiments

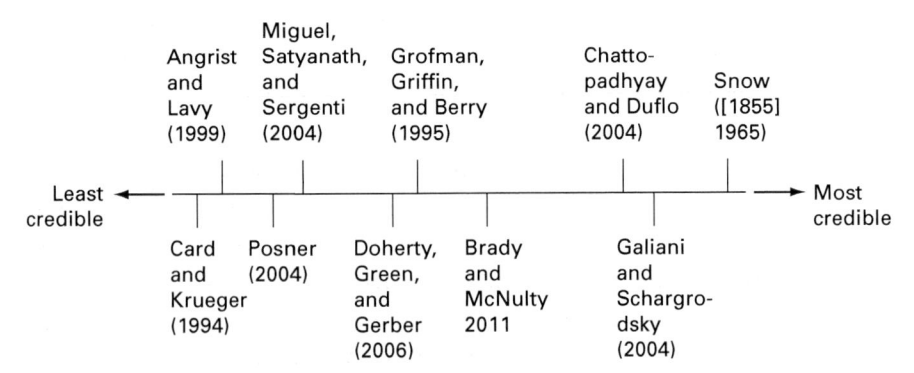

```
                    Miguel,
         Angrist    Satyanath,  Grofman,        Chatto-
         and        and         Griffin,        padhyay     Snow
         Lavy       Sergenti    and Berry       and Duflo   ([1855]
         (1999)     (2004)      (1995)          (2004)      1965)
                │       │          │              │          │
Least  ◄────────┼───────┼──────────┼──────────────┼──────────┼────► Most
credible        │       │          │              │          │      credible
         Card       Posner     Doherty,      Brady        Galiani
         and        (2004)     Green,        and          and
         Krueger               and           McNulty      Schargro-
         (1994)                Gerber        2011         dsky
                               (2006)                     (2004)
```

Figure 9.1 Credibility of statistical models

The most credible analyses are often those that use simple percentage or mean comparisons, and those in which the model of the underlying data-generating process appears most plausible.

Again, our paradigmatic example, Snow ([1955] 1965) on cholera, is located on the far right side of the continuum. The data analysis is based simply on comparing the frequency of cholera deaths from the disease per 10,000 households, in houses served by two water companies (one with a contaminated supply).[45] This type of analysis is compelling as evidence of a causal effect not only because the presumption of as-if randomness is plausible, but also because the broader Neyman model provides a persuasive depiction of the data-generating process (even if Snow did not appeal to this model himself). In two other studies, the model is also quite credible, and the data analysis is simple and transparent. Thus, Galiani and Schargrodsky's (2004) analysis of squatters in Argentina and Chattopadhyay and Duflo's (2004) study of quotas for women council presidents in India both use simple difference-of-means tests—without control variables—to assess the causal effect of assignment. Even here, of course, the modeling assumptions may require further validation; as the discussion above suggested, analysts may need to explore potential violations of noninterference in the Argentina land-titling study (see also Chapter 7). In principle, the dynamic incentives built into the rotation of quotas for female village council presidents could raise similar issues of interference, in the study by Chattopadhyay and Duflo (2004): it may be that potential outcomes in a village not assigned quotas in

---

[45] Snow ([1855] 1965: table 9, p. 86) compares death rates from cholera by source of water supply and thus is coded as having conducted a difference-of-means (difference-of-proportions) test, though he does not attach a standard error to the difference.

one election depend on expectations about the future treatment assignment status, which are engendered by the current assignment of other councils (see Dunning and Nilekani 2010). Still, in Figure 9.1 as in 8.1, these studies are both located on the right side.

This may provide a further lesson about the elements of a successful natural experiment. When the research design is strong—in the sense that treatment is plausibly assigned as-if at random—the need to adjust for confounders is minimal. As Freedman (2009: 9) suggests, conviction arises from the design of the study and the size of the effect. The often strong assumptions behind conventional regression models need not play a role in the analysis.

This observation raises a question about the relationship between the plausibility of as-if random (Chapter 8) and the broader credibility of models (this chapter). Returning to Figure 9.1 and comparing it to 8.1, one notes that there is often convergence between the two figures. As just noted, both the Galiani and Schargrodsky (2004) study of Argentine squatter settlements and the Chattopadhyay and Duflo (2004) electoral study are placed on the right side in both Figure 8.1 and 9.1. For studies that were judged weaker on as-if random assignment and thus were placed on the left side of Figure 8.1, the statistical analysis is correspondingly more complex, resulting in placement to the left in Figure 9.1 as well. Brady and McNulty's (2011) study of voting costs controls for possible confounders such as age; Card and Krueger (1994) also include control variables associated with exposure to minimum-wage laws and with subsequent wages. In such studies, the use of multivariate regression models may reflect the possible violations of as-if random assignment—leading analysts to adjust for the confounders that they can measure. Model-specification issues relevant to Doherty, Green, and Gerber (2006) and Miguel, Satyanath, and Sergenti (2004) were discussed above.

However, the credibility of the model, as coded in Figure 9.1, is not simply derivative of the plausibility of as-if random in Figure 8.1. In the first place, as mentioned above, some studies in which as-if random is plausible nonetheless feature complicated statistical analyses in which the underlying assumptions about data-generating processes are not highly credible. As-if random assignment does not guarantee that analysts will in fact present simple and transparent analyses such as differences-of-means tests.

Yet, there may also be other reasons that the models of the data-generating process are not credible—whether or not as-if random plausibly holds, and whether or not differences-of-means tests are presented. Consider, for instance, Posner's (2004) innovative study, which is ranked quite low on the credibility of the model in Figure 9.1. Here, as-if random may be plausible (see Figure 8.1), and this author does present a simple differences-of-means test: the key piece of evidence stems from a comparison of mean survey responses among respondents in Malawi and those just across the border in Zambia.

There is a complication, however, which is that there are essentially only two random assignments *at the level of the cluster*—living in Zambia or living in Malawi. Yet, the model is specified, and the data are analyzed, as if subjects had been individually sampled at random from the study group and assigned to treatment and control—rather than randomized as two clusters, one of people living in Zambia and the other of people living in Malawi. In consequence, the model of the stochastic process that generates the observed data suffers considerable loss of credibility. Estimators of standard errors based on the assumption of individual-level randomization can lead to misleading statistical inferences in this setting.[46] Note also that at the level of the cluster, estimators of the standard errors are in fact undefined (Chapter 6).[47]

For other studies as well, the position shifts notably between Figures 8.1 and 9.1. Stronger designs *should* permit statistical tests that do not depend on elaborate assumptions. Yet in practice some studies in which assignment is plausibly as-if random nonetheless do not present unadjusted difference-of-means tests. This pattern is reflected in the contrasting positions of the Angrist and Lavy (1999) study in Figures 8.1 and 9.1. Again, the logic of Angrist and Lavy's (1999) regression-discontinuity design implies that treatment assignment is only as-if random near the threshold of the covariate determining assignment; thus, the most defensible way to analyze data from a regression-discontinuity design is through a simple comparison of mean outcomes in the treatment and control groups in the discontinuity sample of schools in the neighborhood of the relevant enrollments thresholds (Chapter 5). Yet, the authors choose to report results from estimation of multivariate models—perhaps because, as Angrist and Pischke (2008: 267) say, estimated coefficients from regressions without controls are statistically insignificant.[48] On the other hand, in Figures 8.1 and 9.1, Grofman, Griffin, and Berry (1995) is an example

---

[46] The ratio between estimated variances assuming clustered randomization and estimated variances assuming individual randomization is known as the design effect; see Chapter 6 for further discussion.

[47] Another inferential and modelling issue that Posner addresses is noninterference: "Indeed, both pairs of villages are so close to each other that several respondents reported regularly visiting friends and relatives across the border in the other village" (Posner 2004: 531). As Posner points out, this may bias against the finding of a difference in intergroup relations on the two sides of the border.

[48] See the discussion in the previous section.

of a study that is evaluated as weak on the criterion of as-if random, yet it compares more favorably in the simplicity of the statistical model employed.[49] Of course, such simplicity may not be justified, given the weakness of as-if random assignment: if unobserved confounders affect the decision of congressional representatives to run for the Senate, a simple differences-of-means test may not provide an unbiased estimator of the causal effect of treatment.

What is the major lesson here? In less-than-perfect natural experiments, in which the plausibility of as-if random is not strong, researchers may feel compelled to control for observed confounders. Indeed, given the absence of true randomization in many of these studies, it is not a bad idea to explore whether statistical adjustment—for example, the introduction of additional control variables in a multivariate regression—changes the estimated effects.

Yet, when these changes are substantial, let the buyer beware (or perhaps more to the point, let the seller beware), because this may point to a lack of as-if random assignment. In such cases, the use of statistical fixes should perhaps be viewed as an admission of less-than-ideal research designs. Post hoc statistical adjustment can also lead to data mining, with only "significant" estimates of causal effects making their way into published reports (Freedman 1983). Because of such concerns, analysts should report unadjusted difference-of-means tests, in addition to any auxiliary analysis.[50] If an estimated causal effect is statistically insignificant in the absence of controls, this should clearly shape our interpretation of the effect being estimated.

9.4 Conclusion: how important is the model?

Social scientists invoke various models to analyze natural-experimental data. Yet, the specification of the model may itself be more or less plausible. Inferring causation from regression may demand a "response schedule" (Freedman 2009: 91–103; Heckman 2000). A response schedule says how one variable would respond, were we to intervene and manipulate other variables; it is a theory of how the data were generated. When the response schedule is not credible, neither are the causal inferences.

---

[49] This raises the interesting question of how to analyze alleged natural experiments in which the treatment is not very plausibly as-if random. Here, consistent with a design-based rather than a model-based approach, I focus on emphasizing the value of transparent and credible statistical analysis when the plausibility of as-if random assignment is high (i.e., in strong natural experiments).
[50] See Chapter 6 for a discussion of how the standard error for the difference of means should be calculated.

As we have seen, there are some limited settings in which analysis based on Neyman response schedules and more standard regression models produce identical results. For instance, with a bivariate regression model and a dichotomous variable for treatment assignment on the right-hand side, the OLS estimator of the coefficient on the treatment dummy is simply the difference of mean outcomes in the assigned-to-treatment and assigned-to-control groups (Freedman 2008a). The usual nominal OLS standard errors—which presume homoskedasticity, that is, equal variances of the errors in the treatment and control groups—differ from the Neyman-based calculations (see Chapter 6). However, adjustments for heteroskedasticity can recover the Neyman variance estimators.[51] Finally, a bivariate IVLS regression, in which a dummy variable for treatment assignment instruments a dummy variable for treatment receipt, produces an estimator that is equivalent to that of the effect of treatment on Compliers that is based on the potential outcomes model.[52]

However, the convergence of estimators based on these different models, in the simplest of settings, does not imply that the models are the same, nor is the choice of models irrelevant. Lack of attention to the credibility of the basic modeling assumptions can quickly lead analysts off track. Defining a plausible model of the data-generating process is the first step in formulating and testing causal hypotheses quantitatively: causal parameters are defined by causal models, and statistical inference about those parameters only makes sense once an explicit sampling model is formulated. For many natural experiments, the Neyman model provides the right starting point, but even there the match between the model and the reality (or lack thereof) should be carefully considered.

The point here is not simply to encourage data analysis or regression diagnostics (although more data analysis is often a good idea). Rather, in any particular application, a priori and theoretical reasoning as well as supplementary evidence should be used to justify the specification of the underlying model. In the case of linear regression, the assumption of homogeneous partial effects may be innocuous; in other settings, it will be wrong, and regression estimators such as IVLS will deliver misleading estimates. Exploiting a natural experiment that randomly assigns units to various levels of X_i—or an instrumental variable Z_i that is correlated with X_i—may not be enough to recover the causal effects of interest, if the regression model that is being estimated is itself incorrect. The model-validation CPOs considered in

---

[51] A lucid discussion of this result can be found in Samii and Aronow (2012).
[52] This is the so-called Wald estimator (Angrist and Pischke 2008).

Chapter 7 may be quite helpful for evaluating key assumptions of the Neyman model or of regression models—for instance, the assumption that unit i's outcome depends only on unit i's treatment assignment status.

In the end, convincing results also come from the strength of the design—and the size of the effect. Hidalgo (2010) and Fujiwara (2009), for example, use a regression-discontinuity design to show that introduction of electronic voting in Brazil increased the effective franchise in legislative elections by around 13–15 percentage points or about 33 percent—a massive de facto enfranchisement.[53] Such results are unlikely to be highly sensitive to modeling decisions, for instance, the use of local-linear regression instead of a difference-of-means test. Indeed, this enormous effect appears in the difference of means in the discontinuity sample; a small amount of confounding is unlikely to account for such a large effect. Here is an example in which conviction arises from the design of the study and the magnitude of the effect. With such convincing design-based research, *ex post* modeling adjustments based on more implausible assumptions about data-generating processes may be beside the point.

Appendix 9.1 Homogeneous partial effects with multiple treatments and instruments

In the text, I discussed the importance of model specification in the analysis of natural experiments. In the case of instrumental-variables linear regression, I placed emphasis not just on standard issues—such as the exogeneity of instruments and the validity of exclusion restrictions—but also on the crucial assumption that exogenous and endogenous pieces of treatment variables have the same causal effects. Thus, to use randomized lotteries to study the effects of overall income on political attitudes, the portion of overall income due to lottery winnings must have the same causal effect as income unrelated to winnings. To use rainfall shocks to study the effect of economic growth on conflict, we must assume that growth induced by rainfall has the same effect as growth not related to rainfall.[54]

---

[53] See Chapters 3 and 5.
[54] In some settings, this assumption of "homogeneous partial effects" may be more plausible than in others. Horiuchi and Saito (2009) use measures of election-day rainfall to instrument for voter turnout in Japan, in a study of the effects of turnout on federal transfers to municipalities; in their discussion of this issue, they suggest that politicians treat turnout shocks that stem from election-day rainfall as if they stemmed from structural factors or systematic features of voters in each municipality (see Exercise 7.2).

This appendix extends that discussion to the case of p treatment variables and q instruments.[55] The matrix version of Equation 9.1 is

$$Y = X\beta + \varepsilon. \tag{9.A1.1}$$

On the left-hand side, Y is an $n \times 1$ column vector. On the right-hand side, X is an $n \times p$ matrix with $n > p$. The parameter vector β is $p \times 1$ while ε is an $n \times 1$ column vector. Here, n is the number of units, and p is the number of right-hand side variables (including the intercept if there is one). We can think of the rows of Equation 9.A1.1 as i.i.d. (independent and identically distributed) realizations of the data-generating process implied by Equation 9.1, for units $i = 1, \ldots, n$.[56] The first column of X may be all 1's, so that there is an intercept. To use IVLS, we must find an $n \times q$ matrix of instrumental variables Z with $n > q \geq p$, such that (i) $Z'Z$ and $Z'X$ have full rank, and (ii) Z is independent of the unobserved error term, that is, exogenous (Greene 2003: 74–80; Freedman 2009: 181–4, 197–99). Exogenous columns of X may be included in Z. The IVLS estimator can be written as

$$\hat{\beta}_{\text{IVLS}} = \left(\hat{X}'\hat{X}\right)^{-1}\hat{X}'Y, \tag{9.A1.2}$$

where $\hat{X} = Z(Z'Z)^{-1}Z'X$.[57]

Note that $\hat{X}$ is the projection of X onto Z and is (nearly) exogenous.[58] On the other hand, X also has a projection orthogonal to Z, which is $e \equiv X - \hat{X}$. Rewriting $X = e + \hat{X}$ and substituting into equation (9.A1.1), we have

$$Y = \left(e + \hat{X}\right)\beta + \varepsilon. \tag{9.A1.3}$$

According to the model, β applies to both pieces. If in truth these pieces have different coefficients, then the IVLS model is misspecified. Dunning (2008c) presents a Hausman-like specification test for use in this setting. However, this test requires an additional instrument and may thus be of limited utility; such specification tests also will not have power against more general alternatives (Freedman 2010b).

---

[55] This discussion draws from Dunning (2008c).
[56] In many applications, we may only require that ε_i is i.i.d. across units.
[57] Equation 9.A1.2 is the usual way of writing the two-stage least squares estimator, $\hat{\beta}_{\text{IISLS}}$. See Freedman (2009: 186–7, 197–8) for a proof that $\hat{\beta}_{\text{IISLS}} = \hat{\beta}_{\text{IVLS}}$.
[58] $\hat{X}$ is not quite exogenous, because it is computed from X. This is the source of small-sample bias in the IVLS estimator; as the number of observations grows, the bias goes asymptotically to zero.

Exercises

9.1) The Neyman potential outcomes model (Chapter 5) assumes "no interference between units" (aka SUTVA). Is this reasonable in the Argentina land-titling study? What kinds of model-validation CPOs would contribute to validating or undermining this assumption?

9.2) An analyst uses data from an alleged natural experiment, in which a large number of subjects are as-if randomly assigned to treatment and control conditions. She gathers data on 20 "pre-treatment covariates" such as age, sex, and so on. She finds that the treatment group is substantially older than the control group, and the difference is highly significant. The researcher comments that "as-if random assignment should balance the treatment and control groups on pre-treatment covariates. Moreover, there are a large number of subjects, lending substantial statistical power. Thus, treatment assignment must not have been as-if random." Discuss this analyst's reasoning. Is the finding evidence against the natural experiment?

9.3) A political scientist conducts a randomized controlled experiment in which 200 units are assigned at random to a treatment group, and 800 units are assigned at random to a control group. She then posits that $Y_i = \alpha + \beta X_i + \varepsilon_i$, where Y_i is the observed outcome for unit i, X_i is a dummy variable for treatment assignment, α and β are regression coefficients, and ε_i is a mean-zero random error term. Finally, she assumes that the ε_i are i.i.d. for all i. Give at least two reasons why this last assumption may be invalid.

9.4) A social scientist is interested in the effects of religion on political participation in Africa. She analyzes data from surveys taken in all 48 sub-Saharan African countries. Controlling for many covariates in a regression model, she finds no relationship on average between strength of individual religious beliefs and political participation. However, suspecting that this relationship might differ in different countries, she runs separate regressions for each country. She writes "interestingly, we found a statistically significant and positive relationship between individual attachment to religion and political participation in Nigeria, Sudan, and the Ivory Coast—all countries in which religion has been substantially politicized in recent years."

(a) Does the evidence suggest that the effects of religious beliefs may be conditional on the country-level politicization of religion? What is a different interpretation of the evidence?

(b) How would one formulate the causal hypotheses under investigation in terms of a "response schedule"? Does the response schedule make sense?

9.5) In your view, which of these statements is closer to the truth?
   (i) Regression analysis can demonstrate causation;
   (ii) Regression analysis assumes causation but can be used to estimate the size of a causal effect—if the assumptions of the regression models are correct.

   Pick one of these two statements and defend your choice in detail. Does your answer change, depending on whether we are analyzing experimental or observational data?

9.6) (Adapted from Freedman, Pisani, and Purves 2007.) A geography test was given to a simple random sample of 250 high school students in a certain large school district. One question involved an outline map of Europe, with the countries identified only by number. The students were asked to pick out the United Kingdom and France. As it turned out, 65.8 percent could find France, compared to 70.2 percent for the United Kingdom. Is the difference statistically significant? Or can this be determined from the information given? Explain.

9.7) In a graduate class, 30 students take a midterm; 10 are left-handed and the other 20 are right-handed. The 10 left-handers score 83 (out of 100) on the exam on average, with a standard deviation of 7, while the right-handers score 89 on average, with a standard deviation of 9. Is the difference between 89 and 83 statistically significant? Explain.

9.8) A key assumption in the Iyer (2010) study of the effect of direct British rule, as described in Chapter 4 and Exercise 4.1, is that there is no "interference between units," which is sometimes described as the stable unit-treatment value assumption (SUTVA). What is meant in this context by SUTVA? How plausible is the assumption? What sorts of model-validation CPOs would contribute to supporting or undermining this assumption? In answering this question, list specific pieces of information that would support or undermine SUTVA.

10 How relevant is the intervention?

A third dimension along which natural experiments can be classified is the substantive relevance of the intervention. In any natural experiment, researchers and readers must ask a fundamental question of interpretation: to what extent do the effects of a random or as-if random intervention in fact shed light on wider social-scientific, substantive, and/or policy concerns?

Answers to this question might be cause for unease, for a number of reasons. For instance, the type of subjects or units exposed to the intervention might be more or less like the populations in which we are most interested. In lottery studies of electoral behavior, levels of lottery winnings may be randomly assigned among lottery players, allowing us to assess the impact of lottery winnings on political attitudes. Yet, we might doubt whether lottery players are like other populations (say, all voters). Next, the particular treatment might have idiosyncratic effects that are distinct from the effects of greatest interest. To continue the same example, levels of lottery winnings may or may not have similar effects on, say, political attitudes as income earned through work (Dunning 2008a, 2008b). Finally, natural-experimental interventions (like the interventions in some true experiments) may "bundle" many distinct treatments or components of treatments. This compounding of treatments may limit the extent to which any given natural experiment isolates the effect of an explanatory variable of greatest interest for particular substantive or social-scientific purposes. Such ideas are often discussed under the rubric of "external validity" (Campbell and Stanley 1966).[1] Yet, the issue of substantive relevance involves a broader question: whether the intervention—based on as-if random assignment deriving from social and political processes—in fact yields causal inferences about the real causal hypothesis of concern, and for the units we would really like to study.

---

[1] Campbell's own usage of external validity relates to a number of these points, though the term is generally used to refer to the ability to project from some sample to broader populations. Thus, external validity sometimes refers to only the first point in this paragraph.

As emphasized in the introductory chapter, such questions have generated criticism of natural experiments. For some commentators, the price of the recent focus on finding instances of as-if random assignment—in which confounding can be obviated, and credible causal inference can be founded on simple and transparent data analysis—is too high. These observers suggest that such a focus threatens to narrow social-scientific research to the point where broad but vitally important research questions—such as, say, the causes and consequences of democracy or development—are not considered. According to this point of view, natural experiments lack substantive and theoretical relevance and are thus undesirable as research strategies. On the other hand, defenders of design-based research suggest that the alternative to such designs is mere speculation. It is far better, they say, to be able to say something credible about causal effects in at least some contexts than in none—even if not all research questions yield themselves to experimental or natural-experimental designs. As Imbens (2009) puts it, "Better LATE than Nothing"—that is, it is better to be able to find credible evidence of a local average treatment effect, i.e., an effect that applies to only one study group or a subset of types in one study, than to be left with the inferential difficulties of conventional observational studies, which may not allow us to say anything definitive about causal relations at all.

Here, as in the introduction, I seek to strike a middle ground between these perspectives. There are two major messages. First, substantive relevance is indeed an important desideratum for natural experiments, as with other research designs. As the critics have emphasized, clever natural experiments in which as-if random assignment is compelling but in which the key intervention has only limited substantive relevance do not meet a high standard of research design. It is therefore especially crucial to understand threats to theoretical or substantive relevance in natural experiments. This chapter emphasizes three potential concerns in this regard:

- *Lack of external validity*, or the extent to which effects estimated for one natural-experimental study group may not generalize to other populations. This is a relatively familiar concern from the literature on research design.
- *Idiosyncrasy of interventions*, or the extent to which the key interventions in natural experiments are unlike the treatments of greatest theoretical or substantive concern.
- *Bundling of treatments*, also known as the "compound treatment" problem, or the extent to which natural-experimental interventions combine various treatments. Such bundling makes it difficult to ascertain which component of the treatment is "doing the work."

This list is not intended to be exhaustive of the issues that arise in connection with substantive relevance. Yet, these three issues can be especially important for natural experiments, for reasons discussed below; thus, understanding these threats to relevance is crucial for evaluating natural-experimental designs.

Second, however, the extent to which these concerns arise depends on the application. Different natural experiments vary in the extent to which the substantive or theoretical relevance of the intervention may be compromised: in many natural experiments, the intervention is highly relevant indeed. Thus, rather than paint a broad-brush negative portrait of the substantive relevance of natural experiments in general—as some critics have done—one should seek to distinguish more relevant from less relevant interventions and to investigate how researchers can bolster the substantive relevance of particular natural experiments.

To give an initial sense of this second point, consider the issue of local average treatment effects. In a natural experiment constructed from a regression-discontinuity design, causal estimates are valid for subjects located immediately on either side of the threshold—such as students who score just above or below a threshold exam score, prisoners who are close to the threshold that triggers assignment to high-security prisons, or near-winners and near-losers in elections. Of course, causal effects estimated for these groups may or may not be more broadly relevant to other kinds of units and other kinds of treatments: while the local average treatment effects analyzed in such regression-discontinuity designs may sometimes be of limited broad interest, in other natural experiments they reflect the impact of very substantively relevant interventions. For some policy questions, the marginal effect of raising or lowering the key threshold is exactly the critical substantive question; in this case, units located just at the key threshold are exactly the units we want to be studying. In other cases, the units located at the regression-discontinuity threshold may not be of special interest, yet effects for those units may plausibly generalize to other populations of interest. Finally, the use of multiple regression-discontinuity thresholds sometimes allows researchers to analyze the issue of heterogeneity empirically.

For instance, recall again the study by Hidalgo (2010), who used a regression-discontinuity design to study the impact of electronic voting machines on de facto enfranchisement and patterns of partisan support in Brazil (see Chapter 3; also Fujiwara 2009). The introduction of electronic voting machines eased the process of navigating Brazil's complex electoral system for illiterate and less well-educated voters, which had contributed to giving Brazil the highest rates of invalid or blank ballots in Latin America prior to the introduction of the reform.

Hidalgo (2010) and Fujiwara (2009) both find that introduction of electronic voting increased the effective franchise in legislative elections by about 13–15 percentage points or about 33 percent—a massive de facto enfranchisement that appears more pronounced in poorer municipalities with higher illiteracy rates. Moreover, this reform also had other quite broad political and policy effects: while Hidalgo (2010) finds that expansion of the effective franchise did not greatly tilt the ideological balance in the national Chamber of Deputies— and may on average have slightly favored center-right candidates, in contrast to simple "class conflict" models of the effect of franchise extension—voting reforms also elevated the proportion of voters who voted for party lists, rather than choosing individual candidates as allowed under Brazil's open-list proportional representation electoral rules. The introduction of electronic voting machines appears to have boosted the vote shares of parties with clearer ideological identities, such as the Workers' Party as well as the Brazilian Social Democracy Party of the incumbent president, Fernando Henrique Cardoso. Finally, the introduction of voting machines led to substantial declines in the vote shares of incumbent "machine" parties in several Northeastern states. Thus, Hidalgo (2010) concludes that the introduction of voting machines contributed to strengthening programmatic parties in Brazil, at the expense of traditional clientelistic parties who had sometimes resorted to fraud to win elections.

In Hidalgo (2010) we find an example of a natural-experimental study that contributes decisively to a "big" question of broad importance in developing democracies, namely, the sources of transitions from more clientelistic to more programmatic forms of politics. Moreover, the key intervention itself—which resulted in the de facto enfranchisement of many poor and illiterate voters—is of substantial interest to scholars of democratization. Many previous researchers have studied the consequences of suffrage extensions that were clearly not as good as randomly assigned—and thus, where it was difficult to separate the effects of suffrage expansion from confounding factors. Here, the natural experiment allows us to identify the causal effects of an independent variable with clear substantive relevance. The intervention is well-defined, so problems with bundling of treatments are not marked, and the key treatment is not apparently unlike other voting reforms or substantive franchise extensions that social scientists may care about theoretically or substantively.[2]

---

[2] This latter point could be debated, however; it may be that suffrage extensions adopted strategically, for instance in response to mass protests, have a different logic and different consequences than those adopted by technocrats or by an insulated judiciary, as was the case in the Brazilian reforms.

Note also that while the population of voters affected by the treatment—those who live in cities with around 40,500 registered voters—is not clearly of idiosyncratic or special interest (as this is a typical size for Brazilian municipalities), the natural experiment provides a number of ways to evaluate this issue of external validity empirically. Interestingly, an earlier reform in 1996 had extended voting machines to cities with more than 200,000 registered voters. Thus, here the effects at two different regression-discontinuity thresholds can be compared. While there are important effects on effective enfranchisement at both thresholds, Hidalgo finds that the effects of the earlier reform are somewhat more muted—suggesting that the reforms are more important in smaller municipalities. Subgroup analysis also suggests that poverty and illiteracy may drive the important effect of voting machines on de facto enfranchisement.

The larger point here is that the key interventions in many natural experiments have clear relevance—while in other natural experiments, threats to relevance may be more pronounced. For practitioners, the key question is therefore how greater substantive relevance can be achieved. For evaluators of the substantive relevance of natural experiments in general, the variance across different applications should also be kept in mind. The rest of this chapter focuses on how natural experiments can best be used to achieve inferences about substantively and theoretically relevant interventions, and especially to develop further the idea of an evaluative dimension based on the variance across different applications.

10.1 Threats to substantive relevance

To consider the substantive relevance of particular natural experiments, it is useful first to discuss challenges that may arise in general. I focus here on three threats to relevance that may be pronounced in many—though not all—natural experiments. Again, these are not exhaustive of the obstacles to greater substantive or theoretical relevance. Yet, each of these threats arises, in one way or another, due to the fortuitous, unplanned, or nonmanipulated character of natural-experimental interventions. Thus, they are particularly important to consider in connection with this kind of research design.

10.1.1 Lack of external validity

The first threat to relevance is the well-known issue of external validity. I use this term as Campbell and Stanley (1966) often defined it: do effects estimated for a particular study group generalize to a broader population of units, that is, a set of units different from those studied in a particular natural experiment? The reason that external validity bears on substantive relevance is that with a natural experiment, "Nature" subjects a particular study group to an intervention; the natural experiment can be used to estimate effects of the intervention for that study group. Yet, whether these estimated effects are broadly relevant for various substantive and theoretical questions depends in part on whether they can be readily extrapolated to broader populations.

External validity poses a challenge for most kinds of research designs, of course. In true experiments in the social sciences, the study group is not usually a random sample from some underlying population.[3] Often, the study group consists instead of a convenience sample, that is, a group of units that have been "drawn" through some nonrandom process from an underlying population. In other studies, one cannot even readily claim that the study group has been drawn from *any* well-defined population. In either case, one cannot confidently project estimated causal effects to a broader population, or attach estimates of sampling error to those projections. In most true experiments, in other words, causal inferences are drawn conditional on the study group—the particular set of units assigned to treatment and control groups. While randomization to treatment and control groups generally ensures that estimators of effects *for the study group* are unbiased (barring differential attrition or other threats to internal validity), whether these effects generalize to other populations is often an open question.

Yet, with true experiments, two factors may ameliorate this situation. First, at least some experiments *are* administered to random samples from broader populations, allowing effects to be projected to the population from which the experimental study group (i.e., the sample) was drawn. Second and perhaps more importantly, many true experiments are relatively amenable to replication. Thus, effects estimated in one substantive context and for one set of units can be estimated in a different context and with a different study group. This sheds some light on whether estimated effects may be generalized to other populations. Widespread experimental replication has occurred in a number of substantive areas—for example, in behavioral economics, where the character of subjects' play in dictator or public goods games has been evaluated and compared in diverse settings (see, e.g., Bowles and Gintis 2011) and in

---

[3] A common exception arises in the case of survey experiments—that is, experiments embedded within survey instruments in which question ordering or phrasing is randomly varied across different sets of respondents. Many sample surveys are indeed administered to probability samples of respondents from well-defined populations.

voter-mobilization studies, where the effects of different types of get-out-the-vote efforts such as telephone calls or in-person contacting have been compared in different elections and substantive contexts (Green and Gerber 2008).[4] This ability to replicate experiments is true in principle, if not always in practice: perhaps unfortunately for the accumulation of knowledge, professional academic incentives seem to favor doing new, original research, rather than seeking to replicate previously established results.

External validity concerns may pose an even greater challenge for natural experiments than for true experimental research, however, for two reasons. First, as in many other research designs, social scientists studying natural experiments do not always work with random samples from well-defined populations. To be sure, there are some examples in which the natural-experimental study group is indeed a probability sample from a broader population. In Angrist's (1990a) study, analysis of the effects of the Vietnam draft lottery is done for a one-percent probability sample of draft-eligible men; data are drawn at random from Social Security Administration records. In other natural experiments, the study group can be seen as a sample from a well-defined population, even if probability methods are not used to draw the sample. Dunning's (2010a) study of the effect of caste-based quotas in India, for example, drew village councils from many subdistrict-specific regression-discontinuity thresholds, across a number of districts in the Indian state of Karnataka. Because the relevant regression-discontinuity thresholds varied across different subdistricts, the natural-experimental study group consisted of village council constituencies that appeared quite representative of the state as a whole, at least on variables measured in the Indian census. Yet, in many natural experiments, the study groups cannot be seen as samples, random or otherwise, from a well-defined population.

Second, however, replication across different populations may be even trickier than in true experiments—due to the fortuitous character of many natural experiments. In the Argentina land-titling study, effects were estimated for the particular poor squatters organized by the Catholic Church in the early 1980s, some of whom were granted property titles and others denied them through the idiosyncrasies of the legal challenges that worked their way through the Argentine courts. It is difficult to know whether the effects found in Argentina—for example, that land titling reduced teenage fertility and increased beliefs about individual efficacy but did not boost access to credit

---

[4] While many studies have been replicated across the US states, get-out-the-vote experiments have also been conducted in state-controlled elections in China, among other settings (Guan and Green 2006).

markets—would also be found in other contexts. Thus, while the natural experiment contributes to undermining key claims found in De Soto (2000), it remains an open question whether property titles might have other effects in different contexts.

Yet, crucially, the ability to replicate results varies across different kinds of natural experiments. Some types of natural experiments are quite amenable to replication, and therefore the external validity of results is, at least in principle, subject to empirical verification. For example, as explored in Chapter 3, an increasing number of regression-discontinuity studies have compared near-winners and near-losers of close elections. This type of natural experiment may be widely replicable across different elections (see Lee 2008 or Sekhon and Caughey 2011 on the US), across types of offices and countries (see Boas and Hidalgo 2011, Brollo and Nannicini 2010, and Titiunik 2009 on city council and mayoral elections in Brazil), and across electoral systems (see Golden and Picci 2011 for an adaptation to open-list proportional representation elections in Italy). In this way, the effects of incumbency on a range of dependent variables may be compared across diverse settings, allowing the external validity of the findings of particular studies to be evaluated empirically.

Replication is also possible across other kinds of natural experiments as well. Chapters 2–4 explored many examples of ideas for natural experiments that have spread from one substantive question or empirical context to another; for instance, weather shocks have been used as instrumental variables for economic growth or inequality in several settings (Miguel, Satyanath, and Sergenti 2004; Hidalgo et al. 2010). The growth and expansion of such methods allows, at least in principle, for results to be compared across diverse contexts, which may shed some light both on how generalizable the effects are and on the contextual factors that might condition them. Thus, as with other threats to relevance we will consider below, different kinds of natural experiments might vary both in apparent challenges to external validity and in our ability to evaluate those threats empirically.

Other potential issues should be mentioned here as well. One important potential threat is publication bias—the tendency of research outlets to publish apparent evidence of causal effects, but not null findings.[5] Of course, this issue is common to other research designs in the social sciences as well. Yet, in natural experiments, the ability to replicate results may be weaker than

---

[5] For evidence of publication bias, see Gerber and Malhotra (2008); also, De Long and Lang (1992).

in other settings, which may make issues relating to publication bias more pronounced. If evidence of an apparent effect is not forthcoming on one trial, the results may not appear in print, while a single striking result may reach publication. Yet, because some natural experiments are difficult to replicate, it may be harder to assess whether an initial result was a fluke.

Two final points are worth making in conclusion to this section. First, while external validity is an important desideratum for natural experiments, in general it is difficult to evaluate the external validity of any single study, without further replication that would allow empirical assessment of the extent to which findings generalize across contexts and populations. Thus, as a criterion for evaluating the relevance of particular natural experiments, external validity may weigh somewhat less heavily than other threats to relevance, except where it seems clear as an a priori matter that the study group is comprised of quite idiosyncratic units. This point will be implicit in ranking particular studies along a continuum of relevance below.

Second, one should also note that conventional observational studies are subject to the same difficulties explored in this section. In many such studies, there is not even a well-defined population from which the study group is drawn; analysts simply estimate effects for the set of units they happen to have at hand. In cross-national regressions, for instance, researchers may talk about estimating effects for an "estimation sample," but it is difficult to conceive of the countries in their data sets as being drawn from any kind of population.[6] Replicating conventional observational studies is also often subject to a host of difficulties, similar to those involved with replicating natural experiments. External validity is difficult to achieve in most social-scientific contexts; natural experiments are no exception to this general rule.

10.1.2 Idiosyncrasy of interventions

The natural experiments surveyed in this book feature many different kinds of treatments or interventions. These include levels of lottery winnings, shocks to economic growth induced by weather patterns, property titles for poor squatters, eligibility for the military draft, incumbency in elected office, and government transfers of resources to particular individuals or municipalities. Analysts have in turn studied the effects of these natural-experimental interventions on a range of outcomes: respectively, political attitudes, civil war,

---

[6] Researchers sometimes talk about hypothetical "super populations" from which samples or populations of countries are drawn, but these metaphysics seem generally unhelpful.

access to credit markets, labor-market earnings, reelection, and electoral turnout/support for political incumbents.

A general question that arises in each of these studies is whether the key intervention in fact illuminates the effects of the causal variables in which researchers are most interested. Put differently, one might say that the causes that Nature deigns to assign at random are not always the same as those that social scientists would most like to study. The extent to which this is true often depends on the questions that analysts seek to answer, of course. Moreover, the possible idiosyncrasy of the intervention varies across different applications. However, it is useful to consider various ways in which natural-experimental interventions may be idiosyncratic—that is, unlike other classes of interventions in which social scientists may be interested—as a way of assessing when this threat to relevance is most likely to arise.

One very broad issue is whether interventions that are randomized (or as-if randomized) are like interventions that are not randomized, e.g., that are intentionally targeted to particular individuals or other units. Consider, for example, the case of government transfers of resources to particular individuals or municipalities. In some natural experiments, these are allocated at random, for instance, through randomized roll-outs (De la O forthcoming); or the allocation is based on formulas that allow the construction of regression-discontinuity designs (T. Green 2005; Manacorda, Miguel, and Vigorito 2011). Analysts are then often interested in the effect of such disbursements on political behavior, such as support for an incumbent or electoral turnout.

Yet, one can imagine that if voters know they have been allocated a disbursement through a random process or a rule-bound formula—and not because an incumbent candidate or party has *chosen* to give them a gift—this could affect their attitudes or behavior. For example, the support for an incumbent induced by these two distinct processes could well differ. This may be because voters' perception of an incumbent's *intention* in disbursing the gift or benefit may differ. Moreover, the kinds of incumbent behaviors often associated with targeted allocations of benefits—such as monitoring of voters by clientelist parties—may be absent in the context of randomized allocations.[7] For this reason, disbursements allocated at random or through formulas might tell us little, more generally, about the effect of disbursements

---

[7] For example, in the Mexican National Program for Education, Health and Nutrition (Oportunidades/PROGRESA) program studied by Green (2005) and De La O (forthcoming), voters were given pamphlets explicitly telling them that their receipt of benefits was not conditional on their electoral behavior or support for the political incumbent.

on political support. If researchers analyze the natural experiment hoping to learn about the effects of discretionary or targeted interventions on political behavior, then the idiosyncrasies of the randomized or rule-bound allocation may pose a challenge.[8]

This issue may arise in some natural-experimental settings and not others, however. In the Argentina land-titling study, property titles were extended to poor squatters by the state; the natural experiment arose because some owners of expropriated land challenged the expropriation in court. Yet, the intervention itself seems very like the intervention that would occur if the state systematically extended *de jure* land titles to many de facto occupiers of public lands—which is precisely the intervention that development scholars such as De Soto (2000) have in mind. Thus, here the natural-experimental intervention does not seem idiosyncratic, for purposes of answering causal questions such as those raised by the work of De Soto. Similarly, incumbency that is due to winning a close election could, for some purposes, be just like incumbency won through commanding a larger share of the vote. Of course, for other purposes, winning office through a close election may be unlike winning office in more dominant fashion.

Issues of idiosyncrasy of interventions may be particularly pronounced in instrumental-variables designs. Here, we may see an especially large gap between the causes that Nature assigns at random and the causes that social scientists would like to be able to assign—because here, units are not assigned by Nature to the key treatment variable of interest but only to a cause of that treatment variable. Thus, as-if random assignment may only illuminate the effects of broader treatments of interest if strong assumptions about the homogeneity of causal effects hold. One example discussed in Chapter 9 pertained to lottery studies, in which levels of lottery winnings are randomly assigned among lottery players. While intention-to-treat analysis can illuminate the effect of lottery winnings on, say, attitudes towards the estate tax or other political preferences, instrumental-variables analysis may not validly illuminate the effect of overall *income* on attitudes—unless the effects of lottery winnings are like the effects of other kinds of income. Yet, social scientists may be most interested in the effects of income, not the effects of windfall lottery earnings. Thus, the possible idiosyncrasies of the instrumental variable are a key issue in evaluating substantive relevance.

Similar issues can arise with other instrumental-variables designs. For instance, weather shocks may have idiosyncratic effects on economic growth—and in turn

---

[8] This point parallels in some ways the discussion in an important essay by Goldthorpe (2001).

special effects on civil conflict—that are unlike the effects on conflict of other sources of economic growth (Chapter 9). With such designs, then, the possible idiosyncrasy of the instrumental variable must be carefully considered when drawing conclusions about the effects of the main causal variable of interest.

10.1.3 Bundling of treatments

A final challenge relevant to substantive relevance is "bundling," also known as the "compound treatment" problem. This issue arises when the treatment contains multiple explanatory factors, such that it is hard to tell which of these factors "does the work" in producing a causal effect. Broad interventions that expose the subjects of interest to an important intervention may appear to maximize theoretical relevance. Yet, the bundling in some such interventions can complicate the interpretation of the treatment. While this aspect of relevance is different from the previous two discussed above, it fits with this discussion because the bundling of treatments can make it difficult to make inferences about the specific treatment of social-scientific interest—which is clearly an issue that bears on the substantive and theoretical relevance of the natural-experimental intervention.

In regression discontinuities based on age, for example, the treatment—say, being just above or just below the 18th birthday—may enable the right to vote in a particular election. This allows analysts to study the effect of voting eligibility on later political participation (see Meredith 2009). But turning 18 years old also enables other behaviors; for instance, the legal age to obtain an unrestricted driving license is 18 in some US states.[9] Whether or not this bundling of the right to vote with other treatments, such as the right to drive, does in fact complicate interpretation of the intervention will vary across applications: it may be innocuous in some settings and more problematic in others.

The problem of bundling also arises in connection with many natural experiments that exploit jurisdictional borders. An illustration comes from the study by Posner (2004), who asks why cultural differences between the Chewa and Tumbuka ethnic groups are politically salient in Malawi but not in Zambia (see Chapter 2). Recall that according to Posner, long-standing differences between Chewas and Tumbukas located on either side of the

---

[9] For example, 18 is the legal age for an unrestricted driver's license in Connecticut, Florida, and Oregon, among other US states.

border cannot explain the different intergroup relations in Malawi and in Zambia. Indeed, he argues that the location of people in Zambia or Malawi is as-if random: "like many African borders, the one that separates Zambia and Malawi was drawn purely for [colonial] administrative purposes, with no attention to the distribution of groups on the ground" (Posner 2004: 530). Instead, factors that make the cultural cleavage between Chewas and Tumbukas politically salient in Malawi but not in Zambia presumably should have something to do with exposure to a treatment (broadly conceived) received on one side of the border but not on the other.

Yet, such a study must face a key question which sometimes confronts randomized controlled experiments as well: what, exactly, is the treatment? To put this question in another way, which aspect of being in Zambia as opposed to Malawi causes the difference in political and cultural attitudes? As discussed in the subsection on independent-variable CPOs in Chapter 7, Posner argues convincingly that interethnic attitudes vary markedly on the two sides of the border because of the different sizes of these groups in each country, relative to the size of the national polities (see also Posner 2005). This difference in the relative sizes of groups changes the dynamics of electoral competition and makes Chewas and Tumbukus political allies in populous Zambia but adversaries in less populous Malawi.[10] Yet interventions of such a broad scope—with so many possible treatments bundled together—can make it difficult to identify what is plausibly doing the causal work, and the natural experiment itself provides little leverage over this question (see Dunning 2008a).[11]

Indeed, it seems that expanding the scope of the intervention can introduce a trade-off between two desired features of a study: (1) to make a claim about the effects of a large and important treatment, and (2) to do so in a way that pins down what aspect of the treatment is doing the causal work.[12] Thus, while Posner's study asks a question of great substantive importance, the theoretical or substantive relevance of the treatment can be more challenging to pin down. Some analysts might view this compound-treatment problem as an

---

[10] In Zambia, Chewas and Tumbukas are mobilized as part of a coalition of Easterners; in much smaller Malawi, they are political rivals.

[11] Clearly, the hypothesized "intervention" here is on a large scale. The counterfactual would involve, say, changing the size of Zambia while holding constant other factors that might affect the degree of animosity between Chewas and Tumbukus. This is not quite the same as changing the company from which one gets water in mid-nineteenth-century London.

[12] As discussed in Chapter 2, many other studies use jurisdictional boundaries as sources of natural experiments; see, e.g., Banerjee and Iyer (2005), Berger (2009), Krasno and Green (2005), Laitin (1986), or Miguel (2004).

issue of identification: i.e., the bundling of treatments does not allow one to discern the singular effect of any of the intervention's distinct components. This is a useful way to think about the problem. The key point here is that different natural-experimental interventions will suffer from this bundling problem to greater or lesser degrees, and the salience of this issue depends on the research questions being asked—for instance, whether the overall intervention or rather only some component of it is of primary interest to researchers.

Studies using jurisdictional borders do not always suffer from this compound treatment problem, for instance, at least not to the same degree. Consider the research by Card and Krueger (1994), who assess the impact of raising the minimum wage on employment in fast-food restaurants. These analysts compare restaurants on either side of the border between the US states of New Jersey and Pennsylvania; the former were subject to an increased minimum wage in 1992. Here, as in Posner (2004), units are compared across a geographic border, and units on one side of the border are exposed to an intervention. In principle, one might suggest that there is also a compound treatment problem here: the minimum-wage law is changing, but there might also be other aspects of the treatment of "being in New Jersey" versus "being in Pennsylvania" that could lead to contrasts between outcomes on the two sides of the border. Yet, here the claim that any differences in employment in firms on either side of the border reflects the discrete impact of the increase in the minimum wage appears more plausible—perhaps because the time-series nature of the data allows Card and Krueger to make pre- and post-comparisons in a narrow window around the date of the new minimum-wage law.[13]

The broad lesson here may be that the problem of bundling must be assessed on a case-by-case basis. This is true of the larger question of substantive relevance as well: just as with dimensions such as the plausibility of as-if random and credibility of the models, one should perhaps think of substantive relevance as a matter of degree. This in turn suggests the usefulness of arraying particular applications along a continuum defined by the substantive or theoretical relevance of the intervention, a task to which I turn in the next section.

---

[13] To use Donald Campbell's language, there is a pre-test and post-test in both treatment and control (i.e., this is a difference-in-differences analysis). Analysts usually describe difference-in-differences as a way to avoid confounding in quasi-experiments, but here it may serve another purpose, which is pinning down what is the treatment (i.e., minimum-wage law).

10.2 A continuum of relevance

The discussion above suggested that threats to substantive or theoretical relevance vary across different applications. While the search for as-if random assignment may indeed narrow analytic focus to possibly idiosyncratic contexts, as critics such as Deaton (2009) and Heckman and Urzúa (2010) have suggested, the extent to which this is true or important varies for different natural-experimental studies.

Just as for previous dimensions of the evaluative typology, it is therefore useful to consider a continuum of relevance along which different studies may be ranked. Figure 10.1 arrays the same studies as Figures 8.1 and 9.1, this time by the substantive relevance of the intervention. Because a number of different criteria help to determine substantive relevance—including external validity, idiosyncrasy, and bundling—and because these studies may do well on one of these criteria but not as well on another, the ordering of studies is once again an inexact science.[14] Moreover, in the study of politics and public policy, what can plausibly be understood as substantive relevance will vary by context, so the degree of subjectivity involved in classifying individual studies is perhaps even greater here than with the previous two dimensions. Again, the goal here is to assess how closely each study approximates an ideal on the criterion of relevance, not to judge the overall quality of each study. Despite these caveats, as a heuristic device it is again useful to rank particular studies, if only to

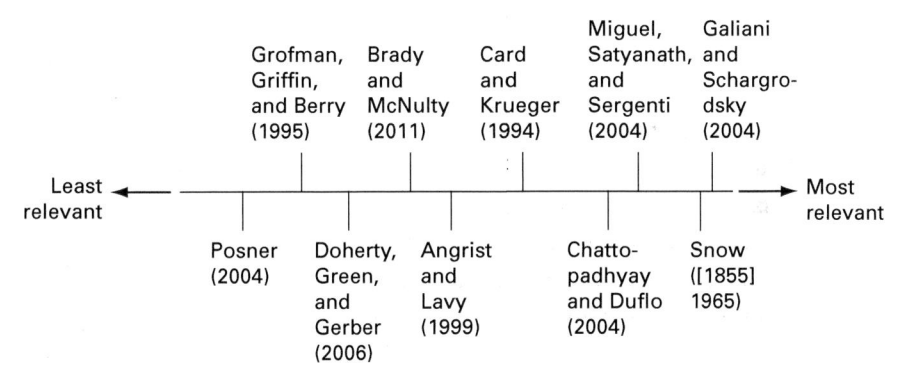

Figure 10.1 Substantive relevance of intervention

---

[14] I have not attempted to assign quantitative weights to each of the three criteria, for example; doing so would give an inappropriate impression of precision in an exercise intended as a useful heuristic.

highlight the substantial variation that can exist along this dimension among natural experiments.

Comparing Figure 10.1 to Figure 8.1 and Figure 9.1, we see some examples of studies in which the placement lines up nicely on all three dimensions. The study by Chattopadhyay and Duflo (2004) not only has plausible as-if randomness and a credible statistical analysis, but also speaks to the political effects of empowering women through electoral quotas. This topic's wide substantive relevance is evident, even when the particular substantive setting (village councils in India) might seem special. Similarly, Galiani and Schargrodsky's study of land titling has wide substantive and policy relevance, given the sustained emphasis of social scientists on the allegedly beneficial economic effects of property titles for the poor. Another of our other paradigmatic examples, Snow's ([1855] 1965) study of cholera, is once again located close to the far right side as well. His findings have remarkably wide substantive relevance—both for epidemiology and for public policy. Research in epidemiology, as opposed to politics, may have another key advantage: given that causes of a certain disease may be the same across a wide range of settings, findings routinely have broad substantive importance beyond the immediate context of the study.

With other studies, however, the placement in Figure 10.1 stands in contrast to 8.1 and/or 9.1. The study of Card and Krueger (1994), for example, while having less plausible as-if randomness and more complicated statistical analysis than others, incisively explores the effects of minimum-wage level, which seems to be of wide substantive importance. The same appears to be true of Miguel, Satyanath, and Sergenti's (2004) study of the effect of economic growth on civil war in Africa: while previous chapters discussed some limitations with regard to the plausibility of as-if random and the credibility of the models, this appears to be a big, important empirical question in a research setting that is often fairly intractable terrain for drawing reliable causal inferences. In contrast, some studies that in Figure 8.1 ranked highly on the plausibility of random assignment might be viewed as involving less substantively relevant treatments. Doherty, Green, and Gerber's (2006) study, for example, is motivated by the desire to learn about the effects of income on political attitudes; yet, the key intervention involves randomized lottery winnings, and lottery winnings may not be like ordinary income. This possible idiosyncrasy of the treatment variable is reflected in the placement in Figure 10.1.

In general, the ordering of studies along the continuum reflects the influence of all three threats to relevance—lack of external validity, idiosyncrasy of interventions, and bundling of treatments. First, with respect to external validity, the studies in the figure vary with respect to the types of units subject to a given intervention. These include voters in the Los Angeles area (Brady and McNulty 2011), fast-food restaurants near the Pennsylvania–New Jersey border (Card and Krueger 1994), children in Israeli schools that have certain enrollment levels (Angrist and Lavy 1999), politicians who move from the House to the Senate (Grofman, Griffin, and Berry 1995), village councils in two districts in two Indian states (Chattopadhyay and Duflo 2004), and ethnic Chewas and Tumbukas in villages near the Malawi–Zambia border (Posner 2004).

Whether the groups on which these studies focus are sufficiently representative of a broader population of interest seems to depend on the question being asked. Card and Krueger (1994), for instance, want to know whether minimum-wage laws increase unemployment in general, so any distinctive features of fast-food restaurants in Pennsylvania and New Jersey must be considered in light of this question. Brady and McNulty (2011) investigate how changes in the costs of voting shape turnout for voters in a specific electoral setting, the gubernatorial recall election in 2003, yet the impact of voting costs due to changes in polling places may or may not be similar across different elections. Angrist and Lavy (1999) study a question of great public-policy importance—the effect of class size on educational attainment—in the particular context of Israeli schools, estimating the effect of class size for students at the relevant regression-discontinuity thresholds. In other settings—such as Grofman, Griffin, and Berry's (1995) study of US congressional representatives and senators[15]—whether the group is representative of a broader population may not be of direct interest.

Next, the degree to which the intervention reflects a key cause of social-scientific interest—an issue captured by the concepts of idiosyncrasy and bundling, albeit in different ways—is another important determinant of placement along the continuum. As noted above, here there may be trade-offs in connection with the "breadth" of a natural-experimental intervention. On the one hand, the relatively broad scope of the treatment is an attractive feature of many natural experiments, compared, for example, to some true experiments. After all, natural experiments can allow us to study phenomena—such as institutional innovations, polling place locations, and minimum-wage laws—that are not routinely amenable to true experimental manipulation.[16]

---

[15] The placement of Posner's (2004) study on the continuum is discussed below.

[16] It is true, however, that some experimental researchers have become increasingly creative in developing ways to manipulate apparently nonmanipulable treatments, thereby broadening the substantive contribution of this research tradition. However, a trade-off may arise between the scope of an intervention and manipulability by experimental researchers.

These phenomena themselves may vary in their breadth and apparent substantive importance, so that some very interesting but somewhat narrow interventions—e.g., the location of polling places (Brady and McNulty 2011) or even class sizes (Angrist and Lavy 1999)—are ranked lower on the continuum than interventions such as minimum-wage laws (Card and Krueger 1994).

On the other hand, some interventions may be so broad as to lose some theoretical and substantive relevance, due inter alia to the issue of "bundling" discussed above. The difficulty raised by this compound treatment problem can vary across otherwise quite similar studies, as discussed above. Thus, we see in Posner (2004) and Card and Krueger (1994) two different studies that exploit jurisdictional borders, yet the bundling of the treatment seems more pronounced in one than in the other: in Card and Krueger, perhaps because pre- and post-comparisons are made within a relatively narrow window, knowing what exactly is the treatment (i.e., the minimum-wage law) seems less difficult than in Posner's study. Bundling can also raise issues in contexts such as the study by Grofman, Griffin, and Berry (1995), who seek to determine whether movement of representatives from more ideologically homogeneous constituencies (US House districts) to those more heterogeneous (US Senate districts, i.e., states) moderates those representatives' voting records in favor of states' median voters. There are a lot of things that distinguish voting in the Senate from voting in the US House (e.g., institutional rules regarding amendments, cloture, etc.), and so the ideological composition of the representatives' districts is not the only treatment. Thus, the issues of interpretation raised by bundling of treatments can arise in many settings.

10.3 Conclusion

When evaluating the success of natural experiments, the substantive or theoretical relevance of the intervention is a key consideration. In the search for situations of apparent as-if random assignment, the analyst must be concerned with whether the explanatory variable thereby generated is in fact interesting and relevant to a wider set of substantive concerns. Clever studies in which this form of assignment is compelling, but that have only limited substantive relevance, are not strong research designs. There is a legitimate concern that too much scholarship might come to focus on discovering ingenious natural experiments, at the cost of larger substantive agendas.

Yet, as we have seen, many natural experiments can successfully illuminate important social-scientific questions. In the best case, natural experiments share many of the advantages of true experiments—because randomization limits confounding—yet they can also reveal the effects of variables that may be difficult to manipulate experimentally. Thus, in the best instance, natural experiments have broad substantive relevance, and they can contribute to causal inferences in ways that neither true experiments nor conventional observational studies may do.

Two final questions are worth posing in conclusion to this chapter. First, can natural experiments be used to answer broadly comparative, cross-national questions about national development, political regime trajectories, or other topics of interest to scholars of comparative political development? It is striking that many of the studies discussed in this book are single-country studies; consideration of the coding of the country in which each study is located in Tables 2.2, 2.3, 3.2, and 4.3 illustrates this tendency. Moreover, the units of analysis are typically at lower levels of aggregation (e.g., municipalities, political candidates, citizens) than the nation-state. Furthermore, in those natural experiments in which countries are compared—for instance, when national borders are used to estimate the effects of nation-level treatments—I have pointed out substantial problems in terms of the credibility of models and especially the specificity and relevance of the "treatments." To be sure, there are a number of cross-national instrumental-variables designs, in which the questions are explicitly posed about broad phenomena such as the effects of institutions on national economic growth or the effect of growth on civil war.[17] In these studies, though, the assumptions that must hold for valid application of the instrumental-variables approach are often found to be implausible.

This does not mean that natural experiments cannot be used to answer substantive or theoretical questions that bear on broader questions of development or regime trajectories, however. Knowing whether property titles engender access to credit markets among poor squatters or military service affects political attitudes is certainly relevant for understanding broader patterns of socioeconomic and political development. Moreover, as pointed out above, some kinds of natural experiments have proven to be quite amenable to replication across varied contexts. Replication can lay the foundation for systematic comparative research, though few researchers as yet appear to have effectively exploited this possibility. Comparing causal effects using similar natural experiments across different countries—for example, through

---

[17] Examples of such studies include Acemoglu, Johnson, and Robinson (2001) and Miguel, Satyanath, and Sergenti (2004).

regression-discontinuity studies on the political effects of federal transfers in various Latin American countries—may thus offer interesting possibilities for future research. Of course, one of the difficulties that would inevitably arise here, when comparing divergent natural-experimental results across contexts, is that the interest then comes to be in the causal effect of the "context"—and this is going to involve nonmanipulated (and perhaps nonmanipulable) variables that are also not randomly assigned. Problems of bundling—what is it about the "context" that leads to different effects in different natural experiments?—would also likely complicate interpretation. Thus, many of the usual bugaboos that limit the validity of causal inferences in observational settings will likely arise. These are tricky issues, and so the jury does seem to be out on how natural experiments will contribute to broad cross-national comparative work.

Second, how can analysts strengthen the substantive relevance of a particular natural experiment? This chapter proposes a number of ideas related to both theory and interpretation. For example, whether the groups on which these studies focus are sufficiently representative of a broader population of interest often depends on the question being asked. The relevance of a given intervention may also depend in part on the research question. Thus, greater sensitivity to issues of external validity, bundling, and particularly the idiosyncrasy of interventions may help analysts use natural experiments to pose and answer appropriate questions. Replication may be a tool for evaluating external validity, while a variety of quantitative and qualitative tools—such as independent-variable and mechanism causal-process observations—may limit problems of bundling and help analysts to isolate what component of treatment is plausibly "doing the work" (Chapter 7).

Of course, substantive relevance is mainly discussed in this chapter in the context of an evaluative framework for assessing the success of any given natural experiment; the emphasis on relevance is meant to underscore that achieving as-if random assignment is not the only important desideratum in natural-experimental research. How to bolster substantive relevance in any particular natural experiment is an important issue and one on which future methodological writing should focus more. What is clear from the survey in this book is that some natural experiments can achieve the best of all worlds—for example, they may combine plausibly as-if random assignment, simple and credible models, and broad substantive relevance. Yet, there may also be tensions and trade-offs between the dimensions of the evaluative framework discussed in Chapters 8–10. The next chapter therefore concludes by discussing the relationship between these dimensions more explicitly, and it focuses on how various qualitative and quantitative methods may be combined to build strong research designs.

Exercises

10.1) Boas, Hidalgo, and Richardson (2011) study the returns to campaign contributions in Brazil. They compare the returns to donations to near-winners and near-losers of close elections, showing that public-works companies that rely on government contracts received a substantial monetary return on their electoral investments in near-winners.
   (a) Evaluate the plausibility of as-if random in this study. What sort of evidence is needed to evaluate the plausibility empirically?
   (b) Consider the three threats to substantive relevance discussed in this chapter: lack of external validity, idiosyncrasy of interventions, and bundling of treatments. Which, if any, of these threats do you think may be most important for this study? Can you think of empirical strategies for evaluating these threats to relevance? Are there other criteria pertinent to the question of substantive relevance that should be considered here?

10.2) Berger (2009: 2) argues that in 1900, "[t]he British divided Nigeria into different regions along the 7°10' line of latitude. Otherwise identical villages were subjected to different tax regimes based on whether they were barely north or barely south of the line. This led to different levels of local bureaucratic capacity formation. Today, a century after the different systems were implemented, differences in government quality persist."
   (a) What makes this study a natural experiment? What are some potential threats to the validity of the natural experiment? What kind of evidence would help validate the natural experiment?
   (b) Discuss the potential contributions of causal-process observations to such a study, including treatment-assignment CPOs, independent-variable CPOs, and mechanism CPOs.

10.3) Miguel (2004) claims that greater interethnic cooperation in Tanzania, relative to Kenya, is due to nation-building activities under Tanzanian leader Julius Nyerere—such as a national language policy and public-school curricula—that de-emphasized tribalism in favor of a cohesive

national identity. Miguel shows that more ethnically diverse communities in Kenya's Busia district provide fewer public goods (such as primary-school funds), while no such contrast exists in Tanzania's Meatu district, located across the shared border between the two countries.
- (a) Does the claim that nation-building fostered interethnic cooperation in Tanzania follow from this empirical test? Why or why not?
- (b) What are potential threats to substantive relevance in this study, and how might they be evaluated?
- (c) Is this a natural experiment? Why or why not? What might be some challenges to valid causal inference?

10.4) Miguel and Fisman (2006: 1020) are interested in how cultural norms influence corruption. They write, "Until 2002, diplomatic immunity protected [United Nations] diplomats from parking enforcement actions, so diplomats' actions were constrained by cultural norms alone. We find a strong effect of corruption norms: diplomats from high-corruption countries (on the basis of existing survey-based indices) accumulated significantly more unpaid parking violations." They refer to this study as a "unique natural experiment."
- (a) What is the treatment variable in this study? Is it plausibly assigned as-if at random? Is this plausibly a natural experiment?
- (b) Consider three threats to relevance: external validity, idiosyncrasy, and bundling. Which of these do you consider to be the most important and why?
- (c) What if diplomats from richer countries tend to have paid parking spaces? What violation(s) of the natural-experimental setup would this imply?

10.5) MacLean (2010) compares ethnically Akan villages on either side of the Ghana–Côte d'Ivoire border. Despite similar political and cultural institutions prior to the colonial period, by the 1990s these sets of villages exhibited "puzzling differences in the informal institutions of reciprocity and indigenous notions of citizenship" (MacLean 2010: i).
- (a) On what basis could such a study be called a natural experiment?
- (b) What sorts of data-set observations and causal-process observations would help to validate as-if random here? What respective roles might they play in establishing the nature of the treatment or linking that treatment to outcomes of interest?

Part IV

Conclusion

11 Building strong designs through multi-method research

This book has sought to provide a comprehensive—though far from exhaustive—discussion of the discovery, analysis, and evaluation of natural experiments. I have emphasized that the strongest natural experiments contribute markedly to causal inference. In the best case, natural experiments allow us to learn about the effects of causes that are difficult to manipulate experimentally, while obviating the substantial problems of confounding associated with conventional observational studies. At the same time, I have underscored the potential limitations of this approach and identified three dimensions on which specific natural experiments may fall short: plausibility of as-if random, credibility of models, and relevance of interventions.

Using natural experiments is not easy terrain. As with other methods, there is no single algorithm for success, even if some types of natural experiments are increasingly replicated across contexts. Natural experiments that are persuasive on one evaluative dimension might well fall short on another; sources of natural experiments that are compelling in one substantive setting or for one research question might elsewhere raise difficult issues of interpretation. In each application, researchers are therefore challenged to provide evidence that can bolster the credibility of the underlying assumptions and enhance the persuasiveness of their findings. This evidence comes in disparate forms, including both quantitative and qualitative data, and deep knowledge of substance and context is often essential. Data collection can also be costly and time-consuming.

This is why the statistician David Freedman (1991) referred to successful natural experiments, such as John Snow's study of cholera, as involving "shoe-leather" research. Design-based research of the kind advocated in this book tends to eschew the technical fixes of model-based adjustment. Yet, this puts the onus on the ability to find and leverage research designs that can compel conviction through the strength of the design. Validating natural experiments usually requires strong substantive knowledge and engagement, and a mix of quantitative and qualitative methods. Moreover, success on one evaluative dimension sometimes comes at the cost of another, and balancing the trade-offs between desiderata is challenging. This takes both preparation and perspiration, and examples that are successful on every dimension may not be common.

Given these difficulties and limitations, it is important to be clear about the potential payoffs of this kind of research. I thus begin this concluding chapter by revisiting the virtues of the approach, discussing several examples of natural experiments that compellingly reverse or affirm the conclusions of conventional observational analyses. If the assumptions are persuasive, then natural experiments can improve the quality of our causal inferences about substantively important questions. Natural experiments are a powerful part of the social-scientific toolkit, and they can contribute markedly to the validity of causal inferences in many substantive arenas.

The major question that analysts using natural experiments—and readers evaluating them—might then ask is how a study's joint performance on the three dimensions contributes to successful causal inference. This also raises the question of the relationship between the three dimensions of the evaluative typology developed in the third part of the book. While the connection between plausibility of as-if random, credibility of models, and substantive relevance has been hinted at elsewhere in the book, here I integrate the discussion further, discussing the interaction between these three dimensions even as I also emphasize that they are independent; that is, no one of these is simply derivative of another. I also underscore that while the discussion here is focused on natural experiments—and specific challenges arise for this kind of research design in connection with the plausibility of as-if random, credibility of models, and substantive relevance—the evaluative framework is also of broader potential utility. Indeed, many kinds of research designs, from the conventionally observational to the truly experimental, can be evaluated using this typology.

I then turn finally to further discussion of the contribution of multiple methods to successful natural experiments. Greater attention to all three evaluative dimensions, and not merely one to the exclusion of the others, can do the most to unlock the potential of natural experiments to contribute markedly to social-scientific research. For each dimension, quantitative and qualitative methods have vital functions; knowledge of context and substance can also contribute to achieving the proper balance in reconciling potential trade-offs between the evaluative dimensions. Thus, multiple methods are crucial for achieving the strongest research designs.

11.1 The virtues and limitations of natural experiments

Strong natural experiments can teach us about causes and effects in ways that neither conventional observational studies nor true experiments can easily do. For purposes of establishing causality, they are often superior to conventional observational studies, because random or as-if random assignment limits confounding from self-selection—which is the hallmark of conventional observational studies. And while true experiments provide the gold standard for limiting confounding, natural experiments allow analysts to study the effects of variables that are difficult to manipulate experimentally. In many natural experiments discussed in this book, the key treatment variables—such as quotas for female village-council presidents in India, voting reforms that extend the effective suffrage in Brazil, or conscription into the military in the United States—are generally infeasible for researchers to manipulate. Thus, natural experiments offer an important methodological alternative to both conventional observational studies and to true experiments.

Natural experiments can be particularly striking when they produce surprising findings that could otherwise be readily explained by self-selection. For example, Galiani, Rossi, and Schargrodsky (2011) find that Argentine men randomly selected for eligibility for the military draft have a greater propensity to have criminal records later in adulthood than men not chosen for the draft, an effect they attribute to the influence of delayed entry into labor markets. If such a finding came from a conventional observational study, it would lack credibility: men who choose to enter the military may be quite unlike men who stay out, so comparing the criminal records of these two groups of men does not readily illuminate the causal impact of military service. For instance, it would also be quite difficult to "control" for unobserved individual attributes that might explain self-selection into the military and also be related to the propensity to develop a criminal record. In contrast, the draft lottery ensures that the comparison groups were symmetric prior to the intervention of military service, so the effects can be credibly understood in causal terms.

Successful natural experiments can also reverse causal understandings drawn from previous conventional observational analyses. For example, as Iyer (2010) points out, straightforward comparisons of parts of India annexed by the British and parts of India that were controlled by native princes during the colonial period suggests positive long-run developmental consequences of direct British rule (Chapter 4). However, British annexation was apparently a selective process, with wetter and more fertile lands being preferentially appropriated by the British. Long-run differences in outcomes could thus reflect these disparate initial conditions, or unobserved confounders with which they are associated. Iyer (2010) thus uses a natural experiment, in which native states in which the ruler died without a natural heir—and were thus annexed by the British during the colonial governor Dalhousie's tenure in office—are compared to native states in which the ruler did not die in office without a natural heir during this period. This comparison suggests that direct British rule actually had a negative effect on development outcomes in India, relative to rule by native states. If the assumptions of the analysis are plausible and the supporting evidence is credible, the natural experiment overturns the conclusions from analysis of conventional observational data.[1]

Other natural experiments discussed in this book have contributed to similar reversals of conventional understandings. Consider the case of property titles for poor squatters. Advocates such as De Soto (1989, 2000) have suggested that *de jure* land titles promote broader socioeconomic development by allowing squatters to borrow money, using their legal property as collateral; this hypothesis has led to major policy reforms in many countries, including Peru, Haiti, and other developing countries. Yet, testing this idea has proved difficult in the absence of randomized evaluations of titling programs: for reasons amply discussed elsewhere in this book, comparing borrowing rates among propertied and non-propertied squatters will generally not provide compelling evidence of the effect of titles. Natural experiments such as Galiani and Schargrodsky's (2004, 2010) in Argentina therefore provide important evidence, suggesting that while titling may reduce household size or have other effects, it does not necessarily boost access to credit. A broader set of complementary institutional or legal reforms may be needed, though of course the natural experiment does not provide evidence on that point. In other substantive areas as well—from the educational effects of class size to the impact of military service—natural experiments have contradicted and helped to overturn results from conventional observational studies.[2]

Of course, persuasive natural experiments are useful even when they do *not* overturn or reverse previous conclusions. We might, for instance, believe that income shapes attitudes over taxation—and we might observe that richer people are indeed more opposed to taxing inheritances. Yet, this does not mean that income causes such attitudes, for reasons discussed throughout this book: unobserved confounders (such as the wealth and conservatism of

---

[1] See Chapter 4 and Exercises 4.1 and 5.1 for further discussion of this example.
[2] See, e.g., Angrist (1990a) for discussion.

parents) could be systematically correlated with both income and political attitudes. Thus, the finding from a compelling natural experiment that boosting one form of income—in the form of lottery winnings—causes lottery winners to turn against the estate tax is an important verification of the conventional wisdom (Doherty, Green, and Gerber 2006). Without strong designs such as natural experiments to confirm such findings, one might well suspect that the prevailing wisdom is not only conventional but also wrong.

In sum, natural experiments can afford social scientists with powerful tools for improving the quality of their inferences about causes and effects. Confounding is a fundamental obstacle to making valid causal inferences, and natural experiments can help markedly in this regard. With natural experiments, the data analysis can be strikingly simple, since the research design does the heavy lifting in eliminating confounding. There are also more natural experiments waiting to be discovered than many researchers may currently imagine. One goal of this book has therefore been to illustrate the usefulness of this approach in a range of contexts. The book has therefore aimed to provide a guide to researchers who wish to discover, analyze, and validate natural experiments, in the service of diverse substantive research agendas.

Yet, applauding the virtues of strong natural experiments is not to gainsay their potential weaknesses. Natural experiments can also have substantial limitations, which this book has emphasized as well. For example:

- Natural "experiments" are observational studies, not true experiments. With natural experiments, the researcher does not manipulate the political and social world in order to assign subjects to treatment and control conditions, and this can bear on our interpretation of the effects analysts estimate.
- In addition, the absence of an actual randomization device determining assignment to treatment and control, in many natural experiments, may present important concerns. To the extent that assignment to treatment is something less than as-if random, analysts may be analyzing something less than a natural experiment, and familiar challenges to valid causal inference from confounding factors may then arise.
- Natural experiments may also vary in the credibility of the statistical and causal models used to analyze them.
- Distinct natural experiments may shed greater or lesser light on the substantive or theoretical problems that motivate their use.

Perhaps the key point here is that different natural experiments vary in whether and how these various limitations are overcome. Rather than applaud or critique natural experiments as a whole, then, the best approach may be to distinguish different natural experiments according to their success in achieving strong research designs.

11.2 A framework for strong research designs

How, then, can strong research designs best be achieved? Any natural experiment, and indeed any piece of research, can be placed in the three-dimensional space represented in Figure 11.1, which repeats the cube displayed in the introductory chapter, though now locating specific studies within the figure. The cube captures the typology around which Part III of this book is structured and suggests three dimensions along which natural experiments may vary: (1) plausibility of as-if random assignment, (2) credibility of the statistical models, and (3) substantive relevance of the intervention. The uppermost corner to the back and right of the cube corresponds unambiguously to a strong

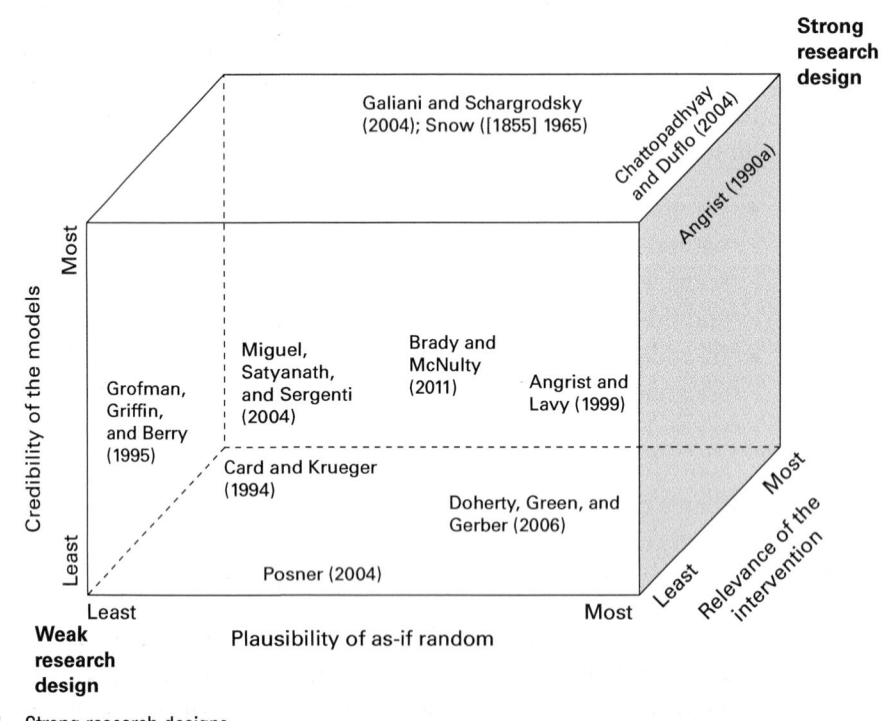

Figure 11.1 Strong research designs.
The figure locates several studies in the three-dimensional evaluative typology.

research design, which is strong on all three dimensions. The bottom corner to the front and left is a weak research design—i.e., furthest from this ideal.

Several broad points should be made in reintroducing this framework. First, this framework may be used to evaluate a wide range of research designs, not merely natural experiments; indeed, the utility of natural experiments can be understood by comparing their placement in the cube to conventional observational studies or true experiments. Second, as the previous chapters have suggested, the three dimensions of Figure 11.1 are interconnected. While some natural experiments will do unambiguously well on all three dimensions, there may be trade-offs between these dimensions of strong research design. Different studies may manage this trade-off in distinct ways, and which trade-offs are acceptable (or unavoidable) may depend on the question being asked. A discussion of the virtues and limitations of natural experiments must therefore consider not only how individual studies fare on each of these dimensions—as in Chapters 8–10 of this book—but also how the dimensions are related to one another. Third, reconciling such competing objectives and thereby realizing the full potential of design-based inference demands substantive knowledge and close attention to context: various methods are needed to achieve greater success on all dimensions.

Finally, as Figure 11.1 suggests, few studies exhibit strength on every dimension and thus rise close to the "strong research design" corner of the cube. This does not in the least imply that the effort to achieve strong research designs is futile. The dimensions on which Figure 11.1 is based should best be understood as aspirational. Like Robert Dahl's (1971) notion of democracy—an idyllic regime that few real-world "polyarchies" achieve—a truly strong research design may be an ideal type. Yet, stronger research designs are clearly more desirable than weaker research designs. Figure 11.1 suggests the dimensions that should be bolstered if stronger research designs are to be achieved. All three of these criteria should matter when we evaluate the strength of a research design. In the rest of this chapter, I turn to developing these themes further.

11.2.1 Conventional observational studies and true experiments

With a view to establishing a baseline, we can situate conventional, regression-based analysis of observational data within the cube. (1) These studies make no pretense of as-if random assignment, so they will be on the far left side. (2) Credibility of the statistical models varies considerably. Given the complex statistical modeling that is common in regression studies, it can readily be argued that the credibility and transparency of statistical models is routinely low, placing these studies toward the bottom of the cube.[3] (3) Finally, such regression studies may potentially allow greater scope in terms of the wider relevance of the analysis. For example, they can focus on macro-political outcomes of enormous importance, such as war, political regimes, and national political economy. Hence, on this third dimension, they may contribute more than natural experiments. Of course, as critics such as Seawright (2010) have suggested, the credibility of statistical models in these studies may be so low that the apparent contribution in terms of wider relevance may potentially be obviated.

To summarize the placement of regression-based, observational studies, they will be at the far left side of the cube and often in the lower part of the cube, reflecting the weaknesses just noted. However, they may be further toward the back, given their potential wider relevance compared to at least some natural experiments. The cube thus brings into focus what is basically conventional wisdom about these regression studies, and provides a useful point of departure for evaluating other research designs.

What about nonregression-based or qualitative observational studies? Like regression-based studies, the plausibility of as-if random may be routinely low, while substantive relevance may vary substantially. Evaluating the credibility of models may be trickier, because such studies do not routinely formulate quantitative or statistical models of the data-generating process. However, explicit or implicit causal models, involving various causal pathways or mechanisms, are often posited. One can likewise evaluate the credibility of these models of data-generating processes, allowing at least tentative placement of nonregression-based qualitative studies in the cube.[4]

True experiments can also, at least approximately, be placed in the cube. (1) Genuine random assignment (and not merely as-if random) is presumably their defining characteristic, though in too many poorly designed experiments it is not achieved. Hence, taking the left-right dimension of the cube as a proxy for the plausibility of randomization in true experiments, many true experiments are not merely at the right side of the cube, but in a sense are well beyond it. For true experiments with inadequate randomization, they will to varying degrees be more toward the left side. (2) The statistical models should in principle be credible and simple, though too often they are not—either because the investigator seeks to correct for a failure of random assignment, or

---

[3] Moreover, the estimation of complex models produces research that is not transparent to readers with a substantive interest in politics but less-than-expert technical knowledge.
[4] Comprehensive location of qualitative or nonregression-based observational studies that do not use natural experiments must be left to future work, as that would take us too far from the focus of this book.

because the temptation to employ elaborate statistical models is so engrained. (3) Depending on the ingenuity of the investigator, these studies potentially have wide relevance, but again they may not. Overall, researchers using true experiments can and should strive for the uppermost corner to the back and right in the cube—which is labeled as a "strong research design"—but they potentially may fall short on any or all the dimensions.

Of course, where true experiments are located in the cube depends also on the details of implementation—and sometimes, similar issues arise for true experiments as for natural experiments. Researchers may in fact have only imperfect control over the manipulation in true experiments—weakening their contrast with randomized natural experiments and leading to issues of interpretation that also arise in the latter. If randomization is faulty, which can sometimes occur due to failures in randomization procedure, as-if random is also not plausible. And the credibility of underlying models and the simplicity and transparency of data analysis depend in part on the training and proclivities of the researcher. Thus, while experiments may in principle reach an ideal position on the first two of the three dimensions (with substantive relevance depending on the application), they may in practice fall quite short—depending on how they are actually implemented.

11.2.2 Locating natural experiments

How, then, do natural experiments fare relative to conventional observational studies and true experiments, and how do different natural-experimental applications fare relative to each other? While the discussion above suggests that the dimensions of the evaluative typology are important for many research designs—for example, the substantive relevance of social-scientific research is often a concern, whether or not a natural experiment is involved—the relationship between these dimensions has special salience in the case of natural experiments. For example, the importance of substantive relevance for evaluating natural experiments should be understood in relation to the other evaluative dimensions discussed in previous chapters, particularly the definitional claim of as-if random—because the causes that social and political processes assign at random or as-if at random may or may not be of broader substantive importance. How do the natural experiments discussed in this book fare when all three dimensions are considered?

Several natural experiments cluster towards the upper-back, right-hand corner of the cube (strong research design)—reflecting the high degree of plausibility of as-if randomization, strong credibility of the statistical model, and wide substantive importance. Studies with true randomization, such as Angrist (1990a) or Chattopadhyay and Duflo (2004), rank very high on the as-if random dimension (indeed, as high as true randomized controlled experiments); thus, they are pushed over to the extreme right-hand side of the front axis of the cube.[5] Other natural experiments in which as-if random is compelling, such as the Argentina land-titling study of Galiani and Schargrodsky (2004) and Snow's ([1855] 1965) study of cholera are also very strong on this dimension—though without true randomization, these are somewhat to the left, relative to the studies with true randomization.[6] The studies in the strong-research-design corner are also characterized by simple and transparent data analysis founded on credible causal and statistical models. (Due to possible violations of the exclusion restrictions necessary for instrumental-variables analysis, the study of Angrist 1990a may be somewhat weaker on the dimension of credibility when the goal is to understand, not the effects of the draft lottery, but instead the effects of military service.) Finally, all of these studies are judged to exhibit broad substantive relevance, featuring interventions the effects of which are important for social-scientific and policy purposes. Studies such as Snow's ([1855] 1965) are paradigmatic precisely because they are situated in this corner, and they are probably more successful on each of these dimensions than many true experiments.

Many other studies discussed above have weaknesses on one or more dimensions, which to varying degrees push them toward the lower-front, left-hand corner of the cube (weak research design). Some alleged natural experiments, such as Grofman, Griffin, and Berry (1995), are so low on the plausibility of as-if random that they should be placed with conventional observational studies; that is, they are not really natural experiments (which does not deny their potential contribution to knowledge). Other natural experiments feature plausible as-if random assignment but are low on the dimension of relevance, either because the treatment is potentially narrow or idiosyncratic (Doherty, Green, and Gerber 2006) or is so broad as to lose theoretical or substantive relevance, due to the problem of bundling (Posner 2004). Finally, the natural experiments vary substantially with respect to the credibility of causal and statistical models, a point discussed at length in Chapter 9.

---

[5] See, however, the footnotes to the discussion in Chapters 1 and 8 of controversies surrounding the randomization of the Vietnam draft lottery. Due to space limitations, the Angrist (1990) study that uses this lottery was not ranked on the individual dimensions in Figures 8.1, 9.1, and 10.1, yet the study has been discussed extensively throughout the book and thus also appears in Figure 11.1. See also the discussion of the assignment procedure used in Chattopadhyay and Duflo (2004) in Chapter 2.

[6] Another study in the cube, Doherty, Green, and Gerber (2006) also features true randomization via a prize lottery; however, lottery players are only randomized to levels of lottery winnings conditional on having bought the same kind and number of tickets.

The previous situating of conventional observational studies in the cube helps underscore an important point about these weaker natural experiments, however. Even natural experiments that are not all the way to the upper right-hand corner of the cube—the strong-research-design corner—may be substantially stronger on the plausibility of as-if random assignment, and perhaps the credibility of models and substantive relevance as well, than many conventional studies. Thus, even relatively weak natural experiments may be stronger on one or more of these grounds than much social science—though of course, the substantive relevance or other dimensions could well be lower for such studies as well. Thus, even natural experiments with some "imperfections" can make valuable contributions to knowledge. Again, the strong-research-design corner of the cube represents an aspiration, which may be achieved to greater or lesser degrees in practice.

Discussion of the cube likewise provides an opportunity to draw together the assessment of the studies that employ regression discontinuities and instrumental variables. Regression-discontinuity designs (1) may have plausible as-if randomness in the neighborhood of the threshold, and (2) data analysis may potentially be simple and transparent, as when mean outcomes are compared in the neighborhood of this threshold. Yet a trade-off can readily arise here. Data may be sparse near the threshold, which together with other factors may encourage analysts to fit complicated regression equations to the data, thus potentially jeopardizing the study in terms of the credibility of the statistical models—as in Angrist and Lavy (1999), which ranks low on this dimension in the figure.[7] As for (3) relevance, with a regression-discontinuity design causal effects are identified for subjects in the neighborhood of the key threshold of interest—but not necessarily for subjects whose values on the assignment variable place them far above or far below the key threshold. Whether a given regression-discontinuity study has broad substantive relevance (as in Angrist and Lavy 1999) or is somewhat more idiosyncratic may depend on the representativeness of subjects located near the relevant threshold.

For instance, to return to an example of a regression-discontinuity design discussed earlier in the book, perhaps recognition in the form of a Certificate of Merit is less important for exceptionally talented students than for much less talented students (Thistlethwaite and Campbell 1960). For students at a middle level of talent and achievement, the salience of the national recognition may be harder to predict; perhaps it gives them an important boost and motivation, while failure to receive this recognition for students at middle

---

[7] See the discussion of this study in Chapter 9 for explication of the reasoning behind the ranking.

levels may weaken their motivation for further achievement. Thus, relevance might be undermined if the regression-discontinuity design produces a somewhat idiosyncratic finding that is only relevant to a specific subgroup—i.e., the group of students near the threshold score for Certificates.[8]

Like regression-discontinuity designs, instrumental-variables designs may also vary substantially on these dimensions, and individual studies may be stronger or weaker on different dimensions. In many cross-national instrumental-variables regressions, substantive relevance may be high. For example, the effect of economic growth on civil conflict in Africa studied by Miguel, Satyanath, and Sergenti (2004), is (3) a question of broad policy as well as social-scientific importance. Yet perhaps precisely because some scholars aim to answer such broad substantive questions in constructing instrumental-variables designs, these designs have significant limitations in terms of both plausibility and credibility. For instance, the instrumental variable (1) may or may not plausibly be as-if random. Moreover, it may or may not influence the outcome exclusively through its effect on the main explanatory variable, and may or may not influence components of this variable, which have idiosyncratic effects on the outcome of interest (Dunning 2008c). Thus, in practice, data analysis in many instrumental-variables designs depends on (2) complicated statistical models, whose potentially questionable credibility may make these designs less compelling than other types of natural experiments. These strengths and limitations explain the placement of the study by Miguel, Satyanath, and Sergenti (2004). As with other natural experiments, instrumental-variables designs may be more or less model based, and they may have greater or lesser success in reaching the strong-research-design corner of the cube.

11.2.3 Relationship between dimensions

The dimensions of Figure 11.1 were discussed separately in Chapters 8–10 because these are distinct evaluative dimensions. Conceptually, whether assignment to treatment is as-if random does not determine whether, for instance, the intervention is substantively or theoretically relevant. Empirically, some studies that did well on one dimension did worse on another; thus, there is no one-to-one mapping from one dimension to another. It is true that there is some relationship between plausibility of as-if random and credibility of models, in

---

[8] Whether the effect for this group of students is meaningful for inferences about other kinds of students may be a matter of opinion; see Deaton (2009) and Imbens (2009) for a related discussion.

that when as-if random is plausible, the analysis may be simpler and more transparent and the underlying models more credible. Yet, Figure 11.1 makes clear that the credibility of models is not simply derivative of the plausibility of as-if random: there are several studies in which treatment assignment is plausibly as-if random and yet the credibility of models is low. This occurs when the posited model does not describe the true data-generating process very persuasively (for instance, when the data are produced through clustered as-if random assignment but individual-level randomization is assumed, as in Posner 2004). Broader choices about models of the data-generating process are distinct from the question of whether social and political processes have generated as-if random assignment.

Yet, the dimensions of Figure 11.1 are related, in that trade-offs between the dimensions can arise. Achieving success on one dimension can sometimes come at the cost of success on other dimensions. As we saw in Chapter 10, for example, critics of experimental and natural-experimental research have suggested that the search for situations of as-if random assignment can narrow research foci to substantively or theoretically uninteresting questions. By the same token, investigations of broad and important questions, such as the relationship between national economic development and democracy, typically feature very nonrandom assignment and many problems of potential confounding, of which the causal and statistical models often feature complicated assumptions that lack credibility (Seawright 2010).

Overall, then, the cube reminds us that good research routinely involves reconciling competing objectives. Achieving (1), plausible as-if randomness, may come at the expense of (3), broad substantive relevance. Alternatively, (3), striving for broad substantive relevance, may occur at the expense of (1), plausible as-if randomness, which may push the investigator toward (2), more complex and less credible statistical models. Thus, the contribution on each dimension must be weighed against the others in evaluating particular studies. The process of developing strong research designs can be understood as the process of astutely managing the trade-offs between these dimensions.

Judgments about coordinating among these three dimensions should rely on deep knowledge of the subject matter and the context of research. From the standpoint both of evaluating natural experiments and making recommendations for conducting them, this component is critical. Adding substantive expertise as a formal dimension would make the typology unwieldy, and it is sometimes difficult to assess investigators' level of expertise simply on the basis of published articles. Yet, substantive knowledge plays a strong role in discovering natural experiments and validating the claim that assignment is as good as random, in generating model-validation CPOs that may contribute to formulating credible quantitative models, and in shaping interpretation of effects in a way that highlights and reinforces the relevance of the study.

In sum, successful natural experiments depend on such substantive knowledge. It is an illusion to believe that mere technique is sufficient to design good natural experiments, just as it is an insufficient basis for regression analysis (Freedman 2009, 2010a). Without a foundation of substantive expertise, a study will routinely make mistakes on all three dimensions.

11.3 Achieving strong design: the importance of mixed methods

Throughout this book, I have underscored the important contributions of both quantitative and qualitative analysis to successful natural experiments. Analysts should use data-set observations—that is, systematic data on outcomes, treatment assignment and treatment receipt, and various pre-treatment covariates for each unit in the study group—to assess empirically the plausibility of as-if random, for instance, by checking for balance on pre-treatment covariates. When as-if random is persuasive, data analysis can be simple and transparent, and it is often supported by credible assumptions about the data-generating process. In this way, quantitative tools are essential for validating the research design and for analyzing the effects of natural-experimental interventions.

The contribution of qualitative evidence to natural experiments must also again be underscored. To reiterate, the qualitative methods discussed throughout this book make a central contribution to constructing and executing natural experiments. Substantive knowledge and detailed case expertise often associated with qualitative research is essential for working with the three dimensions shown in Figure 11.1 (Dunning 2008a). For instance, knowledge of context helps analysts to understand the process of treatment assignment and to validate at least partially the assumptions invoked in quantitative analysis. This knowledge does not come only in the form of systematic measurement of independent and dependent variables for each unit in the study group; instead, it may come in the form of disparate pieces of information that help to motivate the natural-experimental setup. Thus, various kinds of causal-process observations—including what I have called treatment-assignment CPOs and model-validation CPOs—play a critical role in successful natural experiments.[9]

---

[9] In his discussion of Snow's natural-experimental study of cholera, Freedman (2010a) emphasizes the similar view that qualitative methods—an important "type of scientific inquiry"—play an important role.

Data-set and causal-process observations contribute not only to achieving success on each of the dimensions of Figure 11.1 but also to coordinating between them. Consider again Galiani and Schargrodsky's study of squatters in Argentina. Here, strong case-based knowledge was necessary to recognize the potential to use a natural experiment in studying the effect of land titling. After all, squatters invade unoccupied urban land all the time; yet, it is undoubtedly rare that legal challenges to expropriation of the land divide squatters into two groups in a way that is plausibly as-if random. Thus, many field interviews and deep substantive knowledge were required to probe the plausibility of as-if randomness—that is, to validate the research design. As-if random assignment then sets up a persuasive, simple, and transparent form of data analysis that is based on the comparison of average outcomes in the treatment and control groups—i.e., a difference-of-means test. Further qualitative information in the form of model-validation CPOs could also have been used to evaluate the credibility of the model—for instance, information about interactions between titled and nontitled squatters that could have led to possible interference between units (i.e., SUTVA violations). Finally, substantive knowledge is important for interpreting and contextualizing the evidence on the effects of land titling—for instance, the finding that titling boosts beliefs in individual self-efficacy (Di Tella, Galiani, and Schargrodsky 2007)—and also the null effects—for instance, the conclusion that at least in this case, titling does not boost poor squatters' access to credit.

In other examples, case-based knowledge is crucial in many other ways. As with the Argentina land-titling study, substantive knowledge often helps analysts to recognize and validate alleged natural experiment. To mention just two, Angrist and Lavy (1999) not only knew about Maimonides' Rule in Israel but also recognized its social-scientific potential as the source of a regression-discontinuity design, while Lerman (2008) gained insight into the assignment process of prisoners to high-security prisons through many qualitative interviews and sustained observation of the California prison system. Hard-won qualitative evidence can also enrich analysts' understanding and interpretation of the causal effect they estimate. What does property *mean* to squatters who receive titles to their land, and how can we explain the tendency of land titles to shape economic or political behavior, as well as attitudes towards the role of luck and effort in life? Qualitative assessment of selected individuals subject to as-if random assignment may permit a kind of "natural-experimental ethnography" (Paluck 2008; Dunning 2008b) that leads to a richer understanding of the mechanisms through which explanatory variables exert their effects.[10]

In sum, natural experiments are an eminently mixed-method form of research. The best natural-experimental research therefore evidences a trend towards the combination of various methods that has been emphasized by some political scientists as well as scholars in other disciplines. There are many other kinds of multi-method work in the social sciences, with their characteristic strengths and limitations.[11] However, methodologists have not widely noted the importance of multiple methods in successful natural experiments, and doing so has been an important aim of this book.

11.4 A checklist for natural-experimental research

Researchers seeking to use natural experiments in their substantive research may well desire a checklist or decision flowchart that helps with systematic navigation of the issues raised in this book. A rigid or formulaic checklist fits somewhat uneasily with several of the main messages of this book, e.g.: (1) successful causal inference depends on many methods; (2) strong research design demands careful attention to context and setting and especially a close understanding of the process governing treatment assignment; (3) understanding the relevant details is likely to demand close engagement with the substantive terrain being studied. Moreover, the appropriate modeling and data-analytic decisions are going to vary from study to study. For these reasons, many of the key issues may be application specific. Strong research designs cannot be mass produced.

Nonetheless, the broadest messages that this book has sought to underscore can be summarized in the form of key questions that analysts might ask of their data and research design. These questions can indeed form a kind of checklist for researchers using potential natural experiments. These questions

---

[10] The term borrows from Sherman and Strang (2004), who describe "experimental ethnography." See Paluck (2008).

[11] Seawright and Gerring (2008) and Lieberman (2005) recommend using regression models to drive case selection in cross-national research, which can be helpful if the model is correctly specified; they describe a range of case selection techniques based on the relationship of particular cases to a bivariate regression line (or multivariate regression plane). Many scholars have also emphasized the ways in which game-theoretic approaches, statistical modeling, and qualitative fieldwork can be combined in the context of particular research questions.

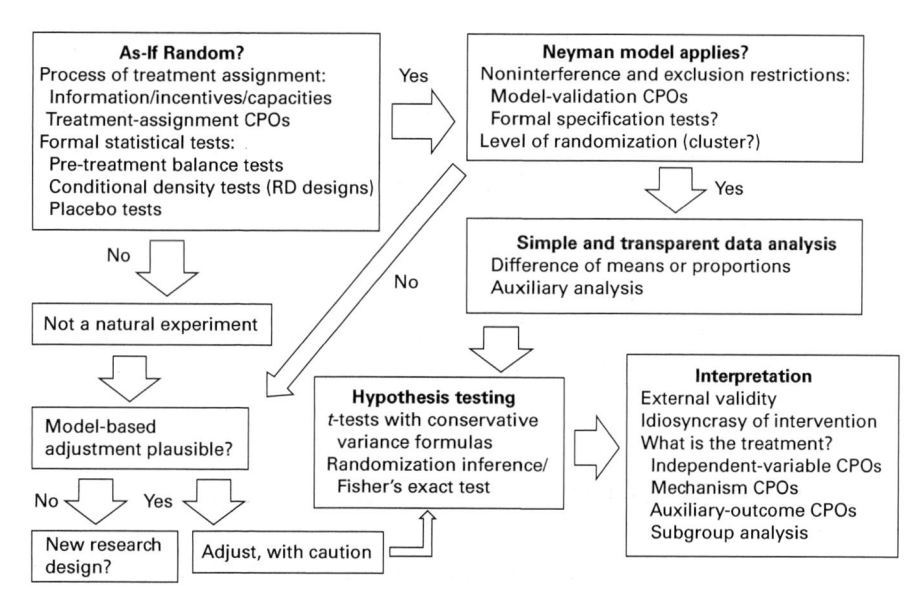

Building strong designs through multi-method research

Figure 11.2 A decision flowchart for natural experiments.

[Flowchart contents:]

- **As-If Random?** Process of treatment assignment: Information/incentives/capacities; Treatment-assignment CPOs; Formal statistical tests: Pre-treatment balance tests; Conditional density tests (RD designs); Placebo tests
- Yes → **Neyman model applies?** Noninterference and exclusion restrictions: Model-validation CPOs; Formal specification tests? Level of randomization (cluster?)
- No → Not a natural experiment → Model-based adjustment plausible? → No: New research design? / Yes: Adjust, with caution
- Yes (from Neyman) → **Simple and transparent data analysis**: Difference of means or proportions; Auxiliary analysis
- **Hypothesis testing**: t-tests with conservative variance formulas; Randomization inference/Fisher's exact test
- **Interpretation**: External validity; Idiosyncrasy of intervention; What is the treatment? Independent-variable CPOs; Mechanism CPOs; Auxiliary-outcome CPOs; Subgroup analysis

and the methods relevant to answering them are depicted in the decision flowchart in Figure 11.2.

The first, foundational question analysts should ask is: does as-if random hold? The answer to this question determines whether the analysis is working with a plausible natural experiment. Even when treatment assignment is apparently truly randomized, as in lottery studies, the veracity of random assignment should be scrutinized carefully: bureaucrats or others implementing random assignment can sometimes make mistakes, and this may compromise the ability to make credible causal inferences based on simple and transparent data-analytic procedures. In the 1970 Vietnam-era draft lottery discussed in the introduction, as mentioned in a footnote there, it was alleged that a failure to sufficiently mix the jar into which 366 capsules had been deposited (one for each day of the year, including February 29) led to systematic underselection of men born in later months of the year.

Analysts considering potential natural experiments, whether randomized or not, should thus first investigate the plausibility of as-if random assignment. This book has emphasized the importance of several kinds of tools, including (i) *close understanding of the process of treatment assignment.* Analysts should consider the *information, incentives,* and *capacities* of units in the study group, as well as other key actors who have control over assignment decisions, to undermine the statistical independence of treatment assignment and potential outcomes (Chapters 7 and 8). Thus, they should ask: (a) Do natural-experimental units have *ex ante* information that they may be assigned to treatment conditions? Do policy-makers know which units are assigned to which treatment conditions, and what treatment units end up receiving? (b) Do units have incentives to self-select into treatment and control groups? Do have policy-makers have incentives to allocate particular units to particular groups? (c) Do units have the capacity to self-select into treatment or control groups, or do policy-makers have the ability to allocate particular units to particular groups?

Answering "yes" to any of these questions does not necessarily suggest lack of statistical independence between potential outcomes and treatment assignment. Yet, it does imply that strategic incentives and capacities may end up undermining as-if random assignment. Thus, if analysts cannot answer no to these questions, they should exercise particular caution before asserting as-if random assignment and before attaching the label of natural experiments to their research designs. (Below, I discuss further the issue of what to do with "less-than-perfect" natural experiments.)

Information relevant to understanding the process of treatment assignment may come in disparate forms and from varied sources, as noted above. I have described the important role of what I termed treatment-assignment causal-process observations in many successful natural experiments (Chapters 7 and 8). More important than the label attached to these nuggets of information, however, is their provenance: generally, treatment-assignment CPOs are deduced from close engagement with the substance and research setting. A variety of research methods—including interviews with policy-makers and natural-experimental units themselves—may be relevant for understanding the context and process of treatment assignment.

Other crucial tools for assessing as-if random include (ii) *formal statistical tests*. The particular tests that are relevant depend on the application and type of natural experiment, but in virtually every alleged natural experiment in which as-if random is asserted, the balance of pre-treatment covariates across treatment and control groups should be formally assessed. Usually, this can be accomplished through presenting a set of t-tests for the difference of means of the pre-treatment covariates across treatment conditions; a complementary strategy is to conduct a regression of an indicator for treatment assignment on an intercept and all pre-treatment covariates, and conduct an F-test of the hypothesis that the coefficients on the pre-treatment covariates are equal to zero.[12] Analysts should keep in mind that one significant *t*-statistic does not make as-if random implausible, if there are many pre-treatment covariates; in expectation, *p*-values should be smaller than 0.05 in 1 out of 20 independent tests. Another potentially useful set of tests examines not just the means but also other aspects of the *distributions* of pre-treatment covariates across the treatment and control groups.[13]

Note that these tests should be conducted at the level of randomization: e.g., if randomization is by cluster, pre-treatment covariates should be balanced at the cluster level. The power of these tests to reject the null hypothesis should also be explicitly considered: failure to reject the null hypothesis of equal means on pre-treatment covariates is not compelling evidence of as-if random if the number of units is small (Chapter 8). (For references and further discussion of statistical power, see, e.g., Gerber and Green 2012.) In this case, other sources of evidence (especially qualitative information on the process of treatment assignment) should take on particular weight in assessing as-if random, but analysts should proceed with caution in alleging a natural experiment. For natural experiments with small study groups or complex designs, analysts may wish to conduct balance tests using randomization inference (Chapter 6).

If close investigation of the process of treatment assignment and formal statistical tests do not rule out as-if random, analysts may well proceed on the assumption that they are analyzing a natural experiment. Note, however, that failure to reject the null hypothesis of as-if random does not confirm the null hypothesis. In natural experiments without true randomization, and even those with true randomization, the possibility of unobserved confounders is always a possible Achilles heel. This should be borne in mind by natural-experimental researchers and their readers when evaluating the results of natural experiments. By the same token, however, apparent failures of as-if random do not necessarily invalidate the main goal of randomization: achieving the statistical independence of treatment assignment and potential outcomes. For example, in the 1970 Vietnam-era draft lottery, the insufficient mixing of capsules appeared to lead to some nonindependence of month of birth and probability of draft eligibility. This does not, of course, imply a correlation between draft eligibility and potential outcomes—that is, the later labor-market earnings (Angrist 1990a) or political attitudes (Erikson and

---

[12] The validity of the *F*-test, however, depends on the joint normality of underlying variables; this restriction is less important when the study group is large.

[13] For instance, standard Kolmogorov-Smirnov tests are easy to implement in statistical packages such as Stata or R.

Stoker 2011) that would materialize in the presence and absence of draft eligibility. The bottom line is that the assertion of as-if random must be defended, to the extent possible, with a priori reasoning and various kinds of empirical evidence discussed in this book (see especially Chapters 7 and 8).

If as-if random plausibly holds, the next step may be to consider the other assumptions of the Neyman urn model (Chapters 5 and 6). Do the causal assumptions of this model plausibly hold—for instance, the assertion that each unit has a "potential outcome" that is invariant to the weather, the moons and the tides, and especially the treatment assignments of other units? The realism of this assumption may be debatable, for instance, in social or political settings in which units in the treatment and control group interact; for example, the behavior of units in the control group may be affected by the behavior of units assigned to the treatment group. Such violations of non-interference, aka the stable unit-treatment value assumption (SUTVA), violate a usual tenet of the Neyman model. Treatment assignment may also have effects on outcomes through channels other than its relationship to treatment receipt, which would violate the exclusion restriction (Chapters 5 and 9). This may be a particular issue when the Neyman model is extended to include noncompliance with treatment assignment, as in instrumental-variables designs or fuzzy regression discontinuities (Chapters 3, 4, and 5). Finally, it is also important to pay attention to the level of randomization in constructing the urn model: if treatment assignment is by cluster, then the appropriate model involves clustered randomization, i.e., the drawing of clusters of potential outcomes from an urn, and data analysis should be based on this model (Chapter 6).

Modeling assumptions are sometimes taken as unverifiable, and indeed causal inference requires maintained hypotheses: the assertions are ultimately not completely testable. Yet, a theme of this book has been the ways in which various kinds of evidence can be brought to bear to assess the credibility of underlying models. For instance, model-validation CPOs can be brought to bear on the question of noninterference: in the Argentina land-titling study with which the book began, such causal-process observations might help in validating (or invalidating) the non-interference assumption by revealing the nature of interactions between titled and untitled neighbors, or the ways in which control-group squatters understood their treatment status relative to treatment-group squatters. Sometimes, such model-validation CPOs may also lead to the generation of data-set observations and systematic testing as well. Other modeling assumptions are sometimes amenable to formal specification tests. As just one example, in Chapter 9, I considered the assumption of homogeneous partial effects across pieces of treatment variables in the linear regression context, and the resulting implications for instrumental-variables analysis; in such contexts, simple specification tests may help to assess whether homogeneous partial effects are consistent with the data (see Appendix 9.1 and Dunning 2008c). Yet, the utility of such tests may be sharply limited: they do not generally have much power against more general forms of model misspecification (Freedman 2010b). That is why this kind of diagnostic has not been emphasized in this book and appears with a question mark in Figure 11.2.

The bottom line, however, is that assessing the credibility of the Neyman model, using both qualitative and quantitative evidence, is an important part of natural-experimental analysis—and of design-based research more generally. In this way, analysts can obtain a closer connection between their causal and statistical models and the empirical reality they are modeling. To be sure, some modeling assumptions are not verifiable, and we are left with only the credibility rather than the truth of the models. Still, focusing more analytic attention on the modeling assumptions seems likely to lead to stronger designs and fewer inferential mistakes.

If the Neyman model holds, then many of the advantages of design-based research can best be captured. Data analysis can be simple and transparent. The difference of means (or proportions) across treatment and control groups usually suffices to estimate a causal parameter of interest, such as the intention-to-treat parameter (aka the average causal effect of treatment assignment). Auxiliary analyses may be presented; for instance, in natural experiments without true randomization, analysts may well want to present the results of multiple regressions of the outcome variable on a dummy for treatment assignment, including pre-treatment covariates. Yet, the results should not change much from the unadjusted difference of means, if as-if random holds (since then the correlation in the data between treatment assignment and pre-treatment covariates should be weak). Moreover, analysts should almost always present the unadjusted difference of means, as this will help readers judge for themselves whether the results stem from the strength of the design and the size of the effect, rather than from model-based adjustment. Hypothesis testing may involve t-tests specifying unequal variances across treatment and control groups, and thus the conservative variance formula discussed earlier in the book; or, randomization tests based on the permutation distribution of test statistics may be used, especially when the study group is small (Chapter 6).

Finally—once an analyst has validated a natural experiment and the basic potential outcomes model, and estimated the average effects of interest using the data-analytic procedures described above—we arrive at the interpretation of the results (bottom right of Figure 11.2). Of course, this presents a somewhat misleading picture of the way real research occurs, since analysts are rightly probably thinking ahead to the interpretation, even as they formulate an initial design to help them answer a research question. Yet, thinking of interpretation as an activity that takes place after analysis of main effects is nonetheless useful, since it focuses attention on the *ex post* evaluation of the success of the natural experiment. Thus, the dimensions considered in Part III of the book, and especially in Chapter 10, may be particularly relevant here. Interpretation of results involves consideration of the three aspects of relevance considered in the previous chapter: external validity, idiosyncrasies of the key intervention, and the degree of bundling of distinct components of the intervention—the "what is the treatment" question.

Here, further data analysis involving both qualitative and quantitative information may also be useful. For example, independent-variable CPOs may help to identify key components of treatment, while mechanism- or auxiliary-outcome CPOs may give some hint both of idiosyncrasies of the treatment and issues related to external validity (Chapter 7). Subgroup analysis may be useful here as well. Are the results stronger for men or for women? For rich units or poor units? Such subgroup analysis should usually be interpreted with caution, particularly if initial hypotheses did not specify differences across subgroups; problems involved in testing multiple statistical hypotheses may arise (and thus *p*-values might be adjusted accordingly, e.g., through Bonferroni-type corrections). Yet, differences across subgroups can also generate new hypotheses for future testing, and can help to evaluate the generality of treatment effects. Thus, such subsequent and auxiliary data analysis bears centrally on issues of interpretation of estimated effects.

What about imperfect designs, such as those in which the assertion of as-if random is not plausible (bottom-left corner of Figure 11.2), or settings in which other assumptions of the basic Neyman model may not hold? If as-if random does not hold, the design is something other than a natural experiment—and the label should be avoided. Does this mean that researchers should not pursue the study? Of course not. As emphasized in the introduction, research questions should drive choices of research methods, and various design tools—from true experiments to conventional observational studies—can be useful in different contexts. Studies in which the key intervention is not assigned at random—as in probably the great majority of social-scientific studies—may also be strong on other dimensions of the evaluative typology in Figure 11.1, lending a further motivation to their pursuit. Yet, causal conclusions drawn from such studies are also substantially less secure than in studies with strong research designs.

One strategy available to researchers, of course, is to adjust the data. It may be useful to distinguish two cases of possible adjustment. In one case, the number of plausible confounders may be relatively small, and the strategy for adjustment driven by some clear and partially verifiable hypotheses about the assignment process. Blattman's (2008) study of child soldiering, for example, suggests that the abduction of child soldiers by the Lord's Resistance Army is as-if random, given the age and region of each potential abductee. The claim is thus that within strata defined by age and region, assignment to abduction is like a coin flip.[14] Notice that here the probabilities of assignment differ across ages and regions, and age and region are probably both related to potential outcomes; so given the assumption of as-if random, the design may be something like a block-randomized experiment, and it is important to calculate within-block estimates of treatment effects and weight across the blocks to arrive at an overall estimate of an average causal effect (Gerber and Green 2012). Of course, one must choose a procedure for doing the weighting; probably the most transparent strategy for adjustment is simply to weight each within-stratum (within-block) estimate by its share of the study group size, though regression can be used to replicate these estimates given correctly specified weights (see Humphreys 2011). The point here is that in some settings, adjustment can be relatively transparent, plausible, and even essential, and analysis should proceed (with appropriate caution), even if the label of natural experiment should not be readily applied.[15]

In other cases, adjustment is harder to justify. Without as-if random assignment, the set of potential confounders may be large, and they may be difficult to measure. Ultimately, the direction and extent of confounding is unverifiable without strong assumptions. Researchers may attempt to identify more and more potential confounders, yet this leads towards "garbage-can regressions" (Achen 2002), and inclusion of irrelevant or poorly measured variables in regression equations may lead to other pathologies, including worsened biases in inferences about causal effects (Clarke 2005; Seawright 2010). We thus move quickly back into the world of model-based adjustment, in which the extent of

---

[14] In the language of some of the literature on covariates, treatment assignment is "ignorable" conditional on covariates. How to do the conditioning, of course, is an important issue discussed throughout this book.
[15] Note that adjusting for blocked randomization by calculating weighted averages is essential, for otherwise estimators of average treatment effects will be biased for the study group (see Gerber and Green 2012: chapter 4, for explication). But in many settings, the analogy to blocked randomization in observational studies may break down: e.g., an analyst alleges that within strata defined by controls, assignment is as-if random; yet the assertion is debatable, and if the wrong confounders are identified or the wrong strategy for controlling for them is used, inference may well go off the rails.

modeling uncertainty is difficult to evaluate and the substantive, causal, and statistical rationale for the models is substantially weaker.

Ultimately, the question of what to do in such challenging settings is not the focus of this book, though it is the focus of a large methodological literature in the social sciences. The point here has instead been to point out some of the difficulties with standard model-based analysis in conventional observational studies—and to highlight the way in which strong research designs can (sometimes) help analysts sidestep these difficulties. The precise dividing line between plausible adjustment and those settings in which adjustment is probably self-defeating is hard to find and will be judged by the scholarly community. But simple and transparent analysis founded on credible models of the data-generating process should be the aspiration. When the research design is strong, as in successful natural experiments, this simplicity, transparency, and credibility can sometimes be achieved.

In closing, it is useful to reiterate some key points. (1) Building strong research designs with natural experiments requires choices about multiple objectives—including compelling as-if random assignment, simplicity of data analysis, and wider relevance. These objectives may be in conflict, and strong research can be understood as the process of balancing astutely between them. (2) Substantive expertise plays a vital role in striking the appropriate balance. Without strong substantive knowledge, moreover, it is unlikely that analysts will achieve strength on any of the three dimensions. (3) Multiple methods, including both quantitative and qualitative tools, make important contributions to successful natural experiments. Natural experiments require substantial "shoe leather" and hard work; and while some natural experiments can be replicated in different contexts, it is unlikely that a one-size-fits-all approach will be successful. Causal inferences cannot be made by algorithm, in natural experiments as in other designs; and especially with natural experiments, substantive knowledge and multiple methods must inform the process of discovery, analysis, and evaluation.

More generally, it seems that many modes of inquiry contribute to successful causal inference. Ultimately, the right mix of methods substantially depends on the research question involved. In every study, analysts are challenged to think critically about the match between the assumptions of models and the empirical reality they are studying. This is as much the case for true experiments and natural experiments as it is for conventional observational studies. Convergent lines of evidence, including various kinds of qualitative inquiry, should be developed and exploited (Freedman 2010a). There may always be a place for conventional regression modeling and matching designs based on observational data, because some interesting and important problems will not easily yield themselves to strong research designs.

Yet, where strong designs are available, the researcher should resist the impulse to fit conventional statistical models to the data from such designs—the assumptions behind which are not validated by the design. At a minimum, the assumptions behind the models and the designs should be defended. As with the many other analytic tasks discussed in this book, this defense is most effectively carried out using diverse forms of quantitative—and also qualitative—evidence. Such approaches can best leverage the substantial power of natural experiments to answer important causal questions in the social sciences.

References

Acemoglu, Daron, Simon Johnson, and James A. Robinson. 2001. "The Colonial Origins of Comparative Development: An Empirical Investigation." *American Economic Review* **91**(5): 1369–1401.

Achen, Christopher H. 1986. *The Statistical Analysis of Quasi-experiments*. Berkeley: University of California Press.

———. 2002. "Toward a New Political Methodology: Microfoundations and ART." *Annual Review of Political Science* **5**: 423–50.

Angrist, Joshua D. 1990a. "Lifetime Earnings and the Vietnam Era Draft Lottery: Evidence from Social Security Administrative Records." *American Economic Review* **80**(3): 313–36.

———. 1990b. "Errata: Lifetime Earnings and the Vietnam Era Draft Lottery: Evidence from Social Security Administrative Records." *American Economic Review* **80**(5): 1284–86.

Angrist, Joshua, Eric Bettinger, Erik Bloom, Elizabeth King, and Michael Kremer. 2002. "Vouchers for Private Schooling in Colombia: Evidence from a Randomized Natural Experiment." *American Economic Review* **92**(5): 1535–38.

Angrist, Joshua D., Eric Bettinger, and Michael Kremer. 2006. "Long-Term Educational Consequences of Secondary School Vouchers: Evidence from Administrative Records in Colombia." *American Economic Review* **96**(3): 847–62.

Angrist, Joshua D., and Stacey H. Chen. 2011. "Schooling and the Vietnam-Era GI Bill: Evidence from the Draft Lottery." *American Economic Journal: Applied Economics* **3**: 96–119.

Angrist, Joshua D., Stacey H. Chen, and Brigham Frandsen. 2010. "Did Vietnam Veterans Get Sicker in the 1990s? The Complicated Effects of Military Service on Self-Reported Health." *Journal of Public Economics* **94**(11–12): 824–37.

Angrist, Joshua D., and William N. Evans. 1998. "Children and Their Parents' Labor Supply: Evidence from Exogenous Variation in Family Size." *American Economic Review* **88**(3): 450–77.

Angrist, Joshua D., Guido W. Imbens, and Donald B. Rubin. 1996. "Identification of Causal Effects Using Instrumental Variables." *Journal of the American Statistical Association* **91**(434): 444–55.

Angrist, Joshua D., and Alan B. Krueger. 1991. "Does Compulsory School Attendance Affect Schooling and Earnings?" *Quarterly Journal of Economics* **106**(4): 979–1014.

———. 2001. "Instrumental Variables and the Search for Identification: From Supply and Demand to Natural Experiments." *Journal of Economic Perspectives* **15**(4): 69–85.

Angrist, Joshua D., and Victor Lavy. 1999. "Using Maimonides' Rule to Estimate the Effect of Class Size on Student Achievement." *Quarterly Journal of Economics* **114**: 533–75.

References

Angrist, Joshua D., and Jörn-Steffen Pischke. 2008. *Mostly Harmless Econometrics: An Empiricists' Companion*. Princeton University Press.

Ansolabehere, Stephen, James N. Snyder, and Charles Stewart. 2000. "Old Voters, New Voters, and the Personal Vote: Using Redistricting to Measure the Incumbency Advantage." *American Journal of Political Science* **44**(1): 17–34.

Arceneaux, Kevin, Donald Green, and Alan Gerber. 2006. "Comparing Experimental and Matching Methods Using a Large-Scale Voter Mobilization Experiment." *Political Analysis* **14**: 37–62.

Banerjee, Abhijit, and Lakshmi Iyer. 2005. "History, Institutions, and Economic Performance: The Legacy of Colonial Land Tenure Systems in India." *American Economic Review* **95**(4): 1190–1213.

Bartels, Larry M. 1991. "Instrumental and 'Quasi-Instrumental' Variables." *American Journal of Political Science* **35**(3): 777–800.

Bell, Robert M., and Daniel F. McCaffrey. 2002. "Bias Reduction in Standard Errors for Linear Regression with Multi-stage Samples." *Survey Methodology* **29**(2): 169–79.

Benjamini, Yoav, and Yosef Hochberg. 1995. "The Control of the False Discovery Rate: A Practical and Powerful Approach to Multiple Testing." *Journal of the Royal Statistical Society, Series B* **57**: 289–300.

Benjamini, Yoav, and Daniel Yekutieli. 2001. "The Control of the False Discovery Rate in Multiple Testing under Dependency." *Annals of Statistics* **29**(4): 1165–88.

Bennett, Andrew. 2010. "Process Tracing and Causal Inference." In Brady and Collier (2010).

Berger, Daniel. 2009. "Taxes, Institutions and Local Governance: Evidence from a Natural Experiment in Colonial Nigeria." Manuscript, Department of Politics, New York University.

Berk, Richard A., and David A. Freedman. 2008. "On Weighting Regressions by Propensity Scores." *Evaluation Review* **32**(4): 392–409.

Black, S. 1999. "Do 'Better' Schools Matter? Parental Valuation of Elementary Education." *Quarterly Journal of Economics* **114**: 577–99.

Blattman, Christopher. 2008. "From Violence to Voting: War and Political Participation in Uganda." *American Political Science Review* **103**(2): 231–47.

Bloom, Howard S., Larry L. Orr, Stephen H. Bell, George Cave, Fred Doolittle, Winston Lin, and Johannes M. Bos. 1997. "The Benefits and Costs of JTPA Title II-A Programs: Key Findings from the National Job Training Partnership Act Study." *Journal of Human Resources* **32**(3): 549–76.

Boas, Taylor C., and F. Daniel Hidalgo. 2011. "Controlling the Airwaves: Incumbency Advantage and Community Radio in Brazil." *American Journal of Political Science* **55**(4): 869–85.

Boas, Taylor C., F. Daniel Hidalgo, and Neal P. Richardson. 2011. "The Spoils of Victory: Campaign Donations and Government Contracts in Brazil." Working Paper 379, Kellogg Institute for International Studies, University of Notre Dame.

Bound, John, David Jaeger, and Regina Baker. 1995. "Problems with Instrumental Variables Estimation When the Correlation between the Instruments and the Endogenous Explanatory Variables is Weak." *Journal of the American Statistical Association* **90**(430): 443–50.

Bowles, Samuel, and Herbert Gintis. 2011. *A Cooperative Species: Human Reciprocity and Its Evolution*. Princeton University Press.

Brady, Henry E. 2008. "Causality and Explanation in Social Science." In Janet M. Box-Steffensmeier, Henry E. Brady, and David Collier, eds., *The Oxford Handbook of Political Methodology*. Oxford University Press.
  2010. "Doing Good and Doing Better: How Far Does the Quantitative Template Get Us?" In Brady and Collier (2010).
Brady, Henry E., and David Collier, eds. 2010. *Rethinking Social Inquiry: Diverse Tools, Shared Standards*. Rowman & Littlefield, 2nd edn.
Brady, Henry E., David Collier, and Jason Seawright. 2010. "Refocusing the Discussion of Methodology." In Brady and Collier (2010).
Brady, Henry E., and John E. McNulty. 2011. "Turning Out to Vote: The Costs of Finding and Getting to the Polling Place." *American Political Science Review* **105**: 115–34.
Brickman, Philip, Ronnie Janoff-Bulman, and Dan Coates. 1978. "Lottery Winners and Accident Victims: Is Happiness Relative?" *Journal of Personality and Social Psychology* **36**(8): 917–27.
Brollo, Fernanda, and Tommaso Nannicini. 2010. "Tying Your Enemy's Hands in Close Races: The Politics of Federal Transfers in Brazil." Working Paper 358, IGIER (Innocenzo Gasparini Institute for Economic Research), Bocconi University.
Brollo, Fernanda, Tommaso Nannicini, Roberto Perotti, and Guido Tabellini. 2009. "The Political Resource Curse." Working Paper 356, IGIER (Innocenzo Gasparini Institute for Economic Research), Bocconi University.
Bronars, Stephen G., and Grogger, Jeff. 1994. "The Economic Consequences of Unwed Motherhood: Using Twins as a Natural Experiment." *American Economic Review* **84**(5): 1141–56.
Bullock, John G., and Shang E. Ha. 2011. "Mediation Analysis Is Harder Than It Looks." In James N. Druckman, Donald P. Green, James H. Kuklinski, and Arthur Lupia, eds., *Cambridge Handbook of Experimental Political Science*. New York: Cambridge University Press.
Burghardt, John, Peter Z. Schochet, Sheena McConnell, Terry Johnson, Mark Gritz, Steven Glazerman, John Homrighausen, and Russell H. Jackson. 2001. *Does Job Corps Work? Summary of the National Job Corps Study*. Research and Evaluation 01-J. Washington, DC: US Department of Labor, Employment and Training Administration.
Cameron, Samuel. 1988. "The Economics of Crime Deterrence: A Survey of Theory and Evidence." *Kyklos* **41**(2): 301–23.
Campbell, Donald T. 1969. "Reforms as Experiments." *American Psychologist* **24**: 409–29.
  1984. Foreword to *Research Design for Program Evaluation: the Regression-Discontinuity Approach*, by William M. K. Trochim. Beverly Hills: Sage Publications.
Campbell, Donald T., and Robert F. Boruch. 1975. "Making the Case for Randomized Assignment to Treatments by Considering the Alternatives: Six Ways in Which Quasi-experimental Evaluations in Compensatory Education Tend to Underestimate Effects." In Carl A. Bennett and Arthur A. Lumsdaine, eds., *Evaluation and Experiment: Some Critical Issues in Assessing Social Programs*. New York: Academic Press.
Campbell, Donald T., and H. Laurence Ross. 1970. "The Connecticut Crackdown on Speeding: Time-Series Data in Quasi-experimental Analysis." In Edward R. Tufts, ed., *The Quantitative Analysis of Social Problems*. Reading, MA: Addison-Wesley.
Campbell, Donald T., and Julian C. Stanley. 1966. *Experimental and Quasi-experimental Designs for Research*. Chicago: Rand McNally.

References

Card, David. 1995. "Using Geographic Variation in College Proximity to Estimate the Return to Schooling." In L. N. Christofides, E. K. Grant, and R. Swidinsky, eds., *Aspects of Labor Market Behaviour: Essays in Honour of John Vanderkamp*. University of Toronto Press.

Card, David, Carlos Dobkin, and Nicole Maestas. 2009. *Quarterly Journal of Economics* **124**(2): 597–636.

Card, David, and Alan B. Krueger. 1994. "Minimum Wages and Employment: A Case Study of the Fast-Food Industry in New Jersey and Pennsylvania." *American Economic Review* **84**(4): 772–93.

Card, David, and David S. Lee. 2007. "Regression Discontinuity Inference with Specification Error." *Journal of Econometrics* **142**(2): 655–74.

Caughey, Devin M., and Jasjeet S. Sekhon. 2011. "Elections and the Regression-Discontinuity Design: Lessons from Close U.S. House Races, 1942–2008." *Political Analysis* **19**(4): 385–408.

Chamon, Marcos, João M. P. de Mello, and Sergio Firpo. 2009. "Electoral Rules, Political Competition, and Fiscal Expenditures: Regression Discontinuity Evidence from Brazilian Municipalities." IZA Discussion Paper No. 4658, Institute for the Study of Labour, Bonn.

Chattopadhyay, Raghabendra, and Esther Duflo. 2004. "Women as Policy Makers: Evidence from a Randomized Experiment in India." *Econometrica* **72**(5): 1409–43.

Clarke, Kevin A. 2005. "The Phantom Menace: Omitted Variable Bias in Econometric Research." *Conflict Management and Peace Science* **22**: 341–352.

Cogneau, Denis, and Alexander Moradi. 2011. "Borders That Divide: Education and Religion in Ghana and Togo since Colonial Times." Working Paper WPS/2011–21/, Center for the Study of African Economies, Oxford.

Collier, David. 2011. "Teaching Process Tracing: Examples and Exercises." Online supplement to David Collier, "Understanding Process Tracing," *PS: Political Science and Politics* **44**(4): 823–30. Available at http://polisci.berkeley.edu/people/faculty/person_detail.php?person=230, downloaded April 7, 2012.

Collier, David, Henry E. Brady, and Jason Seawright. 2010. "Sources of Leverage in Causal Inference: Toward an Alternative View of Methodology." In Brady and Collier (2010).

Conley, Dalton, and Jennifer A. Heerwig. 2009. "The Long-Term Effects of Military Conscription on Mortality: Estimates from the Vietnam-Era Draft Lottery." NBER Working Paper 15105, National Bureau of Economic Research, Cambridge, MA.

Cornfield, J. 1978. "Randomization by Group: A Formal Analysis." *American Journal of Epidemiology* **108**: 100–2.

Cox, David R. 1958. *Planning of Experiments*. New York: John Wiley & Sons.

Cox, Gary W. 1997. *Making Votes Count: Strategic Coordination in the World's Electoral Systems*. Cambridge University Press.

Cox, Gary, Frances Rosenbluth, and Michael F. Thies. 2000. "Electoral Rules, Career Ambitions, and Party Structure: Conservative Factions in Japan's Upper and Lower Houses." *American Journal of Political Science* **44**: 115–22.

Dahl, Robert A. 1971. *Polyarchy: Participation and Opposition*. New Haven, CT: Yale University Press.

Dal Bó, Ernesto, and Rossi, Martín. 2010. "Term Length and Political Performance." Manuscript, Haas School of Business, University of California at Berkeley.

De la O, Ana. Forthcoming. "Do Conditional Cash Transfers Affect Electoral Behavior? Evidence from a Randomized Experiment in Mexico." *American Journal of Political Science*.

De Long, J. Bradford, and Lang, Kevin, 1992. "Are All Economic Hypotheses False?" *Journal of Political Economy* **100**(6): 1257–72.

De Soto, Hernando. 1989. *The Other Path: The Economic Answer to Terrorism.* New York: Basic Books.

———. 2000. *The Mystery of Capital: Why Capitalism Triumphs in the West and Fails Everywhere Else.* New York: Basic Books.

Deaton, Angus. 2009. "Instruments of Development: Randomization in the Tropics, and the Search for the Elusive Keys to Economic Development." The Keynes Lecture, British Academy, London.

Deere, Donald, Kevin M. Murphy, and Finis Welch. 1995. "Sense and Nonsense on the Minimum Wage." *Regulation: The Cato Review of Business and Government* **18**: 47–56.

Dehejia, Rajeev. 2005. "Practical Propensity Score Matching: A Reply to Smith and Todd." *Journal of Econometrics* **125**: 355–64.

Dehejia, Rajeev H., and Sadek Wahba. 1999. "Causal Effects in Nonexperimental Studies: Reevaluating the Evaluation of Training Programs." *Journal of the American Statistical Association* **94**: 1053–62.

Di Tella, Rafael, Sebastian Galiani, and Ernesto Schargrodsky. 2007. "The Formation of Beliefs: Evidence from the Allocation of Land Titles to Squatters." *Quarterly Journal of Economics* **122**: 209–41.

Di Tella, Rafael, and Ernesto Schargrodsky. 2004. "Do Police Reduce Crime? Estimates Using the Allocation of Police Forces after a Terrorist Attack." *American Economic Review* **94**: 115–33.

Diamond, Jared, and James A. Robinson, eds. 2010. *Natural Experiments of History.* Cambridge, MA: Belknap Press of Harvard University Press.

Dobkin, Carlos, and Reza Shabini. 2009. "The Long Term Health Effects of Military Service: Evidence from the National Health Interview Survey and the Vietnam Era Draft Lottery." *Economic Inquiry* **47**: 69–80.

Doherty, Daniel, Donald Green, and Alan Gerber. 2005. "Personal Income and Attitudes toward Redistribution: A Study of Lottery Winners." Working paper, Institution for Social and Policy Studies, Yale University.

———. 2006. "Personal Income and Attitudes toward Redistribution: A Study of Lottery Winners." *Political Psychology* **27**(3): 441–58.

Donner, Allan, Nicholas Birkett, and Carol Buck. 1981. "Randomization by Cluster: Sample Size Requirements and Analysis." *American Journal of Epidemiology* **114**(6): 906–14.

Donner, Allan, and Neil Klar. 1994. "Cluster Randomization Trials in Epidemiology: Theory and Application." *Journal of Statistical Planning and Inference* **42**(1–2): 37–56.

———. 2000. *Design and Analysis of Cluster Randomization Trials in Health Research.* London: Edward Arnold.

Druckman, James N., Donald P. Green, James H. Kuklinski, and Arthur Lupia, eds. 2011. *Cambridge Handbook of Experimental Political Science.* New York: Cambridge University Press.

Duflo, Esther. 2001. "Schooling and Labor Market Consequences of School Construction in Indonesia: Evidence from an Unusual Policy Experiment." *American Economic Review* **91**(4): 795–813.

Dunning, Thad. 2008a. "Improving Causal Inference: Strengths and Limitations of Natural Experiments." *Political Research Quarterly* **61**(2): 282–93.
  2008b. "Natural and Field Experiments: The Role of Qualitative Methods." *Qualitative and Multi-method Research* **6**(2): 17–22. Working paper version: "Design-Based Inference: The Role of Qualitative Methods."
  2008c. "Model Specification in Instrumental-Variables Regression." *Political Analysis* **16**(3): 290–302.
  2008d. *Crude Democracy: Natural Resource Wealth and Political Regimes*. New York: Cambridge University Press.
  2010a. "Design-Based Inference: Beyond the Pitfalls of Regression Analysis?" In Brady and Collier (2010).
  2010b. "The Salience of Ethnic Categories: Field and Natural Experimental Evidence from Indian Village Councils." Working paper, Department of Political Science, Yale University.
  2011. "Ethnic Quotas and Party Politics in Indian Village Councils: Evidence from Rajasthan." Manuscript, Department of Political Science, Yale University.
Dunning, Thad, and Janhavi Nilekani. 2010. "Ethnic Quotas and Political Mobilization: Caste, Parties, and Distribution in Indian Village Councils." Manuscript, Department of Political Science, Yale University.
Duverger, Maurice. 1954. *Political Parties*. London: Methuen.
Eggers, Andrew C., and Jens Hainmueller. 2009. "MPs for Sale? Estimating Returns to Office in Post-war British Politics." *American Political Science Review* **103**(4): 513–33.
Eisenberg, Daniel, and Brian Rowe. 2009. "The Effects of Smoking in Young Adulthood on Smoking Later in Life: Evidence Based on the Vietnam Era Draft Lottery." *Forum for Health Economics & Policy* **12**(2): 1–32.
Elis, Roy, Neil Malhotra, and Marc Meredith. 2009. "Apportionment Cycles as Natural Experiments." *Political Analysis* **17**(4): 358–376.
Erikson, Robert, and Laura Stoker. 2011. "Caught in the Draft: The Effects of Vietnam Draft Lottery Status on Political Attitudes." *American Political Science Review* **105**(2): 221–37.
Evans, William N., and Jeanne S. Ringel. 1999. "Can Higher Cigarette Taxes Improve Birth Outcomes?" *Journal of Public Economics* **72**: 135–54.
Fearon, James D., and David D. Laitin. 2008. "Integrating Qualitative and Quantitative Methods." In David Collier, Henry E. Brady, and Janet M. Box-Steffensmeier, eds., *Oxford Handbook of Political Methodology*. Oxford University Press.
Ferraz, Claudio, and Frederico Finan. 2008. "Exposing Corrupt Politicians: The Effect of Brazil's Publicly Released Audits on Electoral Outcomes." *Quarterly Journal of Economics* **123**(2): 703–45.
  2010. "Motivating Politicians: The Impacts of Monetary Incentives on Quality and Performance." Manuscript, Department of Economics, University of California at Berkeley.
Fisher, Ronald A. 1951. *The Design of Experiments*. London: Oliver and Boyd, 6th edn (1st edn, 1935).
Freedman, David. 1983. "A Note on Screening Regression Equations." *American Statistician* **37**(2): 152–5.
  1991. "Statistical Models and Shoe Leather." In Peter V. Marsden, ed., *Sociological Methodology*, vol. **21**. Washington, DC: American Sociological Association.

1999. "From Association to Causation: Some Remarks on the History of Statistics." *Statistical Science* **14**: 243–58.

2006. "Statistical Models for Causation: What Inferential Leverage Do They Provide?" *Evaluation Review* **30**: 691–713.

2008a. "On Regression Adjustments to Experimental Data." *Advances in Applied Mathematics* **40**: 180–93.

2008b. "On Regression Adjustments in Experiments with Several Treatments." *Annals of Applied Statistics* **2**: 176–96.

2009. *Statistical Models: Theory and Practice*. Cambridge University Press, 2nd edn.

2010a. "On Types of Scientific Inquiry." In Brady and Collier (2010).

2010b. "Diagnostics Cannot Have Much Power Against General Alternatives." In David A. Freedman, David Collier, Jasjeet S. Sekhon, and Philip B. Stark, eds., *Statistical Models and Causal Inference: A Dialogue with the Social Sciences*. New York: Cambridge University Press.

Freedman, David A., David Collier, Jasjeet S. Sekhon, and Philip B. Stark, eds. 2010. *Statistical Models and Causal Inference: A Dialogue with the Social Sciences*. New York: Cambridge University Press.

Freedman, David A., Diana B. Petitti, and James M. Robins. 2004. "On the Efficacy of Screening for Breast Cancer." *International Journal of Epidemiology* **33**: 43–73.

Freedman, David, Robert Pisani, and Roger Purves. 2007. *Statistics*. 4th edn. New York: W. W. Norton, Inc.

Fujiwara, Thomas. 2009. "Can Voting Technology Empower the Poor? Regression Discontinuity Evidence from Brazil." Working paper, Department of Economics, University of British Columbia.

2011. "A Regression Discontinuity Test of Strategic Voting and Duverger's Law." *Quarterly Journal of Political Science* **6**: 197–233.

Fukuyama, Francis. 2011. "Political Order in Egypt." *American Interest*, May–June. Available online as of July 7, 2011 at www.the-american-interest.com/article.cfm?piece=953.

Galiani, Sebastian, Martín A. Rossi, and Ernesto Schargrodsky. 2011. "Conscription and Crime: Evidence from the Argentine Draft Lottery." *American Economic Journal: Applied Economics* **3**(2): 119–36.

Galiani, Sebastian, and Ernesto Schargrodsky. 2004. "The Health Effects of Land Titling." *Economics and Human Biology* **2**: 353–72.

2010. "Property Rights for the Poor: Effects of Land Titling." *Journal of Public Economics* **94**: 700–29.

Gardner, Jonathan, and Andrew Oswald. 2001. "Does Money Buy Happiness? A Longitudinal Study Using Data on Windfalls." Working paper, Department of Economics, University of Warwick.

Gelman, Andrew, and Jennifer Hill. 2007. *Data Analysis Using Regression and Multilevel/Hierarchical Models*. New York: Cambridge University Press.

George, Alexander L., and Andrew Bennett. 2005. *Case Studies and Theory Development*. Cambridge, MA: MIT Press.

Gerber, Alan S., and Donald P. Green. 2000. "The Effects of Canvassing, Direct Mail, and Telephone Contact on Voter Turnout: A Field Experiment." *American Political Science Review* **94**: 653–63.

2008. "Field Experiments and Natural Experiments." In Janet Box-Steffensmeier, Henry E. Brady, and David Collier, eds., *The Oxford Handbook of Political Methodology*. Oxford University Press.

2012. *Field Experiments: Design, Analysis, and Interpretation*. New York: W. W. Norton & Co.

Gerber, Alan S., Daniel P. Kessler, and Marc Meredith. 2011. "The Persuasive Effects of Direct Mail: A Regression Discontinuity Based Approach." *Journal of Politics* **73**: 140–55.

Gerber, Alan S., and Neil Malhotra. 2008. "Do Statistical Reporting Standards Affect What Is Published? Publication Bias in Two Leading Political Science Journals." *Quarterly Journal of Political Science* **3**(3): 313–26.

Gilligan, Michael J., and Ernest J. Sergenti. 2008. "Do UN Interventions Cause Peace? Using Matching to Improve Causal Inference." *Quarterly Journal of Political Science* **3**(2): 89–122.

Glazer, Amihai, and Marc Robbins. 1985. "Congressional Responsiveness to Constituency Change." *American Journal of Political Science* **29**(2): 259–73.

Goldberg, Jack, Margaret Richards, Robert Anderson, and Miriam Rodin. 1991. "Alcohol Consumption in Men Exposed to the Military Draft Lottery: A Natural Experiment." *Journal of Substance Abuse* **3**: 307–13.

Golden, Miriam, and Lucio Picci. 2011. "Redistribution and Reelection under Proportional Representation: The Postwar Italian Chamber of Deputies." MPRA Paper 29956, Munich Personal RePEc Archive, University Library of Munich, Germany.

Goldthorpe, John H. 2001. "Causation, Statistics, and Sociology." *European Sociological Review* **17**: 1–20.

Gould, Stephen Jay. 1996. *The Mismeasure of Man*. New York: Norton, 2nd edn.

Green, Donald P. 2009. "Regression Adjustments to Experimental Data: Do David Freedman's Concerns Apply to Political Science?" Paper presented at the 26th annual meeting of the Society for Political Methodology, Yale University, July 23–25, 2009.

Green, Donald P., and Alan S. Gerber. 2008. *Get Out The Vote: How to Increase Voter Turnout*. Washington, DC: Brookings Institution Press, 2nd edn.

Green, Donald P., Shang E. Ha, and John G. Bullock. 2010. "Enough Already About 'Black Box' Experiments: Studying Mediation Is More Difficult Than Most Scholars Suppose." *Annals of the American Academy of Political and Social Science* **628** (March): 200–8.

Green, Donald P., Terence Y. Leong, Holger L. Kern, Alan Gerber, and Christopher W. Larimer. 2009. "Testing the Accuracy of Regression Discontinuity Analysis Using Experimental Benchmarks." *Political Analysis* **17**(4): 400–17.

Green, Donald P., and Ian Shapiro. 1994. *Pathologies of Rational Choice Theory: A Critique of Applications in Political Science*. New Haven, CT: Yale University Press.

Green, Donald P., and Daniel Winik. 2010. "Using Random Judge Assignments to Estimate the Effects of Incarceration and Probation on Recidivism Among Drug Offenders." *Criminology* **48**: 357–59

Green, Tina. 2005. "Do Social Transfer Programs Affect Voter Behavior? Evidence from Progresa in Mexico." Manuscript, University of California at Berkeley.

Greene, William H. 2003. *Econometric Analysis*. Upper Saddle River, NJ: Prentice Hall, 5th edn.

Grofman, Bernard, Thomas L. Brunell, and William Koetzle. 1998. "Why Gain in the Senate but Midterm Loss in the House? Evidence from a Natural Experiment." *Legislative Studies Quarterly* **23**: 79–89.

Grofman, Bernard, Robert Griffin, and Gregory Berry. 1995. "House Members Who Become Senators: Learning from a 'Natural Experiment.'" *Legislative Studies Quarterly* **20**(4): 513–29.

Gruber, Jonathan. 2000. "Disability Insurance Benefits and Labor Supply." *Journal of Political Economy* **108**(6): 1162–83.

Guan, Mei, and Donald P. Green. 2006. "Non-coercive Mobilization in State-Controlled Elections: An Experimental Study in Beijing." *Comparative Political Studies* **39**(10): 1175–93.

Haber, Stephen, and Victor Menaldo. 2011. "Do Natural Resources Fuel Authoritarianism? A Reappraisal of the Resource Curse." *American Political Science Review* **105**: 1–26.

Hahn, Jinyong, Petra Todd, and Wilbert Van Der Klaauw. 1999. "Evaluating the Effect of an Antidiscrimination Law Using a Regression-Discontinuity Design." NBER Working Paper 7131. National Bureau of Economic Research, Cambridge, MA.

Hahn, Jinyong, Petra Todd, and Wilbert Van Der Klaauw. 2001. "Identification and estimation of treatment effects with a regression discontinuity design." *Econometrica* **69**: 201–9.

Hájek, J. 1960. "Limiting Distributions in Simple Random Sampling From a Finite Population." *Magyar Tudoanyos Akademia Budapest Matematikai Kutato Intezet Koezlemenyei* **5**: 361–74.

Hansen, Ben B., and Jake Bowers. 2009. "Attributing Effects to a Cluster-Randomized Get-Out-The-Vote Campaign." *Journal of the American Statistical Association* **104**(487): 873–85.

Hearst, Norman, Tom B. Newman, and Stephen B. Hulley. 1986. "Delayed Effects of the Military Draft on Mortality: A Randomized Natural Experiment." *New England Journal of Medicine* **314**: 620–24.

Heckman, James J. 2000. "Causal Parameters and Policy Analysis in Economics: A Twentieth Century Retrospective." *Quarterly Journal of Economics* **115**: 45–97.

Heckman, James J., and Richard Robb. 1986. "Alternative Methods for Solving the Problem of Selection Bias in Evaluating the Impact of Treatments on Outcomes." In Howard Wainer, ed., *Drawing Inferences from Self-Selected Samples*. New York: Springer-Verlag.

Heckman, James J., and Sergio Urzúa. 2009. "Comparing IV with Structural Models: What Simple IV Can and Cannot Identify." NBER Working Paper 14706, National Bureau of Economic Research, Cambridge, MA.

Heckman, James J., and Urzúa, Sergio. 2010. "Comparing IV with Structural Models: What Simple IV Can and Cannot Identify." *Journal of Econometrics* **156**(1): 27–37.

Heckman, James J., Sergio Urzúa, and Edward Vytlacil. 2006. "Understanding Instrumental Variables in Models with Essential Heterogeneity." *Review of Economics and Statistics* **88**(3): 389–432

Hidalgo, F. Daniel. 2010. "Digital Democratization: Suffrage Expansion and the Decline of Political Machines in Brazil." Manuscript, Department of Political Science, University of California at Berkeley.

Hidalgo, F. Daniel, Suresh Naidu, Simeon Nichter, and Neal Richardson. 2010. "Occupational Choices: Economic Determinants of Land Invasions." *Review of Economics and Statistics* **92**(3): 505–23.

Ho, Daniel E., and Kosuke Imai. 2008. "Estimating Causal Effects of Ballot Order from a Randomized Natural Experiment: California Alphabet Lottery, 1978–2002." *Public Opinion Quarterly* **72**(2): 216–40.

Höglund, T. 1978. "Sampling from a Finite Population: A Remainder Term Estimate." *Scandinavian Journal of Statistics* **5**: 69–71.

Holland, Paul W. 1986. "Statistics and Causal Inference." *Journal of the American Statistical Association* **81**(396): 945–60.

Horiuchi, Yusaka, and Jun Saito. 2009. "Rain, Elections and Money: The Impact of Voter Turnout on Distributive Policy Outcomes in Japan." Asia–Pacific Economic Paper No. 379, Australia–Japan Research Centre, Crawford School, Australian National University, Canberra.

Horvitz, D. G., and D. J. Thompson. 1952. "A Generalization of Sampling without Replacement from a Finite Universe." *Journal of the American Statistical Association* **47**: 663–84.

Howell, William G., Patrick J. Wolf, Paul E. Petersen, and David E. Campbell. 2000. "Test-Score Effects of School Vouchers in Dayton, Ohio, New York City, and Washington, D.C.: Evidence from Randomized Field Trials." Paper presented at the annual meeting of the American Political Science Association, Washington, DC, September 2000.

Humphreys, Macartan. 2011. "Bounds on Least Squares Estimates of Causal Effects in the Presence of Heterogeneous Assignment Probabilities." Manuscript, Department of Political Science, Columbia University.

Hyde, Susan D. 2007. "The Observer Effect in International Politics: Evidence from a Natural Experiment." *World Politics* **60**: 37–63.

Hyde, Susan D. 2010. "Experimenting with Democracy Promotion: International Observers and the 2004 Presidential Elections in Indonesia." *Perspectives on Politics* **8**(2): 511–27.

Imai, Kosuke. 2005. "Do Get-Out-The-Vote Calls Reduce Turnout? The Importance of Statistical Methods for Field Experiments." *American Political Science Review* **99**(2): 283–300.

Imai, Kosuke, Luke Keele, Dustin Tingley, and Teppei Yamamoto. 2011. "Unpacking the Black Box of Causality: Learning about Causal Mechanisms from Experimental and Observational Studies." *American Political Science Review* **105**(4): 765–89.

Imai, Kosuke, Gary King, and Elizabeth A. Stuart. 2008. "Misunderstandings Among Experimentalists and Observationalists About Causal Inference." *Journal of the Royal Statistical Society, Series A (Statistics in Society)* **171**(2): 481–502.

Imbens, Guido W. 2009. "Better LATE Than Nothing: Some Comments on Deaton (2009) and Heckman and Urzua (2009)." Manuscript, Department of Economics, Harvard University.

Imbens, Guido W., and Joshua D. Angrist. 1994. "Identification and Estimation of Local Average Treatment Effects." *Econometrica* **62**(2): 467–75.

Imbens, Guido, and Karthik Kalyanaraman. 2009. "Optimal Bandwidth Choice for the Regression Discontinuity Estimator." NBER Working Paper 14726, National Bureau of Economic Research, Cambridge, MA.

Imbens, Guido W., and Thomas Lemieux. 2007. "Regression Discontinuity Designs: A Guide to Practice." *Journal of Econometrics* **142**(2): 615–35.

Imbens, Guido, Donald Rubin, and Bruce Sacerdote. 2001. "Estimating the Effect of Unearned Income on Labor Supply, Earnings, Savings and Consumption: Evidence from a Survey of Lottery Players." *American Economic Review* **91**(4): 778–94.

Iyer, Lakshmi. 2010. "Direct versus Indirect Colonial Rule in India: Long-Term Consequences." *Review of Economics and Statistics* **92**(4): 693–713.

Jacob, Brian A., and Lars Lefgren. 2004. "Remedial Education and Student Achievement: A Regression-Discontinuity Analysis." *Review of Economics and Statistics* **86**: 226–44.

Jones, Benjamin F., and Benjamin A. Olken. 2005. "Do Leaders Matter? National Leadership and Growth Since World War II." *Quarterly Journal of Economics* **120**(3): 835–64.

Kennedy, Peter. 1985. *A Guide to Econometrics*. Cambridge, MA: MIT Press, 2nd edn.

Khandker, Shahidur R., Gayatri B. Koolwal, and Hussain A. Samad. 2010. *Handbook on Impact Evaluation: Quantitative Methods and Practices*. Washington, DC: World Bank.

King, Gary, Robert O. Keohane, and Sidney Verba. 1994. *Designing Social Inquiry: Scientific Inference in Qualitative Research*. Princeton University Press

Kish, Leslie. 1965. *Survey Sampling*. New York: John Wiley & Sons.

Kling, Jeffrey R. 2006. "Incarceration Length, Employment, and Earnings." *American Economic Review* **96**(3): 863–76.

Kocher, Matthew Adam. 2007. "Insurgency, State Capacity, and the Rural Basis of Civil War." Paper presented at the Program on Order, Conflict, and Violence, Yale University, October 26, 2007. Centro de Investigación y Docencia Económicas, Mexico.

Kousser, Thad, and Megan Mullin. 2007. "Does Voting by Mail Increase Participation? Using Matching to Analyze a Natural Experiment." *Political Analysis* **15**: 1–18.

Krasno, Jonathan S., and Donald P. Green. 2008. "Do Televised Presidential Ads Increase Voter Turnout? Evidence from a Natural Experiment." *Journal of Politics* **70**: 245–61.

Krueger, Alan B. 1999. "Experimental Estimates of Education Production Functions." *Quarterly Journal of Economics* **114**: 497–532.

Laitin, David. 1986. *Hegemony and Culture: Politics and Religious Change among the Yoruba*. University of Chicago Press.

Lee, David S. 2008. "Randomized Experiments from Non-random Selection in U.S. House Elections." *Journal of Econometrics* **142**(2): 675–97

Lee, David S., and Thomas Lemieux, 2010. "Regression Discontinuity Designs in Economics." *Journal of Economic Literature* **48**(2): 281–355.

Lerman, Amy. 2008. "Bowling Alone (With My Own Ball and Chain): The Effects of Incarceration and the Dark Side of Social Capital." Manuscript, Department of Politics, Princeton University.

Levitt, Steven D. 1997. "Using Electoral Cycles in Police Hiring to Estimate the Effect of Police on Crime." *American Economic Review* **87**(3): 270–90.

Lieberman, Evan. 2005. "Nested Analysis as a Mixed-Method Strategy for Comparative Research." *American Political Science Review* **99**(3): 435–52.

Lindahl, Mikail. 2002. "Estimating the Effect of Income on Health and Mortality Using Lottery Prizes as Exogenous Source of Variation in Income." Manuscript, Swedish Institute for Social Research, Stockholm University.

Lindquist, E. F. 1940. *Statistical Analysis in Educational Research*. Boston: Houghton Mifflin.

Litschig, Stephan, and Kevin Morrison. 2009. "Local Electoral Effects of Intergovernmental Fiscal Transfers: Quasi-experimental Evidence from Brazil, 1982–1988." Working paper, Universitat Pompeu Fabra, Barcelona, and Cornell University.

Lyall, Jason. 2009. "Does Indiscriminate Violence Incite Insurgent Attacks? Evidence from Chechnya." *Journal of Conflict Resolution* **53**(3): 331–62.

McClellan, Mark, Barbara J. McNeil, and Joseph P. Newhouse. 1994. "Does More Intensive Treatment of Acute Myocardial Infarction Reduce Mortality?" *Journal of the American Medical Association* **272**: 859–66.

McCrary, Justin. 2007. "Testing for Manipulation of the Running Variable in the Regression Discontinuity Design: A Density Test." *Journal of Econometrics* **142**(2): 615–35.

References

MacLean, Lauren M. 2010. *Informal Institutions and Citizenship in Rural Africa: Risk and Reciprocity in Ghana and Cote d'Ivoire.* New York: Cambridge University Press.

McNeil, B. J., S. G. Pauker, H. C. Sox, Jr., and A. Tversky. 1982. "On the Elicitation of Preferences for Alternative Therapies." *New England Journal of Medicine* **306**: 1259–62.

Mahoney, James. 2010. "After KKV: The New Methodology of Qualitative Research." *World Politics* **62**: 120–47.

Manacorda, Marco, Edward Miguel, and Andrea Vigorito. 2011. "Government Transfers and Political Support." *American Economic Journal: Applied Economics* **3**(3): 1–28.

Manski, Charles F. 1995. *Identification Problems in the Social Sciences.* Cambridge, MA: Harvard University Press.

Matsudaira, Jordan D. 2008. "Mandatory Summer School and Student Achievement." *Journal of Econometrics* **142**: 829–50

Mauldon, Jane, Jan Malvin, Jon Stiles, Nancy Nicosia, and Eva Seto. 2000. "Impact of California's Cal-Learn Demonstration Project: Final Report." UC Data, University of California at Berkeley.

Meredith, Marc. 2009. "Persistence in Political Participation." *Quarterly Journal of Political Science* **4**(3): 186–208.

Meredith, Marc, and Neil Malhotra. 2011. "Convenience Voting Can Affect Election Outcomes." *Election Law Journal* **10**(3): 227–53

Middleton, Joel A., and Peter M. Aronow. 2011. "Unbiased Estimation of the Average Treatment Effect in Cluster-Randomized Experiments." Manuscript, Yale University. Available at http://ssrn.com/abstract=1803849 or http://dx.doi.org/10.2139/ssrn.1803849.

Miguel, Edward. 2004. "Tribe or Nation? Nation Building and Public Goods in Kenya versus Tanzania." *World Politics* **56**(3): 327–62.

Miguel, Edward, and Ray Fisman. 2006. "Corruption, Norms, and Legal Enforcement: Evidence from Diplomatic Parking Tickets." *Journal of Political Economy* **115**(6): 1020–48.

Miguel, Edward, Shanker Satyanath, and Ernest Sergenti. 2004. "Economic Shocks and Civil Conflict: An Instrumental Variables Approach." *Journal of Political Economy* **122**: 725–53.

Miles, William F. S. 1994. *Hausaland Divided: Colonialism and Independence in Nigeria and Niger.* Ithaca, NY: Cornell University Press.

Miles, William, and David Rochefort. 1991. "Nationalism versus Ethnic Identity in Sub-Saharan Africa." *American Political Science Review* **85**(2): 393–403

Morton, Rebecca B., and Kenneth C. Williams. 2008. "Experimentation in Political Science." In Janet Box-Steffensmeier, Henry E. Brady, and David Collier, eds., *The Oxford Handbook of Political Methodology.* Oxford University Press.

Morton, Rebecca B., and Kenneth C. Williams. 2010. *Experimental Political Science and the Study of Causality: From Nature to the Lab.* New York: Cambridge University Press.

Moulton, Brent R. 1986. "Random Group Effects and the Precision of Regression Estimates." *Journal of Econometrics* **32**: 385–97.

Neyman, Jerzy Splawa, with D. M. Dabrowska and T. P. Speed. (1923) 1990. "On the Application of Probability Theory to Agricultural Experiments. Essay on Principles. Section 9." *Statistical Science* **5**(4): 465–72. Originally published by Neyman in Polish in the *Annals of Agricultural Sciences.*

Nickerson, David. 2008. "Is Voting Contagious? Evidence from Two Field Experiments." *American Political Science Review* **102**: 49–57.

Nilekani, Janhavi. 2010. "Reservation for Women in Karnataka Gram Panchayats: The Implications of Non-random Reservation and the Effect of Women Leaders." Senior honors thesis, Yale College, New Haven, CT.

Paluck, Elizabeth Levy. 2008. "The Promising Integration of Qualitative Methods and Field Experiments." *Qualitative and Multi-method Research* **6**(2): 23–30.

Permutt, Thomas, and J. Richard Hebel. 1984. "A Clinical Trial of the Change in Maternal Smoking and its Effect on Birth Weight." *Journal of the American Medical Association* **251**(7): 911–15.

Permutt, Thomas, and J. Richard Hebel. 1989. "Simultaneous-Equation Estimation in a Clinical Trial of the Effect of Smoking on Birth Weight." *Biometrics* **45**(2): 619–22.

Porter, Jack. 2003. "Estimation in the Regression Discontinuity Model." Manuscript, Department of Economics, University of Madison–Wisconsin.

Posner, Daniel N. 2004. "The Political Salience of Cultural Difference: Why Chewas and Tumbukas Are Allies in Zambia and Adversaries in Malawi." *American Political Science Review* **98**(4): 529–45.

Posner, Daniel N. 2005. *Institutions and Ethnic Politics in Africa*. Political Economy of Institutions and Decisions. Cambridge University Press

Powers, D. E., and S. S. Swinton. 1984. "Effects of Self-Study for Coachable Test-Item Types." *Journal of Educational Psychology* **76**: 266–78.

R Development Core Team. 2008. *R: A Language and Environment for Statistical Computing*. Vienna, Austria: R Foundation for Statistical Computing. Available at http://www.R-project.org

Ramsay, Kristopher W. 2011. "Revisiting the Resource Curse: Natural Disasters, the Price of Oil, and Democracy." *International Organization* **65**: 507–29.

Richardson, Benjamin Ward. [1887] 1936. "John Snow, M.D." In *The Asclepiad*, vol. **4**: 274–300. London. Reprinted in *Snow on Cholera*, London: Humphrey Milford; Oxford University Press, 1936. Page references are to the 1936 edn.

Robinson, Gregory, John E. McNulty, and Jonathan S. Krasno. 2009. "Observing the Counterfactual? The Search for Political Experiments in Nature." *Political Analysis* **17**(4): 341–57.

Rosenbaum, Paul R., and Donald B. Rubin. 1983. "The Central Role of the Propensity Score in Observational Studies for Causal Effects." *Biometrika* **70**(1): 41–55.

Rosenzweig, Mark R., and Kenneth I. Wolpin. 2000. "Natural 'Natural Experiments' in Economics." *Journal of Economic Literature* **38**(4): 827–74.

Ross, Michael. 2001. "Does Oil Hinder Democracy?" *World Politics* **53**: 325–61.

Rubin, Donald B. 1974. "Estimating Causal Effects of Treatments in Randomized and Nonrandomized Studies." *Journal of Educational Psychology* **66**: 688–701.

Rubin, Donald B. 1977. "Assignment to Treatment on the Basis of a Covariate." *Journal of Educational Statistics* **2**: 1–26.

Rubin, Donald B. 1978. "Bayesian Inference for Causal Effects: The Role of Randomization." *Annals of Statistics* **6**: 34–58.

Rubin, Donald B. 1990. "Comment: Neyman (1923) and Causal Inference in Experiments and Observational Studies." *Statistical Science* **5**(4): 472–80.

Samii, Cyrus, and Peter M. Aronow. 2012. "On Equivalencies between Design-Based and Regression-Based Variance Estimators for Randomized Experiments." *Statistics and Probability Letters* **82**(2): 365–70.

References

Seawright, Jason. 2010. "Regression-Based Inference: A Case Study in Failed Causal Assessment." In Collier and Brady (2010).

Seawright, Jason, and John Gerring. 2008. "Case Selection Techniques in Case Study Research: A Menu of Qualitative and Quantitative Options." *Political Research Quarterly* **61**(2): 294–308.

Sekhon, Jasjeet S. 2009. "Opiates for the Matches: Matching Methods for Causal Inference." *Annual Review of Political Science* **12**: 487–508.

Sekhon, Jasjeet S., and Rocío Titiunik. 2012. "When Natural Experiments Are Neither Natural Nor Experiments." *American Political Science Review* **106**: 35–57.

Sherman, Lawrence, and Heather Strang. 2004. "Experimental Ethnography: The Marriage of Qualitative and Quantitative Research." *Annals of the American Academy of Political and Social Sciences* **595**, 204–22.

Sinclair, Betsy, Margaret McConnell, and Donald P. Green. 2011. "Detecting Spillover Effects: Design and Analysis of Multi-level Experiments." Manuscript, Departments of Political Science, Universities of Chicago, Harvard, and Yale.

Skocpol, Theda. 1979. *States and Social Revolutions: A Comparative Analysis of France, Russia, and China*. New York: Cambridge University Press.

Smith, Jeffrey A., and Petra E. Todd. 2005. "Does Matching Overcome LaLonde's Critique of Nonexperimental Estimators?" *Journal of Econometrics* **125**: 305–53.

Snow, John. (1855) 1965. *On the Mode of Communication of Cholera*. London: John Churchill, 2nd edn. Reprinted in *Snow on Cholera*, London: Humphrey Milford; Oxford University Press.

Sovey, Allison J., and Donald P. Green. 2009. "Instrumental Variables Estimation in Political Science: A Readers' Guide." *American Journal of Political Science* **55**: 188–200.

Starr, Norton. 1997. "Nonrandom Risk: The 1970 Draft Lottery." *Journal of Statistics Education* **5**(2). Available at www.amstat.org/publications/jse/v5n2/datasets.starr.html

Stasavage, David. 2003. "Transparency, Democratic Accountability, and the Economic Consequences of Monetary Institutions." *American Journal of Political Science* **47**(3): 389–402.

StataCorp. 2009. *Stata Statistical Software: Release 11*. College Station, TX: StataCorp LP.

Stokes, Susan. 2009. "A Defense of Observational Research." Manuscript, Department of Political Science, Yale University.

Tannenwald, Nina. 1999. "The Nuclear Taboo: The United States and the Normative Basis of Nuclear Non-use." *International Organization* **53**(3): 433–68.

Thistlethwaite, Donald L., and Donald T. Campbell. 1960. "Regression-Discontinuity Analysis: An Alternative to the Ex-post Facto Experiment." *Journal of Educational Psychology* **51**(6): 309–17.

Titiunik, Rocío. 2009. "Incumbency Advantage in Brazil: Evidence from Municipal Mayor Elections." Manuscript, Department of Political Science, University of Michigan.

Titiunik, Rocío. 2011. "Drawing Your Senator from a Jar: Term Length and Legislative Behavior." Manuscript, Department of Political Science, University of Michigan.

Trochim, William M. K. 1984. *Research Design for Program Evaluation: the Regression-Discontinuity Approach*. Beverly Hills: Sage Publications.

UCLA Department of Epidemiology. n.d.-a. "Lambeth Waterworks." In *Brief History During the Snow Era: 1813–58*, UCLA Department of Epidemiology. Available at www.ph.ucla.edu/epi/snow/1859map/lambeth_waterworks_a2.html (accessed March 15, 2012).

UCLA Department of Epidemiology. n.d.-b. "Southwark and Vauxhall Water Company." In *Brief History during the Snow Era: 1813–58*. UCLA Department of Epidemiology. Available at www.ph.ucla.edu/epi/snow/1859map/southwarkvauxhall_a2.html (accessed March 15, 2012).

Van Evera, Stephen. 1997. *Guide to Methods for Students of Political Science*. Ithaca, NY: Cornell University Press.

Waldner, David. Forthcoming. "Process Tracing and Causal Mechanisms." In H. Kincaid, ed., *Oxford Handbook of the Philosophy of Social Science*.

Wooldridge, Jeffrey M. 2009. *Introductory Econometrics*. Cincinnati, OH: South-Western College Publishing.

Index

Always-Treats, definition of, 138
Angrist and Lavy (1999), 76
   credibility of models in, 268–69, 282, 323
   data analysis in, 268
   plausibility of as-if random in, 216, 250, 323
      role of information, incentives, and capacities in assessing, 238
   relevance of intervention in, 268–69, 323
   role of substantive knowledge in, 327
   use of regression-discontinuity design in, 76
Argentina land-titling study (Galiani and Schargrodsky 2004, 2010), 10
   credibility of models in, 280, 281
   data analysis in, 115–17
   model-validation CPOs in, 226
   nointerference assumption in, 119, 260
   plausibility of as-if random in, 250, 322
      role of information, incentives, and capacities in assessing, 237
   relationship to theory of, 316
   relevance of intervention in, 304
   treatment-assignment CPOs in, 213–14
   use of natural experiment in, 10–12
   validation of as-if random in
      qualitative evidence for, 11
      quantitative evidence for, 11
as-if random, 9, 236
   assessment of plausibility of
      role of information, incentives, and capacities in, 236–39
   continuum of plausibility of, 249–52
   definition of, 9
   difficulty of evaluating, 252
   plausibility of, 27
   validation of, 12
auxiliary-outcome CPOs, 209, 224
   definition of, 224
   examples of, 224
average causal effect, 109–12
   for Compliers, 141
   estimation of, 112–15
   intention-to-treat parameter and, 111
   in regression-discontinuity designs, 122
   relevance of, 111
   unobservability of, 112

balance tests
   in cluster-randomized studies, 242
   and statistical power, 241
   use of, 239
Bonferroni correction for multiple comparisons
   definition of, 241
Brady and McNulty (2011)
   credibility of models in, 281
   description of, 55
   plausibility of as-if random in, 251
   relevance of intervention in, 305
bundling of treatments
   definition of, 290, 300

Card and Krueger (1994)
   bundling of treatments in, 302
   credibility of models in, 281
   plausibility of as-if random in, 251
   relevance of intervention in, 304, 305, 306
causal models *see* response schedule
   maintained assumptions of, 256
   role of interventions, 256
causality, 259
   role of manipulation in concepts of, 259
causal-process observations (CPOs), 210
   definition of, 26, 210
   relation to data-set observations of, 211
   stronger and weaker uses of, 228–29
   types of, 26
   uses of, 211
central limit theorems, use of, 171, 173, 186
Chattopadhyay and Duflo (2004), 280
   credibility of models in, 280
   description of, 50
   plausibility of as-if random in, 250
   relevance of intervention in, 304
clustered randomization, 175–86
   adjustment by intraclass correlation coefficient and, 182–84

Index

clustered randomization (cont.)
　analysis by cluster mean and, 179
　　advantages of, 181, 183
　　formal details of, 195
　　problems with unequal cluster sizes of, 201
　　variance of estimator in, 179
　consequences of, 176
　Neyman model and, 175–78
　within-cluster homogeneity of potential outcomes and, 177
Compliers, definition of, 138
compound treatment problem *see* bundling of treatments
conditional density (sorting) tests, in regression-discontinuity designs, 245–46
conditional independence
　definition of, 23
confounders
　examples of, 5–6
　methods of controlling for, 6, 23
　natural experiments and, 118
convenience sample
　definition of, 294
conventional observational studies
　definition of, 16
　evaluation of, 319
counterfactuals
　and causality, 109
credibility of models
　continuum of, 278

data mining
　problems with, 268, 283
data-set observations (DSOs) *see* causal-process observations (CPOs) definition of
Defiers, definition of, 138, 149
design-based research, Rationale for, 4, 24–25
design effect *see* clustered randomization, definition of, 183
Di Tella, Galiani and Schargrodsky (2007) *see* Argentina land-titling study (Galiani and Schargrodsky 2004, 2010)
difference-of-means estimator
　and bias in regression-discontinuity designs, 128–33
　and confounding variables, 118
　examples of analysis using, 13, 115, 279
　standard error of, 168
　　conservative formula for, 191–94
　　exactness under strict null hypothesis of, 194
　unbiased estimation of average causal effects and, 115
Doherty, Green, and Gerber (2006)
　credibility of model in, 273
　description of, 51
　instrumental-variables analysis in, 94
　plausibility of as-if random in, 250
　relevance of intervention in, 304
double crossover, definition of, 137
Dunning and Nilekani (2010), description of, 82

effect of treatment on Compliers
　estimation of, 141–42 *see* instrumental-variables analysis
　instrumental-variables least squares (IVLS) estimator and, 151
　linear regression and, 150–52
evaluative typology
　relationship between dimensions of, 324
exchangeable, definition of, 131
exclusion restriction
　in Neyman model, 120–21
expected value
　definition of, 114
experiments, true
　advantages of, 7
external validity
　of conventional observational studies, 297
　definition of, 290, 293
　in natural experiments, 295–96
　in true experiments, 294–95

Fisher's exact test, 186–90
　Monte Carlo simulations and, 189
fundamental problem of causal inference, 109
fuzzy regression discontinuity designs *see* regression-discontinuity designs
　definition of, 81–82
　examples of, 134–35
　instrumental-variables analysis of, 135
　intention-to-treat principle and, 135

Galiani and Schargrodsky (2004, 2010) *see* Argentina land-titling study
Grofman, Griffin, and Berry (1995)
　credibility of models in, 282
　description of, 60
　plausibility of as-if random in, 252
　relevance of intervention in, 305, 306

heteroskedasticity
　definition of, 181
Hidalgo (2010), 125
　analysis of, 125–26
　description of, 72
　relevance of intervention in, 291
Hyde (2007) description of, 55

Index

hypothesis testing *see* Fisher's exact test
   t-tests and, 171

idiosyncrasy of interventions
   definition of, 290, 298
   in instrumental-variables designs, 299
   randomization and, 298–99
   variation in, 299
independent-variable CPOs
   definition of, 209, 219
   examples of, 219–21
instrumental-variables designs, 87
   analysis of, 135–49
   as-if random assignment in, 152
   assumptions of, 148
   credibility of models in, 101
   definition of, 18
   effect of treatment on Compliers in, 89
      estimation of, 142–43, 154–57
   external validity of, 153
   historical or institutional variation as sources of, 97–101
   key assumptions of, 90, 152, 270
   lotteries as, 94–95
   model- vs. design-based research and, 90
   natural experiments as, 92
   no-Defiers assumption in, 148
   rationale for, 87
   sources of, 91
   standard errors in, 174–75
   true experiments as, 91
   validation of as-if random in, 101
   weather shocks as source of, 95–97
instrumental-variables estimator
   small-sample bias in, 157
instrumental-variables least squares (IVLS) regression, 270
   model specification in, 271
   use of control variables in, 277
intention-to-treat analysis, 87
   definition of, 87
   in the presence of crossover, 138
   reduced-form regression as, 102
intention-to-treat parameter, 111 *see* intention-to-treat analysis
intervention, 29
   relevance of, 29
Iyer (2010), 97
   assumptions of analysis in, 99–100
   description of, 97–100

jurisdictional borders, 175
   clustered randomization and, 175–76, 185–86
   problem of bundling in, 300–02

linear regression models, 263–64
   homogenous partial effects assumption and, 271
   and instrumental-variables estimation, 270
   vs. Neyman model, 152, 264
local average treatment effect (LATE)
   definitions of, 33, 84
lottery studies
   examples of, 49–53
Lyall (2009)
   description of, 55

manipulation, 7
   of experimental treatments, 7
   natural experiments and absence of, 8
matching, 20
   contrast of natural experiments and, 20–21
   definition of, 20–21
mechanism CPOs
   definition of, 209, 222
   examples of, 222, 223
   and mediation analysis, 222
   qualitative methods and, 223
mediation analysis, 38
Miguel, Satyanath, and Sergenti (2004), 95
   assumptions of analysis in, 96
   credibility of model in, 274
   description of, 95–96
   relevance of intervention in, 304
models
   credibility of, 28
   importance of, 283
model-validation CPOs, 209
   definition of
   examples of, 225–28
Moulton correction factor *see* clustered randomization: adjustment by intraclass correlation coefficient and
Multi-method research
   rationale for, 25–26
multivariate regression
   homogeneous partial effects assumption in, 285–86
   limitations of, 265, 267
   rationales for, 263–64

natural experiments, 34
   checklist for, 328
   clustered randomization in, 175–86
   comparative, cross-national questions and, 307
   conceptual stretching and, 34–35
   contrast with conventional observational studies, 15
   contrast with true experiments, 16, 17
   critiques and limitations of, 32–34

natural experiments (cont.)
  data analysis in, 172
  definition of, 15–17
  discovery of, 41–42
  evaluation of, 321
  evaluative framework for, 27, 30–32
  external validity of, 295–96
  growth of, 1–2
  importance of substantive knowledge in, 326
  limitations of, 3
  non-compliance in, 136
    box model and, 138
  qualitative methods and, 4
  quantitative analysis of, 4
  rationale for, 2
  role of chance in, 167
  role of qualitative methods in, 208, 218, 228, 229–30
  strengths and limitations of, 315–18
Never-Treats, 138
  definition of, 138
Neyman model, 107–09, 119 *see* potential outcomes
  assumptions of, 119
  as box model, 112
  box of tickets in, 166
    sampling potential outcomes from, 166
  causal parameters in, 259
  and clustered randomization, 175–78
  contrast with linear regression model, 172
  and counterfactuals, 259
  extensions of, 118
  nointerference assumption in, 119
  non-compliance and, 138–40
  simplicity of, 173
  statistical assumptions of, 112–13, 165–66
  strengths and limitations of, 259
Neyman-Rubin-Holland model *see* Neyman model
noninterference assumption, 119, 260
  examples of, 119
  in regression models, 120, 261
null hypothesis, 186
  strict form of, 186
  weak form of, 190

observational studies, 16
  definition of, 16

placebo tests, 247
  in regression-discontinuity designs, 247
Posner (2004), 57
  bundling of treatments in, 300–02
  credibility of models in, 281
  description of, 57–58

plausibility of as-if random in, 251
relevance of intervention in, 306
shoe-leather research of, 221
potential outcomes, 108–09 *see* Neyman model
pre-treatment covariates, 239
  definition of, 239
probability limits, 157
process tracing, 211
  definition of, 211
publication bias, 296
  definition of, 296
  in natural experiments, 296

quasi-experiments, 18
  contrast of natural experiments and, 18–20
  definition of, 18–20

random assignment, 7
  random sampling and, 113
random sampling, 112
randomization, 6
  rationale for, 6–7
randomization inference *see* Fisher's exact test
randomization tests *see* Fisher's exact test
ratio-estimator bias, 157
reduced-form regression *see* intention-to-treat analysis
regression analysis, 22
  credibility of models in, 23
  limitations of, 22–24
regression-discontinuity design, 130
  average causal effect in, 130
    limit of intercepts vs., 130
regression-discontinuity designs, 18
  analysis of, 121–23
  bias of difference-of-means estimator in, 158–60
  close elections as, 77–79
    plausibility of as-if random in, 79
  definition of, 18, 63
  definition of average causal effect in, 122
  discovery of, 69
  history of, 63
  limitations of, 68, 84
  local linear or global polynomial regressions and, 128, 133–34
  plausibility of as-if random in *see* conditional-density (sorting) tests
  population thresholds in, 72–75
  potential outcomes regression function, 130
  slope of, 159
  role of as-if random in, 64, 67, 122
  selection of bandwidth in, 127
    bias-variance tradeoff and, 127
    algorithms for, 127

shape of potential outcomes regression function
    in, 131
  sources of, 68
  standard errors in, 173–74
  true randomization in, 82–83
  use of age as, 79–80
  use of indices in, 80
  use of multiple thresholds in, 83
  validation of as-if random in, 127
relevance of intervention, 289, 303
  continuum of, 303
  definition of, 289–91
  importance of, 306
  strengthening of, 308
replication
  natural experiments, 295–96
  of true experiments, 294
response schedule, definition of, 23

sampling distribution, definition of, 165
sampling variance, 168
  definition of, 168
  of the difference of means of two independent
    samples, 169
  of the mean of an independent random
    sample, 168
sensitivity analysis, 38
sharp null hypothesis *see* strict null hypothesis
shoe-leather research, 26
  definition of, 26, 208, 221, 229
  examples of, 221
  usefulness of, 313
simplicity of data analysis, advantages of, 105
single crossover, definition of, 137
Slutsky theorem, 157
small-sample bias, 157 *see* ratio-estimator bias
Snow on cholera, 12
  credibility of models in, 280
  data analysis in, 13
  description of, 12–15
  natural experiment in, 13
  plausibility of as-if random in, 13, 243, 250
    qualitative evidence for, 14
    quantitative evidence for, 14
  relevance of intervention in, 304
  role of information, incentives, and capacities in
    assessing, 243
  strengths of study of, 14
  treatment-assignment CPOs and, 214–15
specification tests, 248
  in instrumental-variables designs, 248
stable-unit treatment-value assumption (SUTVA)
    see noninterference
standard error, 165
  definition of, 165
  of the difference-of-means estimator, 169
  i.i.d. assumption and, 171
standard natural experiments, 18
  as-if randomization in, 53–60
  definition of, 18
  sources of, 43
  true randomization in, 48
  use of jurisdictional borders in, 57–59
    limitations of, 58
  use of redistricting as, 59
statistical assumptions, 258
  vs. causal assumptions, 258
statistical independence of treatment assignment
    and confounders, 6, 21
statistical inference, definition of, 258
strict null hypothesis *see* null hypothesis
  definition of, 186, 192
  relevance of, 190
strong research designs, 318
  as aspirational, 319
  definition of, 318
  importance of mixed methods for, 326
  tradeoffs involved in, 319
study group, 108
  in regression-discontinuity designs, 122, 127
  and selection of bandwidth, 127

Thistlewaite and Campbell (1960), 64
  analysis of, 123–25
  description of, 64–67
treatment-assignment CPOs
  definition of, 209, 212–13
  examples of, 213
  in instrumental-variables designs, 218
  in regression-discontinuity designs,
    215–18, 248
true experiments, 320
  evaluation of, 320

unbiased estimator, definition of, 114
unit causal effect, 109
urn model *see* Neyman model statistical
    assumptions

Vietnam draft lottery study (Angrist 1990)
  credibility of models in, 322
  description of, 8–9
  effects in, 8
  imperfect compliance in, 137
  instrumental-variables analysis in, 87,
    143–48
    assumptions of, 269–70, 271
  intention-to-treat analysis in, 87, 88, 144

Vietnam draft lottery study (Angrist 1990) (cont.)
  no-Defiers assumption in, 149
  plausibility of as-if random in, 322, 331
  relevance of intervention in, 322
  study group in, 108, 295

Vietnam draft lottery study (Erikson and Stoker 2011), political effects in, 49

weak form of null hypothesis *see* null hypothesis
  definition of, 192